# "Ask", said.

Conversing with the Lord
Through the New Testament

Michael Holsten

Copyright © 2020 by Michael D. Holsten

All Rights Reserved


Printed in the U.S.A.


**Except where noted**
**Scripture taken from the *New American Standard Bible*®**
**(NASB),**
**Copyright © 1960, 1962, 1963, 1968, 1971, 1972, 1973,**
**1975, 1977, 1995 by The Lockman Foundation**
**Used by permission. www.Lockman.org**

Scripture texts marked NABRE in this work are taken from the *New American Bible, revised edition* © 2010, 1991, 1986, 1970 Confraternity of Christian Doctrine, Washington, D.C. and are used by permission of the copyright owner. All Rights Reserved. No part of the New American Bible may be reproduced in any form without permission in writing from the copyright owner.

Scripture quotations marked ESV are from the ESV® Bible (The Holy Bible, English Standard Version®), copyright © 2001 by Crossway, a publishing ministry of Good News Publishers. Used by permission. All rights reserved.

# Dedication

To all of you who enjoy conversing with the Lord.  And to all of you who have a few things you have been meaning to talk about with Him.  To you this book is dedicated.

# Table of Contents

Acknowledgment ......................................................... f
Introduction ............................................................... g
Matthew ..................................................................... 1
Mark .......................................................................... 48
Luke .......................................................................... 71
John ........................................................................ 116
Acts ........................................................................ 155
Romans ................................................................. 201
1 Corinthians ........................................................ 228
2 Corinthians ........................................................ 258
Galatians ............................................................... 282
Ephesians ............................................................. 293
Philippians ............................................................ 305
Colossians ............................................................ 313
1 Thessalonians ................................................... 321
2 Thessalonians ................................................... 332
1 Timothy .............................................................. 339
2 Timothy .............................................................. 351
Titus ....................................................................... 359
Philemon ............................................................... 365
Hebrews ................................................................ 367
James .................................................................... 390
1 Peter .................................................................. 399

2 Peter ..................................................... 409
1 John ..................................................... 415
2 John ..................................................... 425
3 John ..................................................... 427
Jude ......................................................... 429
Revelation .............................................. 432

# Acknowledgment

Thank You Gracious Lord for the privilege of conversing with You.  Thank You for Your conversation to me and us in Your word.  There are times when listening to You is difficult, but it is always a blessing listening to You and talking to You.  As You know, I believe You have a sense of humor (which I have depended on many times in these conversations).  Thank You for putting up with me and graciously conversing with me, a sinner and by Your grace one of Your servants.  Thank You for the insights, the joy, the humility (whether I needed it or not!).  Thank You for Your calling to put these conversations into print.  Please make them a blessing to all who read this book (they have certainly been a blessing to me).

All that is gold is from You, thank You, Lord.
All that is dross is mine; let it not get in the way, Lord.

To God alone, the glory.

2$^{nd}$ Edition:
Thank you to the wonderful, friendly, caring people at the Irish Stud and Garden near Kildare, Ireland, especially Maria and Caroline who made us feel welcome and have continued to bless us.  The cover picture I took in the Japanese Garden there.  It is truly one of the most beautiful places on the planet.  (And the food is outstanding.)

# Introduction

"There is nothing more worthwhile than to pray to God and to converse with him, for prayer unites us with God as his companions. As our bodily eyes are illuminated by seeing the light, so in contemplating God our soul is illuminated by him. Of course the prayer I have in mind is no matter of routine, it is deliberate and earnest. It is not tied down to a fixed timetable; rather it is a state which endures by night and day." St. John Chrysostom in his Homily 6 on prayer.
(http://prayerfoundation.org/john_chrysostom_homily_six_on_prayer.htm)

He did say to ask. The Lord, that is. That is the foundation of this journal of conversations with the Lord.

Here are some of the places where He said it.

> "Call upon Me in the day of trouble;
> I shall rescue you, and you will honor Me."
> Ps 50.15

> "Ask, and it will be given to you; seek, and you will find; knock, and it will be opened to you. For everyone who asks receives, and he who seeks finds, and to him who knocks it will be opened. … If you then, being evil, know how to give good gifts to your children, how much more will your Father who is in heaven give what is good to those who ask Him!"
> Matthew 7.7, 8, 11

> In that day you will not question Me about anything. Truly, truly, I say to you, if you ask the Father for anything in My name, He will give it to you. Until now you have asked for nothing in My name; ask and you will receive, so that your joy may be made full.
> John 16.23, 24

> These things I have written to you who believe in the name of the Son of God, so that you may know that you have eternal life. This is the confidence which we have before Him, that, if we ask anything according to His will, He hears us. And if we know that He hears us *in* whatever we ask, we know that we have the requests which we have asked from Him.
> 1 John 5.13-15

Now, there are books about prayer. Quite a lot of them. This is not one of them. Neither is this a book of prayers.

In the spirit of St. John Chrysostom, this is a journal of conversations with the Lord. There is, certainly, a lot of asking that goes on in these conversations. The asking is based on the encouragements, invitations, and promises above. In particular, since God promises to grant our requests when we ask according to His will, and since He has shared His will in His word, the conversations are started by God speaking in three passages I have chosen from each chapter in the New Testament.

By using this title, I do not mean to imply that all conversing involves asking. It does seem to me, however, that all my asking needs to involve conversing. There is certainly conversing with the Lord that includes, "Wow, Lord! Are You ever good at that!" Others might include, "Look at this, Lord, just look at this!" Or, "What do You think, Lord?" "What do You want me to do, Lord? I'm having a lot of trouble seeing Your way." "That was amazing, Lord, the way You opened that door that I didn't see. Thank You!" "There seems to be so much darkness, Lord! Turn me to Your light."

My purposes in writing which I hope you will accept and take on as your purposes in reading are, first, for you to be blessed in reading and in some sense for you to participate in these conversations. You will notice that I have included many personal things in these conversations. Perhaps some of them apply to you. If they do not, please feel free as you read to substitute your own personal thoughts. These conversations are meant to give you an opportunity for open-hearted conversation with the Lord. (Because the conversations are in response to communications from the Lord, some topics that He brings up more than once appear in more than one conversation.)

The second purpose I have, is for you to enjoy conversations with the Lord so much that you will (in St. Chrysostom's "state that endures night and day") have conversations with the Lord all through your day, enjoying a fellowship with our Lord that brings humility, openness, faithfulness, delight and joy to every part of your Living. (I have used Living with a capital "L" for the Life that we have by grace in Jesus, as opposed to living that is our body working effectively through the day. Of course, the two are not separate, but I am emphasizing the Life we have in Jesus in the midst of our living.)

The structure of this book is in the order of the New Testament, from Matthew to Revelation, with the chapters in order. There are 260 chapters in the New Testament, the same as the number of weekdays in 52 weeks. So one plan in using this book is to enjoy one chapter of the New Testament a day on weekdays and review or rehearse or rewrite parts you enjoyed to make them more personal on weekends. (To get the full benefit of the context of these passages, you might read the whole chapter in your Bible first.) I have included a phrase for each conversation at the end of each New Testament chapter to help remember each conversation. Feel free to write your own. I intend those to help us carry the benefits of the conversations into the day.

Besides that suggested plan for using this book, I'm sure you can find many others (including looking for Bible passages you like).

However you use this book, I pray that the Lord will make it a blessing as you participate in these conversations and as you enjoy conversing with the Lord throughout your days. I look forward to meeting you, if not here, then there, at home with the Lord.

Michael Holsten

# Matthew

Matthew 1

1 The record of the genealogy of Jesus the Messiah, the son of David, the son of Abraham:
I suppose today, Lord, there would be a "Breaking News!" in the middle of all television broadcasts. CNN would have their local woman or man talk about where You were, Jesus, and what You were doing, while the network put together an hour special on the growing development of the expectation of the Messiah and (just in case the audience didn't have a clue) who David and Abraham were. But through Matthew, You start what You have given us as The New Testament with these simple and powerful words. The record. "This is the way it is!" Thank You, Lord, that You have spoken to my heart in Your word. I suppose I am a person of my culture enough to think it would be a real blessing to see newspaper headlines and special reports on television. But here You are using a Jewish man (who, as a former tax collector for the Romans was not exactly in high society) to carefully start and explain Your great good news from his personal viewpoint of faith, believing in You and trusting You to start Life that leads to You in heaven—for him, for his readers, even for me. Thank You for Matthew. Thank You for Your good news. Father, grant that I get to know Jesus, promised Messiah Whom You have sent, better and better every day, that I might trust Him and Live for You in Him.

5,6a Salmon was the father of Boaz by Rahab, Boaz was the father of Obed by Ruth, and Obed the father of Jesse.
6 Jesse was the father of David the king.
Talk about mysterious ways! There was Ruth in another country, living in sorrow at the death of her husband, not knowing You (and I can almost hear You saying, "Watch

this!"). And You made her the grandmother of King David and ancestress of Jesus. You have an amazing gracious ability to lovingly redirect sorrow to joy. There are a lot of things that I can think of in my life which if I dwell on them produce tears of sorrow. Make some good, some blessing, some joy come from them, Lord. And use me in ways I don't understand today to produce joy and blessing down the road, over somewhere else, that I won't even get to see. But You will be smiling. Thank You Lord.

23 "BEHOLD, THE VIRGIN SHALL BE WITH CHILD AND SHALL BEAR A SON, AND THEY SHALL CALL HIS NAME IMMANUEL," which translated means, "GOD WITH US."
You called Matthew to make it clear that You, Lord Jesus, were the fulfillment of the Old Testament prophecies. Thank You Jesus. In particular thank You for being Immanuel. Some days I get to be with a lot of people and some days I feel alone, Lord. But even when I am with crowds of people, I am alone without You. Be present with me, Lord. Let me know that You, my gracious Lord and God, are with me. Give me grace to walk with You today. Today is a blessing, a joy. Without knowing everything that is coming, I still know today is great because You, Jesus, my Lord and God, are with me. Walk with me, and keep me close to You, please Lord.

For sure. Good news in Jesus.
Use now to produce blessing, somewhere
Walk together


Matthew 2

6 'AND YOU, BETHLEHEM, LAND OF JUDAH,
ARE BY NO MEANS LEAST AMONG THE LEADERS OF JUDAH;
FOR OUT OF YOU SHALL COME FORTH A RULER
WHO WILL SHEPHERD MY PEOPLE ISRAEL.'"

Thank You Jesus for coming. When You talked to crowds You said people were like sheep. "I resemble that remark" seems appropriate. It's easy to wander from something that I have to have, to something else a few months later that I have to enjoy (after I can't remember why I wanted the first thing). Shepherd me Lord. Lead me to pleasures that are blessings in Your gracious will. Grant that I be really satisfied with the blessings You graciously give me. And keep me from wandering off into dumbness, wastes of time, and things hurtful or destructive. Help me to follow You faithfully, gracious Shepherd and Lord.

10  When they saw the star, they rejoiced exceedingly with great joy.
What a joy that must have been, Lord, to walk out into the night and see Your star that You provided still there waiting for them. Father, You provided an unmistakable message of Jesus' coming that was a blessing to the magi and to people now. And You still provide blessings to me that are really wonderful. Help me to see them as clearly as a star. Grant that I remember Your blessings. And grant that I live in joy in every remembrance of You--of Your coming, of Your being here, and of Your blessings that You give me every day.

12  And having been warned *by God* in a dream not to return to Herod, the magi left for their own country by another way.
Father, You not only took care of Jesus, but also of the magi in giving them a clear message of warning. I know You have given me common sense and a healthy Spirit-powered conscience. Sometimes I forget to use them, so help me to use them with Your gift of wisdom so that I live in Your will. And also if You would, please, Lord, guide me, direct me, warn me. Use dreams and my imagination, use other people and their insights, use my memory of Your word and Your will—and please give me Your guidance so that I avoid paths where evil would use me to be hurtful, insulting to You,

or self-destructive, and rather, take the paths You want me to, where I am walking with You.

Sheepishly follow You
Joy in remembering blessings
Listen for Your guidance


Matthew 3

2 "Repent, for the kingdom of heaven is at hand."
Repent—that means I actually have to think about how I am not the person You want me to be (or even that I want to be), that I actually have to think about things I have done, things I have said, desires I have allowed and encouraged. Like going to a garbage dumpster that has not been emptied for a week, and sticking my head in and taking a deep breath. Yuck! But Your kingdom of heaven is really close, it is at hand! Help me to see the wonder and awe of Your kingdom of heaven coming in You, Lord Jesus. Help me to see myself from the point of view of that perfect love and grace. And grant that I recognize my sinfulness and my sins honestly with a feeling of revulsion and sorrow. Give me strength and willingness to repent with the grace You give me by Your coming and by Your kingdom of heaven being right here, close, with You.

8 Therefore bear fruit in keeping with repentance.
Because You help me to see myself honestly, and because You give me grace to repent, and because You give me forgiveness, I am (amazing thought) able to live a new and different life. I am able to live bearing fruit, by Your grace. Gracious Lord, help me to live today bearing fruit. Show me the fruit You want in my life. Stir my desire so that I want to be fruitful with Your fruit all through this day. Keep my attitude of humble repentance strong so that I may be a blessing to others in Your will, with love and thanksgiving to

You for not only showing me my sin, but also leading me to repentance and to serving You.

11 "As for me, I baptize you with water for repentance, but He who is coming after me is mightier than I, and I am not fit to remove His sandals; He will baptize you with the Holy Spirit and fire.
I have met some of those people whom You have baptized with the Holy Spirit and fire. Is it ok if I say sometimes they are scary? Thank You for putting up with me, Lord. There are people who live as if You were in charge of every moment (not meaning You're not, of course), as if You could tell them to drop everything and do something entirely different at any moment. They don't seem attached to things and are willing to give what they have to anyone who needs something. I would like to live with You and for You today, Lord, it's just—is there a middle ground where I could live today while I get more and more used to You being in charge of every ounce of my being and all my time? Then I could kind of grow into Your Holy Spirit and fire plan. Now or never? Trust You? You won't ask me to do mission work in the darkest part of Beverly Hills just yet? (Honestly, Lord!) OK, Holy Spirit fill me and set me on fire to live for Jesus. Help me to trust You absolutely. And if You see my knuckles are white, give me Your comfort and assurance as we fly through this day in Your grace.

Moved to repent
Fruitful service
On fire to live for Jesus


Matthew 4

4 But He answered and said, "It is written, 'MAN SHALL NOT LIVE ON BREAD ALONE, BUT ON EVERY WORD THAT PROCEEDS OUT OF THE MOUTH OF GOD.'"

It seems obvious to me, Lord, that my primary need is nourishment from food.  And when I go to the grocery store the choices (if I am honest and think about what choices people had 50 years ago, and what choices people have in third world countries now)—the choices are mind-boggling!  And yet You tell me that is not my primary need.  Grant that I see that I need, first and foremost, Your word, Father.  And it's not just that I need it to learn and grow, but let me know and rejoice that in Your word is Life.  In Your word is nourishment for me to Live.  Let me see the wonderful, rich nourishment in Your gracious words.  Grant that I listen to You and drink deeply from Your life-giving words, first, last, and every moment in between.

19  And He *said to them, "Follow Me, and I will make you fishers of men."
In Your words, Jesus, You gave the power to do what You invited them to do.  Please empower me to follow You.  I want to be Your disciple, taught by You, walking with You, seeing needs and problems, joys and wonders through Your eyes.  But only by Your grace and power can I do that.  Let me hear You saying to me every morning, "Follow Me!"  Grant that from the first foot out of bed in the morning, I walk with You, using Your power through Your Holy Spirit.  Make me the person You want me to be, Lord, in following You.  What do You want me to be when I grow up?  You keep making the picture larger (more interesting and more difficult) every step in following You.  Your choice.  Thank You, Lord.  Grant that I follow You with the power You give me.

21,22  Going on from there He saw two other brothers, James the *son* of Zebedee, and John his brother, in the boat with Zebedee their father, mending their nets; and He called them.  22 Immediately they left the boat and their father, and followed Him.
See now, there's another thing about following You, Lord.  When I follow You, we always seem to be leaving things

behind. It seems so much more comfortable to stay and to hold onto things and places and people. I am tempted to say, "Are You sure leaving things is so absolutely necessary?", but, of course, I know—You have places for us to go and things for me, that is us, to do. And we can't just stay here and do all You want done. Give me confidence in You to leave what You want me to leave. Give me comfort and assurance in Your presence. Grant that I never hesitate to leave whatever You want me to leave. Being with You is first. Thank You, Lord.

Nourished daily by Your words
Every step, following You
Leaving, with You, again, today


Matthew 5

5 "Blessed are the gentle, for they shall inherit the earth." When I talk to You, Lord, I long for You to be gentle with me! The people I remember well are servants of Yours who were gentle with me. Grant that I be gentle. Exasperation comes so easily to my heart, Lord. Why can't people understand what I mean in what I say, instead of hearing me say something hurtful or of no consequence? Grant that I be gentle in my heart so that my attitude toward people always shows the gentleness that comes from You. Grant that I be gentle in my mind, so that instead of racing into anger and outrage or confusion and incomprehension I can think graciously in the atmosphere of gentleness. Grant that I be gentle in my words, so that others may hear Your healing gentleness. Grant that I be gentle in my eyes and face so that others may see You caring about them and smiling. Grant that I be gentle in my actions so that others may experience walking with You loving them.

6 "Blessed are those who hunger and thirst for righteousness, for they shall be satisfied."

To have You look at me and not cringe. Yes, Lord, I yearn for that. To live a day, each day, completely, unmistakably clear about what Your will is and wanting just exactly that—Your will to be done in me and around me every moment. I want that a lot, Lord. Can You hear that small voice, Lord? Of course You can. The voice in me that says, "Sounds pretty boring to me." Living in Your sunshine and joy, seeing every blessing You give and every opportunity to be a blessing, recognizing Your grace to serve You and using the ability and grace You give me? Not leaving anything undone because of forgetfulness or fear or doubt? Living in joy and satisfaction with You, always? Not boring, Lord. Please grant that, Lord, to me and all the people I love and care about (which, when all is said and done, is a pretty long list, thank You).

14 "You are the light of the world. A city set on a hill cannot be hidden."
Thank You, Lord, for making me a light and part of the light of the world. Your grace to me is amazing. Me, a light! I have a little trouble about the part where I am on a hill and everyone can see me because I can't hide anything. You know, Lord, that there are parts of me that are not perfect, wonderful, or delightful to look at. Cleanse me, please, Lord, so that I am not offensive when people see me. Grant that people see You and Your light when they look at me. It is only by Your grace, I know, that that is possible. So please live through me and shine Your light. On a hill, no hiding, today, only by Your grace—shine Jesus, shine!

By Your gifting, gentle in every way
Satisfied, living with You
Unselfconsciously shining from the hill

Matthew 6

10  Your kingdom come.
Your will be done,
On earth as it is in heaven.
I have said, "Whatever you want." And often I have said it in resignation and exasperation and anger, Lord. Forgive me, Lord, for speaking hurtfully. The problem is that I have some certainty in my heart that "whatever you want" is not going to be good or not going to be what I would choose. Thank You, Father, that I don't have that problem with You. I can say, "Your will be done" in the confidence and certainty that blessings will follow, good things are coming. Every part of Your will is attached to Your blessings and every blessing of Yours is attached to Your will—how cool is that! (In some sense, one-to-one and onto.) Thank You that I can depend on Your will in absolute confidence. And yes, I know that sometimes that means Your will is better (like a lot) than mine, and I may not get what I thought was great and spiffy. Give me joyful submission to Your will in confidence and joy that Your will is always good and always filled with blessing.

11  'Give us this day our daily bread.
What did Paul say, "I live in a world...". Well, I live in a world where the concept of "daily bread" is completely foreign. A goal in life is (clearly advertised, at least) to put aside enough money so that in retirement I won't ever run out of money. Are you kidding! On the one hand, Lord, You know I am really good at spending, and on the other hand, where would I get that much money?! Daily contentment is almost a phrase from a foreign language to most current earth terminology. Push open my heart and mind and vocabulary, Lord, so that I know I need, and I want, and by Your grace I receive what I really need today, with thanksgiving and contentment, without continually trying to push the envelope ("well, could we at least think about what I need for tomorrow?!"). Thank You for being in charge of daily bread, including daily time in which I live. I live only by Your graciously allowing me to be alive, still today. Thank You, Lord.

33  But seek first His kingdom and His righteousness, and all these things will be added to you.
You know how many years I have had a to-do list, Lord. Over the years it has changed from pieces of paper to bound paper to klutzy electronic devices to amazing electronic devices—but it is always a list of things to do.  On the list have been some things about which I really meant well, but …, You know, never got done.  And in all those years, I don't exactly remember putting as the first item, Your kingdom and Your righteousness.  Yes, I can see, that would have been an awfully good idea.  So at least now, on today's list, let that be the first item.  Let me see how to seek Your kingdom and Your righteousness in the choices I make today, in the things I think, in the things I say.  And please fulfill Your promise to manage all the other things, while I enjoy listening to You.  Before the MBA, there You were, thank You Lord, managing quite nicely.

Really, whatever You want
Content and trusting, today
First, seek Your kingdom


Matthew 7

7  "Ask, and it will be given to you; seek, and you will find; knock, and it will be opened to you.
I find it difficult to know what to say, Lord Jesus.  What a promise!  "Ask, and it will be given to you."  Of course, I have a list.  It has been growing through the years.  You know, the one that starts with a 1957 Thunderbird convertible.  (In mint condition, with less than 10,000 miles on it.)  Thank You for smiling, Lord.  Right.  You promise to give good things.  And Your definition of good is a whole lot better than mine, there are always blessings that come from the good things You give.  So, yes, please bless my family with closeness to You.  Please bless the children and grandchildren You have

entrusted to my wife and me—bless them with a strong faith, joy in living with You, and faithfulness in following You all the time.  Bless the poor, provide what they need, keep them close to You, and use them to be a blessing.  Bless me and the people in the United States with good stewardship so that we do not use world resources selfishly to the exclusion of people in other countries.  Please, Lord, stir my heart so that as I begin every day, I may ask for blessings that are good, caring about other people, with thanksgiving for Your generosity and love, and with confidence in Your answering my prayers.  (Yellow.  (Just in case.))

24, 25  "Therefore everyone who hears these words of Mine and acts on them, may be compared to a wise man who built his house on the rock. [25] And the rain fell, and the floods came, and the winds blew and slammed against that house; and *yet* it did not fall, for it had been founded on the rock.
Your words, Lord, are solid rock on which I may depend in all I do.  I hear You saying that's what counts.  Not just that I hear You, not just that I think You are wise and Your words are wonderful, not just that I copy down Your words and organize them.  Help me to get past that, Lord.  Let my thoughts, words, and actions be a direct result of Your words that You speak to me.  Storms are bound to come.  Let me build my life on You and Your words, solid rock no matter what comes.  Grant that I be wise, not in collecting great sayings, not in thinking wise thoughts, not in saying wise things at just the right time (which of course I like), but in doing things that are visibly built on Your words that are blessings and which show wisdom and glorify You.  Then it's ok if storms come—You have that covered, thank You.

29  …for He was teaching them as *one* having authority, and not as their scribes.
Thank You for teaching me, Lord.  You teach me to be gracious and merciful and to live in hope and joy, always.  There are a lot of self-help resources on the web and in books.  Some are written and presented by some very smart

people whom You have blessed with great ability. It just seems so different when I consider smart, psychologically positive, and time-honored stuff. They are all depending on some previous goodness, but You are Goodness. You talk to me in Your word and speak with authority right across the centuries, zap into my life, with certainty, always loving me and caring about me. Thank You that I can depend on You, Lord. Speak to me with authority. Let me depend on Your authoritative grace and love. Blow aside any fog that surrounds me, Lord, and shine Your light into my mind and heart and life.

Ask well
Actions wisely built
Authoritatively loved and taught


Matthew 8

3 Jesus stretched out His hand and touched him, saying, "I am willing; be cleansed." And immediately his leprosy was cleansed.
Thank You, Lord Jesus, for reaching out and touching me. You are so gracious to me as You were touching the man with leprosy. You show me and You tell me that You are always gracious. So whenever I come to You, I may feel discouraged, guilty, joyful or at peace—You are always willing. Always willing to be gracious to me. Thank You for being willing. Other people and I are not so consistent. How wonderful You are, Lord! Give me confidence that whenever I come to You, I will know for certain that You are willing, that You don't hold back waiting for me to convince You. Right now, today, You are willing to love me, to be gracious to me, to touch me with blessing. Let Your willingness always be the light that enlightens my day.

13 And Jesus said to the centurion, "Go; it shall be done for you as you have believed." And the servant was healed that *very* moment.

You gave the centurion what he asked for. And You gave Him Your word to take with him as he headed home. This was not to be a journey of wondering or doubt. "It shall be done for you…" Fill me with faith through Your Spirit, that I will trust You for what I request. Grant that I believe You with unwavering faith—that You will bless me, that You will answer my prayers, and that You will do it in the best possible way with the best possible blessings. I have no reason to doubt You, Lord. Keep me firm in my faith, so that when I bring something to You, I can hand it over to You, and I can be certain that You are then, at that moment, arranging the best possible blessing. I believe You, Lord; You always answer my prayers with Your grace and love, fulfilling Your promises. And when I turn it over to You, grant that I go ahead and move on, with confidence that You have taken my request into Your grace and joy and blessings are on the way.

25, 26 And they came to *Him* and woke Him, saying, "Save *us*, Lord; we are perishing!" [26] He *said to them, "Why are you afraid, you men of little faith?" Then He got up and rebuked the winds and the sea, and it became perfectly calm.

You have given me faith, Lord, so that I can trust You. And still, I have been afraid. In the storms of self-confidence, in the storms of not wanting to be open and not wanting to let go of what I think of as certainties, in the storms of finances, in storms of health problems, in storms of family crises, You know, there are a lot of storms (including some pretty terrific rain storms). Sometimes I have stepped up in faith; sometimes I have wimped out. But in every case You have shown me that You were there, that You were in charge, and that You had the situation well in hand. I suppose it is safe to say there are more storms coming, Lord. Let me live in each day with absolute faith that You can handle every storm and that I can depend on You.  Fill my memory so full of Your storm handling grace in my life and in others, that I consistently, without fail, refer any news of dark clouds on my horizon to You, Gracious, Powerful, Unfailing Storm Handler.

Your willingness, my light
Your answer, my blessing
Your presence, no fear


Matthew 9

6, 7  But so that you may know that the Son of Man has authority on earth to forgive sins"—then He *said to the paralytic, "Get up, pick up your bed and go home." ⁷ And he got up and went home.
Thank You, Lord, for wanting me to know that You have authority to forgive my sins.  I'm glad I can remember wonderful blessings from the past.  On the other hand, when I remember things I have said and done that hurt people and which I feel ashamed about, I am really glad that with Your absolute, eternal authority, You forgave me, You forgive me, You reach into my memory and stand in the shame and pronounce memory shattering, blinding light forgiveness.  So when I have some physical ailment or discouraging event, and I easily slip into feeling separated from You, let me know that no matter what happens, whether I feel healthy or ill, You have touched me with Your gracious authority forgiving me.  Remind me that we are not separated.  Let me see that Your gracious authority keeps us walking together in forgiveness and light even when there is darkness close at hand.

27  As Jesus went on from there, two blind men followed Him, crying out, "Have mercy on us, Son of David!"
In this chapter, Lord, You had Matthew record such wonderful occasions of Your mercy and healing power,

helping the many people who came to You. I come to You for Your mercy today, Lord. You know some parts of my body don't work quite the way I want them to (or the way they worked when I was 18 and didn't really appreciate them). I have made choices that have led me into challenging situations. (What did I do with all that money!?) So it is definitely mercy I ask for, Lord. I don't deserve Your help. It is because You are merciful and loving that I come to You. I know You have been merciful to me in the past. Help me to be responsible and still depend on You, Lord. Grant Your mercy to me in Your good and gracious will. I will be blessed. Thank You, Lord.

36 – 38 Seeing the people, He felt compassion for them, because they were distressed and dispirited like sheep without a shepherd. 37 Then He *said to His disciples, "The harvest is plentiful, but the workers are few. 38 Therefore beseech the Lord of the harvest to send out workers into His harvest."

Yes, Lord. Stressed in a destructive way and having spirits weak, faint, unhealthy, starving—that's what it looks like now as well as then, in newspapers and on CNN. Thank You, Lord that it is Your will to do something about it! Let Your compassion reach to people today. Lord of the harvest, please send out workers to make a difference and bless people today. Send pastors, missionaries, teachers. Send people to speak Your loving word of grace. Send people who are willing to reach out to people in all the places where they are stressed and weak and dispirited. Send workers into Your churches to minister to all who are in need. Send people to be invitational and to bring people to You. Send teachers (even in the midst of national and world-wide confusion about how schools should operate) who care about students more than about money or jobs, who care about learning more than about tests, who care about Living more than about helping students make a living, who care about helping students to use their talents and gifts to be a blessing while they are making a living. Father, send workers into the harvest!

Remember! Forgiven.
Mercy by Your grace
Send workers


Matthew 10

16 "Behold, I send you out as sheep in the midst of wolves; so be shrewd as serpents and innocent as doves.
The people I know don't seem like wolves, Lord, and I thank You for that. But I meet people while traveling who appear to be sharp of tooth. And, of course, if I watch commercials, some television shows, or (ugh!) the news, it is easy to see wolves when I am looking for them. So grant that in all my relations with people I show Your love and at the same time stay shrewd. Grant that I use intelligence, listening with thinking. Grant that I use the wisdom that You have given me with clear perception of what is happening around me. Grant that I be prudent, focused on the calling You have given me. Grant that I live among wolves without taking in any wolf habits or customs. Let me be pure in faith trusting You, showing Your love to others, unmixed with selfishness, ("it's all about me"—give me a break!), or arrogance (thinking I'm the reason I'm blessed—sheesh!). Since it is here that I live, thank you, gracious wolf-managing Shepherd, for being with me.

25 It is enough for the disciple that he become like his teacher, and the slave like his master. If they have called the head of the house Beelzebul, how much more *will they malign* the members of his household!
Do I have enough education? Have I learned enough? I know I'm still growing up, how much longer? But it is easy for me, Lord, to use measures that are not part of Reality. The real measure You show me is to become like You.

Please grant that today I grow closer to becoming like You in recognizing the blessings from my Father, in trusting my Father in every moment and situation, in stepping out into this day with Your purposes, in using Your gifts, in rejoicing and rejoicing! You are wonderfully patient with me, let me be patient, Lord. You live in unity with Your Father glorifying Him. Let me live in unity with my Father and glorify Him in all I think and say and do today. Like You, yes Jesus, let me be like You.

31 So do not fear; you are more valuable than many sparrows.
Am I good enough? Where does my value come from? I'm afraid I haven't done enough and that I have missed things that I should have seen and done. So thank You, Lord, for saying that I do not have to fear. You give me value. Let me be aware today that all my value comes from You in Your grace because You have chosen me, called me, gifted me, sent me into this place and this time. Help me to relax, knowing my value does not come from my doing enough, but from Your grace, forgiveness, and love. I feel a little uneasy having a value compared to sparrows, but then I know You really enjoy all You have created a lot, including sparrows. So whatever value You give me, that's ok with me. Being given value by You is all the satisfaction I need.

Loving, shrewd, unmixed
To be like Jesus
Unafraid, valued, satisfied


Matthew 11

27 All things have been handed over to Me by My Father; and no one knows the Son except the Father; nor does anyone know the Father except the Son, and anyone to whom the Son wills to reveal *Him*.

Please, Jesus, reveal Your Father to me. I can feel with Thomas saying, "Show us the Father". You have brought me into You, Father, Son, and Holy Spirit at my baptism. Whenever You talk about Your Father, I feel like I am getting to know Him better. You have told me that my Father is willing to have me talk to Him directly, because He loves me. So as I live in the faith that You have given me today, bring me closer to my Father. Open me to know my Father. Let me see my Father as the One Who cares about me so much that He sent You to bring me to Life, so that I can Live with You, my Father, and Your Spirit now and always. Thank You Father that I can know You through Jesus Your Son. Thank You that I can talk to You and depend on You. Grant that I grow closer to You, by Your grace through my Savior and Lord.

28 "Come to Me, all who are weary and heavy-laden, and I will give you rest."
There are times when I get home and flop in a chair, and I really feel weary. I don't notice perhaps as easily that I am weary in my spirit, until I find myself thinking about some frustration or about something that appears at the moment to be impossible, and I find myself sighing (if not out loud, at least inwardly). You know the frustrations that I feel. The ones I sublimate and stick behind some other loud noticeable feelings. Thank You for inviting me to come to You for rest. Here I am, Lord. I come to You today. And I admit that I am weary. There are burdens that I carry inside that (when I think about it) are heavy. Grant me rest, Lord. Grant that I remember throughout this day that I can turn those feelings of weariness and those heavy burdens over to you, and that I can have rest in You not just for a moment, sitting beside the path until we move on. But help me be close to You so that I have rest with You, unburdened Living!, every step of the way, throughout this day. (And thank You, Gracious Lord of unburdened Living, for being available tomorrow, too.)

29, 30 "Take My yoke upon you and learn from Me, for I am gentle and humble in heart, and YOU WILL FIND REST FOR YOUR SOULS. ³⁰ For My yoke is easy and My burden is light."
I have enjoyed learning, Lord. Through the years, I have learned a lot. All things considered, I prefer to learn without butting my head against a brick wall and finding that I need to change direction. (But a phrenologist would enjoy my bumps, right?!) I hear about a lot of plans from colleges that arrange learning to be extremely practical. Your plan is very simple—take Your yoke on and learn from You. I'm glad Your yoke is easy, Your burden light, and when I learn from You I don't necessarily have to keep bumping into brick walls. Help me take Your yoke on today, Lord. As a yoke on an animal limits movement to the one productive, desired direction, limit me to Your desired direction, to be productive as You desire—in my thinking, in my feeling, in what I say and do. Learning with rest. By Your grace, I'm ready, Lord. (And You provide the scholarship! What a deal! Thank You!)

See my Father
Rest in You
Yoked to learn


Matthew 12

12 "How much more valuable then is a man than a sheep! So then, it is lawful to do good on the Sabbath."
Your logic, Lord, is gracious, of course. "So then" since the Pharisees would help their sheep, it is lawful to do good to people. It seemed so clear to the Pharisees that rules came first. And if I look closely, there are things I let get in the way of doing good. "Lord, You know how I am supposed to balance my time in a healthy way." "Lord, You know how I am supposed to be careful how I use the money You have given me." And "Lord, You know how You have told me to be healthier, and not overdo." Bilge water! Open my eyes

and my heart so that I can see the good that You prepare for me to do with a willing and open and enthusiastic heart. Grant that I do not let anything get in the way of good that You want me to do. Especially not other good things.

21 "AND IN HIS NAME THE GENTILES WILL HOPE."
There are a lot of names self-presented as available today in which I supposedly could hope. There are political names—if I just commit my allegiance (and I'm sure they would like some money) to them, there is hope for the future! There are self-help authors—if I just organize my life according to their instructions, there is hope for the future! And movie stars, and music groups, and spiritual and philosophical gurus. Thank You, Lord, that I might come to know your gracious name. Isaiah was right, hope is in You. Of course, I left out the most attractive name of all—that is mine. What an ego trip! No. In Your name, Lord, I hope. Not the "just maybe, possibly" hope. But the "my hope is built on nothing less" hope. The absolute confidence in today and every day to come, because I can depend on You hope. Let nothing pull my hope away from You, gracious Lord, Who are in charge of today and all tomorrows.

50 "For whoever does the will of My Father who is in heaven, he is My brother and sister and mother."
When I look in my family tree, I find people I didn't know I should know, from places I didn't knew existed. It's very big right now, Lord, to find ancestors. Some people would like to think that they have kings and queens in their ancestry. Thank You for simplifying this—I am part of the family of a King: You. Grant that I see my Father's will now and every day. Give me wisdom to follow His will. By Your grace, grant that I will carry out my Father's will, well and to His glory. Fill me, Lord Holy Spirit, so that my will is completely taken over by my Father. Thank You, Lord Jesus, that I can be part of Your family. (So is it from You I get my liking for sauerkraut and black olives? (Not necessarily together.))

Your permission: Do good.
Name of hope
Family of Your will


Matthew 13

11  Jesus answered them, "To you it has been granted to know the mysteries of the kingdom of heaven, but to them it has not been granted.
It is a mystery to me, Lord, Your Kingdom.  I am so raised in a society that has good things depend on hard work, occasionally on noble birth or knowing the right people, but mainly on hard work.  Open to me the mysteries of Your Kingdom.  You have shown me that You love me and forgive me and take me into Your family, not because I am somebody or have done great stuff, but because You are Somebody and have done great things for me.  You have shown me that I come into Your Kingdom only by Your grace.  Open the eyes of my heart so that I may continue to see that all that happens in Your Kingdom is also by grace, not just getting in.  It is so easy for me to fall back, now that You have brought me in, to depending on my efforts for good things to happen.  Convince my spirit that all of Living in Your Kingdom is still, always, only by Your grace, and that I may confidently depend on You for all blessings.  Open to me Your Kingdom mysteries still today.

23  "And the one on whom seed was sown on the good soil, this is the man who hears the word and understands it; who indeed bears fruit and brings forth, some a hundredfold, some sixty, and some thirty."
Let me be fruitful, Lord.  Thank You for Your word sown in my heart.  The hard ground and shallow soil is close by, and the thorny cares and troubles of the world still try to entangle me and choke me.  Keep me in Your good soil, Lord.
Protect me from every deathly grip of care and trouble.
Grant that I trust You to take care of those.  And live in me

and work in me so that the fruit that You want is produced through me. Let it be to Your glory, not mine. I suppose it is very human of me to say, "Let's make it a hundredfold, Lord." However You want to use me, let me be fruitful to Your glory. All praise and glory be Yours, Lord!

31 He presented another parable to them, saying, "The kingdom of heaven is like a mustard seed, which a man took and sowed in his field"
And then the mustard seed becomes the largest plant in the garden! Yes! Let Your Kingdom grow, Lord! There seem to be so many forces at work to pull people away from depending on You. Self-help. Be your own person. Carpe Diem. And yet, You tell me in Your word that Your Kingdom is growing. Thank You, Lord! Let it grow! Bring growth to Your Kingdom in my lifetime. In this day, reach people, bring them away from themselves, away from distractions, away from fear—bring them to You. Bless them and all Your people in growing in faith. Bless Your Kingdom growing in my church family, in my community, in my family. Thank You Lord for Your Kingdom growing Now.

Mystery: Even me, still
Fruitful: As You desire
Your Kingdom: Grow it now


Matthew 14

16 But Jesus said to them, "They do not need to go away; you give them *something* to eat!"
You have an amazingly optimistic opinion of what I can do. I can feel with the disciples if they said, "Who, me!?" But, of course, You knew what You were doing. And You know now how You want to use me. What do I have to give to people who are poor, to people who are discouraged, to people who are afraid and angry? It is not immediately obvious to me what I have to give, and yet You continue to put me in

situations where I have the opportunity to give, and when I look, there You are encouraging me. Grant that I have what You want me to give by Your grace. Grant that I trust You to Live through me and to make, what looks to me not nearly enough, just what is needed in Your gracious provision. It is true that I would rather have You show me what I have that You want me to give, before the time comes to give it. But You really enjoy pulling it out of the hat, so to speak, just when it is needed, so that I approach every surprising moment, with confidence in You. Way to go, Lord!

27 But immediately Jesus spoke to them, saying, "Take courage, it is I; do not be afraid."
I know that in this culture, brave is in, and fear is not. But if I look closely at myself (and perhaps others) most of the time when I am angry, I have chosen anger instead of what I really feel which is fear about something. Fear that I'm not good enough. Fear that something is out of control. Fear that anything I say is going to be wrong. The disciples were not looking for You to be walking on the water to them. And often I am not looking for You when I turn a corner and find that I am afraid of something. Yet, there You are. No matter what the situation is that is making me afraid, there You are. And I can still hear You saying, "Take courage, it is I; do not be afraid." That's really why I can take courage, isn't it Lord? Because it is You. Help me to see that it is You. Open my heart to have confidence whenever I feel threatened, because You have shown me how gracious and caring You are to me. You are my gracious Lord and Savior. Help me to live without fear and with courage—because it is You!

33 And those who were in the boat worshiped Him, saying, "You are certainly God's Son!"
So there they were in the boat. You appeared and You weren't a ghost. You walked on water and Peter walked on water. You got in the boat and the wind (which had been really obnoxious) stopped. And did they call CNN to document the event? Did they discuss possible reasons

why they had not really seen what they had just seen? No. It was obvious to them—they worshiped You. So You have blessed me in many ways. I can think back and remember wonderful blessings. I can keep my eyes open, and see Your blessings today. I can listen to Your word and experience Your blessings. Keep me healthy in spirit so that when those things happen, I worship You. I praise You. I thank You. I recognize You, gracious Lord and Savior. I just worship You!

Ready to give, trusting
No fear: It's You
Wonder, joy, blessing—worship


Matthew 15

27, 28 But she said, "Yes, Lord; but even the dogs feed on the crumbs which fall from their masters' table." [28] Then Jesus said to her, "O woman, your faith is great; it shall be done for you as you wish." And her daughter was healed at once.
She was a Gentile, Lord Jesus, but she was convinced You were able and willing to bless her. I come to You as a Gentile also, and You have told me that I am included in Your family, wonder of wonders! (What joy Jewish people can have!) There are times when I cry to You, "Help me!" Grant that I ask with faith. Grant that I ask with great faith to believe that You are gracious, You are able to help me, and that You want to bless me. Grant that whenever I come to You, whenever I talk to You, and especially whenever I ask for Your merciful help, that I ask faithfully believing that You will answer my prayer and bless me. Thank You that I can depend on You in faith, Gracious Lord Jesus!

31 So the crowd marveled as they saw the mute speaking, the crippled restored, and the lame walking, and the blind seeing; and they glorified the God of Israel.

As the people watched, You were blessing and blessing and blessing. What a sight it must have been! People with no hope were restored to life and hope by Your grace. And they glorified God. You are blessing people today, Lord. People receive amazing healing from Your grace through doctors, physical therapy, hospitals, medicine, and not least, directly by Your grace. Let me recognize Your blessings. Glory to You Lord for Your great love to us. And I know You have blessed me through doctors and medicine and in the hospital—You have touched my life and given me good health. I really have reason to glorify You, Lord. Grant that every day as I get up, I glorify You for Your great blessings of health and for Your great blessing of another day. Let my heart sing with praise and glory to You, O Lord!

37 And they all ate and were satisfied, and they picked up what was left over of the broken pieces, seven large baskets full.
You cared about those people who were with You, Lord! You cared about their physical needs. You wanted to satisfy them with food. So You miraculously provided for them. Wow, Lord, to have seen thousands being fed with such little food. By Your grace, plenty. And they were satisfied. They were blessed physically. Yes, You have blessed me, You continue to provide for me. And when I go to the grocery store I have choices that would boggle the mind of kings and queens. Then I go home and eat, and, sometimes, I forget to be satisfied. I'm sorry, Lord. How You have blessed me! It's ok for me to be satisfied! Grant that when I eat, when I receive Your blessings, that I will be satisfied. Satisfied as in, thank You, Lord, that was really good, I'm not hungry anymore. (And I can stop eating things I don't need—satisfied is good. I don't need being stuffed. I don't need gooey things (at least not often).) Help me be satisfied, Lord. And please, Lord, bless those people who do not have enough (any) food. Use me and others to provide Your blessings of satisfaction for them, also.

In faith, "Help"
See Your blessings: Glory to You
Blessed and satisfied


Matthew 16

16, 17  Simon Peter answered, "You are the Christ, the Son of the living God." ¹⁷ And Jesus said to him, "Blessed are you, Simon Barjona, because flesh and blood did not reveal *this* to you, but My Father who is in heaven.
There are a lot of other choices that people have made about You, Lord.  How can people read about You, recognize the promises You fulfilled, hear what You have done, and speak gibberish about You being a good person?  But before I get too righteous, if You are the Christ promised, Messiah come to save us, and the Son of God Who is I Am, how can I think unfriendly, unkind thoughts, say acrimonious and ungentle words, and do some of the dumb things I do?  Please, Father, reveal Your Son to me again today.  Please reveal Him to my heart as well as my head, to my will as well as my thinking, and please let my recognizing Him show in all my thoughts, in all my words, and in all my actions today and forever!

18  I also say to you that you are Peter, and upon this rock I will build My church; and the gates of Hades will not overpower it.
We celebrate history of buildings and congregations, Lord.  We celebrate anniversaries of congregations and Your servants' work in early days in this nation.  And it is wonderful to celebrate Your grace in those ways.  But it doesn't take building committees or anniversary committees to build Your Church.  You do the building.  Thank You, Lord, for building Your Church.  Wow!  How You have built it during the last couple thousand years!  There are times when dire predictions of stagnancy get printed about Your Church these days.  It is not Your Church that is stagnant.  It

is us! Thank You for continuing to build Your Church now, today. Bless me and those I know and love, that we do not opt out of the gracious work You are doing by moaning and groaning. Build Your Church, and according to Your gracious will, by Your Spirit, use me and us.

24  Then Jesus said to His disciples, "If anyone wishes to come after Me, he must deny himself, and take up his cross and follow Me.
OK, I admit, the temptation is to say, "Is there some other option, Lord? Are You sure that's the only way?" I want to follow You. When I read about Matthew walking away from his job, leaving everything and following You, I can feel a sense of zeal awake in me. (But to be honest, I also like stories with happy endings, with riding off into the sunset singing.) So I recognize Your calling as seriously difficult. (And again, in honesty, impossible for me to do.) So Gracious Lord, help me. Let my desire not be some romantic whim, but true zeal given by Your Holy Spirit. As I grow to honestly know myself through the years, help me to deny myself. Grant that I use the fruit of Your Spirit—self-control. Grant that I do not take up my cross by surfing the net shopping for just the right cross that I think fits me, but rather let me walk with You with the cross You give me. Only by Your grace. Only by Your power. Grant that I follow You faithfully, today.

Show You revealed
Build Your Church
Deny. Take. Follow


Matthew 17

5  While he was still speaking, a bright cloud overshadowed them, and behold, a voice out of the cloud said, "This is My beloved Son, with whom I am well-pleased; listen to Him!"

That does sound like a scary experience, Lord. On a mountain. Saw Moses and Elijah, and You, Lord, shining like the sun. And then hearing You, Father, speaking from the cloud. Yes, Lord Jesus, I will listen to You. It's true that there were other voices the disciples had listened to in the past, and there are certainly a lot of other voices to listen to now. Please keep me focused in my hearing, Lord. Let no other voices of "I want" or "I need" or "Most people, of course…" or "Don't you think, just this once, …" or "I'm too tired to listen", let them not get in the way or distract me, Lord Jesus. Grant that I listen to You in Your word, through Your Spirit in Your servants, in my conscience, in my memory of Your grace and blessings. Grant that I listen to You and obey You, follow You, Live in You every moment. Thank You, Lord Jesus, that I may listen to You.

20 And He *said to them, "Because of the littleness of your faith; for truly I say to you, if you have faith the size of a mustard seed, you will say to this mountain, 'Move from here to there,' and it will move; and nothing will be impossible to you.
The disciples wanted to help, but their faith was too small to serve You as they wanted. I have prayed for people to be blessed. It is Your will that decides if they will be blessed and how. Your good and gracious will I depend on and trust always. Yes, I would like to pray for people and for them to be healed (like right then!). I believe You want me to pray for people. I believe You have a good and gracious will. And I believe that You want me to pray with great faith. So please, Lord, grant me great faith, that in all my prayers nothing will be impossible because You can bless wonderfully, immediately, eventually, however You want. With Your gift of faith, when I pray for people, I depend on You and believe that You will bless them right then with the blessing that is absolutely the best, in Your grace and love. Thank You for answering my prayers.

27  However, so that we do not offend them, go to the sea and throw in a hook, and take the first fish that comes up; and when you open its mouth, you will find a shekel. Take that and give it to them for you and Me."

"I have a right to …" It's a very common attitude where and when I live.  And thank You for the rights that I and others have.  We are certainly blessed.  So it is kind of far out, to pray to You, Lord, to help me to not claim all my rights.  You had a right not to pay the tax.  You had a right to have the tax takers respect and recognize You.  But Your desire was to not offend them.  How very gentle and kind You are, Lord.  Ok, help me not to offend people.  Even when I have a right to something, to respect, to receive help, whatever—grant that I not offend people.  Help me find ways to be gentle and gracious and not offend others.  Open my heart and mind so that I think more of others than of my rights.  (And if it involves money, would You, please, have the money arrive some other way, since I really don't like to fish?)

My privilege and blessing, Lord:  Listening to You
Believing You give the best, always
My best right:  To be gracious


Matthew 18

14  So it is not *the* will of your Father who is in heaven that one of these little ones perish.

Thank You Father for Your gracious will.  Bless the little ones.  Bless the children whose parents are abusive—bring them to safety, joy, and Life in You.  Bless the children who were not wanted—grant them life and Life with loving people who want them.  Bless the children whose lives are damaged by their parents' bad habits—give them recovery and joy in You.  Bless the children who get to school hungry—provide for them, and change their situation with Your blessings.  Bless the children who get to school having been taught at home that education is not important—

reteach them the value of education and lead them to use the abilities You have given them.  Bless the children who get to high school having had some teacher (heal the teacher, Lord!) tell them they are dumb or can't do math—rescue them and help them to be valued and to value themselves and to believe in the abilities You have given them to learn.  Bless the children whose parents don't bring them to You—bring the children (and the parents, even kicking and struggling) to You and Your grace and Life.

19, 20  "Again I say to you, that if two of you agree on earth about anything that they may ask, it shall be done for them by My Father who is in heaven. [20] For where two or three have gathered together in My name, I am there in their midst."
What a responsibility, Lord!  First let me frequently gather with others in my family, friends, or church in Your name.  To gather in Your name is a joy and a privilege.  And then bless us in our asking.  Open our hearts and minds and spirits so that gathered in Your name, Jesus, we ask for Your blessings, in agreement, wisely, imaginatively, in faith.
There are so many to pray for.  Poor, government, church leaders, family, sick, homeless, those suffering injustice, those who are different from me in some way that I don't understand.  Mission workers, counselors, teachers, those inventing new blessings, those who guide finances of cities, companies, countries.  Grant that we ask for stuff that is good in Your definition of good.  And grant that we always ask with faith, certain of Your blessings in answer to our prayers, and with thanksgiving for all You so graciously give.

21, 22   Then Peter came and said to Him, "Lord, how often shall my brother sin against me and I forgive him? Up to seven times?" [22] Jesus *said to him, "I do not say to you, up to seven times, but up to seventy times seven.
Thank You, Lord for the privilege of forgiving those who sin against me.  I want it to help them (even when it takes a moment or five to unclench my jaw from gritting my teeth)

and it sure helps me. You are so gracious to forgive me, thank You, Lord. Help me to never hold back from forgiving. It is indeed tempting to hold on to some things with an attitude of "God will get you for that!" But I know that just gives me ulcers and isn't what You want. So no matter how many times she or he says things that hurt, no matter how many times they do things that are dumb and seem hurtful to me, keep my counting mechanism turned off, and grant that with all my heart, by Your grace, in Your name, I forgive.

Children: Protected. Healed. Alive
With Jesus, asking well
Forgive through me


Matthew 19

4-6 And He answered and said, "Have you not read that He who created *them* from the beginning MADE THEM MALE AND FEMALE, [5] and said, 'FOR THIS REASON A MAN SHALL LEAVE HIS FATHER AND MOTHER AND BE JOINED TO HIS WIFE, AND THE TWO SHALL BECOME ONE FLESH'? [6] So they are no longer two, but one flesh. What therefore God has joined together, let no man separate."

Thank You, Gracious Father for joining my wife and me. We have things in common and we have things that are different, and it seems a miracle to us that You brought us together. Thank You! Continue, please, Lord, to graciously draw us together, to keep us close to each other and to You. There are a lot of attacks that come against us. Thank You for money, it's just that we manage to be stressed about it. Keep us in Your will, in good stewardship, with joy in giving and with absolute trust together, in You. Be present in every stress with Your grace and peace. Grant us joy together in You today. Let us see the blessings that You have put in our lives and around us. Help us to be an example to encourage others. (When she has really had it with me give her patience and healing. (And it would be really nice if You would arrange it so that everything I say, she hears as positive and loving, even if there were some drips of gook that I inadvertently allowed to get mixed up in my communicating!))  Thank You Lord for us.

14  But Jesus said, "Let the children alone, and do not hinder them from coming to Me; for the kingdom of heaven belongs to such as these."
Bring children to You, Lord.  Thank You for loving children.  Give children good Christian examples in the midst of the horrid ones they see in movies and on television.  Bless children with loving parents or others who bring them to You in baptism.  Who read Your word to them.  Who pray with them and teach them to talk to You in prayer.  Bless children who have so much it threatens to get in the way between them and You.  Bless children who have so little that it threatens to get in the way between them and You.  Bless children who are in poor health with healing, strength, faith, and joy in You.  And please grant that I never do anything to hinder a child from coming to You.

25, 26  When the disciples heard *this*, they were very astonished and said, "Then who can be saved?" [26] And looking at *them* Jesus said to them, "With people this is impossible, but with God all things are possible."
Your disciples, of course, were part of a culture that believed that the richer a person was, the closer that person was to You.  It was a shock to them that riches could get in the way.  And, ok, I have had times when I saw or met someone and I unconsciously put the person in the "impossible" category.  Thank You that it is most certainly not up to me to judge impossible or possible.  Thank You that You are in charge of that.  And thank You, Gracious Father, that with You all things are possible.  Thank You that every person I see and meet is in Your "possible".  Thank You that saved does not depend on how good we are, how smart, how responsible, how good looking (phew!), or any of that stuff.  Only on Your

grace in Jesus. Reach out with Your gracious "possible" again, now, today.

Us, close, in You
For children, open the way to You
Your "possible", bringing people


Matthew 20

15 Is it not lawful for me to do what I wish with what is my own? Or is your eye envious because I am generous?'
Thank You, Lord, for giving Your gift of eternally Living with You, to people by grace. I can believe that there might be some of Your people in the Old Testament times who went through great trials and tribulations enduring in trust in You to the end of their lives, who would look at my life and think I had nothing to go through the way they did. No "heat of the day". Thank You for giving us all the same gift of Life in You. On the other hand, I admit that there are people who seem to be living lives of evil and destruction. Reach them, Lord, and help me not to be in the least envious or dismayed because of the 11th hour conversions that You graciously achieve. When we all come home to You, we can rejoice and give thanks together for Your love (even if someone looks surprised to see me there).

26 It is not this way among you, but whoever wishes to become great among you shall be your servant.
I hear You saying, Lord Jesus, that a great goal I can have in my life is to serve others. Thank You for opportunities I have had to help people. Open my eyes, please, Lord, to see the opportunities You give me today to serve others and be a blessing. Help me to listen and pay attention to needs others have. Grant that I don't disdain opportunities You give me because they are small and menial, or large and challenging. Let me depend on You for all strength, wisdom, joy, and love to be a blessing as You desire and to serve

others and You effectively. Keep my heart and mind in peace, because I don't need to be in charge, You will be able to do just fine, without my help.

31  The crowd sternly told them to be quiet, but they cried out all the more, "Lord, Son of David, have mercy on us!" "Lord, have mercy"—not just something to sing or say on Sunday morning, but yes, Lord something that applies to me. It's not just physical problems that I have, although there are some of those. I need You, please, to open my eyes so that I see You clearly and see the evil in the small choices I make, so that I may by Your grace and power choose Life in all the choices I make. And I need mercy because I have sinned in things I have said and done, and I carry a burden of guilt. Be merciful to me, Lord (even if some days I seem to need more than my share). Forgive me for my sins. Take away the guilt that I carry and give me healing and peace and Your wonderful joy in Living newly now in this clean fresh day and hour and year. Let my life demonstrate thanksgiving for Your gracious and generous mercy. Thank You for Your mercy!

Only joy in Your generosity
See opportunities and serve
Mercy: Yes, on me


Matthew 21

9  The crowds going ahead of Him, and those who followed, were shouting,
"Hosanna to the Son of David;
BLESSED IS HE WHO COMES IN THE NAME OF THE LORD;
Hosanna in the highest!"
To see You coming into Jerusalem, Gentle, Holy King! What a sight! You are the Son of David, the Christ, the Fulfillment of our Father's promise! And the people were shouting "Hosanna!" I use that word in worship, and sometimes I

forget what it means: Be propitious! Be favorably disposed! Be benevolent! Yes, Lord, please look on me with Your favor. Have a good and gracious will toward me, also, now. These many years later, I still ask that same thing, because I know I am a sinner. It is only by Your good and gracious will that You can bless me. Thank You, Lord. Today, grant that I do not forget Your grace and love toward me. Grant that I remember that also today, You are answering my prayer, my "Hosanna!"

16 ...and said to Him, "Do You hear what these *children* are saying?" And Jesus said to them, "Yes; have you never read, 'OUT OF THE MOUTH OF INFANTS AND NURSING BABIES YOU HAVE PREPARED PRAISE FOR YOURSELF'?"
There You were, coming down the road, and what was appropriate by grace on this great day in the history of the world, was not to get out an autograph book or a picture for You to sign, not to unload onto You some problems that were going on at the time, but only to praise! You were fulfilling the promises that Your Father had made through the ages. And the time had come to recognize You as Fulfillment and King and just praise You and praise God, our Father, for You. I know You are here, now. I have asked Your help in many ways. Remind me to spend at least equal time just praising You. Gracious Father, prepare praise in me, in my heart today. With the things I do, let there be praise to You. In the things I think, let there be praise to You. In all I say, please Lord, let there be praise to You. You are here. You have forgiven me and blessed me with Life in You. Praise to You!

43 Therefore I say to you, the kingdom of God will be taken away from you and given to a people, producing the fruit of it.
I don't celebrate people losing Your kingdom, Lord. Yet, thank You for including me in the people to whom You have given Your kingdom. Thank You for forgiveness and faith in You. Let me demonstrate Your grace by producing fruit, as

You desire. I don't see fruit ahead in this day. It doesn't exactly stand out clearly. But You can see it coming, so help me to recognize every opportunity to be fruitful for You. Let me not disappoint You. Let me never be distracted from faithfulness to You, so that I slip into unfruitfulness. Let Your Kingdom today have the wonderful scent of blossoms proclaiming fruitfulness in all the people to whom You have given Your Kingdom.

Hosanna, also today
Praise, yes, in today
Tending fruitfulness


Matthew 22

20, 21 And He said to them, "Whose likeness and inscription is this?" [21] They said to Him, "Caesar's." Then He said to them, "Then render to Caesar the things that are Caesar's; and to God the things that are God's."
As Caesar provided coins and international structure for people to use, You have blessed us with life and all things good. Bless me in using all that You have given, with an awareness and appreciation that they come from You. It is hard some days to see the girders and duct tape (!) that You used in providing this planet, the beautiful land, the structure of commerce and community and education. Help me to rejoice in all You have provided. Grant that I am a good steward of what You have given. Help me to see how to return Your gifts to You with praise and thanksgiving by sharing the encouragement and hope You have given, by using the faith You have given openly, and by sharing money and things You have given me with those who need them. May I please, Lord, honor You in all the ways I use what You have given me.

37  And He said to him, "'YOU SHALL LOVE THE LORD YOUR GOD WITH ALL YOUR HEART, AND WITH ALL YOUR SOUL, AND WITH ALL YOUR MIND.'
Thank You for letting me know that the great privilege I have is the privilege to love You, Lord.  Grant that I may use this privilege today.  Let not sin get in the way.  Keep distractions away.  Fill my heart, that with undivided heart I may love You.  Let Your grace completely enliven my soul so that I love You as Your creation to whom You have opened eternity.  And capture all of my mind, so that in my thinking, planning, and doing today I love You in all I do.  Let my love for You grow each day.  Let not fears nor concerns for myself get in the way of loving You, my Lord and God, always.

39  The second is like it, 'YOU SHALL LOVE YOUR NEIGHBOR AS YOURSELF.'
I hear You saying, Lord, that I can love the people around me as I love myself.  Help me to rejoice in the value and eternal joy that You have given me, so that I love myself in a good and proper way (without any selfishness).  Grant that I do not love myself too little, by forgetting how You have redeemed me and made me Your own.  Grant that I do not love myself too much, by thinking about myself with vanity and pride.  And then let my care, concern, and love for other people be based on that healthy love and on Your grace so that my "neighbors" may recognize Your love through me.

Steward:  Using gifts, generously
Undivided heart:  Loving You
Loving me and others, well


Matthew 23

8  But do not be called Rabbi; for One is your Teacher, and you are all brothers.

Thank You, Lord, for being my Teacher. I have had very good teachers, and I have enjoyed learning a variety of things. The thing is, when I listen to You, I feel like I am Your only student. You care about me. You have so much for me to learn. I feel like I have learned a lot, and then I get older and look back and it seems that I have a lot more to learn. Grant that I am a willing and able student. Help me to listen to You when You teach me through Your word, through other people, through experiences, through talking to You and listening to You. Grant that I put into practice what I learn, not learning so that I pile knowledge higher and deeper, but learning to follow You better, more faithfully, and with love for my fellow learners. Let there be no arrogance to my learning from You, Lord, but only humble, loving following You.

10 Do not be called leaders; for One is your Leader, *that is*, Christ.
I remember the leader You provided on the hike in Glacier National Park to the Salamander Glacier. He was an expert, knowledgeable and friendly, helpful and gracious. The trail was filled with breathtaking views. And I have been blessed with other guides who were also masters in their areas. But You are the only One that is my Guide, my Leader, my Master in all of life. No matter what comes up, no matter where I am, You are my Guide. Lead me, Lord. Thank You for being available on every path. When I am on the wrong path, pull be aside, point me in the right direction, and help me get on the right path with Your leadership (yes, a kick in the rear is acceptable). When I am on the right path, keep me moving (more mountain tops are coming, so I don't have to just stand on this one), give me strength in body, mind, and heart, stamina in my spirit, joy in my soul to keep up with You. I depend on You, my Master, Leader, and Guide in every moment of this day.

37 "Jerusalem, Jerusalem, who kills the prophets and stones those who are sent to her! How often I wanted to

gather your children together, the way a hen gathers her chicks under her wings, and you were unwilling.
OK, I admit it, I have a slight tendency (!) to stay by myself, away from crowds and groups. And I am sure that I also have resisted You when You have graciously wanted to gather me to others You have already brought close to Yourself. I'm sorry, Lord. Don't give up on me! Gather me every day closer to You. Bring me closer to Your people. Help me not to be so fixed on my list of all the wonderful things I want to do for You, that I miss being gathered in this day by You, so that You can use Your list of all the wonderful things You want to do for me and through me. Thank You, Lord, for not giving up on me.

Open to learn and to do
Following You, my only Guide
Closer to You: Your list


Matthew 24

14 This gospel of the kingdom shall be preached in the whole world as a testimony to all the nations, and then the end will come.
Thank You for this promise, Lord. Make it happen soon! Send Your gospel to all people in all nations in every corner of this world. Motivate Your people to support the work of reaching to people with Your gospel. Provide for all those who are proclaiming Your gospel. Protect them from evil. Open doors for more of Your servants to reach those who have not heard Your gospel. Grant Your gospel faithful hearing by the power of Your Spirit, so that people in every nation around the world will come to You and to Your gift of Life. And since one corner of the world is where I live, please grant that my life and words show and share Your good news of Your gospel to the people I see and meet today and every day.

24, 25  For false Christs and false prophets will arise and will show great signs and wonders, so as to mislead, if possible, even the elect. $^{25}$ Behold, I have told you in advance.
Thank You for the heads up, Lord. There are certainly a lot of "This is it! Satisfying life is here!" messages available now. Inform my hearing. Give me clear sight. Let no invitation, message, distraction enter me and lead me astray, away from You and Your gift of Life. Let me find in Your word all the signs and wonders of Your grace and love that I need for joyous Living with You and in You now. Grant that I begin every day in the confidence that You have told me. You are quite aware of what is happening today. There is nothing new and beyond Your understanding. Keep me faithful to You in the joy and confidence You have given me, Gracious Lord.

42  "Therefore be on the alert, for you do not know which day your Lord is coming."
When I know someone is coming, then we can go to the store and I plan to be ready. Even a little early, in case they come before the appointed time. You have graciously told me that You are coming, Lord. Help me be ready! Keep me in Your word. Feed me and nourish me in times of worship. Open my heart and mind so that I talk with You throughout this day and each day. It doesn't seem like all of the conditions have been quite fulfilled for Your coming Lord, but there I go forgetting that it is not up to me. In any case the day for my coming to You is certainly coming one day, and it could be today. Grant that I am alert, that I am ready. Let me be so close to You in Living and loving today, that when I go around a corner and find You there waiting for me I will rejoice and be satisfied.

Your Gospel sent and faithfully heard
Undistractedly close to You
Ready

Matthew 25

23 His master said to him, 'Well done, good and faithful slave. You were faithful with a few things, I will put you in charge of many things; enter into the joy of your master.'
You have entrusted to me gifts, abilities, and blessings, Lord. Thank You! Grant that I will be a good steward of Your gospel, believing You, trusting You always and sharing with others Your gospel, with faith that You will bring results You want. Grant that I use the abilities You have given me wisely and with the energy and time You have given, so that I will accomplish what You want and be a blessing to others. Grant that I will recognize the blessings You have given, Lord, that I will demonstrate thankfulness to You and use them well. Let me use everything You have given me with faith so that all the things You have given are multiplied in their use by Your grace to Your great glory, Lord.

34 "Then the King will say to those on His right, 'Come, you who are blessed of My Father, inherit the kingdom prepared for you from the foundation of the world.'"
I look forward to being on Your right, Lord, not because I am sinless or good or worthy because of anything I have done or will do, but only by Your gracious blessing, Father. "Blessed of My Father"—yes, thank You, Lord. I am blessed to have You send Jesus, my Savior. I am blessed to have You take my sins on You, Jesus, and I am blessed by receiving forgiveness from Your sacrifice. I am blessed, Lord Holy Spirit, by Your giving me faith so that I can believe Your gospel, receive forgiveness, and trust You to Live in me today. Only because I am greatly blessed, do I earnestly look forward to inheriting the kingdom You have prepared. Because You have prepared it, I know it will be wonderful beyond my wildest imagination. Thank You, Gracious Lord.

40 The King will answer and say to them, 'Truly I say to you, to the extent that you did it to one of these brothers of Mine, *even* the least *of them*, you did it to Me.'

This is really terrific, Lord! You know I would like to go back in time and be there when You were ministering so I could shout from the back of the crowd, "Way to go, Lord!" Or perhaps I could fix lunch for You and Your disciples one day. But lacking that (even though some science fiction is no longer fiction, I suspect You have a lock on time), it is wonderful that You give me the opportunity to do things for You now. Things that I do for other people I can be doing for You. What a concept! To do for You today! You give a whole new meaning to getting up in the morning. Grant that I remember and rejoice in everything I get to do today, that I do things for You by doing things for my family, friends, and strangers I meet. No matter what people say today, I will see You smiling.

Using Your gifts well
Blessed: Thank You
Doing things for You


Matthew 26

26 – 28 While they were eating, Jesus took *some* bread, and after a blessing, He broke *it* and gave *it* to the disciples, and said, "Take, eat; this is My body." [27] And when He had taken a cup and given thanks, He gave *it* to them, saying, "Drink from it, all of you; [28] for this is My blood of the covenant, which is poured out for many for forgiveness of sins.
Thank You Lord for the Passover. Thank You, Lord Jesus, for making the Passover a blessing for me so that I can be strengthened for Living. You have said You give Your people Your body and blood for the forgiveness of our sins. Please grant that I come to worship in repentance and confidence in You. And please grant that I receive Your gifts so that I will walk with You in each day and live forgiven, in new Life, every day. I look forward to receiving Your wonderful gifts; make them powerful in me so that I will serve

You effectively today. Please grant that I recognize You in Your gifts and receive Your gifts with joy and satisfaction.

38  Then He *said to them, "My soul is deeply grieved, to the point of death; remain here and keep watch with Me."
The disciples had trouble being actively alert with You, as You wrestled with the burden You carried, Lord Jesus. I would like to say I can do better. But the truth is, after starting the day You give me, by talking to You, and listening to You in Your word, I often forget to be in touch with You during the day until evening, unless there is some problem or attack or need. Help me to be alert with my head and my heart through the day so that I can recognize beauty in Your world with You, so that I can feel joy with You in Your blessings, so that I can actively lean on You, Your grace and Your wisdom, at every choice and decision, so that I can be aware of Your presence whenever I meet people or spend time with them. Please grant that I be alert, actively seeking Your presence whenever I am tempted or discouraged. Thank You, Lord, that You are alert and blessing me even when I lose focus on You and Your sustaining love and grace.

63, 64  But Jesus kept silent. And the high priest said to Him, "I adjure You by the living God, that You tell us whether You are the Christ, the Son of God." ⁶⁴ Jesus *said to him, "You have said it *yourself*; nevertheless I tell you, hereafter you will see THE SON OF MAN SITTING AT THE RIGHT HAND OF POWER, and COMING ON THE CLOUDS OF HEAVEN."
Promises upon promises You gave in the Old Testament, Lord—Messiah was coming. Then when You came, Jesus, some recognized You as the Fulfillment of all the promises, while some were holding out for their own version of what the Messiah should look like and sound like. You have made it clear. You are the Christ, the Son of God. Not a good person. Not a great leader. Not an inspiring prophet. You are the Fulfillment. All the promises come to reality in You. Thank You for making clear that you are the Christ

sent from God to give me forgiveness and new Life. Grant that I Live in satisfaction in You and in looking for Your great and awesome return.

Nourished by Your Meal
Actively alert throughout this day
You are the One, now and then


Matthew 27

12  And while He was being accused by the chief priests and elders, He did not answer.
Thank You Lord Jesus for being silent. What gracious strength, Your silence! Because if You had not been silent, the truth would have taken a long time and been very difficult. The truth was that You were taking the burden of my guilt. The truth that could have been spoken was that You were suffering for all my sins, for all my brokenness, for all my selfishness, for all the hurtful things I have said and done, for all the good and right and wonderful things that I have failed to do. The truth would have taken a long time and they would not have believed it. And they particularly wouldn't have liked or believed the part of the truth You could have spoken—that You were carrying the burden of their guilt as well. Thank You, Jesus, for carrying my burden to the cross. Thank You for being silent.

40  ...and saying, "You who *are going to* destroy the temple and rebuild it in three days, save Yourself! If You are the Son of God, come down from the cross."
It seemed so reasonable to them. If You were the Son of God, then You could just avoid the whole thing, use Your power to blow away all Your persecutors, and with blinding light show Who You were. (Definitely a plot favored by Hollywood.) But the truth was, it was because You were and are the Son of God that You chose, loving me and all people, to suffer for us, to give us forgiveness, to arrange a

proclamation of "Not Guilty" and "Righteous in the Lord" for us. The point of Your life was to be there, then, on the cross—for me, for us, even for those at the foot of the cross. Thank You, Gracious Lord Jesus! Thank You for staying on the cross!

46 About the ninth hour Jesus cried out with a loud voice, saying, "ELI, ELI, LAMA SABACHTHANI?" that is, "MY GOD, MY GOD, WHY HAVE YOU FORSAKEN ME?"
You have cried out from the cross in anguish, in suffering beyond human understanding, and so that I could get the point. Yes, I know why. It was because of me. When I look back over yesterday or over the years, I like to remember the high points. I like to remember warmth, goodness, truth, and blessing (and maybe recognition times). What I don't like to remember is all the times when I chose to be forsaken by God. When I chose my way instead of Yours, Lord. When I knew what You wanted, but I was afraid, or lazy, or foolishly liked my idea better. Every time I said, "Yes, Lord, but what I would really rather do is …" I have so much trouble following Mary's example, "Let it be according to Your will." Yes, Lord, I know why. Thank You for being my Substitute, for taking what I deserve. Thank You, my Gracious, Wonderful Savior and Lord!

Your grace:  Love in silence
Your grace:  Staying on the cross
Your grace:  Taking my place


Matthew 28

9 And behold, Jesus met them and greeted them. And they came up and took hold of His feet and worshiped Him.
Thank You Jesus for meeting me still today. Thank You for being here with me. Thank You for speaking to me in Your word. Thank You that I can remember verses in which You have touched me in the past and experience Your presence.

Help me to take hold of You with my heart and my head and all of my being today.  Grant that I worship You in this day with the great joy that You are forever alive in power, grace, glory, majesty, and eternal light.  Please meet me along the way in this day.  Lift my spirit beyond the painful news of the day, beyond the to do list (and the file of old to do lists that I am trying to forget)—lift my spirit to see You Who are Life and to listen to Your Life-giving greeting today.

18, 19  And Jesus came up and spoke to them, saying, "All authority has been given to Me in heaven and on earth.
[19] Go therefore and make disciples of all the nations, baptizing them in the name of the Father and the Son and the Holy Spirit...
"Therefore"!  How wonderfully You say that!  Like, it's all taken care of.  No doubt about it.  Because You have all authority, Therefore!, Be going.  Send me going into today for You.  Send me by Your authority to hope, to love, to be patient, to care, to see needs, to encourage, to help, to speak of the joy I have in You.  Let Your Therefore! ring in my ears, in my heart, in my thoughts and in my words.  Use me to be a blessing.  Grant that some part of my day, today, may be effectively useful in blessing others in becoming or being disciples.  "What will people think (!) if I demonstrate dependence on You in all I say and do?"—let joy in You shine so brightly through me that people think You are great, gracious, God, Savior, and Lord.  Direct my day with Your authority and Your Therefore!

20  ...teaching them to observe all that I commanded you; and lo, I am with you always, even to the end of the age."
You say things, Lord Jesus, in such a way that I can step out confidently into today.  When there is the death of someone I love, Your "always" is there to sustain me—the eternal reality underneath the thin reality in which I live.  Through death, there is going home to be with You.  But (selfishly) here I am.  OK.  It's ok for me to miss loved ones that have gone home to You.  It's ok to let this be a time when I think about

dying, leaving all the people I know, leaving all this stuff that at some point in time seemed important. It's ok to think about a time when nothing matters except You and Your love. Let me carry with me some of that focus while I walk on through the days You give me: You are most important. You are wonderfully, graciously essential to each breath I take. And bless me in living in the amazing confidence that while I live and breathe, even though the reality I live in seems thin and shaky sometimes, You promise to be with me Always. Always now. Always then. Always forever.

Meet me today
Living in Your Therefore!
Here, now, always

# Mark

Mark 1

15 And saying, "The time is fulfilled, and the kingdom of God is at hand; repent and believe in the gospel."
It was the right time for the people who came to John the Baptist. Now is the right time for me, Lord. I repent of my sins. Thank You for the good news of Your gospel. Thank You for coming and living and dying for me. Help me always to believe You came, and are here, and forgive me, and give me life with You now and forever—help me believe that more than I believe the weather report (not terribly difficult) or the news or even that I am alive and breathing. You are more certain than life.

18 Immediately they left their nets and followed Him.
Yes, Lord, I want to follow You. You know what question is in my heart, "How large a suitcase can I bring?" Yep, that's me, Lord. I have difficulty going anywhere without taking a lot of stuff with me. What I hear You saying is that there are some very definite things I need to leave behind. Give me a clear vision of You calling me every day. Give me a joyful and willing spirit to follow You every day. And give me also a clear understanding and willing spirit about what to leave behind.

35 In the early morning, while it was still dark, Jesus got up, left *the house*, and went away to a secluded place, and was praying there.
Thank You Lord Jesus, for Your example. You show me that Your will is for me to have time alone for praying. As You know I have difficulty managing my (Your gift of) time. It gets full so easily. I tend to jump into the day with a passing word to You, "Good morning, Lord. Good to see You. I think

I've got today taken care of. See You later." (Get real!) Please give me courage and faith to carve out time for prayer every day, trusting You to make the rest of the time enough for whatever else I need to do. And open my heart and mind so that in that prayer time, I will talk to You and listen to You, without letting anything else intrude into my thinking (woolgathering be gone!). Let me experience You with me, Father, Jesus, Holy Spirit, as I talk to You and listen to You.

I'd rather believe the Good News
Leave and follow
Time to listen (and talk)


Mark 2

3  And they *came, bringing to Him a paralytic, carried by four men.
You received those men who brought someone to You, Lord. Thank You for receiving me when I bring people to You in prayer. Those people I see who don't look blessed or happy, touch them Lord with Your grace and joy. Those people I know who are suffering some frustration or illness, bless them, Lord, with healing. And people that I think about with frustration or anger (people who thoughtlessly litter with beer cans, wrappers, trash, people who block crosswalks!) help me to bring those people to You also, Lord. With all my heart (please, Lord) I bring them to You. Bless them all.

5  And Jesus seeing their faith *said to the paralytic, "Son, your sins are forgiven."
It is so easy for me to see the physical needs I have and others have, Lord. You graciously take care of the big problem first. When You answer my prayers and everyone's prayers, please, first, Lord, forgive us and wash us clean. Help us to see without the blinders of sin and selfishness, so that we see our needs in the light of Your love and grace.

How bright and clear things are Lord, when You first wash me with forgiveness.

25  And He said to them, "Have you never read what David did when he was in need and he and his companions became hungry?"
They were supposed to read their Bible and apply it to the time in which they lived.  So, I'm sure You want me to read the Bible and apply it to now.  Open my mind and heart, Holy Spirit, so that I may hear You speaking to me in Your word.  And grant me recall of what You have shown me in Your word, so that I may apply Your wisdom with devotion to Jesus and love for my Father to all that I see, experience, and say and do today.

Bring all to You for blessing
Wash me so I may see clearly with love
Remembered Word alive for now


Mark 3

4  And He *said to them, "Is it lawful to do good or to do harm on the Sabbath, to save a life or to kill?" But they kept silent.
If I am willing to look closely, Lord, I can see that I sometimes box myself in by rules.  I claim understanding of Your will, but I use it to keep me separate from opportunities to love people.  I'm sorry, Lord.  Open my box.  Let me live in fresh new ways, loving people as You give me opportunity.  Let no fear or laziness on my part keep me boxed in and separated from loving others.  Open my eyes to see the good that You have prepared for me to do.

17  And James, the *son* of Zebedee, and John the brother of James (to them He gave the name Boanerges, which means, "Sons of Thunder")…

I find myself, Lord, looking for things that people do wrong. Blame comes so quickly to my lips. Harshness in my voice communicates that someone is doing something wrong (or at least not the way I would do it). Forgive me, Lord. Let my attitudes and words and voice show Your love and concern. Let me look for and find blessings to value and honor in the people around me. And if I am frustrated and angry, let me always turn to You, call on You to be present, and trust You to deal with the people and situation that bother me.

18 And Andrew, and Philip, and Bartholomew, and Matthew, and Thomas, and James the son of Alphaeus, and Thaddaeus, and Simon the Zealot.
You saw zeal in the heart of Simon. Sometimes zeal is scary to me. (There is this voice inside saying, "How do these people live in this real world that I live in?!) I meet people who are zealous for a cause. I even meet people who are zealous for You, Lord. Open my heart to zeal, Lord. Grant that I practice "reckless abandonment" as You desire. [Thank You for Oswald Chambers, Lord.] Grant that I may leave fear behind, recognize zeal with joy, and follow You zealously, putting You absolutely first in my life.

Open my box
Thunder: Yours, not mine
Trusting, loving, zealous.


Mark 4

19 But the worries of the world, and the deceitfulness of riches, and the desires for other things enter in and choke the word, and it becomes unfruitful.
This really sounds like the twenty-first century, Lord. Of course, I would like to think that I'm not that bothered, but then You help me to see and I realize it is not a huge amount of anxiety that is the point. It is not the lure of millions and billions. The lure of thousands (or an extra $25) will be just

as effective. And I don't want a lot of things. (Just a lot of books!) Help me not to be anxious about family members who need Your help. Help me to love them and entrust them to Your loving care. Remind me every morning that I can trust You to provide for me, and help me to refrain from telling You what is included in "provide". Let me see things that You have given with thanksgiving and grant that I will be a good steward of all that You have given me. Keep me free from all these anxieties so that nothing gets in the way of my bearing fruit as You desire. And if I hear a choking noise from Your word, give me a clear view of my anxieties.

24  And He was saying to them, "Take care what you listen to. By your standard of measure it will be measured to you; and more will be given you besides."
You give me two ears and one mouth, and still I do find myself tuning people out. I suppose I'm so used to tuning out commercials, that I hurtfully use that ability with people. I'm sorry, Lord. Help me to really listen and hear what people say. Help me hear the feelings, the joys, the frustrations people have. Give me patience, to listen to people with Your love. Grant that I give my time and attention with a caring attitude when I listen to people. And when I have an opportunity to hear something derogatory or evil, grant that I choose a measure of zero attention, and that I do not take in evil that is spoken. Thank You for being in charge of which is which.

41  They became very much afraid and said to one another, "Who then is this, that even the wind and the sea obey Him?"
You are so kind and gracious to listen to me talk to You, Lord. You speak to me in Your word. Help me not to slip into familiarity, breeding contempt. Help me remember You with great awe, to wonder who You are, so great, so powerful, so gracious, so loving, beyond my wildest imagination, and yet living in my heart and life. You are

more that I can ever take in, Lord. Thank You, gracious Lord, for being You.

No room for anxiety
Caring listening
You are awesome!


Mark 5

10  And he *began* to implore Him earnestly not to send them out of the country.
The evil spirits knew the jig was up. They recognized absolute authority and power when they saw You. Grant that I recognize in You not only mercy, grace, love, and joy, but also all authority and all power over evil, over every situation I hand over to You in prayer, and over me and all that I am and all that I have. You have all authority to bless me and others, so when I talk to You, Lord, let me do that with confidence in You and obedience to You.

19  And He did not let him, but He *said to him, "Go home to your people and report to them what great things the Lord has done for you, and *how* He had mercy on you."
There have been those times, Lord, when I was in the shoes of Walter Mitty, and I imagined going with You and being Your great representative, saving people, helping people with nobility and courage (and being recognized for being some great poobah!). And You keep telling me, "Go home, be a blessing there." OK, by Your grace, Lord, in the daily things at home and in my daily schedule, grant that I serve You and let others know what great things You have done for me and how You have had mercy on me. (And blow away the figments of my Walter Mitty imagination with the strains of Tchaikovsky's 1812 overture in the background.)

36  But Jesus, overhearing what was being spoken, *said to the synagogue official, "Do not be afraid *any longer*, only believe."
You have an amazing ability to hear really bad stuff and not take it in, Lord.  There are bad things swirling around waves of TV, radio, and various other media and social whatnot.  Help me not to take them in.  Grant that I do not sink into fear and depression from the news and information that is around, but rather that I believe You to be in charge, here and now, in all of those problematic situations.  And believing in You, grant that I dwell in confidence, and that I press on, walking with You and living in peace.

Recognize authority to bless
What the Lord has done
Overhear, no fear, only believe


Mark 6

8  And He instructed them that they should take nothing for *their* journey, except a mere staff—no bread, no bag, no money in their belt—
I'm glad You don't send me on journeys telling me to take nothing along.  The reason I like pants with lots of pockets is that I can take lots of stuff with me wherever I go.  And in general it is a lot easier to depend on experience, education, money, and how many books (or e-books) I can carry—than it is to depend on You.  Forgive me, Lord.  Help me not to let anything distract me from depending on You.  Thank you for experiences, education, money (and especially books!), but on the journey every day, let me depend only on You with joy, confidence, and enthusiasm.

13  And they were casting out many demons and were anointing with oil many sick people and healing them.
Thank You, Lord, that it is Your will to cast out demons.  They have not gone away, of course.  It isn't quite as popular

today to talk about demons and really mean evil angels.
And yet they are surely here. Protect me and all my loved
ones from demons, please, Lord. Cast them out of our lives.
Especially the ones in my life that I have invited in. Ych! Fill
us with Your Holy Spirit to the exclusion of all evil spirits, and
grant that I and we give no room for evil. Grant that we
avoid temptation by Your grace and ever keep watch so that
we do not welcome any evil spirits.

50 For they all saw Him and were terrified. But immediately
He spoke with them and said to them, "Take courage; it is I,
do not be afraid."
That does not sound like my favorite place, Lord, in the early
morning hours, after a sleepless night, in the dark, on the
sea that has a reputation for quickly developing bad weather.
But there are dark places that I have been in my spirit and
yes, Lord, I will take all the courage You want to give me. In
every dark time, in every time of fear, let me know that You
are close, walking by, not tossed about, in the sunshine,
smiling, loving me, available, so that I do not have to be
afraid.

Nothing, with You, is plenty
Welcoming, with Your discernment
Be my sunshine, in every storm.


Mark 7

6 And He said to them, "Rightly did Isaiah prophesy of you
hypocrites, as it is written:
'THIS PEOPLE HONORS ME WITH THEIR LIPS,
BUT THEIR HEART IS FAR AWAY FROM ME.
The Pharisees really worked hard to do religious actions.
They had lost the why. Help me to see why I do things,
Lord. Grant that I do not take in any of the world's "whys" as
motivation for the things I do in Your will. Touch my heart
please, Lord, and forgive my rote, unthinking words and

actions. When I have the opportunity to serve You, help me to see You with me, so that I am not depending on some personal motivation of goodness in me. Gracious Spirit set fires of love and worship in my heart so that going to church, praying, and loving people come only from the fire of Your presence in my heart and my love for You, gracious Lord and God.

8,9 Neglecting the commandment of God, you hold to the tradition of men."
9 He was also saying to them, "You are experts at setting aside the commandment of God in order to keep your tradition.
It isn't reasonable! It only makes sense to… . You know, Lord, those voices are very loud in me. When I try to put other people first or make some small sacrifice (or large) of what I want, there come those voices. The temptation I feel is to say, "What You really meant, of course, was …". Help me, when I feel my reasonable, makes sense, motor start, to turn it off, and listen to You. And then reset the defaults in my reasonable, makes sense, motor to Your will. In all my thinking and wanting and depending on tradition, let me hear and obey only You.

30 And going back to her home, she found the child lying on the bed, the demon having left.
Now that took guts! She walked away from You. You spoke a word of blessing. She believed You. She went home. When I hear You speak a word of blessing, Lord, please grant that I also will listen, believe You, and walk on in faith, knowing that is taken care of. No going back with, "Lord, have You taken this into account? You're really sure, Lord? You know a lot of people say that …". When I see Your will in Your word, grant that I talk to You, take in Your gracious will, depend on it, and walk on into the day, in confidence in Your grace.

All my "whys" from You

Not now, Reason
Hearing, believing, walking on


Mark 8

1 In those days, when there was again a large crowd and they had nothing to eat, Jesus called His disciples and said to them...
You gave them a chance to step out in faith and suggest that You give the people what they needed. They had previous experience with You in a similar circumstance. It seems to me that I have failed to learn from the experiences You have given me, Lord. By now, I have seen You bring people to faith. I have seen You provide help from sources I didn't know existed. I have seen You touch me and others with love from people that didn't appear to be loving. So when You give me a chance to step out and trust You to deal with a problem, help me to remember. Help me to step out in faith that You are there using me and blessing people by Your power.

11 The Pharisees came out and began to argue with Him, seeking from Him a sign from heaven, to test Him.
"Lord if You want me to do that, have a check for $100 come in the mail tomorrow." I haven't exactly said that, Lord, but it's been close. And I can still hear You sighing. Help me to listen to You, Lord. (There have been those times, Lord, when You finally used a 2x4 to get my attention. I'd really like to avoid that, Lord.) Help me look in my heart and see Your Holy Spirit leading me, calling me to follow You. Help me to make real sacrifices that will be a blessing. Grant that I don't need a sign (or a 2x4), just the joy of listening to You and following You.

34 And He summoned the crowd with His disciples, and said to them, "If anyone wishes to come after Me, he must deny himself, and take up his cross and follow Me.

I feel with Peter, Lord. Always sunshine, success, acceptance, good health, and joy. Well one out of five is pretty good. You tell me I can have joy in You always, even if not the others. Walk with me, Lord, and help me to follow You when the way ahead looks dark, unsuccessful, full of rejection, and possible suffering. Help me to see what in me I need to deny. Grant that my enjoyment of sunny days and peaceful living not keep me from recognizing the cross that is mine or from picking it up and carrying it. Grant that I recognize the sunshine of Your love and the peace You give as I carry the cross You show me today, walking every step with You.

Stepping out in faith
Listening to You
Walking in Your sunshine


Mark 9

5,6 Peter said to Jesus, "Rabbi, it is good for us to be here; let us make three tabernacles, one for You, and one for Moses, and one for Elijah." 6 For he did not know what to answer; for they became terrified.
There are things, Lord, that happen in my life, and I feel like I need to say something to You. It's not that I heard You say words to me, but I, with Peter, am responding to some event. For Peter the event didn't fit anything in his experience and all the disciples were terrified. When I have things happen that I can't fit into my understanding, when there are blessings so wild that I have trouble taking them in, Lord, please give me confidence to talk to You. Forgive me if I babble without understanding. There is no event outside Your experience, so direct my words and thoughts in conversation with You, that I will have confidence in You, relax in You, live in peace in You, and know that I have come to the right Person.

35 Sitting down, He called the twelve and said to them, "If anyone wants to be first, he shall be last of all and servant of all."

What are children taught now, Lord? How to get ahead. How to be somebody. How to succeed. Be first? A lot of people will sign up for that. And yes, Lord, I have been there. But Your plan is really far out and weird. Pick the group I want to be first in; then find a way to serve everyone in that group. Sheesh! I'm sorry Lord that I have trouble fitting that square peg into the round holes in my heart. Change me, Lord, change my heart. Help me to want to serve others. Help me go against the enormous flow of current civilization and desire to be humble and of service. Help me leave the "first" part up to You, and give me the opportunity to serve in whatever way You want. There I know You will give me satisfaction.

43 If your hand causes you to stumble, cut it off; it is better for you to enter life crippled, than, having your two hands, to go into hell, into the unquenchable fire.

One of the jobs with the surest longevity is a job in the health industry. And that, Lord, I suppose is because we (translate I) really want to have our bodies healthy. You showed Your concern for how people felt in their bodies by healing people, so I know You understand my desire to be healthy and I know You care about me. Still, help me to realize what comes first. Surely a healthy body is useless if I cannot live in Your gift of life with You, now and forever. Grant that I put as much time, effort, and focus on my health in relation to You as I do on my physical health.

In any event, You're the One to talk to
Satisfaction in serving
Living or dying, healthy in You


Mark 10

8  AND THE TWO SHALL BECOME ONE FLESH; so they are no longer two, but one flesh.
What God has joined together.  You have made us one.  Thank You for the joy You have given us.  And, ok, there are times when I wish You would Bless my other half when she doesn't think the way I do.  And there are times when my other half wishes You would Bless me because I don't think (and she would add feel) the way she does.  So, since You have made us one, since You have blessed us and given us joy and wonder in life and worship together, please give us patience, a listening caring ear and heart, and a desire to bless each other in every way.  Grant that we enjoy peace and satisfaction in You and serve You faithfully, together.

15  Truly I say to you, whoever does not receive the kingdom of God like a child will not enter it *at all*.
"Ooh, You made this for me?  Thank you!"  With surprise, joy, trust, and expectation that this will be continuingly wonderful.  Let me accept Your gift of Your kingdom with these beautiful child attitudes.  Help me, Lord, avoid the "Let me see if I have room in my schedule" and "What is this going to cost me?" attitudes more common to adults.  Let me enter each day with surprise, joy, ooh, and great expectations.

48  Many were sternly telling him to be quiet, but he kept crying out all the more, "Son of David, have mercy on me!"
It is so easy, Lord, to decide Your agenda for You.  To decide whom You should bless, and how.  Help me to get out of the business of being Your private agenda secretary.  You have made it clear that You answer prayers so that we receive the best possible blessing.  (I'm sorry that I (and we) have such selfish and limited ideas about what is the best possible blessing for us and others.)  Let me bring each person I can think of, each need I am aware of, to You, and grant that I let You bless with reckless abandon as You desire.

Listening, caring
Joy with ooh!
Trusting Your agenda


Mark 11


9  Those who went in front and those who followed were shouting:
"Hosanna!
BLESSED IS HE WHO COMES IN THE NAME OF THE LORD."
How I receive someone depends on whom he represents. When I get a call from a representative of the East Snowshoes Barn Door and Investments company asking me to invest money (no offense to barn doors, which are important) I don't take them seriously.  Grant that I receive You with thanksgiving and joy, and that my recognition of Who You are and Whom You represent shows in my face and in all my words and actions.   Help me always, Lord Jesus, to honor You and rejoice in Who You are because You represent our Father in heaven.  Thank You that I am always blessed by the Father in Whose name You come.

17  And He *began* to teach and say to them, "Is it not written, 'MY HOUSE SHALL BE CALLED A HOUSE OF PRAYER FOR ALL THE NATIONS'? But you have made it a ROBBERS' DEN."
Partly a quote from Isaiah 56.7, let this verse be a reminder to me, Lord, that You have prepared the church where I worship as a place to talk to You.  Thank You that I can talk to You anywhere, but especially thank You that I know You come to talk to me and listen to me in the house of worship to which You have called me.  May I always come to speak, sing, and listen, to You.  Grant that I remember, no matter where I am in my life, there You are.

28 And *began* saying to Him, "By what authority are You doing these things, or who gave You this authority to do these things?"

The scribes, Pharisees, and elders were disturbed. Their lifestyle was being threatened. There are times when I have asked You something that sounds very much like that question. "You want to change my life, my life-style? You want to change what I do, where I live? What authority, …?" And then I remember, "Oh, right, You have all authority. And You always make changes to bless me or make me a blessing." Grant that I honor You and always welcome Your exercising Your authority in my life. (And when I have white knuckles (!), help me to relax and trust You.)

Receiving You with honor
There You are
Authority to change


Mark 12

14 They came and said to Him, "Teacher, we know that You are truthful and defer to no one; for You are not partial to any, but teach the way of God in truth. Is it lawful to pay a poll-tax to Caesar, or not? "

The world often presents me with two choices and (sneeringly) asks me to pick one. Open my eyes to see that Your choice is not necessarily one of the ones that the world offers. In fact it usually isn't. When I hear "only two choices" or "only three possibilities", let me remember to ask You to show me what Your choice is, because Yours is always best. And if Your choice is to do something that is unpopular, help me to be faithful to You even when it is unpopular.

Whatever choice You want me to make, grant that my motives be and be seen to be love for You and desire to do Your will. Keep me safe from appearing to do the right thing for the wrong reason.

27 "He is not the God of the dead, but of the living; you are greatly mistaken."
I often do not know how to think about life after death, but thank You Lord that I can be sure that I will be living after death. And thank You that I know that those whom I love and miss are also living in You and that we will be together in Life. Grant that I always live in confidence and hope looking beyond death to Life. Keep me from using Life after death as an excuse for not helping people in need here and now. And yet, in all the opportunities that You give me to be a blessing to others now, grant that all help and love and assistance be clear windows showing Your love now and Your loving gift, in Jesus, of joyous Life after death with You forever.

30, 31 "AND YOU SHALL LOVE THE LORD YOUR GOD WITH ALL YOUR HEART, AND WITH ALL YOUR SOUL, AND WITH ALL YOUR MIND, AND WITH ALL YOUR STRENGTH.' 31 The second is this, 'YOU SHALL LOVE YOUR NEIGHBOR AS YOURSELF.' There is no other commandment greater than these."
Wow, Lord, that is beautiful, huge, and scary! But You have made it clear that this is Your will, so here I am asking You to please grant that I love You today with all my heart, wanting nothing more than You and Your gracious will in all my life. Grant that I love You today with all my soul. My eternal being is a gift from You and is satisfied only in You. Grant that I show eternal joy and satisfaction in all I do today. Grant that I love You with all my mind, thinking well, with Your wisdom, and in Your gracious will. Grant that I love You with all my strength, my strength of character, my emotional and physical strength, (all gifts from You), always walking in Your light. And grant that I love those around me, especially those who need mercy, by Your grace and power with Your wisdom. Fill my days with love for You and for people.

Your choices

Showing now, Life then
Days full of love


Mark 13

6 Many will come in My name, saying, 'I am *He*!' and will mislead many.
You were certainly right about that, Lord! Many have come. There are many now. Thank You, Lord, for the many people who love You, Jesus, and who have different cultural approaches to worship and prayer and living in You. Help me not to be put off by differences that are not misleading. Enrich my experience with You by letting me know Your people who have backgrounds different from mine. And then there are the others. The ones that claim to follow You and want me to change in a way that leads away from You and Your grace and Your love. Grant that I recognize them, and recognized the distinction between those who are different and faithfully following You and those who are different and going away from You. Help me not to be afraid of caring about people. Give me the confidence that You can tell the difference and will lead me to walk with You faithfully today.

8 For nation will rise up against nation, and kingdom against kingdom; there will be earthquakes in various places; there will *also* be famines. These things are *merely* the beginning of birth pangs.
Help me to have an attitude and actions of mercy toward those suffering. Grant that I never see disasters as events that can pull me away from You. We live in a world that is broken in many ways. Let us recognize disasters as part of the brokenness. Grant that all people experience a wake-up call when terrible things happen. Open our eyes to see You, not as a vengeful God, but as our Gracious Lord bringing us another step toward the beginning of Life without tragedy, pain, suffering or disasters. Touch our minds and our hearts

so that with everything that happens we are brought closer to You with growing confidence in Your grace and in the new Life You are preparing for us with You.

37 What I say to you I say to all, 'Be on the alert!'"
Grant, Lord, that I not be distracted by evil or stuff or worries of the world. Help me not to get so used to the brokenness of the world that I fall asleep with an attitude that nothing matters. Let me live without hyperventilating with an attitude that everything is terrible and to be feared. Grant that I walk with You in each day listening to Your calling me and alert to Your direction and warnings. Help me look ahead to the Light and Joy coming while I am alert to the rocks and curves on the path now. Grant that I enter every day looking to You, waiting expectantly, watching for You to step into every room I am in, into every moment of time I enjoy. Grant that my heart and my ears ever listen with joy and expectation for Your step in the hallways and pathways of my life.

Different together and different apart
Disasters, drive me to You
Listen for Your step


Mark 14

6 But Jesus said, "Let her alone; why do you bother her? She has done a good deed to Me.
What better use is there for the highest of honors, the very best I have, than to give it to You, Lord, for Your use. You are worthy! Let my words and actions, my attitudes and desires, all give honor and glory to You. You are worthy of far more than I can ever say or do or give. Let nothing hold me back from giving You the very best I have and the best I am every day. Now when it comes to other people, they don't seem to use the same common sense I use. They don't seem to do things the way that I know would be a

blessing. If I could just give them a little guidance. (What is amazing, Lord, is that I have actually thought those thoughts! Incredible! Beyond arrogant, I seem to think that everyone should be like me, have my understanding, and do things the way I do. How narrow-minded, blind to Your gracious love to a variety of people, and in fact boring! Please forgive me, Lord.) Help me to rejoice in all that others do for You. Grant that I appreciate all the good that others do. Let me recognize others and their Living for You with thanks, with words of celebration, and with worship of You.

13 And He sent two of His disciples and said to them, "Go into the city, and a man will meet you carrying a pitcher of water; follow him.
The disciples had grown to the point where they didn't ask how You could know what would happen after they went into the city. They went. (A *man* carrying a jar of water! You've got to be kidding, Lord.) You send me, Lord, into each day asking me to trust that You will continue to lead me. You grant that I can make commitments trusting that You will provide for me and lead me. Thank You, Lord. Please grant that, listening to You, I take first steps, in the direction I hear You calling me, always trusting You to lead me on the rest of the steps You want me to take, even if I can't in my wildest imagination figure out where You are leading me. Keep me safe from every attitude of "Well, just a minute, Lord, where are You leading me!" and "I would really like You to explain to me what is coming and how You are going to manage this, Lord!" Let me know and rejoice that it is enough to get up. To go into the city. To start.

31 But *Peter* kept saying insistently, "*Even* if I have to die with You, I will not deny You!" And they all were saying the same thing also.
They are not alone, Lord. I would like to think, Lord, that I can manage stuff, like living in today. After all, I have several spreadsheets that deal with many of the concerns that I am currently dealing with. (!) You remind me that I am

a sinner and that I need You, every moment. Yes, I resist thinking of myself as helpless. And yet, I know You can see me clearly. Those weak spots in my faith muscles. Those enormous holes in my "clear" vision of what is going on around me. Forgive me, Lord, for brash, unfounded arrogance. Grant that I depend on You, consciously, throughout the day, with a continuing conversation in which I listen to You and talk to You. And grant that in every battle with temptation, discouragement, or vanity I turn to You (no weakness, no holes, no blind spots!) for all strength, all guidance, all victory.

Our best, to You
Without knowing, going
See You, depend on You, rejoice in You


Mark 15

2 Pilate questioned Him, "Are You the King of the Jews?" And He *answered him, "*It is as* you say."
If that were the charge against Jesus it wasn't nearly bad enough. (It should have been "someone pretending to be God!" Jesus had even said He was the "I am", invoking the very name of God.) If that were a statement of faith, it wasn't nearly good enough. (Certainly King of the Jews, but King of the universe—Jews, Gentiles, every people and country, every idea and thing. And Savior, and Lord.) Gracious Lord, let all my statements and choices and actions show that I claim with joy and satisfaction and confidence that You are the Christ, Messiah, the Son of God, my King now and forever, and my Lord.

14 But Pilate said to them, "Why, what evil has He done?" But they shouted all the more, "Crucify Him!"
Pilate would not have believed You, Lord, if You had told him. It wasn't because of evil You had done. It was because of evil I have done. Without knowing it, Pilate was

pointing to me.  I have mixed feelings about this, Lord.  I'm sorry You carried my sins.  I'm also very thankful that You carried my sins.  Thank You for not stopping time so that You could list all the evil in answer to Pilate's question.  It would have sounded terrible.  Of course, it might have led them to think about themselves.  But Pilate didn't seem to be very open to think about himself as part of the answer to his own question.  So You didn't stop to explain.  Thank You, Lord.  Thank You for going on, even though everyone there should have known that the answer had to do with them, then and there, as well as every person here and now.  Thank You for carrying my burden so that I am free from the burden of my sin now and forever.

38  And the veil of the temple was torn in two from top to bottom.
You have shown me and people from every generation that the way is open to talk to You, listen to You, to worship You.  Amazing!  Doctors—it might take a week or two or three.  Customer service—it might be today, but of course it might not be the department I need (that will be tomorrow (unless they are on vacation)).  But because of Jesus, Your door is open to me, and when I look in, You are smiling at me.  Wow!  Grant that I think about and appreciate with wonder and awe the privilege that I, a sinner, have to talk to You, to listen to You, to worship You, to receive Your Word and blessings.  And grant that I use the door that You have opened frequently with joy and thanksgiving!

Recognize and see:  More than that
I am why
Open door policy


Mark 16

2  Very early on the first day of the week, they came to the tomb when the sun had risen.

They were not coming for a celebration, for the end of Holy Week, or anything pleasant. Yet they came. Because they loved You. I would like to always be walking into victory and celebration and joy, Lord. I would like everything I do to be interesting and obviously worthwhile and helpful to others. I would like to proceed into each day with people around me welcoming me and telling me how much they appreciate all that I do. I would like, Lord, when I see people in need with problems and difficulties, to be able to just point to them and have You zap them with healing, provisions, solutions, and joy. But it doesn't seem to work that way. So give me courage and enduring love for You, so that I will walk on into things that I expect to be unpleasant, problematic, and lonely out of love for You. Grant that I rejoice in You in every day, even when there is grief and uphill struggle involved with each step.

5 Entering the tomb, they saw a young man sitting at the right, wearing a white robe; and they were amazed.
It's not that I expect You to have angels appear to me often in my life, although I think I may have met some once. But keep me open, Lord. If You want me to meet my guardian angel that will be fine. When I say that, though, Lord, I see the women running away afraid. So meeting an angel may be very scary. Still, Lord, keep me open in my attitudes to listen for Your voice from those around me. There are amazing examples of love when I keep my eyes open and look. They may not be angels, but there are young people who are gracious and kind, there are busy working people who take time to care about others, and there are retired people who show Your love by using time in giving and caring in new and selfless ways. Turn all my amazement at Your grace and love and joy into a continuing expectation of Your presence with me every day and an attitude of love and joy with all the people around me every day.

7,8 But go, tell His disciples and Peter, 'He is going ahead of you to Galilee; there you will see Him, just as He told you.'" [8] They went out and fled from the tomb, for trembling and astonishment had gripped them; and they said nothing to anyone, for they were afraid.

They said nothing to anyone. Let fear not get in the way of my sharing the joy and love I have in You and feel toward You with other people. We live in shells, trying to protect ourselves from others' witnesses. If I lean toward trembling and astonishment when I see people giving so much of themselves (and feel afraid they might ask me to join them), I'm sorry. If I feel nervous when I see and hear people I don't know giving You honor and glory, I'm sorry. And if I am amazed when I see people in great need smile and thank You for providing for them, I'm sorry Lord. Let me take in joy from Your love shown through other people, let me open the door into each day expecting joy (without any astonishment), and let joy show in my words, my face, and my actions, to Your glory.

In darkness, listen for Your voice
Expect Your presence
Let joy shine

# Luke

Luke 1

17 It is he who will go *as a forerunner* before Him in the spirit and power of Elijah, TO TURN THE HEARTS OF THE FATHERS BACK TO THE CHILDREN, and the disobedient to the attitude of the righteous, so as to make ready a people prepared for the Lord."
We spend a lot of time and energy, Lord, being prepared. Way beyond Boy Scouts, we, in this culture where I live, work to be prepared for a job, a career. We prepare for health problems with health insurance. We prepare for dying with burial insurance and life insurance for family members left behind. We prepare for retirement (or at least we are supposed to). And the education and insurance sectors are truly enormous. But are we prepared for You, Lord? The temptation is to be prepared in the same way—insurance. Do what we need to do to insure everything is ok. Sheesh! Give us a clear vision of the preparation we need. Let us see that all of our lives, alone, with families, working, we need Your gracious attitude adjustment. Grant that we have an attitude of putting You first no matter what else is going on. Grant that we recognize Your grace in Jesus, and live in confidence in You every day. Grant that we be ready for You, Lord, not insured, but rejoicing in Your love and Life-giving blessings.

38 And Mary said, "Behold, the bondslave of the Lord; may it be done to me according to your word." And the angel departed from her.
I suppose there were always a lot of choices. It just seems like there are an awful lot of them now, Lord. As children grow up, some lean toward being an astronaut, some a fireman, some a rock star, some a high school math teacher (ok, not so many of those). Bless us today, Lord, with

Mary's inspired, simple, gracious attitude.  May it be done to us, Lord, according to Your good and gracious will.  Guide us in the paths of Life that You set before us.  Bless children in knowing You and trusting You implicitly.  Bless young people with hearing Your calling above the wild din of the world.  Bless people in working years with letting You set the course so that they will be a blessing as You desire.  And bless retired people with trusting You to use them in new and different ways following You. Bless them with taking in satisfaction, serving You, right to the time You call them home.  You are very good at this, Lord.  You are gracious and loving, and You provide us with what we need to serve You.  May it be done to us according to Your word.

78, 79  Because of the tender mercy of our God,
With which the Sunrise from on high will visit us,
[79] TO SHINE UPON THOSE WHO SIT IN DARKNESS AND THE SHADOW OF DEATH,
To guide our feet into the way of peace."
Because of Your mercy, Lord, John the Baptist came.  Thank You for Your loving intention and desire to visit us with Your Sunrise from on high.  There is still darkness and the shadow of death.  It seems clear in places of war and turmoil around the world today.  It seems clear in natural disasters.  It seems clear when terrorists attack people for their twisted and perverse reasons.  The darkness may not seem so clear when families struggle to talk to each other or when someone is living alone without anyone seeming to care, but it is still there.  We each need You, Lord to guide our feet into the way of peace.  Please do that, Lord.  No matter what the darkness or shadow is, light up our lives with Your presence.  Bring the Sunrise of Your grace into our hearts.  And guide us into Living in Your way of peace.

Ready, with You and for You
According to Your word, also now
Guide us on Your way of peace

Luke 2

9, 10  And an angel of the Lord suddenly stood before them, and the glory of the Lord shone around them; and they were terribly frightened. [10] But the angel said to them, "Do not be afraid; for behold, I bring you good news of great joy which will be for all the people.
Whether it is a certified letter or a special report announcement on television, it is easy, Lord, first, to be afraid. Afraid of bad news. What has happened now!? What is this going to cost? How is this going to change (mess up) my life? I guess people today, with the shepherds, are not accustomed to someone interrupting our life with good news. So thank You for saying, "Do not be afraid". Help people today, truly to relax. Open our hearts, still in this time. Bless those people who have decided Your good news is only for "those religious people". Let the "for all the people" ring clearly and effectively open the hearts of all people. Let me and all Your people live in the great joy that You bring, Lord Jesus. And let that joy be so infectious that all the people will hear Your good news of great joy.

13, 14  And suddenly there appeared with the angel a multitude of the heavenly host praising God and saying,
[14] "Glory to God in the highest,
And on earth peace among men with whom He is pleased."
I have been blessed, Lord, with going to some great concerts, but that must have been a humdinger! And Your message was clear—to the shepherds, to Mary and Joseph, to me and people today. You are indeed glorious and worthy of praise for fulfilling Your promise and sending Jesus. The thing that takes some listening and mental chewing is the part about peace. For the shepherds, living in a land ruled by Rome, I suspect peace was a dream that seemed impossible. For our time, when CNN is ready to identify the hot spots of conflict for the week, worldly peace seems rare at times. Help us today to recognize Your peace

that You give in Jesus to fill our hearts. Help us to recognize Your grace by which You make a people pleasing to You. Grant that people today value Your peace that You give us with forgiveness in Jesus—Your peace that allows us to Live in joy and closeness to You, no matter what is happening in the world—grant that people value Your peace more than Christmas snow and lights and presents and family gatherings. Grant that we enjoy Your peace, by Your gracious favor, in all the days of the years You give us.

30 – 32 For my eyes have seen Your salvation,
31 Which You have prepared in the presence of all peoples,
32 A LIGHT OF REVELATION TO THE GENTILES,
And the glory of Your people Israel."
It is certainly hard to see in the dark. Getting up in the middle of the night and trying to find something, trying to see where the dog is on the way to the bathroom. And You have prepared such wonderful blessings for people through Your grace and love in Jesus. Some people live in darkness and have never seen them. Some of us have seen them and then allow darkness from the world—worries, frustrations, fears, uncertainties—to hide them from us. Shine Your light, Lord! Let me see Your grace, joy, and salvation again! Let all people see what You have prepared in Jesus and His love. Send Your Spirit to bring light to all Gentiles and to all people of Israel. Open our eyes to see the revelation of what You have prepared in Jesus then and now and forever.

No fear: Good news—joy!
Treasure: Peace for Living!
Light: See Your blessings!


Luke 3

3, 4 And he came into all the district around the Jordan, preaching a baptism of repentance for the forgiveness of

sins; ⁴ as it is written in the book of the words of Isaiah the prophet,
"THE VOICE OF ONE CRYING IN THE WILDERNESS,
'MAKE READY THE WAY OF THE LORD,
MAKE HIS PATHS STRAIGHT.

It is amazing, Lord, when we have someone come over to stay with us, how we do straighten up!  There are piles that I have seen, looked at with resignation, and allowed to grow, that suddenly are unacceptable!  (Particularly to herself.)  So I hear You saying that I need to look inside at obstacles I have allowed to occupy space in my heart and mind.  Help me to repent of my sins, Lord.  Show me, Holy Spirit, the obstacles that I have allowed to exist.  Grant me the enthusiasm and power and wisdom to actually do something about them, by Your grace.  I rejoice that You are coming again, Lord Jesus.  Help me not to procrastinate and wait until then to suddenly think about making the way for Your coming straight.  Grant that, by Your grace and Spirit, I check the path and straighten up, daily.

8  Therefore bear fruits in keeping with repentance, and do not begin to say to yourselves, 'We have Abraham for our father,' for I say to you that from these stones God is able to raise up children to Abraham.

More than words, I hear You saying.  It is easy to go through the form of speaking words of repentance, but also kind of holding on to an attitude of "You do realize, Lord, who I am!  I have been a faithful follower of Yours for at least 2 (10, 71, 97) years now.  So surely that's enough."  Hogwash!  Fruits.  Let there be continual newness in my thoughts, words, and actions, so that repentance is not just something that is appropriate in conversations with You, but something that shows in changes that, by Your grace, happen in my life.  Remove all darkness from me, Lord, and grant that I may Live in the newness of Your Light, fruitfully.

10, 11  And the crowds were questioning him, saying, "Then what shall we do?" ¹¹ And he would answer and say to them,

"The man who has two tunics is to share with him who has none; and he who has food is to do likewise."
In comparison, giving 10% sounds pretty good, Lord. You have truly given me so much, Lord. Sometimes I forget, Lord, that there are people in the world, and many in this country, who if they were asked to list what they "have", could not list more than ten or twenty things. Help me to be responsible in sharing not just money, but also clothes, (the closet is really very full!), food, other stuff, electrical energy and other consumable energy. Help me to use resources on this beautiful planet You have provided, in such a way, that there are resources available for others who need them. Two tunics? Give one. Keep me from fear and hoarding. Fill me with a spirit of generosity every day, with thanksgiving for all You give me.

Obstacle removal: Daily
More than words: Fruitful changes
No fear: Generous sharing


Luke 4

3, 4 And the devil said to Him, "If You are the Son of God, tell this stone to become bread." ⁴ And Jesus answered him, "It is written, 'MAN SHALL NOT LIVE ON BREAD ALONE.'"
I have no idea what it was like, Jesus, to resist that temptation to just create bread when You were hungry. I (and most people in this country) have no idea what it is like to be hungry. A lot of us eat when we are not hungry and we support a food industry that provides astounding choices of food. Eating is high on our list of priorities and sometimes ahead of whatever is in second place. Help us to be clear in our priorities. Help us enjoy Your gifts of food with thanksgiving to You. Help us eat responsibly, so that we don't let food make us unhealthy because of eating too much or eating from a menu that is way out of balance. Grant that above all we recognize that the point of living is not eating,

but Living for You, Jesus, to the glory of God, enjoying food and the other blessings God gives us, with our first priority being loving and serving our Gracious Lord and God.

6 – 8  And the devil said to Him, "I will give You all this domain and its glory; for it has been handed over to me, and I give it to whomever I wish. ⁷ Therefore if You worship before me, it shall all be Yours." ⁸ Jesus answered him, "It is written, 'YOU SHALL WORSHIP THE LORD YOUR GOD AND SERVE HIM ONLY.'"

Yes, Lord, I remember times when I have sung out (if only to myself) "If I were king!"  I see problems and needs and it is sometimes easy to believe that anyone with common sense would realize that my solutions to the problems are really fairly obvious.  And yes, I know, I avoided courses in political science, so I don't know what (dastardly) immediate or long term effects would come of my solutions.  Thank You for showing me that even You left it up to Your Father in heaven.  When I am tempted to want to be in charge of the world, help me remember Who is in charge of the world. When I am tempted to want power from a sense of anger and frustration, help me remember Who has all power with a complete sense of love and joy.  Let every desire to power and control and fixing, lead me to worship You, Gracious Father.  Thank You for being in charge.

9, 12  And he led Him to Jerusalem and had Him stand on the pinnacle of the temple, and said to Him, "If You are the Son of God, throw Yourself down from here…And Jesus answered and said to him, "It is said, 'YOU SHALL NOT PUT THE LORD YOUR GOD TO THE TEST.'"

The Lord has promised to take care of us, so it doesn't matter what we do.  Right!  I think of myself as a fairly quiet person, Lord.  And then I remember those Walter Mitty episodes I have from time to time, where I am Noticed and Valued and Famous and in Great Demand because I have just saved the world (or some notable part of it) again.  Good grief!   Thank You, Lord for promising to take care of me.

Thank You for Your guardian angel in charge over me. Help me not to be a problem case. Help me to listen to You and use Your wisdom. Help me to be a blessing to others, but not from a desire for fame and adulation. Help me not to put myself in harm's way by my habits of thought, entertainment, eating, drinking, reading, listening to people, ignoring people, or anything else. Grant that I take in satisfaction, Living for You and serving You, with the blessings and opportunities You (wisely) provide.

Eat responsibly. But first...
You are King. Thank You.
Serving boldly, in Your will


Luke 5

5 Simon answered and said, "Master, we worked hard all night and caught nothing, but I will do as You say *and* let down the nets."
Thank You for Your servant, Simon Peter, Lord. "We've really already tried that which You are suggesting, Lord, but..." I have found myself telling You all that I have done. I have given in to the temptation to tell You why what You are saying won't work for me. Please forgive me, Lord. Please, grant that I will develop my ability to use "but" appropriately. "I have tried this, Lord, but..." But I will listen to You and do what You tell me to do. But I will follow Your suggestion. But I will let You take over and give me direction (even though I am pretty sure I know best—Sheesh!). Help me to faithfully and boldly put "but"s in my thinking when I hear You calling me to change something. Help me to see, with confidence, the blessing You are preparing for me (it doesn't actually have to be two boat loads of fish, although I'm sure Peter, James, and John appreciated that). Grant that even when I'm tired after really trying, I will still do as You say, Gracious Lord.

16  But Jesus Himself would *often* slip away to the wilderness and pray.

There You were.  Living on the planet You created.  Divine and human.  Blessing people, teaching people, healing people, loving people, calling people to new life.  You were faithfully carrying out the Mission.  And yet, in the midst of this world, broken as it was then and now with sin, You found it important to take time to put Yourself apart from the action, the ministry, the crowds, the individuals, and go off alone, to the wilderness to pray.  I am really not doing well at regularly taking the opportunity during the day to slip away to some wilderness spot in my mind or heart or place to follow Your example.  If that was important to You, Wow!, I must really need this.  Help me to look for moments during the day to step aside and talk to You.  Let me recognize moments when I can choose to pray to You, Father, and talk about what is going on and ask Your guidance and blessing for what is ahead.  As surely as I talk to myself and others during today, grant that I include You in my conversations that You will include me in Your guidance, fellowship, and joy.

32  I have not come to call the righteous but sinners to repentance."

Some of those people You met, Lord Jesus, were absolutely sure that Messiah was coming to tell them what wonderful lives they were living.  They expected a "Keep up the good work!"  And, of course, they were kind of ticked when You didn't do that.  I can feel with that.  It would be nice if when I talk to You, You would tell me how wonderfully I am doing, using Your grace and love, effectively Living as You want me to.  (More than a hint of arrogance, right, Lord?)  Must You always call me to newness?!  Right.  Help me to be honest with myself.  Forgive me for my sins also in my feeling and my thinking and my assuming and my hurting my arm patting myself on the back.  Open my eyes to see the newness that You want for me.  Open today to be new as You want.  Grant that my satisfaction comes, not in hearing "Keep it up!", but in finding doors You open and in using the grace and power You give to do the new, the joyous, the blessing, rather than the pretty good that I am tempted to be satisfied with.

But...Your way
Time to step aside and talk
Satisfied with Your new


Luke 6

30  Give to everyone who asks of you, and whoever takes away what is yours, do not demand it back.
You have graciously given so much to me, Lord. You have taken care of me through years when it was obvious where things were coming from and years when it was difficult to look ahead and see where things were going to come from. But always You have given me the privilege of giving. Thank You for convincing me that if I give first, what remains will be enough for me. Yes, there are times when I waver. Forgive me for not trusting You always. Forgive me for not being as generous with others as You are with me. Show me how to choose wisely with Your generous love in giving. There are so many wonderful people serving You in so many great charities, and I would like to give to all of them. Show me how to give wisely and still be available to help all who ask for help, whom You want me to help.

35, 36  But love your enemies, and do good, and lend, expecting nothing in return; and your reward will be great, and you will be sons of the Most High; for He Himself is kind to ungrateful and evil *men*, 36 Be merciful, just as your Father is merciful.
I have difficulty, Lord, imagining anyone I know as an enemy. There are people who seem to do things thoughtlessly, and I feel hurt by the choices some people make though. And there are times when I feel unjustly

treated. (Not on purpose. I'm afraid I think it's just dumbness or lack of caring.) I think, in my life, those are the people that You give me to love with Your gracious love. Help me to treat them with respect and love and caring. Grant that what I think about them and feel about them is full of Your mercy. I don't think they are evil. Help them, Lord, to realize that there are hurtful consequences of their actions. Bless them so richly with Your love and grace that they will reach out to others with an attitude of love and caring. Thank You for Your mercy. Please grant that in all my thoughts and words, I will always be merciful.

45  The good man out of the good treasure of his heart brings forth what is good; and the evil *man* out of the evil *treasure* brings forth what is evil; for his mouth speaks from that which fills his heart.

Yes, I was afraid that was where my mouth was getting that stuff. It would be nice if my mouth only let out things that were filtered by the teaching I have received, and the spiritual growth You have graciously provided. If there were a filter built in. But sure enough, it's what is in my heart that slips right out through my mouth. So, Lord, create a new heart within me. If I accumulate some crud during the day, cleanse my heart before the new day dawns. And fill my heart with Your Holy Spirit, with joy in You, with wonder and awe in Your love, with satisfaction in You and in the life and calling You have given me. Let my mouth speak from a heart full of Your love and blessings, no matter where I am, no matter what is happening, and no matter what anyone else says. Help my mouth by filling my heart completely, to the exclusion of all junk and crud and arrogant twaddle.

Blessed to give
Given mercy to be merciful
Heart filled to speak


Luke 7

4  When they came to Jesus, they earnestly implored Him, saying, "He is worthy for You to grant this to him"
So here come these elders representing the centurion to You, Lord Jesus, and as they ask You to help the centurion, they (what a great example!) assume You are the right person to come to.  They assume that this problem is in Your authority and something that You deal with.  And they assume that You are capable of providing this blessing.  What a terrific attitude!  When something goes wrong and I have to call someone, sometimes it takes a while to find the right person, agency, department.  Help me to always talk to You, Lord, with the absolute confidence that whatever the difficulty, problem, disaster, need, joy, or celebration, You are the One to talk to.  Grant that I always talk to You with absolute confidence that You are able to deal with whatever problem or joy I am facing.  No matter what it is in my life, Lord, You have authority.  Thank You for being in charge and thank You for being willing to listen to me no matter what (mess or joy) I need to talk about.

35  "Yet wisdom is vindicated by all her children."
Thank You, Lord, for Your wisdom.  Thank You for granting Your wisdom, Lord Holy Spirit, to Your people.  I know You have given me wisdom.  It's just that sometimes I am afraid that I don't appear to others as someone acting in wisdom.  I really don't want to give Your wisdom a bad reputation.  So, Lord, please help me to be completely open to Your wisdom.  Grant that I let Your wisdom into every particle of my being.  Control all of my thoughts and actions with Your wisdom, Lord.  And grant that Your wisdom will be visible to others through me, so that I am one of the children of Your wisdom through whom vindication comes to Your glory and praise.

41 – 43  "A moneylender had two debtors: one owed five hundred denarii, and the other fifty. $^{42}$ When they were unable to repay, he graciously forgave them both. So which of them will love him more?" $^{43}$ Simon answered and said, "I

suppose the one whom he forgave more." And He said to him, "You have judged correctly."
I actually forget how much You have forgiven me, Lord. Days pass, time goes on, and it's easy to slip into an attitude of thinking about what You have done for me lately. Bless me with a memory full, not of the dumb and hurtful things I have done, but of Your mercy and grace and forgiveness to me in each of the days that I have received from You. Help me remember Your blessings, and let the memory of Your mercy keep multiplying my love for You in new and fresh ways. You are wonderful, Lord! Bring me past believing in You, trusting You, recognizing You, and rejoicing in You. Bring me all the way to loving You with my whole heart. Let me think about You and love You in all I think and feel and say and do. Grant me this fulfillment, Lord: Loving You.

You are the One to ask
Wisdom, visible, to Your glory
Always: Loving You


Luke 8

15  But the *seed* in the good soil, these are the ones who have heard the word in an honest and good heart, and hold it fast, and bear fruit with perseverance.
Thank You, Lord for Your word. Thank You for sending it to us. Keep sending it to those who have not heard Your gracious word. And then, Lord, grant that we handle Your word with faith. There are a lot of words available on a lot of topics. Let us recognize Your word with faith believing that You are personally talking to us. Help us today also to trust You. Grant that we are honest with ourselves and recognize our sins. Grant that we receive forgiveness from Your gracious hand. And then send us into each day, holding Your word fast in our hearts. Let us not leave home without it. Put Your word into our hearts so that we desire You to be graciously and lovingly part of each moment in our days.

Grant that we will be fruitful serving You with perseverance through every trial and difficulty. Let us glorify You with loving, fruitful Living in this and every day.

21 But He answered and said to them, "My mother and My brothers are these who hear the word of God and do it." There was a time when I lived close to my relatives, Lord, my family. And maybe some people still do. It just seems like a lot of families move on as generations go on, to widely separated parts of the country. We get to some holidays and perhaps there is a great desire that appears in our hearts to get together again. You make it much simpler, Lord. Family—we are Your family as we hear the word of God and let that word rule in our lives. To be in Your family, Lord, is to be in a great family! Thank You for making Your people Your family. We are a big family in You, Lord. And the joy we have is that we don't have to go long distances to celebrate with our families. Wherever here is, You graciously are here, too. Help us to recognize with joy and satisfaction the family that we, Your people, are, with You, here. Help us to celebrate Your family that we are by Your grace, this week.

35 *The people* went out to see what had happened; and they came to Jesus, and found the man from whom the demons had gone out, sitting down at the feet of Jesus, clothed and in his right mind; and they became frightened. We have dreams of the way life is supposed to be, of the way things are supposed to work, of miracles of healing, of wonder and awe. But, truth be told, we mostly don't expect to actually see those things happen in the here and now where we live. When the Gerasenes saw them, they were afraid. I suppose we might be afraid, too, if there were a day with no accidents, no angry comments, no selfishness, no hurt feelings. If it were my day, I think I would start to seriously wonder! And yet You are blessing people, Lord, You are healing people, You are giving strength for trials, deliverance from evil, joy in the midst of chaos and

sadness—right now, there You are, doing those things. Give me and all of us eyes to see the wonders of Your grace and love still, now, Lord. Thank You for protection from accidents, thank You for patience with other people (especially when I'm tired, Lord). Thank You for unselfishness by the power of Your Spirit. Thank You for endurance and understanding. And thank You for miracles whether we see them or not. No fear! You are still touching lives with Your eternal goodness, today. Praise to You, Lord!

Your word: Fruitful in me today
A family to enjoy
Goodness and joy are welcome today


Luke 9

23, 24  And He was saying to *them* all, "If anyone wishes to come after Me, he must deny himself, and take up his cross daily and follow Me."  24 For whoever wishes to save his life will lose it, but whoever loses his life for My sake, he is the one who will save it.
Yes, Lord, I want to follow You. I want in this day to be with You throughout the day. You really know how to help me see Your light in the midst of the hoopla that is going on today. More than one advertisement leans on "It's all about you!" to get people to buy something. And denying myself is not my beginning point of choice. So please help me, Lord, to turn over to You all of my life. Grant that I do not go through this day grasping for what I want, for satisfying my feelings and desires. Grant that I let go and give myself in this day over to You. Help me to recognize the challenges and burdens that You want me to carry—give me strength in Your grace to take my cross and not one that looks appealing to me. Help me not to carry my cross with an attitude of looking for approval and attention. But grant that I follow You, completely letting You be in charge of my

thinking, wanting, choosing, speaking, giving. Thank You for Frances Havergal's "Take my life and let it be, Consecrated Lord to Thee, Take my moments and my days, Let them flow in ceaseless praise."

35  Then a voice came out of the cloud, saying, "This is My Son, *My* Chosen One; listen to Him!"
It is a lot easier, Lord, to recognize You, praise You, and worship You than it is to listen to You.  You say such difficult things.  Just when I think, "Right, Lord, things are getting easier and smoother," You let me see more clearly that I need to take a path that goes uphill.  But, yes, You are right.  I really do want to listen to You, Lord.  Help me to listen.  Let nothing get in the way.  Not busy-ness, not selfishness, not family, not serving You, and especially not fear.  Grant that I listen to You in Your word every day.  Help me to listen, not gritting my teeth, squinting with one eye, afraid of what You are going to tell me.  Rather grant that I listen, knowing that You love me, knowing that You are leading me, knowing You have a purpose for me, knowing that You are in charge, and especially knowing that all satisfaction in my life comes from listening to You and following You.

48  ... and said to them, "Whoever receives this child in My name receives Me, and whoever receives Me receives Him who sent Me; for the one who is least among all of you, this is the one who is great."
I love the children You have graciously given to me, Lord.  They are a blessing.  And I love all the children I have had the privilege to teach.  (It is true that there are one or two (hundred) things I may not have liked and wanted to change in their lives.)  And now, children today have been born into a very different world from the one I came into.  Help me to receive every child I see, every young person I meet, every person You bring into my life, from whatever generation—grant that I receive them in Your name.  Let me see each child, each person as a person whom You love, with You walking alongside.  Especially help me to receive young

people who have (help them, Lord) gotten angry or bitter or impertinent. Let me receive them into the space of my life, shining Your light of love and peace and joy. Let us together receive You and Your love.

Lord, let me Live, losing my life in You
Recognizing, listening, following, satisfied
Receiving children with love


Luke 10

2  And He was saying to them, "The harvest is plentiful, but the laborers are few; therefore beseech the Lord of the harvest to send out laborers into His harvest.
Thank You, Gracious Lord, for wanting people to come to You. The harvest is certainly plentiful today. How very many people there are who do not appear to know You. And there are many who have heard of You and have chosen the other path of selfishness and accumulation. Send laborers, Lord. Send Your servants to effectively touch the lives of people distant from You. Love people into Your kingdom through Your servants. Send laborers into this country and into every country where the harvest is waiting. Send pastors, teachers, missionaries, and every calling You desire. Create congregations of Your people everywhere around the world. And bless Your congregations with Your powerful word of Gospel reaching effectively through them to bring the harvest to You. Choose from among Your people those whom You want to send. Use Your people to touch the lives of those waiting to be in Your harvest. And, yes, Lord, in Your grace, use me, too.

21  At that very time He rejoiced greatly in the Holy Spirit, and said, "I praise You, O Father, Lord of heaven and earth, that You have hidden these things from *the* wise and intelligent and have revealed them to infants. Yes, Father, for this way was well-pleasing in Your sight.

In every age, Lord, there have been really smart people who have written or taught with excellence. And yet, You have chosen men and women, young people, boys and girls who were not blessed with great educations or renowned wisdom, but who absolutely trusted You. Thank You for education. Thank You for wisdom, wise sayings, and helpful thoughtful people. But grant that people today receive Your grace and unending joy and Life through the simple, uncomplicated way of hearing Your Gospel and believing You. Create a people, also today, who trust You for forgiveness, for love, for peace and for joy from You, Father, Jesus, Holy Spirit. (Of course, if You want to let wise and intelligent folks come to trust You more than wisdom and intelligence, that would be ok, kind, and gracious, too.)

36, 37 Which of these three do you think proved to be a neighbor to the man who fell into the robbers' *hands*?" [37] And he said, "The one who showed mercy toward him." Then Jesus said to him, "Go and do the same."
It's not that I have seen a lot of people beaten up by robbers by the side of the road (although I have seen people lying by the side of the road), but there are so many people who need so much help today, Lord. It's hard to know where to start. It's easy to say that I feel mercy toward others. Like having an extra coat but never actually giving it to anyone. Grant that I put the mercy that You have created in me (responding to Your forgiveness) into action. "The one who *showed* mercy." Help me to show mercy. Let me see with Your gracious insight where, when, to whom, with what I may give mercifully Your love and caring. Reach people, with Your powerful love, from Your bountiful supply, through me.

Call, send, harvest
Absolute trust, still today
Following You, showing mercy

Luke 11

2 And He said to them, "When you pray, say:
'Father, hallowed be Your name.
Your kingdom come.
Thank You, Lord Jesus, for teaching us to pray. Father please let Your name be made holy and recognized as holy in us, Your people. Grant that we glorify Your name by what we think and say and do. May Your kingdom come now, Father. Grant that Your kingdom, that flows from Your throne of mercy in Jesus, by Your Spirit include us and explode around and through us in this place and time and through Your people and Your gospel around this planet. Sometimes it seems hard to see Your kingdom coming, growing, exploding with joy and grace here and now, Father. Thank You for promising that Your word is always effective by Your grace. Thank You that at this moment there are people moved by Your Spirit whom You are bringing into Your kingdom. Bless those people, here, there, with joy in new Life. And bless us with joy and satisfaction living in Your kingdom. Let it never be with complacency but with wonder, thanksgiving, and infectious joy.

8, 9 I tell you, even though he will not get up and give him *anything* because he is his friend, yet because of his persistence he will get up and give him as much as he needs. ⁹ "So I say to you, ask, and it will be given to you; seek, and you will find; knock, and it will be opened to you. "Why didn't you give me one of those?" "You didn't ask." We know that's true, Lord. And yet we forget to ask You. You are so ready to have us ask. Thank You, Lord. Help us to remember to ask. Grant that we do not sit sulking physically or spiritually thinking You don't care. Grant that trusting You, we will ask. I think we have been somehow encouraged not to ask. There is a message of "Be satisfied!" that comes to us. So when You say, "Ask", I first think of myself—healing for ills, for me and my wife and family, ability to eat without gaining weight, and an unlimited electronic space for storing books, ability to afford (free would be nice) all the books I want, and the ability to read very quickly and remember well (all the good) that I read. Better: Help people who are sick, alone, homeless, impoverished, discouraged, depressed, lacking in opportunity to work, living without enthusiasm or joy or hope, and especially those who do not know You. Open my heart that I will ask well. Stir my imagination and trust in You that I will ask largely and wisely. Fill me with enthusiasm that I will seek creatively and to Your glory. Guide me in my knocking that I knock on doors that open to Your great and wonderful blessings to me and through me to others. Thank You for being so generous and ready to give, in answer to my prayers.

13  If you then, being evil, know how to give good gifts to your children, how much more will *your* heavenly Father give the Holy Spirit to those who ask Him?"
I feel a little like You are saying I can ask (with confidence) to be on the first flight to Mars. Ask for You to give me the Holy Spirit! I remember when You said through John the Baptist that we will be baptized with Holy Spirit and with fire. [Matt. 3.11] Is it ok if I say that sounds kind of scary, Lord? But You are the Lord. You have shown Your love to me in Jesus, Immanuel, God with us. So fill me with faith and trust in You. Relax my tight-fisted grip on myself and my life. Open my heart and my mind. And give me Your Holy Spirit, Lord. Whatever You want is good and right and blessed. Burn what needs to be burned, and set me on fire in Your Spirit to serve You in the moments of this day. I'm hanging on to You, Lord. Go for it!

Grow Your kingdom
Faithfully asking largely
On fire with Your Spirit

Luke 12

**11, 12** When they bring you before the synagogues and the rulers and the authorities, do not worry about how or what you are to speak in your defense, or what you are to say; **12** for the Holy Spirit will teach you in that very hour what you ought to say."

What will I say to people? How will I manage to speak in a way that honors You? How can I speak truthfully without hurting people? When is it that I speak in such a way that it touches someone's heart and that person can be drawn closer to You? It's hard for me to know, Lord. Even if You provide training for me in speaking or teaching with Your word, it is more than is in me to be a blessing the way You want. So thank You, Gracious Lord for Your wonderful promise. Grant that I will not worry about what to say. Guide me in words, guide me in timing, guide me in speaking in the right place. Teach me what You want me to say, Lord Holy Spirit. You know the time, place, and words You want. Speak through me. Whether it is my family, with friends, in a social time, in a formal time—grant that I do not worry, but only trust You to be with me and give me Your words to be a witness and blessing, Holy Spirit, Gracious Lord.

**29 – 31** And do not seek what you will eat and what you will drink, and do not keep worrying. **30** For all these things the nations of the world eagerly seek; but your Father knows that you need these things. **31** But seek His kingdom, and these things will be added to you.

I remember our son, when going to a restaurant (he was albeit young) saying he wanted French fries, the meal choice was unimportant, as long as it came with French fries. I am really close to that, Lord. It's not that I worry about having enough to eat and drink (ok, maybe sometimes). The message of the world is very strong on "Do you have enough stuff?" "Do you have what you need" (translate, "want"). Thank You, Father for knowing all the things I need. Help me to see clearly and remember that that is not the point.

Those are "comes with". Keep my heart focused on what is important, essential: Your kingdom. Grant that my choices and delights in this day be in Your kingdom. Let me Live and enjoy this day inside Your kingdom and use time in a way that furthers Your will in Your kingdom. Help me to leave it up to You that what You choose to come with Your kingdom are the things I need. (So when I budget, let me do it with confidence, humility, and trust in You, knowing the main thing is not the spreadsheet (although spreadsheets are really cool, Lord, thank You!).)

37, 38 Blessed are those slaves whom the master will find on the alert when he comes; truly I say to you, that he will gird himself *to serve*, and have them recline *at the table*, and will come up and wait on them. ³⁸ Whether he comes in the second watch, or even in the third, and finds *them* so, blessed are those *slaves*.
It seems like a long time, Lord. I feel like we are in the third watch at least. A lot of history has rolled along. Books (printed, and now as ebooks) have multiplied with stuff that has happened. Science (discovering the wonders You have put for us to see) and mathematics (enjoying the logical bones of Your wonders) have grown by leaps and bounds. What makes being alert easy is to recognize Your wonderful blessings. Help me to recognize (some) books as great blessings from You. Help me to see science and math as means to appreciate Your gracious wonders. And grant that in this day I will spend time (amidst the thinking, saying, and doing) remembering Your grace that makes life a Life Lived with You. Keep my heart open and yearning for Your loving presence. Even more than noticing dings from texts or emails or phone calls, keep my attention ever open and alert to You, Your love, Your grace, and Your coming.
Maranatha! [Come, Lord! 1 Cor. 16.22]

Your time, place, words
No worry: Comes with
Alert: Listening through the noise

Luke 13

20 And again He said, "To what shall I compare the kingdom of God? [21] It is like leaven, which a woman took and hid in three pecks of flour until it was all leavened."
There are so many different kinds of people, Lord. How will Your kingdom approach all the different peoples in all the parts of the world? TV reaches a lot. Internet reaches a great number. But there are a lot more. Your kingdom is like leaven that keeps touching more and more of the flour until it touches every part. Grow Your kingdom, Lord. Grant that Your kingdom will grow to touch people of every language with Your gospel. Send Your word with the power of Your Spirit to reach people who have not heard Your good news in Jesus. Reach people around the world, but also in this country who have not been invited to Life with You. And please, Lord, as Your kingdom grows, touch those people who have heard Your invitation and put it on a pile where it got buried or wasn't taken seriously. Empower Your leaven to bring people everywhere to Life.

29 And they will come from east and west and from north and south, and will recline *at the table* in the kingdom of God.
I have trouble picturing the celebration You are preparing, Lord. It sounds like there will be a lot of us, which is really great! And outside, perhaps, in a wonderful garden of Yours? Or in a magnificent, very large hall? And I have to admit, I don't have practice reclining to eat, but You will give us a chance to practice and enjoy that, I'm sure. But whether I can picture it or not, I am looking forward to it. Thank You, Lord, for wanting us, Your people, to be with You. Thank You for Your love now in this pre-celebration period. Help us to focus on You with us in each day. Help us think of You with thanksgiving and joy when we eat now. And grant that our anticipation and eager desire looking

forward to the celebration then, will color our Living with love for others and with joy in You, in all the now that You give us.

35  Behold, your house is left to you *desolate*; and I say to you, you will not see Me until *the time* comes when you say, 'BLESSED IS HE WHO COMES IN THE NAME OF THE LORD!'"
I have had times, Lord, when I have been so focused on doing something that I have not wanted anyone to interrupt me.  And I'm afraid I have not always been open, compassionate, and loving when someone tried to get my attention.  I'm sorry.  I don't ever want to be so preoccupied that I tell You, "Not now!"  Grant that I will always be open to You.  Your talking to me and touching my life and heart is always a blessing and never an interruption.  Grant that I never stray into anything that makes me not want Your company.  Blessed are You, Jesus.  Bring the joy of Your presence into every part of my day, today, Gracious Lord.

Graciously touch all
Anticipation infectious with joy
Yes, welcome anytime


Luke 14

11  "For everyone who exalts himself will be humbled, and he who humbles himself will be exalted."
I don't mind being humble, just so I get credit for it, Lord.  Yuck!  It is easy to think about myself, what I want, what I enjoy, how other people should see me and recognize me.  That's the way it was at that dinner party You went to, Lord.  People were showing that they thought a lot of themselves.  Thank You for C. S. Lewis' "Humility is not thinking less of yourself, but thinking of yourself less."  You don't want me to put myself down as worthless—thank You, Lord.  Help me to spend time thinking about other people.  Help me to think about Your wonderful grace and creativity in making such

wise, interesting, gracious, helpful people. Help me to spend time recognizing Your love in other people. Grant that I think about what others need and ways to be a blessing and help them. When I do think about some ache or pain or need or want that I have, help me to (quickly) turn those over to You, thank You for listening, and trust You so that I can get back to the much more important things You have given me to do.

16, 17 But He said to him, "A man was giving a big dinner, and he invited many; [17] and at the dinner hour he sent his slave to say to those who had been invited, 'Come; for everything is ready now.'
It is very easy, Lord, for me to think of my time as my own. I have good and prudent reasons for choosing the priorities I am using (it sounds like such a good excuse!). Can Your "now" be my "just a little later"? Later today, next week, next year... . It is easy to say, "I give You my life Lord, to use as You will (as long as I get to say when)." Help me to give You the right to say, "Now!", whenever You choose. Grant that I do not obfuscate or dilly dally. I know that You are very good at timing and blessing. Please accept not only my heart and my will, but also my clock. Use them all to Your glory in Your good and gracious "now".

33 So then, none of you can be My disciple who does not give up all his own possessions.
Boy is that an idea that is out of this world! First we spend time working on an education, then we spend time using it (hopefully) to earn money and participate in the great blessings (according to us) that are available, and then we buy really elaborate and complicated alarm systems to protect all the stuff that we have spent time getting. Give up my possessions? My mind is quick to say, "And then what?" But that's not up to me, is it? My loyalties cannot be attached to stuff if I am going to follow You. So, yes, Lord, please take all the stuff. I turn it over to You. If You want me to use it, fine. If You want me to give things away, direct me. Grant me absolute faith that You are quite capable of

providing for me, whatever I need. Grant that I follow You faithfully without my cargo pants pockets stuffed with things that I have trouble leaving behind and without a full backpack of things I have chosen. You choose, Lord (loosen my white knuckle grip). There are wonderful blessings of stuff, but Your blessings are best, and Your choices are always the most satisfying. Thank You for being in charge of stuff.

My attention: You in charge
My time: You in charge
My stuff: You in charge


Luke 15

20, 21 So he got up and came to his father. But while he was still a long way off, his father saw him and felt compassion *for him*, and ran and embraced him and kissed him. [21] And the son said to him, 'Father, I have sinned against heaven and in your sight; I am no longer worthy to be called your son.'
Yes, Lord, I have found myself in a far country. I do something or I say something, and I realize that I am a long way from You. I don't even need to look to see if You are frowning, I can feel in my heart that I have pushed You aside and taken over for a while. It feels so horrible when I realize where I am and what I have done. Because it is not just someone I have hurt by what I said or did, I have sinned against You. Please grant that I recognize when I sin, when I push You aside, when I try to take over, when I let anger get in the way of love and indignation in the way of patience. Thank You for always looking for me. Thank You for wanting me back. Please forgive me for my sins. Please accept me back into Your house as Your humble servant. Thank You, Gracious Lord!

**22, 23** But the father said to his slaves, 'Quickly bring out the best robe and put it on him, and put a ring on his hand and sandals on his feet; 23 and bring the fattened calf, kill it, and let us eat and celebrate.'

There are those people who have hurt me, Lord. Yes, the temptation is sometimes really strong (!) to stuff those times into my Permanent Memory Register ("Well! If that's how you feel! …"). Help me always to be looking at people with an attitude of readiness to forgive. Grant that I am ready and generous with my best smile and most loving voice toward all that hurt me. Grant that I never hold back, but always have forgiveness in my heart toward every person that ever sins against me. And no matter whether someone asks for forgiveness or not, grant that I absolutely let go of anything done to me. Whether they come back or not, grant that I always have a smile in my heart ready for them. Thank You for the privilege of forgiving "those who trespass against us". Let my heart and voice be filled with mercy, forgiveness, and welcome—always.

**31, 32** "And he said to him, 'Son, you have always been with me, and all that is mine is yours. 32 But we had to celebrate and rejoice, for this brother of yours was dead and *has begun* to live, and *was* lost and has been found.'"

Let me get this straight. I do what's right. He does what's wrong. And when he comes back, we all celebrate. (The words, "I don't *Think* so!" lurk in my heart and mind, ready to jump out.) You have blessed us with really nice worshiping congregations, and then You want to let just anybody in!? How much I need to grow, Lord. I really need to give that Policeman of the Universe outfit over to You. It doesn't fit, and it feels uncomfortable. Thank You for bringing people to You. There are still people like Saint Paul who are running away from You as fast as they can, and You snatch them and bring them to You. Wow! Are You good at that or what! Help me not to sniff and shuffle. Grant that I rejoice with You at every member of Your family. Grant that with a full heart I celebrate Your grace and Your love reaching people. Help me to celebrate with the confidence that if You brought me in, anyone else You want to bring in is perfectly ok.

Forgive, accept me
My heart: Mercy, forgiveness, welcome
Your celebrations: Participating joyously


Luke 16

9 "And I say to you, make friends for yourselves by means of the wealth of unrighteousness, so that when it fails, they will receive you into the eternal dwellings."
What a lot of things there are to do with money, Lord! Vacations, second homes (third?), cars that have internet and whistle Dixie, first homes with more square feet than the population of at least half the small communities of the United States. I know, those are not necessarily bad things, Lord. But You have an amazing plan for using wealth. You give us the privilege of using wealth (whether it is a little or a lot) to support ministries that bring people to You, so that we participate in creating eternal friendships, by Your grace. Thank You Lord that we get to use money now to support ministries of Your Gospel and when You take us home, we will meet friends in eternity whose lives we have had the privilege of touching by Your grace. Please keep this vision clear for Your people. Bless us with wisdom in using all the money You give us. Fill our hearts with generosity. And give us a sense of enthusiastic anticipation as we look forward to meeting those new eternal friends.

13 "No servant can serve two masters; for either he will hate the one and love the other, or else he will be devoted to one and despise the other. You cannot serve God and wealth."
When is it that people decide that the main thing in life is making a living rather than Living? At home watching parents? In school listening to friends? Deciding on which courses to take to achieve a major that will make a success

of life? For those of us who are past all that, please, Lord, help us to refocus our devotion and love. Help me to begin every day rejoicing that You are my Master and Lord, and grant that everything I do every day I do listening to You, by Your power, with Your wisdom, for You, to be a blessing, and to Your glory. And please bless those who are in the process of (knowingly or otherwise) deciding the main thing in life. Grant that they see the light of Life in You. Help them to Choose Life rather than just living. Among the military and educational recruiters that come to young people, send Your Holy Spirit and recruit young people to choose a career of putting You first, then, lifelong, and eternally.

29 "But Abraham *said, 'They have Moses and the Prophets; let them hear them.'"
You have had people make suggestions to You, Lord, throughout history of the ways that You should reach people. Have the skies open up, and Jesus comes walking down a crystal gold stairway with the vast choirs of heavenly angels singing in magnificent eight part harmony. That would be nice. Have an old friend (or enemy) rise from the dead and sit down in the room and tell of Your grace that they are enjoying (or miss dreadfully). And You just smile and keep saying that if people don't meet You in Your gracious word, they will never find You. Bless Your word in effectively reaching people today. Open people's hearts and minds to meet You in Your gracious love. Send Your word to every nook and cranny of this world to touch people with Life and bring them to You. Use Your people to speak, carry, support and send Your word as You graciously and powerfully desire. Let the good news in Jesus ring out around this world in our lifetime.

Wealthy with eternal friends
Life is You first
Your word: Attractive, effective, Life-giving

## Luke 17

10 "So you too, when you do all the things which are commanded you, say, 'We are unworthy slaves; we have done *only* that which we ought to have done.'"

When I watch football, Lord, it is so obvious to me. There is a defensive player who makes a tackle. He is paid jillions of dollars to make tackles. But when he makes a tackle, he struts around the field pounding his chest like he is the most wonderful person in the world. That seems, to me, obviously dumb. But when I remember to do something loving for someone, or resist buying something that I obviously can't afford, there I am (strutting) thinking that I deserve extra credit from You. (Equally dumb, right?) Help me to be thankful for Your revealed will. Grant that I recognize opportunities to serve You and be a blessing. Grant that I am effective in sharing Your love and joy. And then help me to be really, really clear that You are the One Who gets the credit—Your grace, Your mercy, Your love, Your word—not me.

15, 16 Now one of them, when he saw that he had been healed, turned back, glorifying God with a loud voice, [16] and he fell on his face at His feet, giving thanks to Him. And he was a Samaritan.

I really appreciate the opportunity to talk to You, Lord, and listen to You, and ask You for blessings. You have given me such wonderful encouragement to ask You, and You stir my imagination with Your word. So I do ask You a lot. And I trust that Your gracious will still abounds today, and that You are answering my prayers. I do, however, sometimes (like most of the time?) forget to thank You for answering my prayers. There are some prayers that You answer, and Zap! there is the answer in help, healing, encouragement, deliverance, understanding, opportunity... . I'm probably a little better at remembering to thank You then. But there are also those prayers which I pray in absolute confidence that You are helping someone, or making Your word a blessing, or guiding Your people—when I don't exactly see You answering my prayer. I know You listen to me. I know that You answer my prayers, giving the best blessing always. So, Gracious Lord, help me to remember *Always* to thank You. As I begin to pray each day, grant that I remember to thank You for answering all the prayers from yesterday, because surely, You have indeed answered them. Thank You, Lord for answering all my prayers. Thank You for the answers I see. Thank You for the answers that are coming in ways different from what I imagined. Thank You for the answers I don't see. (And thank You for answering, "No, Michael, I love you," when I ask for something that from Your clear and excellent point of view is actually, pretty dumb.)

20, 21  Now having been questioned by the Pharisees as to when the kingdom of God was coming, He answered them and said, "The kingdom of God is not coming with signs to be observed; [21] nor will they say, 'Look, here *it is*!' or, 'There *it is*!' For behold, the kingdom of God is in your midst."
It is easy, Lord, to be taken in by the idea that Your kingdom shows most clearly in the places where there are the most magnificent church buildings, or the largest congregations, or the greatest music (whether it's rejoicing with J. S. Bach or a wonderfully stirring modern chorus). I suspect Your people today, as well as the Pharisees then, would really like to see Your kingdom visibly glorious, giving glory and honor to You, so that the large number of people who don't know You would see it and be attracted. You have, however, made clear several times that that is not the plan You are using. So thank You, Lord, for Your kingdom in our midst. Thank You for Your kingdom being inside Your people. Thank You for Your kingdom appearing in small and quiet ways where people love and care for others, where people endure suffering and difficulties with Your strength, and where people step out in faith in You and carry out ministries without fanfare or spotlights. Let Your kingdom come through me in whatever way You would like, today.

Obedience: All credit to You
Prayers: Answered. Thank You.
Your kingdom: (here)


Luke 18

1 Now He was telling them a parable to show that at all times they ought to pray and not to lose heart.
I remember, Lord, when written communicating was by letter. Then wait for a couple weeks to get an answer. One could call, but long distance was something of a luxury. Now if my browser isn't ready to use in three seconds I start getting testy. I easily find myself slipping into wanting immediate gratification. Order the food, drive up, pay and pick it up. I hear You saying that Your gift of prayer is not designed to fit my timing preferences. Keep it up, You say. Don't lose heart, You say. So help me, Lord, to avoid putting prayer in the package in my heart with instant ordering, instant communication, and things happening on my scheduling. Thank You for answering some of my prayers faster than I can say thank You. Many times, there You are, prayer answered, Zap! You are very gracious, Lord. Grant me patience and trust and perseverance in prayers that don't seem to get an immediate response. If You want me to know the answer is "No", please let me know and I'll stop. If I don't get a "No" from You, give me strength and satisfaction in continuing to pray, knowing that Your gracious will is always to answer prayers with blessings (even if that is not precisely the blessing I asked for).

16, 17 But Jesus called for them, saying, "Permit the children to come to Me, and do not hinder them, for the kingdom of God belongs to such as these. [17] Truly I say to you, whoever does not receive the kingdom of God like a child will not enter it *at all*."
There are those little children in Sunday School singing, "Jesus loves me this I know". More powerful than a

speeding locomotive! You are so wonderful, Lord, in reaching children and letting them know that You love them. It's easy to think of earthquakes, and other disasters, wars and other terrible events as having great power on earth. But the faith of a child, trusting You is awesome, thank You, Lord. The temptation comes to adults to think, "Well, if they only knew the trials and tribulations…". Help us to see the real power in the simple (uncomplicated), joyous, unselfconscious faith of children. Help adults (like me) to avoid trying to bring children into a more "mature" faith. Grant that we let go of the years, the trials, the fears, the uncertainties, and just join the children, enjoying You, loving You, and trusting You.

41 "What do you want Me to do for you?" And he said, "Lord, *I want* to regain my sight!"
There was no hesitation. The blind man sitting by the roadside begging had had some time to think about it. He *Really* wanted to see again. If You asked me that, Lord, I don't think I am as ready to answer. I can name several aches, pains, and things for which I take pills. I can think of family members who need particular, wonderful blessings. There are injustices in this country and in my community that are in need of extermination. And yes, I would like help with all those things. But since Living with You is not limited by the temporary hurts, dumb things, injustices, and other examples of evil that are visible today, I think if You asked me what I want You to do for me it is this: Gracious Lord bless Your Gospel that it will be effective in me, through me, through all Your people, all over the world—bringing people to Life and giving us all great joy and satisfaction in Living with You now and forever.

Praying. Knowing: Answer coming.
Joining children, trusting You.
Gospel. Life. Joy. Satisfaction.

Luke 19

3 – 5 Zaccheus was trying to see who Jesus was, and was unable because of the crowd, for he was small in stature.
⁴ So he ran on ahead and climbed up into a sycamore tree in order to see Him, for He was about to pass through that way.
⁵ When Jesus came to the place, He looked up and said to him, "Zaccheus, hurry and come down, for today I must stay at your house."
Yes, Lord, there have been times when I have gone to see someone who was famous. And then I had a memory to file away. (So that years later I could tell students or offspring, "Yes, there was that time when …".) But I don't remember going with the excellent purpose that Zaccheus had. He went to see Who You were. Not just to see You. And You knew he wanted more than to see You, so You invited Yourself over to his house. Help me, Lord, to have an attitude of wanting to see Who You are. Grant that in listening to Your word, reading Your word, praying, talking to You, I will want to get to know You. Please, Lord, invite Yourself in to where I live that I may know You. I believe You love me. I believe You care about me. Even if I have something planned, invite Yourself in to my heart, and grant that without fear, with joy, I may get to know You.

10 For the Son of Man has come to seek and to save that which was lost."
Thank You, Lord Jesus, for coming to save people who are lost. With all the digital maps available, it is becoming hard for people to admit that they are lost. And particularly it is hard for people who are trying to convince everyone around them that they know what they are doing, to admit in any way that they might not know what they are doing, that they are not where they want to be, and that they are lost and in need of You finding and saving them. Help them, Lord. Help people to be lost. Bless all those people who do not know and believe that You are their Savior and Lord—bless them with a sense of being lost, even in the midst of all the

success, accomplishments, and adulation they might have. And please save them, Lord. Please also, Lord, when You see me heading down a path of thought or words or disgruntlements that You know leads away from You toward the darkness of being lost, rescue me. Open my eyes. Use Your gracious 2 by 4 if necessary. Please grant that in this day and every day I will rejoice that You found me and brought me to You.

13  And he called ten of his slaves, and gave them ten minas and said to them, 'Do business *with this* until I come *back*.'
17  And he said to him, 'Well done, good slave, because you have been faithful in a very little thing, you are to be in authority over ten cities.'

Thank You, Lord, for all that You have given me. I am blessed in many ways. Sometimes it is easy to just sit and be satisfied without recognizing that Your words are meant for me, now. "Do business, until I come." Help me, Lord, to see how to use everything that You have given me, to do the business of Living and blessing in this time waiting for You to come. When I leave the house I remember to make sure I have keys, sunglasses, possibly hat or coat, backpack, … . Grant that I remember to take all the blessings You have given me. The love, the caring, the joy (visible on my face would be nice!), the wonder, the delight in doing something. As I engage in the business of living, let me be faithful in using what You have given me so that I am Living while I am living and so that others are blessed and encouraged.

Knowing Jesus
First lost, then found
Blessed, and in business


Luke 20

17  But Jesus looked at them and said, "What then is this that is written:

'The stone which the builders rejected,
This became the chief corner *stone*'?
Thank You, Lord Jesus, for being the chief corner stone of Life for me and all Your people. Build me on You, Lord, please. You are the Foundation for all of my being. I see people build their lives on assumptions that having stuff is what is important, being respected (or feared) by others is what is satisfying, being famous is what makes life worth living. Shaky ground, Lord! Grant that everything in my life be built on You, Lord. Everything I want. Everything I enjoy. Everything I encourage. If there is anything in my life that doesn't fit or refuses to be built on You, let it fade quickly away from my life. Let the Light of Your love shine through all my being and thinking and saying and doing, so that it may be clear that You are my Foundation, now and forever.

26 And they were unable to catch Him in a saying in the presence of the people; and being amazed at His answer, they became silent.
Trying to catch You saying something wrong! That seems so obviously stupid. And yet, You know, Lord, there have been those times when I find myself saying, "Are You sure about that, Lord?" If I don't understand what You are saying to me or if I find it hard (read excruciating) to do what You are leading me to do, help me to be silent and listen more. I know You are loving me. I know You are blessing me and others through me. I know You know exactly what is the best possible blessing. When my idea of the best possible blessing doesn't seem to coincide with Yours, help me to listen more, knowing Who You are, trusting You for leading me in Life in the midst of life, depending on You always (especially when I am amazed and discombobulated).

37, 38 But that the dead are raised, even Moses showed, in the *passage about the burning* bush, where he calls the Lord THE GOD OF ABRAHAM, AND THE GOD OF ISAAC, AND THE GOD OF JACOB. 38 Now He is not the God of the dead but of the living; for all live to Him."

What a joy, Lord! Not that the Sadducees seemed to appreciate what You had to say. But when I think of those who have died besides Abraham, Isaac, and Jacob, like Your parents, St Frances of Assisi, my family members who have died—I look forward to seeing them all, Lord. All live to You. Thank You, Lord. You are keeping them in Your gracious care. I may not understand exactly how You are doing that, but to know that You are doing that is a comforting, exciting blessing. Please use this encouragement to bless all of us who miss people who have died. And please use this encouragement also to bless all of Your people who die. Let them know that You are still in charge, and that they can entrust themselves to You past death into Life after life. (And as I get closer to that time, thank You Lord, that I may have that confidence and joy as well.)

Corner Stone of my Life
Listen: You are blessing
God of the living


Luke 21

28 "But when these things begin to take place, straighten up and lift up your heads, because your redemption is drawing near."
Surely, they have begun, Lord. The things that You talked about that need to take place before You come back. There have been amazing things in the heavens, supernovas that grab people's attention. There have been natural disasters. The earth seems to be warming, seas rising. We have had plenty of wars. So if all we have to see is the beginning, Lord, this is a good time to pay attention. Help Your people to straighten up, to remember Whose they are, to celebrate Your grace and love. Bless us that nothing distract us from standing straight in each day with faith in You, depending on You. And grant that we look forward to our redemption

getting close.  For some of Your people it means that they will see You coming before they die, for some after they die.  Whichever it is, Lord, let us live each day in faith and joyful anticipation.

34, 35  "Be on guard, so that your hearts will not be weighted down with dissipation and drunkenness and the worries of life, and that day will not come on you suddenly like a trap; [35] for it will come upon all those who dwell on the face of all the earth."
The day of Your coming, Lord, is getting closer.  Perhaps for some people it seems so long since Your first coming, that Your second coming doesn't seem so real anymore.  There are certainly a lot of heavy things that try to put debilitating weight on our hearts.  Keep the focus of Your people on Your coming and grant that we do not dissipate our love and joy in You, by falling into temptations to evil or even falling into temptations to focus on good things instead of You.  I can imagine people in Capernaum worrying about the fish supply dwindling or the storms ruining the fishing.  And the people in Jerusalem concerned about the downturn of tourists visiting or the economy not supporting the purchase of all the things available in Jerusalem.  Hasn't changed, Lord.  Here we are, and worries of life are readily available.  Grant that they do not weigh down our hearts.  Grant that every day when we get up we practice faithful guarding by looking for any weights sticking and every night before retiring do the same.  Grant us faithful joy in You for continuous, effective sticky weight removal.

36  "But keep on the alert at all times, praying that you may have strength to escape all these things that are about to take place, and to stand before the Son of Man."
Stuff is coming, Lord.  You are clear about that.  One choice, of course, is to tune out, bury our heads in the sand, and think about other things.  Not a wonderful plan!  Bless Your people, Lord, that we recognize that bad things are going to happen before Your return.  Grant that we have the courage

from You to actually look and see what is happening, not with fear, but with recognition that we are getting closer to Your coming. And give us, please, Lord, the strength to escape evil crud that is popping up, exploding, and darkening the landscape of the world in which we live. Protect Your people from evil, Lord, and keep us faithful through everything that happens, that we will stand before You, washed in Your mercy and grace, protected by Your power, filled with Your Spirit, sliding into Home with great joy and anticipation.

Straighten up. Joy coming
No sticking, heart guarding
Strength, deliverance from evil


Luke 22

13 And they left and found *everything* just as He had told them; and they prepared the Passover.
Were they surprised, Lord? They left You. They followed Your directions. As they walked into town, there was the man carrying the jug on his head (the way women normally did). They talked to the owner of the house and sure enough, he had a room for You to use. Had they gotten to the point where they left You sure that everything You said was going to happen as You said? So I guess I say that thinking about me. Have I gotten to the point where I believe You know what is going to happen for me so I can trust You to guide me and direct me? I want to be there, Lord. Help me to listen to You with the confidence that I can take You at Your word. Grant that I will depend on You to use me to be a blessing (even if when I look in the mirror in the morning, I don't see how). Grant that, when I hear You giving me a way to bless people, I don't doubt Your willingness to give me strength and wisdom to carry out Your plan. As I live today, and You keep blessing me, and You keep giving me joy and satisfaction serving You, and You keep walking with

me in the little things—shopping, working, eating, reading—keep me smiling, Lord. Let me look like—"no surprise, yup, the Lord is here, that's the way He works, just like always." (Even when I feel an amazed, "Way to go, Lord!")

19  And when He had taken *some* bread *and* given thanks, He broke it and gave it to them, saying, "This is My body which is given for you; do this in remembrance of Me." Sometimes to remember someone a statue is built. Sometimes a new building at the university is funded. Sometimes it's a street renamed or a star on the sidewalk. Sometimes there is a picture carefully framed in the living room.  There are a lot of ways people choose to remember someone special.  You tell Your people, Lord, to remember You by partaking of a meal where You give Your body and the new covenant in Your blood.  So, bless Your people, Lord.  Help us to remember You.  In remembrance of You, Lord let us Live in the days You give us.  Let us Live by Your power, by Your grace, in Your will.  Let us glorify You, our Father, Your Spirit.  Let remembrance be something that flows from the meal You give us into every part of our thinking, feeling, speaking, and doing.  Let remembrance be in the joy that we carry into every day.  Let remembrance show in the love that we have toward others.  Let remembrance shine so brightly that others are drawn to You, so they can remember You, here and through eternity.

40  When He arrived at the place, He said to them, "Pray that you may not enter into temptation."
This is not the most common prayer for people, Lord.  You know that.  More commonly the prayer is, "Let me give in enough to temptation so that I will enjoy it but not so much that You will be very angry."  We human beings would like to be separate from temptation to live with You, but not so far from temptation that we forget what temptations are like. Ouch!  Whether it's spending time with the person who is not the one to spend time with, or going to a bookstore or shopping on the internet, or going to the clothes store, the

electronics store, or the store where everything costs only twice as much as what is available. Or saying things on social media without any limits since everybody does it. Lord, the list seems endless. Before we get hooked, before we want to get hooked, before we think about getting hooked by some temptation, grant us power and grace and determination to talk to You. Grant that we rejoice in Your Spirit Whom You have given to us. Grant that we Live grateful for the angel protection You provide. We, Your people, ask You, with real, whole-hearted desire, to bless us with not entering any temptation. Help us to see temptations for what they are—hooks to pull us away from You. Grant us courage and confidence in You to know that there are those who are powerful who are trying to pull us away from You, and at the same time grant us certainty that You have the power and desire to keep us safe with You. There is a lot off to the side of the path, loud, attractive, and inherently evil. Keep us on Your path, walking only in Your joy and peace and love.

Always trustworthy. No surprise.
Let our remembrance show
Your path: Avoiding temptation


Luke 23

5 But they kept on insisting, saying, "He stirs up the people, teaching all over Judea, starting from Galilee even as far as this place."
Thank You, Jesus, how true their accusation was. Of course, they thought that was a bad idea. But how wonderfully, You stirred people's hearts and minds with the joy of Your coming. You changed people's lives, and that really made the chief priests and elders very angry. Thank You, Lord for stirring up people today. Stir Your people with Your Holy Spirit. Be present with Your people and stir us to new Living with You. Stir our hearts with joy and satisfaction

in You even in the midst of normal (possibly mundane) days and events that sometimes try very hard to discourage us. Let the wonder and fire of Your presence so change us that we may be Light to the world around us (even if some who like darkness choose to respond with anger). Keep us stirred, Lord (never shaken).

14 ...and said to them, "You brought this man to me as one who incites the people to rebellion, and behold, having examined Him before you, I have found no guilt in this man regarding the charges which you make against Him.
Pilate seemed to enjoy politics more than truth, Lord. But even he is clear that there was no guilt in You. Thank You for his statement so that what happens is only because of Your gracious sacrifice for us. Guilt—there is a lot of it. People through the ages have known Your will one way or another and chosen their own will instead. It's easier to think about people in the Old Testament than it is to think about me when it comes to guilt. Lord, I admit, I have contributed plenty of guilt to the load that You carried. I am sorry for choosing my own will instead of Yours, for choosing unwisely and hurtfully, and especially for trying to make it on my own instead of trusting You. Thank You for carrying my guilt, even if Pilate could not see it. Thank You for sacrificing Yourself so that I am forgiven, Gracious Jesus.

35 And the people stood by, looking on. And even the rulers were sneering at Him, saying, "He saved others; let Him save Himself if this is the Christ of God, His Chosen One." You had sent prophets, Lord, to make clear the reason Messiah was coming. But the rulers twisted the message. The point was not for You, Jesus, to save Yourself. It never was. You came for me, for all people. We are the ones who needed saving. Thank You for putting up with the hurtful comments by the rulers and many others. Thank You for completing Your mission of sacrifice and even of rejection on the cross so that You can offer forgiveness and New Life in You to all people. Thank You for giving Your gift of salvation

to Your people. Grant that we never forget we are saved. We are not inoculated so that we will be generally ok. We are not helped by Your example to be good. We are saved from eternal separation from God, and given the gift of Life with You now and forever. Help us to Live in the joy and satisfaction of being (not helped, blessed or just guided, but) Saved.

Keep stirring, Lord
My guilt. Your forgiveness.
Not helped. Saved.


Luke 24

8, 9  And they remembered His words, [9] and returned from the tomb and reported all these things to the eleven and to all the rest.
There I am in some place of worry or turmoil. And like the women, I remember Your words to me about peace and joy and trusting You. They remembered that You promised to rise to Life again, and what had seemed like nonsense at the time or at least something very difficult to understand, suddenly became clear. They looked around them and realized they were in the wrong place and returned from the tomb. Help me, Lord, to remember Your words of Life. Help me to remember Your promises, Your peace, Your joy. And let me be overwhelmed, not with worry and confusion and despair, but with Your words that bring Life to me always. Lead me from the places where I wander in doubt, to walk with You in the places of peace and confidence that You choose. Because You have promised to be alive forevermore, I can live in places of Life throughout this day. Thank You, Lord.

25 – 27  And He said to them, "O foolish men and slow of heart to believe in all that the prophets have spoken! [26] Was it not necessary for the Christ to suffer these things and to

enter into His glory?" ²⁷ Then beginning with Moses and with all the prophets, He explained to them the things concerning Himself in all the Scriptures.

Thank You, for Your Holy Spirit, Lord. Thank You for explaining Your word to me and to Your people. Perhaps it is because it is so easy to find bad news around us that our hearts are slow to believe the wonderful Good News. The Good News that You have risen and that by rising You are with us to give us new Life with You today even here where there is bad news. We don't actually mean to focus on bad news of disasters and traffic and strained relations and people who are in need of help, it's just that we accept them as normal background noise in our hearts, while we are about other things. Let our hearts be so fast that we recognize joy with You now, and that we pray for all those who need Your loving care. Let us be fast of heart so that we live with the background music in our hearts of rejoicing and John Philip Sousa and Tchaikovsky's 1812 Overture as we enjoy Living this day with You.

32 They said to one another, "Were not our hearts burning within us while He was speaking to us on the road, while He was explaining the Scriptures to us?"

There are quite a few ways, Lord, as You know, of getting heartburn. (And it is true that I have tried quite a few of them.) But what an experience the disciples had! They were walking along thinking and feeling like their Lives were over, and here You come to walk with them. And You could have just said, "Whoa! Don't give up! Here I am!" Instead You took them back to the Scripture that they knew and showed them how they were supposed to expect You to die and rise from the dead. How often You must look at me and us today thinking, "Why are they walking around with gloomy faces? Why aren't their hearts burning with joy and hope and satisfaction?" It just seems so easy, Lord, to let the agenda for the day, the weight of responsibilities, the concerns for ourselves and for others pull our hearts and attention into a dark muddle and away from You and Light and Joy.  You have given Yourself into eternal death for us and risen so that we can now Live with You in joy and confidence every day.  Open Your word to us again, Lord.  Explain Scriptures to us, as we read Your word, as we worship You and listen to Your word, as we remember Your word that You have put into our hearts.  Set our hearts on fire, Lord so that the world's darkness, gloom, anger and hopelessness will be afraid to get too close to us (fearing that they might, Whoosh!, be swallowed up in the blazing joy of Your resurrection presence with us.)  Risen Lord Jesus, Light of the world, Fire of Joy, enflame our world with the joy of Your victorious presence, and use us to keep the fire going.

Remember:  To choose where
Fast hearts:  Music of joy
"Victory!" our song shall be (today)
["Rise, ye children of salvation", Justus Falkner, tr. Emma F. Bevan]

# John

John 1

4 In Him was life, and the life was the Light of men.
5 The light shines in the darkness,
   and the darkness has not overcome it.  (NABRE)
I don't think much about being alive, Lord, until something doesn't work right, and then I think about dying and wanting to enjoy more living now.  I forget that Life is so much more than waking up and cleaning, dressing, eating and doing.  It is wonderful to have the sun up early in the summer, and it seems as if that is the light in which I live.  Help me, Lord, to enjoy Your gift of sunshine but still recognize that there is darkness all about.  Help me to recognize that the Light that Lights up my life is from You, from Your Life.  When I feel the darkness of discouragement, disappointment, frustration, and temptations to despair and to dwell in anger and resentment—grant, Lord, that I recognize darkness for what it is and grant that I live in the joyous confidence that darkness has not and will not overcome the Light You are and that You bring to me.  Let me live in the darkness-searing power of Your Light 24/7, awake, asleep, at work, at home, alone, in fellowship, in joy, and through every attack of temptation and evil.

12, 13  But as many as received Him, to them He gave the right to become children of God, *even* to those who believe in His name, <sup>13</sup> who were born, not of blood nor of the will of the flesh nor of the will of man, but of God.
My mother was wonderful, and both my parents were terrific—blessings from You, Lord.  But to be born of You, Gracious Lord, this is a gift of great heritage and life-long Life in You.  Thank You, Lord.  Bless us, Your people, that we recognize we are Your children.  I have albums of pictures of relatives (and incredibly old cars and dresses)

that give me an attachment to family and place and background. Help me carry in my heart the album of attachment to Your family, the place You give me, and a background that grows with Light and joy and wonder every day expanding without end into eternity. Let me always walk with You, Lord Jesus. Thank You for graciously coming into me. Keep me strong in my faith. I believe in You. I trust in Your name. Help me to make that belief and trust real in all I think and say and do. Thank You for bringing me into Your family. (What a family picture!)

16 – 18 For from his fullness we have all received, grace upon grace. [17] For the law was given through Moses; grace and truth came through Jesus Christ. [18] No one has ever seen God; the only God, who is at the Father's side, he has made him known. (ESV)
From Your fullness, Lord Jesus, we have received Your blessings that we do not deserve. You have rescued us, Your people, from sin and eternal death. There are ways to get help for people in other ways. There is unemployment insurance. But it has a limit. There are loans (readily available!). But they have to be paid back! From Your fullness (How wonderful and loving You are!) there is no limit. Grace upon grace. You have given us what we did not deserve, forgiveness and new Life. And in this day, today, You give us more. You never tell us an end date. (After that, you're on your own!) Never. In the grace that You give us, Lord Jesus, grant that we know Your truth and Live in the wonderful truth You show us; the truth about You, our Father, Your Spirit. And yes, Lord, make God known to us. You are the only One Who can. Grant that in Your grace, we may Live by the Spirit and honor our Father.

Living in the Light
By Your gift: In Your family
And we see grace

John 2

11 This beginning of *His* signs Jesus did in Cana of Galilee, and manifested His glory, and His disciples believed in Him. They knew, Jesus, that You were the One they were waiting for. And yet, beyond what they expected, they saw You provide excellent wine to be a blessing to the marriage couple. Perhaps it seemed to them, a ray of heavenly light suddenly flashed on You. They recognized Your glory and You blessed them with faith. Show us the excellent You provide for us, Lord. We can find brokenness and evil if we look for it. Help us not to look for it. Help us to always look for the excellent that You provide: In the beauty of nature, in the care and loving of people, in our families. Help us to recognize Your excellent blessing in old masterpieces of art and literature, and in new inventions as well. Cars that make it difficult to have an accident (of course people will find ways!). Computers that fit in our pockets and provide vast amounts of information. Help us to see Your blessing, Your excellence, Your love, and Your glory. Use even Your blessings of things to stir our faith so we recognize You and believe in You.

16, 17 ...and to those who were selling the doves He said, "Take these things away; stop making My Father's house a place of business." 17 His disciples remembered that it was written, "ZEAL FOR YOUR HOUSE WILL CONSUME ME."
OK, Lord, there have been times when I visit a church that I cringe and wonder if You are going to come and have Stuff fly out the front door. Help us to have zeal for Your house. Grant that we never allow selfish gain to creep into Your holy house of worship and prayer. Thank You for the many opportunities You have given us to support Your work of ministry. Grant that every mention of money in church, by missionaries, by ministries seeking funding, by stewardship representatives—grant that it all be worship. Grant that all requests and all giving be clearly, faithfully part of our worship of You. Help us never to separate appeals for funds

from the heartfelt worship we offer You in giving.  Grant that we, Your people, be cheerful givers.  Grant that we give with sacrificial hearts and enthusiasm so that no ministry of Yours is without the support that You want it to have.  Let us have zeal in worship, in prayer, in loving, and in giving, to Your glory.

22  So when He was raised from the dead, His disciples remembered that He said this; and they believed the Scripture and the word which Jesus had spoken.
Thank You, Gracious Lord, for showing how we may listen to You and remember Your word and grow in faith and trust in You in the process.  Grant that we may so delight in Your word that we read, learn and inwardly digest all that You have for us on a daily basis.  You have arranged that we remember those things that we consider important.  Please grant that we so drink in Your word that we treasure it and put it in the Important File location in our memory, so that we really can remember what You have shown us in Your word.  It seems like, when years go by, what You have said to us in Your word has more and new applications.  Help us to keep remembering and applying the word You have given us, through all the time You give us, that we may Live the new Life You have given, with joy and power, praising and honoring You.

In excellence:  Recognizing You.  Believing.
Giving as worship
Remembering.  Believing.  Applying.


John 3

16, 17  "For God so loved the world, that He gave His only begotten Son, that whoever believes in Him shall not perish, but have eternal life. [17] For God did not send the Son into the world to judge the world, but that the world might be saved through Him."

Listening to people, Lord, it's like some people are riding on a train heading north and they believe all trains run north and south until they see a train coming from the east and crossing in front of them going west. Some people have a picture of You where You are watching to see if You can catch them in doing something wrong, and they are spending their time explaining (to You or themselves) why they are not doing anything wrong. You come to us from an entirely different direction—so loving the world, giving Your only-begotten Son, inviting people to receive Life by believing in Jesus. Open the hearts of people to see You not as Judge but as Savior. There is so much in this broken world that perishes (or doesn't work the way intended) including parts or functions of bodies through age. Thank You, Lord, that we may believe in You and be certain that our end is not perishing, but eternal Life with You.

33 He who has received His testimony has set his seal to *this*, that God is true.

"Real people, not actors" the advertisement says (actors, of course, not being real people). There are amazing things that companies do, Lord, to try to get people to buy stuff. And testimonies by people who have enjoyed the stuff is popular. But that is because You showed that the way to have people come to know You is to get to know someone who has set his seal to the fact that You are true by receiving Jesus. You have blessed me that way, Lord. I have met many people who show their faith in Jesus, who show that they trust You to be true, loving, and gracious. Thank You, Lord, for all those people You have brought into my life (or whose lives I have been blessed to cross). By Your grace I also have received Your testimony, Jesus, and I set my seal (by Your power Lord Holy Spirit): You are my Gracious God and Lord and Savior. Use my testimony, my seal as I cross other people's lives. Let the glow and wonder and awe of Your grace remain at every crossing.

34 For the one whom God sent speaks the words of God. He does not ration his gift of the Spirit. (NABRE)
OK. That is really terrific, Lord. Because I need You, Holy Spirit, to keep coming to me and keep filling me. It would be terrible if You had a limit, "Oops, you have exceeded your use of My Spirit for today (or this week or year), you'll have to wait now." Thank You Lord Holy Spirit for dwelling in me. As I listen to the words of God in Your word and from Your servants, grant that I continue to grow in faith, grant that I continue to come close to You. Grant that I face challenges and trials, not with renewed intestinal fortitude (I think I have used that up some time ago), but depending on You, Spirit of God. Grant that I face choices and decisions, not depending on research and asking around, but depending on You and Your guidance. And grant that I face joys and wonders and blessings, not with smugness and self-satisfaction, but with thanksgiving and praise to You, Gracious Spirit of Life.

From Your love direction: Life, imperishable
Gracious glow at every crossing
Growing in Your Spirit. For today.


John 4

13, 14 Jesus answered and said to her, "Everyone who drinks of this water will thirst again; [14] but whoever drinks of the water that I will give him shall never thirst; but the water that I will give him will become in him a well of water springing up to eternal life."
It's not just that people are thirsty, Lord, although there are a lot of people in the world who don't have any or enough clean water (please help them Lord). But there are people who seem satisfied for a while, and then a new plan for living turns up and they turn to that to try to satisfy their needs. Please bless me with such satisfaction in You, Lord and in the water You give me to drink, that I recognize that I am satisfied, life-long and forever, in You. Please bless those

people who appear thirsty for satisfaction in life but go from one plan to another—bless them with coming to You. Let them see You offering Life-giving water, springing up to eternal life. Let the water You give to me and all Your people, bubble up through us so that people can see those whom You have satisfied, and be drawn to You for the satisfaction that needs no new plan. Ever.

19, 20  The woman *said to Him, "Sir, I perceive that You are a prophet. [20] Our fathers worshiped in this mountain, and you *people* say that in Jerusalem is the place where men ought to worship."

Yes, Lord, I have tried that. When You talk to me about something that I don't want to talk about, when You make clear to me Your will about giving over to You something that I want to hold onto, when You show me something that I should get rid of—then I try the same plan that the Samaritan woman used, I try distraction. "Say, Lord, I've been meaning to talk to You about a question that has been puzzling me…" "By the way, Lord, what do You think about …?"  Of course, this does not fool You, You get that look of patiently waiting for me to stop obfusticating and listen. I'm sorry, Lord. When I try that sidestep distracting plan, ring my bell and let me know to just stop and admit my sins and listen to You. Thank You for bringing the Samaritan woman back to You. Please bring me back to You, Gracious Lord, whenever I foolishly try to slip away. Thank You for caring enough to outwait me.

23, 24  "But an hour is coming, and now is, when the true worshipers will worship the Father in spirit and truth; for such people the Father seeks to be His worshipers. [24] God is spirit, and those who worship Him must worship in spirit and truth."

It is easy, Lord, to feel good about going to worship, and then to participate in the worship with exuberance all the while thinking about the dinner, the ball game, the family, the concerns, the choices to make, … . You are Spirit, Lord.

Grant that with my whole entire spirit I be present in worship. Grant that with all my mind and heart, I will be open to You, focused on You and not on me and my schedule. Grant that my mouth and voice operate only in connection with my spirit, so that with my whole heart I am listening, loving You, worshiping You, and receiving Your blessings. And when I take the time to talk to You during the day, please grant that I be present with You in spirit conversing with You. If I use words that I or someone else prepared, grant that I do not just mouth or remember the words. Even when I repeat prepared prayers, grant that they be meaningful to me, through me, with my spirit. Grant that in every worship opportunity, I worship You in spirit and in truth, by Your grace.

Satisfaction: Needing no new plan
No sidestepping: Listen
Worship: Wholeheartedly present


John 5

6 When Jesus saw him lying *there*, and knew that he had already been a long time *in that condition*, He *said to him, "Do you wish to get well?"
I'm sure You see me many times stewing and mulling things over in my mind, or frustrated and uncertain, trying to figure out what to do or how to deal with something. And then I hear You a little bit like that man at Bethesda. He must have wondered why You would ask him if he wished to get well. But he was so focused on himself, he had hardly noticed You. That's my problem. Thank You for Your patient asking if I would like Your help. Of course, I should have started with talking to You instead of myself when I was frustrated and puzzled. Please help me to remember whenever I need help, that it is ok to need help, that I don't have to sit and stew, trying to come up with something myself, and that first I need to talk to You. Grant that I seek Your guidance, help,

and power with a humble spirit and an open heart, certain of Your understanding and Your gracious ability to bless me, whatever the situation may be. (And if Your patient voice doesn't get my attention, Lord, it's ok with me if You give me a whack on the side of my head—sorry if that is necessary!)

24 "Truly, truly, I say to you, he who hears My word, and believes Him who sent Me, has eternal life, and does not come into judgment, but has passed out of death into life." Thank You, Lord for Your word. Thank You for working faith in my heart. Please grant that I may rejoice today and every day that I have eternal life because of You. The end of this world is coming, I know (and some days it seems pretty close). Keep me in the confidence that by Your grace I have passed out of death into Life now and forever. Please bless Your people with that confidence and joy through every difficulty, especially those who are suffering persecution and trials. And Gracious Lord, please bless all our families and friends with effectively hearing Your word and coming to believe You, Father, in Jesus Your Son, so that they, too, may have eternal life—that we may rejoice together with You in that Life beyond death.

39 You search the Scriptures because you think that in them you have eternal life; it is these that testify about Me. It used to be that there were a few sources of information—the library and some family or community elders. Now, Lord, You have graciously made so many sources available. Searching for information is easier, but also can take hours depending on how many places a person looks. And what people are searching for is something satisfying. Bless people that they will search in the right place. Lead people to Your word. Thank You for making Your word available to people. Grant that they find You in Your word. Bless those people who don't know what they are looking for, who think they are looking for peace or the perfect place to live (that will solve everything) or the perfect job (that will solve everything) or the perfect spouse (that will solve everything)

or ... . Show them, Lord, that they are looking for You. And grant that through Your word, through Your people, even through trials and tribulations, that they will find You (Who are lovingly with them all during their searching).

Yes, I'd like Your help
Confidence in unending Life
Finding You, Life


John 6

5, 6 Therefore Jesus, lifting up His eyes and seeing that a large crowd was coming to Him, *said to Philip, "Where are we to buy bread, so that these may eat?" 6 This He was saying to test him, for He Himself knew what He was intending to do.
Thank You Lord for knowing what You intend to do, blessing us. There are times in my life when I hear You asking me what are we going to do now? Now that this has happened. Now that it isn't clear where the money is coming from. Now that he or she is pulling away from giving and receiving love. Now that the work situation has changed, and it doesn't appear that I will be able to continue in that place. Thank You that the answer always is, "Lord, You know." Help me always to remember when I feel that question growing in me, to trust You, to come to You, depend on You, to ask You. You know, Lord. Work your gracious will through me. Provide for me in Your gracious will. Provide for others. Bless us, Your people with confidence, trusting You, so that we do not stumble when questions arise, but only and always believe in You, trust You, depend on You.

15 So Jesus, perceiving that they were intending to come and take Him by force to make Him king, withdrew again to the mountain by Himself alone.
It really wasn't enough! That was the problem, Lord, right? There are a lot of people through the ages that would have

been glad to have throngs of people come and make them kings. But they were missing the point. Help me never to miss the point, Lord. Bless me and us, Your people, Lord, that we recognize that being king isn't enough. Touch the people You are reaching, and let them know that calling You Great and Wonderful and the Great Role Model is just an insult. Help us all to realize that we are keeping You at a distance with those words. Rather open our hearts and minds, souls and being so that we name You Lord, God, Savior, Only-begotten, and yes, King—our Gracious God, now and forever.

47, 48 Truly, truly, I say to you, he who believes has eternal life. [48] I am the bread of life.
Help us, Lord, to live as those who have eternal life. You have graciously given to Your people faith that we might believe in You. We believe that You are our Savior, true God and true Man. And by the power of Your Holy Spirit, You give us eternal Life. It is hard on a daily basis, with clocks ticking, lists of things to do appearing, sirens going past, and frustrations showing up—it is hard to always recognize that we have eternal Life. Grant that in all the things that happen each day in living, the Life You have given us shows up. Grant that the joy of Life shows in our faces, our words, and the choices we make. Grant that the faith we have in You shows in the peace in our hearts in the midst of turmoil and doubt. Grant that we recognize You, the Bread of Life, and that You are with us in the eternal Life we have now. And let others see that we Live with You in the eternal Life You give us now, as we listen and speak and love.

No doubt: You know.
Lord. God. And King forever.
Life showing through in life.

John 7

7  The world cannot hate you, but it hates Me because I testify of it, that its deeds are evil.

I live a life that seems to fit in, Lord.  There are some people that I see during the week.  There are people that I see on weekends.  There are things I do during the day, places I go... .  Some people seem to like me.  Some ignore me.  But to the best of my knowledge, no one hates me.  Do I fit in too much, Lord?  Help me to see what I think and say and do in the Light of Your grace, through Your eyes.  Grant that I recognize opportunities that You give to stand up for You and for the truth that You give.  Grant that my goal in life is not to fit in comfortably, but to demonstrate in every part of my life that I Live for You.  Help me never to be afraid that someone might not like what I say or think because it comes from You and is different from the world.  Grant that I Live in the uniqueness that is You and Your will whether it generates hatred from others or not.

38, 39  "He who believes in Me, as the Scripture said, 'From his innermost being will flow rivers of living water.'" 39 But this He spoke of the Spirit, whom those who believed in Him were to receive; for the Spirit was not yet *given*, because Jesus was not yet glorified.

Thank You, Lord Jesus for giving Your Spirit to me and all Your people.  Please let those rivers of Living water flow from my innermost being.  Grant that nothing I do or say or think slows the river or pushes it around.  As I begin each day, grant that I look for and depend on Your grace in the river flowing in that day.  Grant that the river flows continuously, and that I do not try to turn it off and on depending on where I am or the people I am with.  Grant that the Living water will continue to nourish me that I will be healthy, strong, and able to serve You well by Your direction and power.  And please grant that the flowing river You put in me will get other people wet with the Water of Life You give.  Let the water spread and be part of a mighty water graciously washing through and nourishing this time in which I live.

50, 51 Nicodemus (he who came to Him before, being one of them) *said to them, $^{51}$ "Our Law does not judge a man unless it first hears from him and knows what he is doing, does it?"
Nicodemus had listened to You, Lord. It was hard. He found it difficult to understand You. But he listened and took in the Life You gave him. And then he was amazed that others wouldn't listen. They were full of themselves and telling You what You ought to do. I'm afraid I see a resemblance to me there, Lord. I am ready, often, to come to You full of what I know about You, full of what I see happening, full of my wants and thoughts about the way You could just fix a few (or a lot) of things. I have difficulty coming to You and just Listening. Bless me with a hearing loss for things around me. Turn off the noise of my thinking and wondering and worrying and urgencies. Let me just listen to You. Help me not to listen with an attitude of "Yes, Lord, I think that fits in with what I understood back then …". I know You love me. I know You know what is going on now without me bringing You a list. Grant that I just listen to You.

Living differently: Liked or hated.
Delighting always, in Living water
Listening to You. Now.


John 8

7 – 9 But when they persisted in asking Him, He straightened up, and said to them, "He who is without sin among you, let him *be the* first to throw a stone at her." $^8$ Again He stooped down and wrote on the ground. $^9$ When they heard it, they *began* to go out one by one, beginning with the older ones, and He was left alone, and the woman, where she was, in the center *of the court*.

It is so easy, Lord, to throw stones. "Obviously that person is wrong and immoral!" From watching people drive (pretty scary, sometimes), to listening to and examining political wannabees, to listening to people talk (glowingly) about their exploits, to thinking about what other members of the family have done. It is so easy, Lord, to see what other people do wrong and cast stones of blame. Help me to remember Your writing in the ground. Were You writing the sins of the people around You? Before I reach for blame to throw around in accusations or innuendos, grant that I remember who I am. Grant that I remember my sins. Help me especially not to be quick to blame people for what I don't like in myself. Help me to remember Your grace and Your love, not blaming the woman who was guilty. Help me to remember that You don't spend the day looking for things I do wrong and hitting me over the head with words of accusation. Grant that whatever I toss be from Your supply of forgiveness, patience, love, caring, and encouragement.

12  Then Jesus again spoke to them, saying, "I am the Light of the world; he who follows Me will not walk in the darkness, but will have the Light of life."

Thank You Lord for sunshine. It is wonderful to walk in light and feel the warmth of Your gift of sunshine. And yet there is indeed still darkness. "What is happening?" "What should I do?" "Which choice is the right one?" "How can I live in that situation?" "How can I stop this hurtful habit?" "Where is hope, joy, encouragement, or satisfaction?" In the midst of the sunshine, it can seem, Lord, as if we are wading through a thick darkness. Bless Your people, Lord. Grant that we follow You faithfully. You are the Light in every darkness. We will walk in Your Light as we walk with You. Keep us close to You. When we see the darkness creeping in, grant that we draw closer to You. Let us never fall behind to be swallowed up in darkness. Let us see Your Light, Gracious Lord. Grant that Your Light will cut through all darkness around us. That we will see clearly Your will, Your love, Your encouragement and hope and joy. Wherever we are, keep us close to You, and let Your Light shine in.

31, 32  So Jesus was saying to those Jews who had believed Him, "If you continue in My word, *then* you are truly disciples of Mine; ³² and you will know the truth, and the truth will make you free.

I have times, Lord, being in Your word, delighting in You and Your word. It's the "continue" I sometimes have trouble with. The, not just for a moment, not just for this morning, not just when I feel like it, but always continuing in Your word. Help me to Live and continue in Your word. When I am tempted to set down Your word from my heart or mind so that I can take up something else (to guide or direct or empower), grant that I hear Your words again "continue in My word". Grant that I be Your disciple, following You faithfully, continuously, not once in a while when it is convenient to my situation or time or preference. In Your word, show me the truth—about myself, about others, about the blessings around, and about the world around, and about You and Your grace and Your love. Make me free of sin that clings so closely, free of quick words spoken harshly, free of seeing everything from a selfish point of view. Make this day a day filled with Your word and Your truth and Your gift of freedom.

Throwing only love
Following You in Light
Continuing in Your word


John 9

1-3  As He passed by, He saw a man blind from birth. ² And His disciples asked Him, "Rabbi, who sinned, this man or his parents, that he would be born blind?" ³ Jesus answered, "*It was* neither *that* this man sinned, nor his parents; but *it was* so that the works of God might be displayed in him.

Perhaps I think the disciples' attitudes were strange, but are mine better? I certainly fall into the temptation to look at people who are handicapped or suffer from some birth defect or who have a permanent result of an accident and feel afraid. It's hard to understand my attitude, Lord. I don't want to think about how hard it is for that person to live? I don't want to imagine that something like that could happen to me? I am uncertain how to talk to the person in a normal caring (not patronizing) way? Help me, Lord. These are certainly my problems, not theirs. Let Your blessings of respect, love, fellowship, and caring listening come through me. Bless people who struggle physically, with Your love and with the help they need. Grant them the joy of living independently, depending on You. Let all of my being communicate joy in You, available in fellowship with other people, whether they struggle with special physical or mental handicaps or just the normal physical and mental handicaps that I can find in myself.

25 He then answered, "Whether He is a sinner, I do not know; one thing I do know, that though I was blind, now I see."
It was very clear for that man what had happened to him. It was clear what he had to say to other people. There are other people whom You have blessed in amazing and miraculous ways, who inspire people by their testimony. I am not aware of that kind of miraculous event in my life for me to use in inspiring others. Help me to see what You have done. Help me to recognize the many times You have touched me with Your grace and love and help and rescue. Grant me grace and willingness to share those experiences with others. Use that to be a blessing to others. Not that I want recognition or notoriety, but since You have blessed me a lot, it's a shame to let Your grace and love go unnoticed. Help me not to hit people over the head with My Witness. But open the way for me to share with others lovingly, the way You have blessed me, so that Your blessing will keep multiplying.

38  And he said, "Lord, I believe." And he worshiped Him.
When I recognize the wonderful ways You have blessed me, Lord, help me to do more than hold onto them in an organized list in my head or heart.  Open my memory to recognize Your blessings with joy.  And beyond joy, let me see You and believe in You, trust You, depend on You in this day of remembering.  Most of all, Lord, let the memories of Your grace and blessings lead me through remembering and past trusting You all the way to worshiping You.  You have given me opportunities to worship You with Your family in a congregation.  But You give me daily opportunities to remember You through blessings You have given me, and to worship You.  You are great and greatly to be praised, Lord.  Let me grow with a worshiping heart.  Let me mature with giving all of myself to You in worship.  Holy Spirit, stir my spirit to reach out to You with joy and wonder at Who You are, Father, Son, and Holy Spirit.  Grant me times of quietly recognizing You, loving You, trusting You, and worshiping You today.

Sharing joy with love
Recognizing and sharing Your grace
Remembering, believing, worshiping


John 10

4  When he puts forth all his own, he goes ahead of them, and the sheep follow him because they know his voice.
It is so wonderful to hear a familiar voice.  Arriving at an air terminal, getting off the bus, coming to a meeting and not expecting to know anyone.  I have no doubt that You talk to us, Your people, on a regular basis.  You talk to us in Your word, through Your servants, through our conscience, and if we hand our imagination over to You, in our imagination.  Help us always to hear You, Lord.  Help us to recognize Your voice.  Grant that we recognize Your voice with joy and

satisfaction, as a welcome Friend (not with an attitude of "Good grief, here He comes again, what have I done?") Grant that we hear Your voice on days when there are challenges and frustrations. Grant that we hear Your voice on days of joy and awe. Grant that we hear Your voice when we are worn out and when bubbles of enthusiasm keep coming from our heart. When we hear Your voice, grant that we follow You without hesitation. Thank You, Lord for the joy of hearing Your voice.

9, 10  I am the door; if anyone enters through Me, he will be saved, and will go in and out and find pasture. $^{10}$ The thief comes only to steal and kill and destroy; I came that they may have life, and have *it* abundantly.
The picture comes to my mind, Lord, of a wall with a lot of doors. As one person opens a door, he can see a dark and stormy scene. Another door shows a gray rainy day. Another a stark, rocky landscape. And then there You are, opening a door, and You show a sunlit, glowing, awesome landscape which Albert Bierstadt would have enjoyed. Thank You for coming that we may have Life. Sometimes it seems like things are in short supply. Thank You that Life is abundant. Grant that in this day I live not in a fearsome shortage of Life, but in the joy of Your gift of abundant Life. Fill me with confidence that Life is so abundant, I may share it freely and with reckless abandon.

27 – 29  My sheep hear My voice, and I know them, and they follow Me; $^{28}$ and I give eternal life to them, and they will never perish; and no one will snatch them out of My hand. $^{29}$ My Father, who has given *them* to Me, is greater than all; and no one is able to snatch *them* out of the Father's hand.
Thank You, Gracious Lord, for giving us Life. Help us to live in the present, not worrying about the past. Grant that we turn that over to You with repentance and trust that You will make things a blessing. Thank You that we don't have to worry about the future. We are in Life with You now, and we will be then. Help us to Live each day in the confidence that

days that come are in Your power and grace. Grant that we never fear that anything will happen to destroy the joy we have of Life with You. You are holding onto us. Grant that we so trust You to hold onto us in the future that we may put all the energy and ability and gifts You give into now, without holding back anything, just in case.

Hearing Your voice
Living and sharing abundant Life
Spending time, confident in You


John 11

25 - 27   Jesus said to her, "I am the resurrection and the life; he who believes in Me will live even if he dies, [26] and everyone who lives and believes in Me will never die. Do you believe this?" [27] She *said to Him, "Yes, Lord; I have believed that You are the Christ, the Son of God, *even* He who comes into the world."
Thank You, Jesus, for Life in You. Thank You for faith. Grant that in every day, my words and attitudes and actions testify that You personally are the Resurrection and the Life. Let nothing make me waver from the joy and satisfaction that I have in You. When problems and illness threaten, grant that I remain strongly in faith trusting You for all Life now and beyond death. Bless the people around me so they may recognize You personally as the Christ, the Son of God, the One they can trust now and through death. Use me to demonstrate that faith (of course, I would like that to be without actually being in turmoil, trouble, darkness, or death—but whatever is the blessing You want, Lord, You are in charge, and I trust that You will bless me and bless others through me by Your grace). Thank You for the certainty that I will not end in death, but in Life with You. Thank You, Lord, for being Life for me and for all of us.

37 But some of them said, "Could not this man, who opened the eyes of the blind man, have kept this man also from dying?"

Oh, Lord, I'm sorry. I know I have said that or something close to it, if not out loud, somewhere inside. Who am I to judge You?! Why did that person have to suffer? Why did that bad thing happen? Why do bad things happen to good people? It comes so easily to the lips and hearts of Your people. Forgive me. Forgive us, please, Lord. Help me to see the things that happen, not as occasions to judge You, but as opportunities to love and pray for and support people with the love and care that You give us to share. Be present with people who are suffering, Lord. Bless them with encouragement, strength, hope, and confidence in You. Help me not to be afraid to recognize suffering. Grant that I see the frustrations and problems around, not with judging, but with compassion. Use me to be a blessing as You desire. Thank You for giving me and all Your people the strength and power through Your Holy Spirit to live and Live with or without suffering, and to reach out to others and be a blessing.

43 – 45 When He had said these things, He cried out with a loud voice, "Lazarus, come forth." 44 The man who had died came forth, bound hand and foot with wrappings, and his face was wrapped around with a cloth. Jesus *said to them, "Unbind him, and let him go." 45 Therefore many of the Jews who came to Mary, and saw what He had done, believed in Him.

We have such dramatic events to get people's attention. With loud noises, fireworks, smash!, bang!, whoosh!. What those people saw was You, Life, speaking, and death giving way. They saw and believed in You, as their Lord of Life. You are still speaking Life in the face of death in people's hearts, in times of hopelessness, in hospitals, in hearts empty of love, in the midst of worry and fear. Grant that people see and believe in You. Grant that people recognize You as the One who brings Life to every person who is walking in the valley of the shadow of death.  Grant that people believe and receive Life that changes their lives and leads them through death to joy with You forever.  And when my foot slips into worry, when my steps enter places of shadow, when my heart is near the doors of doubt and discouragement, let me see You.  Let me hear You speaking Life in the face of death.  Fill my heart with joy and confidence in seeing You and Your blessings, and with Your Spirit bring me to believe in You with all my heart, with all my being.

Recognizing You, Who are Life
Opportunity to care
Believing You, Who speak Life


John 12

3  Mary then took a pound of very costly perfume of pure nard, and anointed the feet of Jesus and wiped His feet with her hair; and the house was filled with the fragrance of the perfume.
What can I do for You, Lord?  Mary chose to offer You a costly gift with a loving action.  You are with me.  You walk with me.  You love me, which is amazing to me (of course, I think I'm pretty nice, until I look into Your eyes, and I realize how far I am from good, nice, or ok).  Thank You for choosing to love me.  Thank You for choosing to walk with me.  Thank You for revealing Yourself to me, Gracious Lord, Savior, my God and my King forever.  What can I do for You?  The best I have has holes and rather smells.  With Your grace, enable me to give You all I have.  Help me to give You my life; be in charge, Lord.  Let me pour out, every day, my life before You.  Use me as You will, to Your glory.  Grant that I may honor You with all that I am.

**14, 15** Jesus, finding a young donkey, sat on it; as it is written, ¹⁵ "FEAR NOT, DAUGHTER OF ZION; BEHOLD, YOUR KING IS COMING, SEATED ON A DONKEY'S COLT."

Sometimes I have looked out the window, and yes, I have shuddered as I see people coming. I have been afraid that people would bring problems that I could not imagine how to fix or solve. I have been afraid that I had done something wrong. I have been afraid that they might use my time telling me all the things I needed to fix in my life and the changes I needed to make. But You, when You came, picked a sign of peace and humility. Help me to always delight in Your coming. Grant that I am open to Your company every moment of every day. You are my Lord and King, Gracious Jesus. Thank You for wanting to come into my life. Help me never to receive You with protective armor on, but with heart and life open to Your fellowship and love.

**26** If anyone serves Me, he must follow Me; and where I am, there My servant will be also; if anyone serves Me, the Father will honor him.

When the visiting dignitary comes, his entourage comes with him. You have invited me to serve You, Gracious Lord, and come with You. Thank You for calling me. Help me to remember that I am not in charge of planning the day's trip. I have tried that, and find that You have gone a different direction. Help me to listen to the travel plans for the day. Help me to be flexible when You open doors that I didn't see, so I can come with You. Thank You that I may serve You, Lord. Help me to remember that as I am serving You, we are together, in the same place. Where You are, that's where I am, in Your company. Grant that I serve You with joy and confidence today, recognizing Your presence and depending always on Your gracious love.

Let me honor You, Lord
Open to Your loving company
Your plan. Your presence. Your love.

John 13

8 Peter *said to Him, "Never shall You wash my feet!" Jesus answered him, "If I do not wash you, you have no part with Me."
With Peter, Lord, I want to have a relationship with You, where I do Wonderful things for You, where I accomplish Great tasks for You (and, of course, what I mean is, by my power, so I can be a Great servant of Yours!). But that's not the relationship You offer me. You come to me to serve me. I can only have a relationship with You where I am in total need, and You are my Savior, the One Who serves me and brings me to Life. Help me, also today, to humbly accept Your love and Your gift of Life as Your unworthy servant. Help me to accept being completely humble before You. I want to bring great gifts to You, Lord. Help me to give the only gift I have—myself. Take me, Lord, and make me Your servant by Your grace, by Your strength, with Your wisdom, with Your gift of faith. Grant that in this day I rejoice in the relationship I have with You. Grant that I depend on You, keeping completely clear of every temptation to depend on myself, to be arrogant, to find value in myself apart from You. Thank You for the wonderful relationship You give to me, being with You, now and every day.

14 If I then, the Lord and the Teacher, washed your feet, you also ought to wash one another's feet. ... 20 "Truly, truly, I say to you, he who receives whomever I send receives Me; and he who receives Me receives Him who sent Me."
Thank You, Lord, for this opportunity, this assignment. By Your Love and Self-giving, You not only show us, Your people, how to live, You also empower us. Give us the power we need today to serve one another. Show us today the people around us who need encouragement. Give us the words and actions of encouragement that will be a blessing. Show us the people that need assistance. Give us the wisdom and willingness to use what You have given us

so that we may be of assistance.  Show us the people who need caring and love.  Let us share the love and caring that You have given us with those who need them.  Show us people who need to be rescued.  Work through us to reach them so that through us, either today or over time, they may receive the gift of Life in You.  Thank You for the privilege of washing each other's feet.  Help us not to be put off by any smells that we happen to encounter in the process (ours or theirs).

35  "By this all men will know that you are My disciples, if you have love for one another."
We print a lot of information and advertisements to attract people to come to worship, Lord.  Make those a blessing.  But help us always to remember the method You have created for people to be attracted to You and to Your Church.  Forgive us for so focusing on trying to find ways to love people outside the Church that we forget to love each other.  Help us to see other faithful followers of You not as competitors, but as family, as disciples of Yours with us.  Help us not to resist Your loving ways of making us a blessing to each other.  Help us to be open to each other, to listen to each other, to care about each other.  Inside our congregations and outside our congregations, let us truly love each other so that other people may see and know that we are Your disciples.  Make us the full color, 3D, dynamic, surround sound, 24/7 advertisements filled with love that You want us to be.  Let all people know, and come to You.

Served and serving
Washed and washing
Loved and loving


John 14

13  Whatever you ask in My name, that will I do, so that the Father may be glorified in the Son.

Help me, Lord, to want well. Little children learn to ask while going through stores. They don't have a lot of sense of what is a blessing. And I do suffer, I know, from the temptation to want things that have batteries, cords, or chips in them. You have graciously given me the ability to want. Send Your Spirit and guide me in my wanting so that I will want that which is good, so that I will want fervently by Your grace, and so that I will want that which glorifies Your Father. Filter my asking, so that everything I ask for will give You, Father, the joy of satisfaction in what Jesus does in answering my prayers. Help me to focus, not on myself, but on others. Thank You, Lord Jesus, for the privilege of praying, knowing that You will do all I ask that will glorify Your Father. Stir my asking with Spirit powered wanting well.

16, 17  I will ask the Father, and He will give you another Helper, that He may be with you forever; <sup>17</sup> *that is* the Spirit of truth, whom the world cannot receive, because it does not see Him or know Him, *but* you know Him because He abides with you and will be in you.
Thank You Father, for giving me Your Spirit. Lord, Holy Spirit, Gracious Helper, please help me. Help me to see how much, and all the ways, I need Your help. Help me to recognize You, to see You. Keep me from participating in the blindness of the world. Help me to live each day in faith in You, in Jesus, without fear. Help me to converse with You throughout the day, so that I may have the joy of walking with Jesus to the glory of my Father. Help me worship— touch my spirit and guide me in truth, that I may rejoice in worshiping You every day and particularly in fellowship with others of Your family. Help me to rejoice in what You give me to do and help me to see how to bless others. Help me to depend on You for all the resources I need to be a blessing whether it is money or time or words of encouragement, or fellowship and love. Help me remember that You are my Help and that You are with me always. Grant that I depend faithfully on You in joy and wonder throughout each day.

26, 27  But the Helper, the Holy Spirit, whom the Father will send in My name, He will teach you all things, and bring to your remembrance all that I said to you. $^{27}$ Peace I leave with you; My peace I give to you; not as the world gives do I give to you. Do not let your heart be troubled, nor let it be fearful. Thank You Jesus for speaking to me in Your word.  Thank You for giving Your peace to me.  I read Your words, and my heart is lifted up.  Trouble and fear flee from my horizon.  And then I get busy, and I forget, and trouble and fear sneak back.  Gracious Holy Spirit, Helper Divine, please work in me every day, throughout each day.  Help me to remember.  Not just with my head, but with my heart.  Help me to remember the peace I have from my Lord so strongly that when I step out in word or action I am stepping in the certainty of the Peace I have in my Savior and Lord.  More than any collection of sayings or good feelings, let the Peace from Jesus be the overruling theme and vision and power in my life.  Help me Remember.

Wanting well with enthusiasm
Helped. Dependable. Available.
Remembering Peace. Now.


John 15

5  I am the vine, you are the branches; he who abides in Me and I in him, he bears much fruit, for apart from Me you can do nothing.
I have tried, Lord.  Forgive me for trying to keep You in just certain ("religious") parts of my life.  (Like saying I only need to eat, sleep, and breath on Mondays and Thursdays.)  Be present in my life every day, Lord.  Keep me open to You every moment of every day.  When I am tempted to pick up some project, task, job without looking for Your presence, let my alarm bell go off.  Grant that in every way, in every day, I abide in You.  Help me to expect to be fruitful from being

with You, in every part of my life—working, socializing, resting, being with family members, reading, doing chores, surfing the internet, shopping. Remind me that I get to do everything with You. I don't think of all those things as opportunities to be fruitful. So, help me Lord to open my thinking, and grant, abiding in You and You in me, in every part of this day, that I bear fruit for You.

10, 11 If you keep My commandments, you will abide in My love; just as I have kept My Father's commandments and abide in His love. [11] These things I have spoken to you so that My joy may be in you, and *that* your joy may be made full.
It's easy to look at commandments as what I am not supposed to do. But then I miss the point. Before smart phone apps that show us how to get from one point to another, before GPS devices, before (I suspect) maps!, You showed the way, the path, the road to follow, so that people could abide in You and in Your love. Help me to see Your will as the way to enjoy being close to You. Grant me faithfulness in Living with You and for You. Thank You for wanting there to be real joy in my life. The joy I have in You is truly satisfying. Grant that I recognize that all joy comes from You, and make my joy indeed full in You.

16 You did not choose Me but I chose you, and appointed you that you would go and bear fruit, and *that* your fruit would remain, so that whatever you ask of the Father in My name He may give to you.
Thank You, Lord, I'm glad You're in charge of that. I am often caught up in the urgent. I would like things I do to be long-lasting blessings. But I know I don't have the power to make that happen. Thank You for graciously appointing me to bear fruit. Grant that by Your fellowship I be fruitful, as You would like. And grant that there be long-lasting good and blessing that comes from what I do. When I think of the blessings that I have received, some of them didn't look like blessings at the start. Some were small things to start with.

Use what I think and say and do, and make them a blessing, whether I can see it or not. Take out anything that comes from me that gets in the way, and create blessing, joy, and fruit that remains.

Ready to be fruitful
Enjoying being close to You
Grace preserved fruit


John 16

14, 15  He [the Holy Spirit] will glorify Me, for He will take of Mine and will disclose *it* to you. <sup>15</sup> All things that the Father has are Mine; therefore I said that He takes of Mine and will disclose *it* to you.
Thank You, Lord Jesus for Your Holy Spirit. Thank You for coming, Gracious Holy Spirit. Bring us what Jesus has for us. Bring us guidance, food, encouragement, Gospel, wisdom, joy, Life, fellowship—bring us that which is the Father's, which belongs to Jesus. The disciples were not ready for everything at once. We certainly are not either. As we grow by Your gracious ministry, Lord Holy Spirit, bring us more and more. It is a temptation to think that we get to a certain point of procedure or learning or witness or something and then that's it, we have come into the group of Your Finished People. Hogwash! Keep us growing in fellowship with You. Help us not to be afraid that You always have more for us. (It's like seeing someone coming along the street and saying, "Oh, there he is, and he always wants to talk so much!") But You bring us joy and news from Home! Help us always to be open to receiving more in satisfying, stretching, challenging, wonderful, growing, joyous fellowship with You in Jesus and our Father, Lord Holy Spirit.

22 Therefore you too have grief now; but I will see you again, and your heart will rejoice, and no one *will* take your joy away from you.

The disciples missed walking with You, Lord Jesus. But You showed them the vision of seeing You again and Living in joy unending. There are times when we miss You greatly. We see darkness and we would like to sit with You in the Light of Your presence. We feel uncertainty and would like to be holding Your hand and walking in the certainty of Your visible company. We feel joy in You and with You and then some temptation or grief or sadness or darkness washes over us and our joy seems hard to find. Bless us with the vision of being with You then. Bless us with the certainty of rejoicing with You. Bless us with the wonder of joy never leaving, never growing dim, never seeming far away. As we Live with You now, in the midst of times of uncertainty and darkness, grant us hope, joy, and confidence with the vision of Living with You then in joy unending.

23, 24 In that day you will not question Me about anything. Truly, truly, I say to you, if you ask the Father for anything in My name, He will give it to you. [24] Until now you have asked for nothing in My name; ask and you will receive, so that your joy may be made full.

But Lord, I have a list of questions I have been saving up to ask You when I see You! (I will not miss them, will I, Lord? They will disappear in joy and satisfaction.) I think the temptation some of us have now, is that we think of "asking" as an intrusion, an interruption of Your Kingly busy "day". We think of asking as something appropriate for those special times of the day or in special places. And here You are openly, graciously, magnanimously encouraging us "Ask!" OK, thank You Lord, for showing us Your will in Your word. Thank You for showing us so many blessings to ask for. Remind us to ask. As we read your word and recognize Your loving will, as we walk through the day and see needs and hurts that people have, as we live and breathe and know that You (challenging thought) want to use us to answer others' prayers, remind us to ask. Remind us to trust our Father, to depend on You and ask in Your name, and to have faith that as You have promised, we will receive blessings by Your grace in answer to our prayers, to our great wonder and Life-sustaining joy.

Open:  Receiving more
Joy with You, unending
Trusting, asking, receiving


John 17

1 – 3  Jesus spoke these things; and lifting up His eyes to heaven, He said, "Father, the hour has come; glorify Your Son, that the Son may glorify You, [2] even as You gave Him authority over all flesh, that to all whom You have given Him, He may give eternal life. [3] This is eternal life, that they may know You, the only true God, and Jesus Christ whom You have sent.
Please, Lord, grant us Your gift of eternal life.  Father, include us in those You give to Jesus.  Grant Lord Jesus, that we may know the only true God and You, Jesus.  There are many claimants to being first, to being god.  Large groups of people, voting with their hearts, heads, and lives choose another god.  Bring them to You, Lord.  In our living, we meet a lot of people.  But there are few that we get to know well.  Grant that we may know You, Lord, now by faith.  Grant that we may know You, Life, Love, Joy, Peace, Goodness, Creativity, All that You are.  It will take being made new, Lord.  Make us new here and at home with You there.  It will take time, and eternity, to get to know You—please grant us that privilege, Lord.  Grant that we may know You, Lord, and Jesus, Your Anointed One.  Expand our "knowing" so that we may, in Your gracious plan, be fulfilled and satisfied forever, knowing and loving You.

11 I am no longer in the world; and *yet* they themselves are in the world, and I come to You. Holy Father, keep them in Your name, *the name* which You have given Me, that they may be one even as We *are*.

Thank You Gracious Father for bringing us into Your name at our baptism. Thank You that we are not outside trying to live in the darkness. Thank You that we may Live in the Light and Joy and Life of Your name. Help us, Your people, to recognize that we are all people of Your name, people in Your name. Your Spirit has made us alive in You, praises be to You! Keep us delightedly in Your name. Help us to recognize each other as Family, people in Your name. Make us one by Your grace in Your Spirit, and grant that we recognize with joy, love, respect, wonder, and awe each other as one in You, in Your name. We desire to be one as You are, Lord. We have a ways to go. Bless us here in the world, and let us grow in fellowship in You until the day when we will truly enjoy perfect fellowship with You and with each other as You are truly One.

15 I do not ask You to take them out of the world, but to keep them from the evil *one*.

There are times, Lord, when I would just as soon that You just took me out. Out of the world. Out of the frustration. Out of the terrible things that happen around me, around our country, around our world. Evil appears to be alive and ferociously well and active. Of course the trouble is when a line is drawn separating good from evil, the line goes through me. So while we, Your people, are here, keep us from the evil. It's not just the evil that we can see on CNN in some distant place. (But keep Your people from that.) It's not just the evil that we can hear about in our neighborhood and in our communities. (But keep Your people from that, please also, Lord.) Keep us from the evil that is as close to us as our thoughts and our feelings. Keep us from the evil that tries to stand between us and the people we know and love. Keep us from the evil that tries to discourage us and drag us into depression and despair. And especially keep us from the evil that tries to make us independent from You, that tries to pull us from You, that tries to keep us from seeing Your love and mercy and forgiveness and joy and Life.

Satisfaction: Knowing, loving You
One in Your name: Becoming one.
Keep us from the evil.


John 18

10  Simon Peter then, having a sword, drew it and struck the high priest's slave, and cut off his right ear; and the slave's name was Malchus.
The first problem I have, Lord, I admit, is that I carry a loaded weapon with me wherever I go. Not a gun, but a mouth, an attitude, words practiced with hurtfulness. I see someone doing something and I see injustice or an abrogation of my rights or of fairness, and zap! I pull out my loaded weapon without waiting for You to take care of the situation. You have given me peace and patience, Lord Holy Spirit, please keep them strong and healthy in me. Make them faster than my trigger mouth. Help me to use them faithfully, often, willingly, joyously, trusting You. Help me to give myself to You including all my rights and privileges in trust, joy, sacrifice, and delight. Grant that I do not jerk any of that back just because I see or hear something I don't like. Let me be so practiced in speaking love and using an attitude of patience, that they come (Zap!) first by Your grace in every situation I face this day and each day.

17  Then the slave-girl who kept the door *said to Peter, "You are not also *one* of this man's disciples, are you?" He *said, "I am not."
I can remember times, Lord, when I was in some group, and a leader was pointing out how extreme the behavior of some people was that they let their "religion" get in the way of everything they did. And then the leader would say, "None

of us would be that extreme, would we?" Of course, there was never a long wait for an answer. It was rhetorical. But my silence in the days afterward was deafening. Help me, Lord, not to value relationships with other people over my relationship with You. Help me not to be politically correct at the cost of faithfulness to You. Grant that I stand up for You, hold firmly to faith in You, not with an attitude of standing on street corners hitting other people over the head with Your grace. But grant that I do not with words or silence let people think that working cooperatively and accomplishing important work is more important than my faith, either. Let not fear of ostracism lead me to deny You, Lord. Grant that by my words and actions I always give enough evidence so that I could be convicted of faithfully following You.

33, 34 Therefore Pilate entered again into the Praetorium, and summoned Jesus and said to Him, "Are You the King of the Jews?" 34 Jesus answered, "Are you saying this on your own initiative, or did others tell you about Me?"
Pilate came "that close"! He asked the right question of You, Lord. And You gave him a chance to realize that he needed to know the answer for himself, not just as a judge. But he backed off and became political. Help people today not to be afraid to ask You Who You are. Protect people from the enemy when they finally have the opportunity to get to know You. Help them not to back off into "Just asking, for informational purposes only". When people meet You in Your word or in one of Your servants or in times of great need, help them to meet You with an open heart so that they can ask for their own, personal, eternal benefit. Show them that You are the One they have been seeking all their lives. Show them that You are the Savior they really need. Show them that You are the Source of Life that is filled with joy unending. Show them that they can trust You in every challenge and difficulty of life. Bless people so that in that moment they let go of fear and self-preservation, and come to You, and into Life forever.

Zap! Patience first.
Faithfully Yours, clearly first.
Asking and receiving You, personally.


John 19

12  As a result of this Pilate made efforts to release Him, but the Jews cried out saying, "If you release this Man, you are no friend of Caesar; everyone who makes himself out *to be* a king opposes Caesar."
Choosing friends is an important part of the life You give us, Lord.  Whether "friend of Caesar" was an honored group that Pilate liked belonging to or not, it is true that we make attachments with people and things.  Help us to make attachments in friendship, Lord, that will not draw us from You.  Bless us so that the relationships we have with people and groups do not cause us to have to choose them or You.  Help us to examine the relationships we have, with Your insight, so that we will remain faithful to You in the causes we support, the organizations we work with, and the people we want close in our life.  Grant that our Life in You will be a blessing through us to all the people and groups whom we have given permission to claim our time and friendship.  Whether it is to things or people or groups, Lord, let all our yeses be in Your gracious will.

25  Therefore the soldiers did these things.
But standing by the cross of Jesus were His mother, and His mother's sister, Mary the *wife* of Clopas, and Mary Magdalene.
Lord those were gutsy people who stood there in love for You.  When I look at myself, I have difficulty seeing myself like that.  Forgive me for the times I have shown myself to be in the vast number of Your followers who were not there.  Grant me Your gift of strong faith so that I Live in a way that shows I love You.  Let the words that I speak in worship and caring and frustration and anger not contradict each other.

Grant that I begin each day with a moment in front of Your cross, recognizing that no matter what the winds of the world may bring, I want more than anything else, to be with You, to love You, to stand up for You. Let nothing I do or say today give anyone an impression otherwise.

27  Then He *said to the disciple, "Behold, your mother!" From that hour the disciple took her into his own *household*. How gracious You are that You took care of Your mother, even from the cross. John writing of himself is matter-of-fact in his simple statement of taking Mary into his own household, his own family. You knew You could trust John. And still You entrust people to our care. You give us people to love. Help us to hear You, Lord. Help us to take You as seriously as John did. Whether You give us someone in our family to love and take care of or a friend or whether You give us someone in our congregation or a stranger we meet today, help us to hear You speaking to us. Grant that we respond with the same straightforward love and trustworthy faithfulness that John showed. There seem to be so many people who need Your love and Your help today, Lord. The thought of taking care of all of them is truly scary. Help us to hear You speaking to us individually, giving us the person or persons You want us to take care of, trusting You to provide through us all the love and joy and hope and fellowship and provisions that are needed. And help us to trust that You will also entrust the many others who need Your love to others of Your faithful family. Thank You for the privilege of loving those You entrust to us, on Your behalf.

Friendships, mutually Yours
Standing up for You, today
Privileged to love


John 20

8, 9  So the other disciple who had first come to the tomb then also entered, and he saw and believed. ⁹ For as yet they did not understand the Scripture, that He must rise again from the dead.

It is really terrific, Lord, that we don't have to understand in order to believe. There are a lot of things that I don't understand about Your love and Your sacrifice and Your grace and power that enables me to Live with You now. And yet You give me the privilege of believing that You love also me, here, now, these centuries later. Thank You that I may believe that Your sacrifice frees me from sin and makes me new in You. Thank You for enabling me to believe that You give me Your grace to Live with You now and power to serve You and be a blessing. Help me always to remain firm in faith, trusting You, stepping out into each day, even when I don't understand all that happened then or all that is happening now. Keep me strong in faith to serve You and to rejoice in Living with You now. I trust You, Lord, that if it will be helpful to me to understand, You will make that happen. In the meantime, grant that my head not get in the way of my heart rejoicing in You and walking with You throughout this day.

19  So when it was evening on that day, the first *day* of the week, and when the doors were shut where the disciples were, for fear of the Jews, Jesus came and stood in their midst and *said to them, "Peace *be* with you."

You always know just what to say, Lord. They had a lot of conflicting feelings flying around, and peace is what they needed. I would like to say that in these modern times, with Your word available to read and hear, it is different. Not true. We know You are risen. We know You love us and take care of us. We know You are trustworthy. What we sometimes don't know is what that means, exactly, in connection with what is happening today. So, yes, Lord, please speak Your word of peace to us, today. In the midst of busyness, speak peace to us. In the midst of confusion about how to speak out with courage for what is right and at the same time respect the people to whom we speak, speak Your peace to us. In times where people are tired and at the same time desire to be responsible without laziness, speak Your wisdom and peace. Be present with us, Gracious Lord, and let us Live with You in Your peace.

21, 22 So Jesus said to them again, "Peace *be* with you; as the Father has sent Me, I also send you." [22] And when He had said this, He breathed on them and *said to them, "Receive the Holy Spirit."

People have been sent for a lot of reasons, Lord, from children to the store to emissaries of a King. And they are sent with what they need to accomplish their mission. Thank You, Lord for giving us what we need, as we are sent by You, into this day. Only You know what we need, so You give us Your Spirit. Holy Spirit, take away all fear from our hearts. Show us the people You want us to bless. Fill us with faith that we may trust You to give us all we need to be a blessing. Open our minds and hearts to listen to others, to feel with them, to rejoice and to grieve with them. Grant us energy, enthusiasm, and joy to carry out the mission You entrust to us. Help us always to be conscious, with every breath, that we have been breathed on, empowered, and sent.

Essential: Believing, not understanding
Speaking peace to us
Breathed on, empowered, sent


John 21

7 Therefore that disciple whom Jesus loved said to Peter, "It is the Lord." So when Simon Peter heard that it was the Lord, he put his outer garment on (for he was stripped *for work*), and threw himself into the sea.

There are times, Lord, when I'm minding my own business, and letting my thoughts wander, and then I get an idea! And

I realize that it's a very good idea. I could do that! That would be a blessing! (Now psychologists can explain this by my subconscious working on a problem without me knowing what it was doing and coming up with the idea, but I know different.) It's You, Lord. You graciously reach in and open a door. And I feel a sudden sense of joy in Your presence, Lord. Thank You! It's not so much that I want You to fill me in with all the good ideas that I should be aware of (although that's also ok, Lord). But help me, Lord to be aware of Your presence. When You open doors, when You let me meet Your servants who share their joy of Living with You in the midst of daily travels, when You bring a song to my heart— grant that I recognize You and with the humility of Peter, rush to Your side in joy and thanksgiving.

19  Now this He said, signifying by what kind of death he would glorify God. And when He had spoken this, He *said to him, "Follow Me!"
It is not clear to me yet what kind of death will take me from this world to You, Lord. And, truth be told, I'm not entirely sure I want to know just yet. But as years pass, I know, as the retirement counselor once said, the next big event after retirement is dying. Thank You, that it's ok to talk about, Lord. Thank You that You still are in charge all the way through dying. In the many (or not so many) days ahead here, help me to keep focused, not so much on dying or what kind of death will take me Home, but on following You. Let each day be filled completely with following You. Help me to entrust to You the days of going Home. And right now, grant me the joy and confidence to spend all the time, energy, and wisdom You give me in walking with You. Thank You that today I can be about what You give me to do with Your gifts and power. Grant that I take in all satisfaction now, in following You.

21, 22  So Peter seeing him said to Jesus, "Lord, and what about this man?" [22] Jesus said to him, "If I want him to remain until I come, what *is that* to you? You follow Me!"

Right!  Help me to remember that there are a lot of (like most) things that I am not in charge of.  The temptation is very great, Lord, to look around and point out to You the things that need to be fixed, the things in people's lives that don't seem right, and various other really splendid ideas I have.  And the truth of the matter is, that You are doing very well being in charge, and You don't exactly need me to arrange Your "to do" appointment schedule for You.  Thank You for being in charge, Lord.  My following You does not involve worrying about or trying to arrange other people's lives, (even though the temptation is certainly strong).  Help me to recognize the limitations I accept in following You along with the wonderful enormous, joyful, and fulfilling opportunities You give.  Thank You for the people around me today.  Grant that I will follow *You* faithfully, in company with the others You give me, with Your gifts and to Your glory—today.

Joy in Your presence
Satisfaction now, following You
Great opportunity in a limited agenda

# Acts

Acts 1

6  So when they had come together, they were asking Him, saying, "Lord, is it at this time You are restoring the kingdom to Israel?"
My kind of question, Lord.  Restoring the kingdom to Israel!  That was the best they could think of, and they were ready!  And truly, Lord, I would like to ask sometimes, "Is this it, Lord?  Can we move directly on to the good stuff?  Can we bring an end to suffering, pain, tragedies and disasters?"  There is a place in my heart where I imagine living in good health, having enough money (but not too much to distract (I'll let You know when it's too much, Lord)), singing hymns (a strong tenor voice would be nice), taking walks through beautiful parks with You.  Help me, Lord, not to give up on now.  Help me raise my vision, my desires, my expectations for this time.  Keep me focused on living with You in joy, even if today isn't the day of restoration and deliverance that we, Your people, long for.

8  But you will receive power when the Holy Spirit has come upon you; and you shall be My witnesses both in Jerusalem, and in all Judea and Samaria, and even to the remotest part of the earth."
I'm going to need a lot of power, Lord.  I don't often feel like a witness.  And while I enjoy traveling, I don't think You are calling me to travel to the remote places on the earth to witness to You.  I know You were talking to Your apostles in the words of this passage.  At the same time, I hear You talking to the rest of us, Your people.  The part about "you *shall be*" sounds a little scary, but then You are clear that the power to do what You want comes from Your Spirit Whom You give to us.  So, help me not to wait for some trip to a foreign country or a stage where I am called upon to speak

my faith. Grant that I will be powered by Your Spirit to witness for You now in all the things I do and say (and think) today.

14 These all with one mind were continually devoting themselves to prayer, along with *the* women, and Mary the mother of Jesus, and with His brothers.
The next most important thing to being with You, Lord Jesus, was prayer. There are a lot of Your people now. You have touched us and made us Yours. What a picture You give here! "These all"—that would certainly be a large group now! Can You imagine us all "with one mind"? Well, of course You can. The question is can *we* imagine ourselves with one mind? Help us in our imagination, Lord. Help us to see ourselves in Your large and wonderful family. And then grant that we see clearly what we are devoted to. It appears in this country, that might be holding a smart phone in our hand and communicating with someone somewhere or with several someones in various places. Grant that we focus that devotion on a much more blessed and more certain communication with You, carrying on a conversation with You throughout each day in all that we do. (And while we are conversing with You, help us to remember to listen, also.)

Time to live with You here
Witness starts in Spirit power
Conversation throughout the day


Acts 2

11,12 "...Cretans and Arabs—we hear them in our *own* tongues speaking of the mighty deeds of God." 12 And they all continued in amazement and great perplexity, saying to one another, "What does this mean?"
It means You really care about me, Lord, that You communicate Your word of grace and love to me in language

I can understand. I am caught up in daily language from inside that is filled with "shoulds". I am distracted by thinking about things that need to be fixed in my world and in (other) people. But You care enough to speak to me in my heart, making Your love clear. Help me to hear You. Grant that I spend more time rejoicing in Your grace and love than in trying to figure out how to "fix" people. Help me to hear You in Your word. You have blessed me with various translations and paraphrases of Your holy word so that I can hear You speaking in my language. Thank You Lord. And there are more people who need to hear You speaking in their language, Lord. Please bless those working to translate and bring Your word to everyone, everywhere. Use me to help and support Your work of speaking Your grace and love to all people.

25 For David says of Him,
'I SAW THE LORD ALWAYS IN MY PRESENCE;
FOR HE IS AT MY RIGHT HAND, SO THAT I WILL NOT BE SHAKEN.'
You have given us the privilege of good friends, Lord. Thank You. And I do enjoy spending time with friends. Thank You for the joy and unity You have given me and my wife in marriage. And even then, to have a friend (even a wonderful, loving spouse) always present—well, it might get to be too much (You know that I know this because she told me so(!)) But to have You with me always, what a privilege, Lord! Ok, I admit, there are times when I might feel constrained or nervous, when something happens and I start to get righteously indignant, and looking at You I would realize it's one or the other. Or when temptation comes close and part of me wants it to come closer. But, help me to stay in Your gracious will, Lord. And grant me the wonderful comfort of Your presence always so that I am sure that nothing can come that will shake me away from You and joy and Life. Be at my right hand, Lord. Grant that all my attitudes, words, and actions be with Your power, in confidence in You, and encourage Your continued smiling.

37, 38 Now when they heard *this*, they were pierced to the heart, and said to Peter and the rest of the apostles, "Brethren, what shall we do?" ³⁸ Peter *said* to them, "Repent, and each of you be baptized in the name of Jesus Christ for the forgiveness of your sins; and you will receive the gift of the Holy Spirit.

"What shall we do?" is a question that stays fresh and vital in every generation. Sometimes it is just a mundane question about what to do after a storm with damage. Sometimes it is a question about raising children. Sometimes it is a question of what to do for a job and making a living. But sometimes, Lord, it is still about what to do when people realize they are sinners and that they are a long way from You. The answer to problems with plumbing, children, and jobs can be involved. There are forms to fill out, information to give, things to learn—complicated. But thank You Lord, that when we recognize our need to be close to You, the answer You give is simple. Be baptized. In the name of Jesus. Receive forgiveness. And receive the gift of Your Spirit. Please bless those who need forgiveness and Your Spirit, Lord—bring them to You. And bless those who have been baptized, Lord—set our days on fire with joy by Your presence, Holy Spirit. Let us burn with joy and love in serving You in the new day You give us today.

Speak to us in our language
With You present, never shaken
Spirit powered living


Acts 3

12 But when Peter saw *this*, he replied to the people, "Men of Israel, why are you amazed at this, or why do you gaze at us, as if by our own power or piety we had made him walk? I know that asking for humility is dangerous, Lord, because I suspect it is one of Your favorite prayers to answer. And honestly, I have a lot to be humble about. Still, keep me

humble, and remind me that whatever blessings happen to people I care about, reach out to, or touch are from You, not from me.  Help me to see needs and problems that people have each day.  Open my heart to reach out with simple prayers for help, always with the certainty that it is a privilege You give me to notice what to pray for.  I have the humble privilege of calling Your 911.  You are the One Who graciously touches people's lives in answer to prayer.  You give me the great satisfaction that blessings are multiplying in those answers You give.  So with joy and thanksgiving I recognize, I am Your humble servant, use me as You desire.

16  And on the basis of faith in His name, *it is* the name of Jesus which has strengthened this man whom you see and know; and the faith which *comes* through Him has given him this perfect health in the presence of you all.
As Peter pulled him up, the man believed that through the name of Jesus he would be healed.  Help me, Lord, never to use Your name in my speech as if it made me or my words important.  Your name, Jesus, is still powerful today.  In the midst of radio, television, and publications filled with claims of greatness for various people, let Your name still be known and recognized as the name that blesses.  Yours is still the name that heals.  Yours is the name that lifts hearts and spirits to joy and satisfaction.  Grant that I always depend in faith in Your name for all blessings and for all answers to prayers.  Thank You Father, that I may pray in Jesus' name and depend on Your grace through Him.

19  Therefore repent and return, so that your sins may be wiped away, in order that times of refreshing may come from the presence of the Lord.
Thank You Father for Your promise.  As I confess my sins again today, and trust in Your grace through Jesus, keep me close to Jesus, and send me times of refreshment.  I don't have to have a second home on Maui to have times of refreshment (which is really good, since I don't exactly like that much water!).  But I do need refreshing, Lord.  How can

I feel stale and lethargic entering a day, when Your grace is new every morning? Better than wrapping the scent of pine trees, the grandeur of mountain vistas, the wonder of the first day of summer vacation from school into a multidimensional virtual reality experience, grant that I rejoice in Your presence. Grant that I may listen to You and talk to You in new, fresh ways. Grant that today, in the midst of frustrations and confusions I enjoy Your excellent, wonderful refreshment!

Touch people, use me
Jesus, The name of blessing
The Lord Who refreshes


Acts 4

12  And there is salvation in no one else; for there is no other name under heaven that has been given among men by which we must be saved."
Only in Your name, Jesus. There are a lot of people who have tried many other methods, and many people including me have tried depending on themselves or something else. Of course, it really helps to know that we are sinners. Some people are so busy working to reach their goals and keeping a positive (winning!) attitude that they don't have time or room to recognize that they are sinners. I don't usually have that problem. Although there are times when, I admit, I find myself thinking that I am actually pretty good. Keep me in reality! Give me a clear view of myself, Lord. Help me to see my need for You. Keep me focused on Your cross, on Your taking my sins and paying for them, reminding me that I have forgiveness through You and I need nothing else. And let all people see that they are lost in a dark forest of sin and selfishness. Let them know Your name and Your grace so that they may believe in You and be saved. Deliver them from depending on themselves or some deception from the enemy. Thank You for Your saving name!

13  Now as they observed the confidence of Peter and John and understood that they were uneducated and untrained men, they were amazed, and *began* to recognize them as having been with Jesus.

"Who have you been with!? Listen to your language!" I suppose, Lord, that parents have been saying that for a great many years. (I can read a book and start to sound like one of the characters!) Help us, Your people, to sound like You. Grant that we listen to You in Your word, in hymns, in sermons, through other people, and that our words and actions show it. Grant that we may live in fellowship so closely with You, that people we meet expect to be introduced to the One we are with. Grant us so clear a view of today in the light of that Far and Blessed Country that others recognize our view as coming from You. Let the question, "Who have you been with?" have an obvious and clear answer for everyone that meets us.

20  "For we cannot stop speaking about what we have seen and heard."

I remember those times, Lord. I had been to the mountains or the ocean or Huntington Library. And for weeks, all I could talk about was what I had seen. I would show people pictures. There were the souvenirs to show people. Give me that joy, Lord, in what I see and hear in You. Fill me with Your Spirit so that I can share the peace and love and joy I have received from You. It seems like there are extremes, Lord. On the one side there is being obnoxious so that people want to avoid me. On the other side is being so quiet that no one knows the joy You have given me. Guide me down the middle, Lord. Let my words glow with joy in You throughout every day. Let nothing get in the way to stop my speaking and living in peace from You. When trouble or suffering or change comes into my life, push them off to the side so that I will continue to speak and show what I have seen and heard in You. And thank You, Gracious Lord, for all Your other people who bless me with their speaking and showing what they have from You.  Let the light and joy we have from You keep bubbling, Lord.

Clearly lost.  In You, saved.
Companion of Jesus!
Joy:  Sharing what we've seen


Acts 5

16  Also the people from the cities in the vicinity of Jerusalem were coming together, bringing people who were sick or afflicted with unclean spirits, and they were all being healed.
You used Your people in those first days to be a great, miraculous blessing to others.  You have used many saints since then in similar ways.  Use me as one of Your people today to be a blessing.  Yes, I would appreciate it, Lord, if when I pray for You to heal someone, You would heal them of everything that is wrong with them, completely curing them.  That would be great, Lord.  And I know You can do that, not because of anything in me, but only because of You and Your power and love and authority.  If that is Your will, great, Lord.  If that isn't Your will right now, I am sure it is Your will to give Your best blessings to that person with Your caring love.  I know that it is Your will to use me to be a blessing.  I don't know all the ways You want to do that.  But I trust You, Lord.  Use me as You will, and bless all those who come to You who are sick or afflicted.

18-20 They laid hands on the apostles and put them in a public jail.  [19] But during the night an angel of the Lord opened the gates of the prison, and taking them out he said, [20] "Go, stand and speak to the people in the temple the whole message of this Life."
I haven't had that experience, Lord.  I have had people ignore me.  I have had people walk away and not talk to me again.  I don't feel called on to stand on the street corner and

tell those that pass by all about the new life that You give, Lord.  And yet I believe You call me to encourage people in the new life You give.  I believe You call me to show that life and to use words when necessary.  Let me be an encouragement to others.  Let my heart and mind be so focused on You and Your love and joy and peace that my face shows it.  Grant that my listening, noticing, words, and actions bring encouragement from You to all around me.

39  But if it is of God, you will not be able to overthrow them; or else you may even be found fighting against God."
There are times, Lord, when it looks like Your Church is not growing the way You want.  It doesn't seem to be exploding the way it did after Pentecost.  It doesn't seem to be reaching people here where I live.  And there are people in my church who seem content with having their names on the church list, and that's it for them.  Yuck!  Thank You for the assurance that no one will be able to destroy Your Church.  Bless the churches of Your Church today that they be effective in bringing people to You.  Grant that they will be effective in encouraging Your people to be alive in You and to be a blessing as You desire.  Thank You, Holy Spirit, for being here, now, today.  Make Your Church strong and vibrantly alive in bringing Life to those who are dead.

Sick, afflicted—now blessed
Use me to show Life, encourage, and bless
Bring the dead to Life


Acts 6

2,3  So the twelve summoned the congregation of the disciples and said, "It is not desirable for us to neglect the word of God in order to serve tables. [3] Therefore, brethren, select from among you…
Thank You, Lord for sending Your servants to bring us Your word and grace in preaching, teaching, and leading in

worship. Bless them, Lord. Fill them with Your Spirit. Make them effective in Your calling. Let nothing get in the way of their service. There is administration still today that needs to be done in Your churches. Call those whom You have chosen for that service. And if there is anything that I can do to help, please show me what You would like me to do. Keep those who bless me with Your word ever prominent in my prayers. Bless them with Your love, effectiveness in service, and joy and satisfaction in all they do.

12 And they stirred up the people, the elders and the scribes, and they came up to him and dragged him away and brought him before the Council.
Why is it so easy for people in churches to grumble about those who are helping in the churches? I have fallen into that temptation, and I am sorry, Lord. Please bless all those who serve in helping ways in Your churches. Bless them so that they are not discouraged. Bless all Your people that we will say and do things to support those who help in Your churches. Keep me focused in my prayers that I give them my prayer support as well as my thanks and encouragement. Protect all who serve in Your churches from the attacks of evil, especially from attacks which are really directed at You and Your grace.

14 For we have heard him say that this Nazarene, Jesus, will destroy this place and alter the customs which Moses handed down to us.
Yike! THE most common and very effective complaint for 2000 years—"we've never done it that way before". Your Gospel brings new life to me, to all Christians. And I suppose it would be handy and convenient if that new life came in a once and for all, same for every person, receive it when you become a Christian, never to be changed again, package. Such, however, Lord, I know is not the case. At least You certainly have brought newness to me, over and over again, through the years. I admit, there were times when I thought, "OK, this is it! Now I've got it!" Only to find

out some years (or days) later that, actually there is a lot more to learn, there are new ways to grow. Help me, Lord, to be open to Your newness. Your mercy is new every morning, and often in new packages and new formats. Thank You! And bless Your people that we all are open to the newness of Your grace even if it means changing some custom or worship plan that we are Really Attached To.

Bless the servants of Your word
Encouragement without grumbling
By grace, new (not a four letter word)


Acts 7

1  The high priest said, "Are these things so?"
Help me, Lord, to listen for those rare times, when someone actually asks me about my experience with You. Grant that I don't miss any of those times. Take all fear away, and Holy Spirit give me the words You want me to use to let other people know the ways You have blessed me. Since, in this day and age, people are not willing to have me start when I was born, or start at the time of Abraham as Stephen did, help me to speak of Your gracious blessings briefly, but with joy and thanksgiving. And for the rest of the time, help me to use the simple, "How are you" questions that people speak (generally not expecting me to tell them how I am, of course), to share some one recent blessing that You have given (joyfully, briefly).

10  And rescued him from all his afflictions, and granted him favor and wisdom in the sight of Pharaoh, king of Egypt, and he made him governor over Egypt and all his household.
If I am going to let people know how You have blessed me, help me, Lord, to focus on Your blessings every day. There are a lot of little things every day, like breathing (visiting in the hospital to see life without regular breathing makes me see how much a blessing it is!), seeing the beautiful world

You have created, walking, thinking, eating, talking (and texting). But there are those other times. Help me to remember those times when I have found myself saying, "Wow, Lord, that was wonderful! Thank you for this blessing!" Help me to remember them all. Help me to be visibly thankful so that others can enjoy Your mercy and grace as well. And if I forget to remember problems and frustrations in the process, that's probably ok with You, too.

39 Our fathers were unwilling to be obedient to him, but repudiated him and in their hearts turned back to Egypt. When I consider the history of Your people, Lord, I recognize not only wonderful blessings, grace, and mercy, but rebellion, fear, and selfishness. Help me to learn from previous mistakes and sins, so that I don't have to learn everything by personal dumbness and hardheadedness. Of course, there are quite a few things that I have learned that way. (And I accept the fact that if I am heading for a disastrous fall, I would prefer that you use a 2x4 to get my attention rather than my continuing on to disaster.) But what I would really like is to listen to You and hear You and follow You away from dumbness and selfishness and into blessing. There are things that claim to be gods today, and try to draw people (me) away from You. Grant that I resist those temptations. Grant that by Your grace I give You my whole heart and all my being every day, with obedience and joy, following You faithfully. (My heart, occupied by You completely, no vacancies.)

Since you ask, blessed!
Recognizing and remembering blessings
Occupied. No vacancies.


Acts 8

1 Saul was in hearty agreement with putting him to death.

And on that day a great persecution began against the church in Jerusalem, and they were all scattered throughout the regions of Judea and Samaria, except the apostles. For me, sitting here, able to talk to people about You, with many opportunities to worship with other Christians, it seems strange to think about persecution. But there are many Christians also now, Lord, who are persecuted for believing You and trusting You. Bless them Lord. Protect them from evil. Rescue those depending on You in persecution, in Your gracious will, Lord. Help me to remember my sisters and brothers in the faith, and continue to support them in bringing them to Your throne in prayer. Bless those people who are afraid of being persecuted and who hold back from following You faithfully. And grant that I Live, following You, Lord, in such a way that I give enough evidence to be convicted of being one of Your followers, if there ever would be persecution here.

19 "Give this authority to me as well, so that everyone on whom I lay my hands may receive the Holy Spirit."
It is great to be one of Your people, Lord. To be forgiven, to be blessed with joy, to have new life—this is great. Now if I could serve You in a way that other people would all look up to me and say, "What a wonderful person you are!", why that would be …, well it would be terrible, actually. And the temptation does come, Lord, to want people to think I am somebody special, important, prominent. It wasn't something bad he wanted to do. Just, "Lord let me zap people with Your Spirit!" But—not Your plan! Forgive me, Lord, for going down that path. Touch people with Your Spirit in the ways You desire. And keep me in joy and satisfaction in the Life You give me, in the calling You give me, serving You and being a blessing to others, without in any way desiring people's compliments or accolades. Joy is enough.

30 Philip ran up and heard him reading Isaiah the prophet, and said, "Do you understand what you are reading?"

How could Philip be a blessing? He listened to the man. He listened to find out what was going on in this man. He listened to see how You were reaching out to Him, Gracious Spirit. Help me to listen, Lord. If I am going to care about people and be a blessing, first I need to listen. Help me to restrain my need to tell people all my experiences and feelings (and how important they are). Keep me from dumping on people all the things that I think they need to know (so that they can be, well I suppose, like me). Open my ears and my heart, so that I hear people. Use me to be a blessing based on listening. Let me listen well and reach out to people where they are living, so that I can help people—be like You.

Bless persecuted Christians
Joy is enough
Caring, listening, and blessing


Acts 9

6  But get up and enter the city, and it will be told you what you must do.
No debate. No discussion period. Sometimes I come to You expecting a discussion period. I even expect You to listen to my reasoning. Sheesh! I suppose, Lord, that I even expect You to deliver Your messages to me in fancy envelopes with Your return address clearly indicated so that there is no mistaking Your message. "It will be told you" sounds like I need to be awake and alert and to be listening with faith, so that I will hear You speaking to me in whatever method You choose. (And since You included a donkey in Your communication system, I can see that I need to be open to a variety of methods!) Help me to let go of my "Your message needs to fit in this box" filter and my "Your message needs to fit in my schedule" filter and all my other filters. Lord, grant that I ask for Your guidance openly and honestly. And when I have asked Your help, grant that I

listen, not as if I were going to consider Your suggestions, but with whole-hearted readiness to take in Your will and follow up with confident obedience.

8  Saul got up from the ground, and though his eyes were open, he could see nothing; and leading him by the hand, they brought him into Damascus.
It really is only when I know that I can't see, that You are able to show me the way, Lord.  So often, it seems, I really think I've got this taken care of.  I can see where I am going.  The day is well planned.  There may be a few things that I don't understand, but if I don't think about them, it will probably be all right.  Right.  Help me to know what I don't know, to see the blur in my vision, to recognize my limits, and to begin each day asking You to enable me to see.  Open my eyes to see what You want me to see.  Show me the choices, the words, the attitudes, the joys that You want to use as a blessing in this day.  Grant that I recognize, celebrate, and relax in Your leading me by the hand, with absolute confidence in You, Gracious Lord.

13  But Ananias answered, "Lord, I have heard from many about this man, how much harm he did to Your saints at Jerusalem.
Thank You, Lord, that You are willing to listen to my fears.  I have a lot of "Yes, Lord, but…" attitudes.  The world has many appearances that frighten me.  Sickness, financial problems, "But what if"s.  Thank You for listening and not zapping me with lightning (which You would, of course, have every right to do!).  Thank You for Your patience.  Grant that I recognize my fears as fears, which You have lovingly told me to let go of.  Enable me to let go and hear Your direction and encouragement with openness, without whining, and with faithful, trusting acceptance and compliance.

Thank You for not making suggestions
See that I don't see so I can see
Held by You, letting go

Acts 10

14 But Peter said, "By no means, Lord, for I have never eaten anything unholy and unclean."
I have my dividing walls, too, Lord. There are people whom I have difficulty accepting. You have graciously broken open a lot of those walls that kept me separate from others. Thank You, Lord. I am amazed that You keep showing me more walls that I have unconsciously built, dividing me from others. Thank You for showing me. Break them down, Lord. There are so many assumptions that I have made. I suppose from where I grew up, and with whom I grew up. Help me, Lord, to recognize them. Grant that I hold onto the blessings You have built in my life. And yet, grant that I will be open to other people (without the necessity of their having the "right" values, habits, preferences (that is to say, mine)). Thank you, that I can enjoy people who live lives that seem very different (and sometimes in scary ways) from mine. You came, Lord Jesus, for all. And You made that clear. Help me to be open to all the people around me with love and generosity and no wall building.

19 While Peter was reflecting on the vision, the Spirit said to him, "Behold, three men are looking for you."
Wow, Lord, there are certainly times when I am perplexed, and I would really appreciate your coming and talking to me, Lord Holy Spirit! I think about Your word. I look at some choices I have. It just doesn't seem clear to me, sometimes, what Your will is. It might be clear what I think is good (at least for now). But what will be good later on? How can I be truly satisfied? How can I bless people the way You want, and quit measuring things by what satisfies me? There are times when I get up in the morning that You give me a clear vision of what would be really good. Stay with me during the day, Lord. After I start the day and actually open my eyes, after I recognize the agendas that other people have and

what they expect of me, after I look around and see the things that I didn't exactly finish yesterday, stay with me, Lord. It would be ok if You would put the world on pause, turn on Your "Yes I'm still with you, now listen up" multicolored light from heaven. Please step in, speak to me, blow away the confusion, and let me see and do Your will, by Your grace. (And it would be ok if You give me a couple minutes to digest what You tell me before You take the world off pause.)

33 So I sent for you immediately, and you have been kind enough to come. Now then, we are all here present before God to hear all that you have been commanded by the Lord."
What an attitude! You have something to tell me, Lord. Go ahead. I'm completely open to whatever You have to say to me. That's the attitude I want every time I come to worship, Lord. And every time I read Your word. And every time I pray and listen to You. Help me to listen. Use Your remote to turn off the noise from old hurts and griefs, the noise from should and should haves, the noise from that automatic thought protector device that wants to know how this fits with what I am already thinking and doing. Please turn them off, Lord. Give me this attitude of openly listening to You, please, Lord in every quiet or busy moment in the day. And also when I pray and listen and worship let me remember I am listening to You, the One who is Joy, Grace, and Love. I know You love me, Lord, let me listen, hear, and take in Your gracious word and will.

Life—without walls
Speak, let me hear
Attitude adjusted to Open


Acts 11

**18** When they heard this, they quieted down and glorified God, saying, "Well then, God has granted to the Gentiles also the repentance *that leads* to life."

I understand a little bit what they were saying, Lord. As in, "Lord, there You go. You've done it again! I certainly never expected that!" You have such a bigger imagination, so much more gracious than I have. You surprise me. Help me, Lord, to allow You to be You and not to try to fit You into my box for You. Grant that in all the new, surprising things You do, I don't fall behind pouting and stamping my feet. Grant that with the disciples I just accept You being gracious in surprising and wonderful ways (as, of course, other people have regularly been surprised at how gracious You are to me when I have said and done things that don't fit Your gracious family.) And grant that I catch Your gracious attitude in all I do and say (help those around me not to die of shock!)

**23** Then when he arrived and witnessed the grace of God, he rejoiced and *began* to encourage them all with resolute heart to remain *true* to the Lord.

When I see people doing something new, differently from the way I do things, my temptation is to put in my two cents about how they can improve things a lot (by doing it my way!). Help me, Lord, to emulate the wisdom and gracious actions of Barnabas. When I see some new blessing, grant that I rejoice (in You, with thanks for Your blessing) and encourage people. When I listen to people, I don't seem to hear enough encouragement. I recognize that one of the things I look forward to, and don't get quite enough of, is encouragement. Make me an encourager. Let me see the opportunities You give me to recognize people and encourage them. Show me Your blessings in other people, and give me words to encourage them to enjoy Your blessings and remain faithful to You. Thank You for encouraging us every day, Lord. Let us encourage each other.

28  One of them named Agabus stood up and *began* to indicate by the Spirit that there would certainly be a great famine all over the world. And this took place in the *reign* of Claudius.
You arranged for them to know about it ahead of time so the relief could be timely. I tend to hear about disasters fairly soon after they happen. You let me know, not so that I despair over bad things happening, but so that I can help, right, Lord? The thing is, there are so many opportunities to give to provide relief for people suffering. Please touch people's hearts to be generous toward those in need, Lord. Provide for those people who suffer disasters through the giving of Your people. And grant me wisdom to know which needs You have called me to help with gifts and relief. Multiply the resources of Your people to meet the needs that seem so great.

Surprisingly gracious
Encouraged to encourage
Giving directed by grace


Acts 12

5, 11, 16  So Peter was kept in the prison, but prayer for him was being made fervently by the church to God.    When Peter came to himself, he said, "Now I know for sure that the Lord has sent forth His angel and rescued me from the hand of Herod and from all that the Jewish people were expecting."    But Peter continued knocking; and when they had opened *the door*, they saw him and were amazed.
I remember that great story, Lord, which You have used to bless me: The farmers asked their pastor to pray for rain the following Sunday. But on the next Sunday the pastor didn't pray for rain, so the farmers asked him after the service why he had not prayed for rain. Of course, he told them it was because no one had brought an umbrella. These people were amazed when You answered their prayer, and brought

Peter out of prison. The Jewish people were strong in their expecting, but the church didn't seem to be expecting an answer. I talk to You, I hand things over to You. And some of them are situations that are so wildly difficult that I'm afraid I don't really expect You to fix them. Help me in my expecting. Grant that when I ask Your help and turn things over to You, that I truly expect, with Your gift of faith, that You will deal with that problem, at just the right time, and make it a blessing as You desire. Lift up my spirit from every poor me or poor us or poor them to great and joyous expectations of Your blessings.

23 And immediately an angel of the Lord struck him because he did not give God the glory, and he was eaten by worms and died.
It is amazing to me, Lord, that more people are not struck down today. Ok, that was probably a trifle arrogant. Herod really liked being told how great he was, and I have accepted credit for things that I know were not because I am so great, but only by Your grace. Help me to remember that all good comes from You. Not by luck or chance or probability, but by Your grace. Grant that I give You credit and praise for every blessing. And especially, if I receive a compliment, let me openly and honestly direct the credit to You. Thank You for letting me take part in Your events of blessing.

24 But the word of the Lord continued to grow and to be multiplied.
Thank You, Lord for Your word. Thank You for giving Your word today with Your desire that it continue to grow today and be multiplied. So please make Your word effective today in my heart and life. Make it effective in my parish and community. Make it effective in my family and in my friends. Make it effective across the United States. And make it effective around the world wherever it is given, proclaimed, lived, and shared. May Your word always grow and be multiplied.

Expect well
Give You the credit
The word of the Lord, growing


Acts 13

2 While they were ministering to the Lord and fasting, the Holy Spirit said, "Set apart for Me Barnabas and Saul for the work to which I have called them."
Thank You Lord, Holy Spirit, for calling servants to the work You have for them. Please call men and women today to serve You in preaching and teaching, in ministering to adults and young people and children, in starting new churches and guiding and nurturing existing churches, in reaching people around the world and bringing them to their Savior, Jesus. Please give joy and certainty and provision to all whom You call. Please touch the hearts and minds of young people. Bring them into Your word. Bless them in worship, Bible study, and through Your people, leading them into Your gracious, wonderful, and effective service.

23 From the descendants of this man, according to promise, God has brought to Israel a Savior, Jesus.
The joy You give me to share, Father, is that You kept Your promise that You had given throughout the Old Testament. You sent Messiah. You sent Him in the person of Jesus. And you sent Him to be the Savior of Israel, of all Your chosen people, of all the Greek and Roman people that Paul talked to, and of all the Gentiles in the world to come. Thank You, Lord that since I find myself among the line of Gentiles, You also sent Jesus to be my Savior. Thank You that I can listen to all the promises of grace and love in Your word and know that You are also thinking of me. Thank You, Jesus for saving me from my self-willed attitudes, from my desires to do things my way without listening to You, from my guilt and

the separation from You that I deserve. Thank You for including me in Your Life-giving promise.

43  Now when *the meeting of* the synagogue had broken up, many of the Jews and of the God-fearing proselytes followed Paul and Barnabas, who, speaking to them, were urging them to continue in the grace of God.
They knew the law of God. They tried hard to obey Your law. The wonderful change was that now they knew Your grace in Jesus. My conscience is good at reminding me of when I have not obeyed Your will, Father. And then there are those many days when I spend my time and effort trying (often with great success) to avoid thinking about how I focus on myself without listening to You and without recognizing my living without You. Grant that I live this day and every day continuing in Your grace which You have given in Jesus my Savior and which You have given me through Your Holy Spirit. Grant that I rejoice in Your grace and in the privilege of continuing to Live, graciously brought to Life by You.

Call and empower Your servants
Me, too
Continue in Your grace


Acts 14

3  Therefore they spent a long time *there* speaking boldly *with reliance* upon the Lord, who was testifying to the word of His grace, granting that signs and wonders be done by their hands.
The response of the mission team to the resistance in Iconium was to spend more time there and rely on You, Lord. I don't face that kind of resistance. But I meet people who seem to resist any message about You and some people who resist any kindness from me. Grant that I remember the mission team in Iconium, and that my words

of joy and thanksgiving in You do not depend on a survey of what people want to hear. Grant that my attitude and words every day depend only on You and Your daily love and grace. Please help me to keep going on the path You have for me. And grant that in every conversation and in every attitude toward people I rely, not on my own ability or great well of niceness (it is, unfortunately, sometimes empty!), but on You and Your grace and Your love through me (never empty! Thank You!).

15 ...and saying, "Men, why are you doing these things? We are also men of the same nature as you, and preach the gospel to you that you should turn from these vain things to a living God, WHO MADE THE HEAVEN AND THE EARTH AND THE SEA AND ALL THAT IS IN THEM."
Getting too much credit is a bad thing. It's very nice, Lord, when people tell me that I have done something well. But You are in charge. Whether it's rock stars, movie stars, football or baseball greats, they are people (who have gifts and talents from You, and most of them have put in a lot of hard work.) You are the One Who gives talents and gifts and uses people to be blessings to others. Let my actions and conversations let people know that all goodness and worth come from You, not from me. Let those who are famous in the world, know and show that You are the Source of all true greatness. And when I give credit and compliments to others, let me do it with the certainty that all blessing that comes to me from others comes from You. So grant that I give You credit (and praise) at the end of each day for all the blessings I have seen and received.

22 ...strengthening the souls of the disciples, encouraging them to continue in the faith, and *saying*, "Through many tribulations we must enter the kingdom of God."
I do exercise (some, when I remember) but here is the strength that is really important, Lord. Strengthen my soul. Keep me strong so that I continue faithfully today. Help me not to moan when I see difficulties ahead. Grant that I

recognize the strength You have given me. Help me to remember that the strength of my soul is not for sitting peacefully reading or watching TV. You have given me strength for every trial, every weight that tries to crush my soul. Grant that I use the strength You give me. Not with vanity, but with honest, thankful recognition of Your grace. And if I can speak an encouraging word to help someone else have their soul strengthened, please speak that word through me. (Thank you for all those who speak Your words to strengthen me.)

Persisting. Boldly. Your grace.
For all good, glory to God
Souls, strong with encouragement


Acts 15

3 Therefore, being sent on their way by the church, they were passing through both Phoenicia and Samaria, describing in detail the conversion of the Gentiles, and were bringing great joy to all the brethren.
Thank You, Lord, for all the missionary groups and helping agencies that You have sent to bless people with Your Gospel. Bless them with confidence and joy in the calling You have given them. Stand by them in every difficulty. Stir Your people around the world to support the ministries which You call into being. Bless Your outreach ministries that they will be effective in all their ministry for You. Reach people through them and bring them to You. Thank You for the reports that they send. Grant that I and all Christians may listen to the joyful reports of all You are doing today in reaching people. And may we be filled with joy by their reports so that we will live in faithful witness to You and with an attitude of invitation to all people around us. Use us also to reach and bless people, bringing people to You and eternal joy.

11  But we believe that we are saved through the grace of the Lord Jesus, in the same way as they also are."
The bad news, You tell us, is that there is nothing we can do that saves us.  The good news, You tell us, is that it is everything that You do graciously for us that saves us.  Thank You for Your grace, Lord Jesus.  I would like to think that I am a pretty good person, that I have tried really hard to be the person You want me to be, and that therefore You ought to take me to heaven.  I would like to think that, but there are so many times when I see who I really am, Lord.  And I think about how far I must seem to You from Your holy and perfect will.  So thank You, Lord, that You give me what I do not deserve.  Thank You that You do not give me what I do deserve.  Your gift of Life by Your grace is so wonderful, Lord!  When I feel discouraged or doubts and darkness attack, please grant me certainty that Your grace never changes, and that I may always depend on You.  Unite Your Church today in the joy and power of Your saving grace.  And help me to remember when I look at other people (and am tempted to think how far they are from Your will)—help me remember, except for Your grace, that's what I look like.

15  With this the words of the Prophets agree, just as it is written…
Thank You for Your word, Lord.  Thank You for the example of Your servants depending on Your word.  Please grant that I will read and study Your word guided by Your Holy Spirit and that I will grow in understanding of Your will.  So, ok, I say that to You.  The point is, don't I know!, help me to see when!  Give me so strong a sense of priority connected to reading Your word and listening to You that I will make time for You.  It's easy to say, "I have a really busy schedule today, Lord, how about tomorrow?"  But then "tomorrow" never comes, because it's always busy.  If it was important for the apostles to listen to You in Your word, let it be important for me.  I do make room for things that I think are important.  Work, TV, eating, sleeping, family—hopefully not in that order.  If I need to kick something out of my schedule,

let me see what it is and give me the courage to do it. Guide me and make my time in Your word a blessing. Show me tools and plans that will help me to effectively listen to You. And please bless all the leaders of Your Church that they will be informed and inspired by Your word in the power of Your Holy Spirit to guide Your Church with Your wisdom.

Living in the joy of Your growing Kingdom
Life lived by grace
Timely, Spirit-opened word


Acts 16

7 And after they came to Mysia, they were trying to go into Bithynia, and the Spirit of Jesus did not permit them.
I remember times when I really thought something was good, Lord. I was looking forward to it. It looked very much like a great blessing from You. But You had something better for me. Just because something is good, it is not necessarily in Your will. You know I have trouble with that, Lord. Sometimes it is because I see someone else having some thing or experience, and they even share what a blessing it is. It is so easy to say, "That looks good for me, too, Lord." But You know there are other, different, better blessings that You want for me. So please guide me, Lord, with Your Spirit, so that in all my choices I choose not only that which is good, but that good which You want for me, at that place, at that time. Thank You for not letting me be satisfied with something only good, when You have an excellent blessing You want to give me.

10 When he had seen the vision, immediately we sought to go into Macedonia, concluding that God had called us to preach the gospel to them.
I'm a little busy right now, Lord. You know I have said that to You. I get so focused on what I am doing, I want to bring it to completion because it seems an integral part of the plan

for success for the day(!) Then I hear You calling me to some action, to remember to do something, and I want to put Your item on my to do list in what I consider an appropriate place. Ouch! I'm sorry, Lord. When I hear You calling me, when You show me what You want me to do, grant that I have the same immediacy that Luke and Paul and the group with them showed. Help me avoid "Just a minute", "I'll be right there", "Hold on for a sec", and "Right! (when I get around to it)". May I always be open to hear You, and when I hear You, may I immediately seek to do Your will, knowing that Your plan for success in the day is always better than mine!

25 But about midnight Paul and Silas were praying and singing hymns of praise to God, and the prisoners were listening to them.
When things don't go well, my temptation, Lord, is to complain, find someone to be angry at, and possibly sink into depression. It is so clear to me that my clear idea of the plan for today and for the world (in my particular vicinity) is really terrific. And this, that is not going well, is a serious impertinence in that plan! However, I see that You have a different plan(!) Praying and singing hymns of praise. Right. I admit, that was not high on my list of what to do when things don't go well. Imagine, unplugging righteous indignation and self-centeredness, and praising You, right then, with the dark clouds building overhead. What a thought! So when things don't seem to be going the way I think they should, please Lord, open my heart to talk to You and even sing praise to You. So fill my songs of praise with Your gracious presence that all grousing and complaining dissolves and gives way to joy and confidence in You.

The in Your will, kind of good
The immediate now
Hearty, prayerful songs of praise

Acts 17

6 When they did not find them, they *began* dragging Jason and some brethren before the city authorities, shouting, "These men who have upset the world have come here also"
Your people are still being persecuted today, Lord. Protect them from those who are threatened by Your grace and love. Deliver Your people from those attacking them. Give all those, who are being persecuted for their faith, joy and strength in You. Bless me and all Christians who have never suffered any persecution with awareness of those persecuted and with open, loving, prayerful hearts supporting our brothers and sisters in these times of persecution. Bless the persecutors, Lord, including those (very large group indeed) who persecute Christians by considering them invisible and of no account. And please, Lord, grant that Your people everywhere will continue, with enthusiasm and power from You, to upset the world every day.

11 Now these were more noble-minded than those in Thessalonica, for they received the word with great eagerness, examining the Scriptures daily *to see* whether these things were so.
What a terrific approach to Your word, Lord! Great eagerness! It is so easy to think of "time for Bible reading" each day as, "Well, I should do that." Or, "I'll get around to it." Or possibly, "Yes, I can manage 7 and a half minutes now, I think." Eagerness! A reason to get up in the morning! The feeling we have when we are getting up to go on vacation! The feeling we have when we get to go to our favorite store (Best Buy, Barnes and Noble—here I come!) With that eagerness, Lord, bring us daily to Your word. Lead me (and all Your people) to examine Your word, to eagerly see what You have for us each day. Lead us to put together Your word to us, from different parts of the Bible, with the guidance of Your Holy Spirit. Let us see in every day that

Your Good News is indeed true, also for us, wherever we are, now.

29  Being then the children of God, we ought not to think that the Divine Nature is like gold or silver or stone, an image formed by the art and thought of man.
It seems that people have always tried to define You, Lord, in terms of what they liked. Gold, silver, terrific statue, whatever! And still people try to picture You in "success terms": Three piece suit (only worn for meetings, of course), condo in Cancun, home in Switzerland, summer place in the Catskills, growing business on the internet. I certainly have done my share of trying to map out for You how I think You ought to do things: help the helpless, heal the sick, mess up the lives of the mean and selfish, and bless Christians with life with no worries. But You insist on ignoring all those success pictures we create. Bring me and people today to Your picture of success: New life, so new it can only be shown by Your resurrection from the dead, Lord Jesus. New life, so new we cannot imagine what wonderful opportunities You will give us to be Your representatives of love and newness to the helpless, the sick, the mean, the selfish, and the worried. Open us to Your success story: new life in You.

Upset the world
Eagerness in Your word
Success: New life in You


Acts 18

8 Crispus, the leader of the synagogue, believed in the Lord with all his household, and many of the Corinthians when they heard were believing and being baptized.
It seems to me, Lord, that his household believing in You with Crispus is natural and reasonable. A few generations ago, it seemed like that might have been fairly common. But

it doesn't seem so common—it doesn't seem fair to assume that today. So, please bless my family, Lord. Please bless them with strong faith, with a vital worship life, and with serving You with the gifts You have given them by Your grace and power. Let Your gift of faith spread through all the members of my family in the generations to come. And I ask this not just for my family but for the families of everyone in my worship family and in all Your churches. Give our families joy and enthusiasm in living with You and for You by Your grace, now and as You graciously continue to grow our families in the future.

9 And the Lord said to Paul in the night by a vision, "Do not be afraid *any longer*, but go on speaking and do not be silent.
Should I say Your name, Lord Jesus, in my conversation with people as the One I talk to regularly? Should I recognize Your blessings in my speaking with other people? Should I put in a "May Jesus bless you" instead of a "take care" when I say goodbye to people? I hear You saying a resounding, "Yes!" in this passage. Open my eyes and heart to see all the opportunities You give me to not be afraid, but to go on speaking. Let my life speak of You in the loving and caring I show, but also let me not be silent. Touch people with blessing through the words that I say, gracious Lord, throughout this day.

21 But taking leave of them and saying, "I will return to you again if God wills," he set sail from Ephesus.
It is easy, gracious Lord Jesus, to make commitments based on calendar space, scheduling openness, financial availability, and 23 or so other practical factors. But I hear You saying that to be faithful to You, they are not the factors that top the list when I think about making a commitment. The first one is, "Lord willing." You are in charge. I may not be here tomorrow. I am in Your hands. And I say that with thanks and joy and confidence in You. So help me, Lord, not to get distracted by the calendar, the clock, or my

perceptive (!) view of the future. Grant please, Lord, that I make clear in my attitude and in my speech, that I make commitments, "Lord willing."

Growing family of faith
Speaking without fear
Lord willing


Acts 19

13  But also some of the Jewish exorcists, who went from place to place, attempted to name over those who had the evil spirits the name of the Lord Jesus, saying, "I adjure you by Jesus whom Paul preaches."
It doesn't work, Lord Jesus, to like You and try to use You without knowing You. Bless those people who want to like You as a great moral teacher, who want You to be an example to them, their children, and everyone else, who want to have You take care of world problems, who want You as a safety net in their lives, but who do not want You, personally, to come into them and to be their Savior and Lord and to be in charge of their lives. Bless them, bring them to You. Bring them over the line into real Life, into joy eternal, loved by You and loving You, now and forever.

17  This became known to all, both Jews and Greeks, who lived in Ephesus; and fear fell upon them all and the name of the Lord Jesus was being magnified.
There are people who use Your name in their speech, but do not know You, and are not afraid of misusing Your name. I hear them around me, Lord. Please bless them with proper fear falling upon them. Please let them know that You are more than a word to make them sound important. Let them know that You are here, now, listening to them. Please give them the grace to be ashamed. Let them know You as the One Who loves them and cares about them. And call them

to You so that Your name be magnified more and more also today.

27  Not only is there danger that this trade of ours fall into disrepute, but also that the temple of the great goddess Artemis be regarded as worthless and that she whom all of Asia and the world worship will even be dethroned from her magnificence."
The silversmiths had a very clear insight. If the Gospel is true, then there are some things that are worthless. So, Lord, help me to see clearly in my life what is worthless. If the Gospel is true, if You are my Savior that washes me clean from sin and gives me Your gift of Life, if You are the Lord, my Lord, now and forever, if You are in charge of my life, and if I want to honor You and serve You in everything I do and every choice I make (and all those are indeed true) then there are things that are valued a lot by the world that are not valuable to me. Open my eyes with Your insight. Show me what I can do without, Lord. Keep me focused on what is of value to me and others now and forever. Let nothing worthless remain.

Way beyond good
Your name be magnified
Nothing worthless


Acts 20

2  When he had gone through those districts and had given them much exhortation, he came to Greece.
Your plan for Paul as he was visiting the people he had met and served was that he give them much exhortation. You worked through him to console, encourage, and strengthen those people. You give me the privilege of seeing people, sometimes frequently, sometimes only rarely. I have my agendas, I suppose for those visits—find out what has been happening, tell them all my news. Help me to remember

Your agenda, Lord. So whenever You give me an opportunity to visit people, to see family or friends, give me also words and actions that console, encourage, and strengthen those people. And since a lot of contact I have with people is now using one of the cool electronic gizmos You have arranged, help me to recognize those contacts as opportunities also to serve You and console, encourage, and strengthen those whom I touch. Electric encouragement!

5 But these had gone on ahead and were waiting for us at Troas.
The support system. Paul had one that You provided. Your servants today need a support system as well. You have blessed me through servants of Yours in these days. Help me recognize myself as part of their support system. Use me to communicate thanks for the blessings I have received through them. Use me to care about them and help them be good stewards so that they do not burn out. Show me how I can be supportive for Your servants who minister to me here and for Your servants in many missionary and helping agencies around the world, as You give me opportunity. Provide a healthy support system for each of Your servants whom You have called to serve Your people. Relatives, friends, strangers, and especially those who are being served. Reach through them to love Your servants and bless them with great joy in their service.

22 And now, behold, bound by the Spirit, I am on my way to Jerusalem, not knowing what will happen to me there.
You call Your servants on to new assignments according to Your gracious will. You do know, that I want them all to not grow old, to not have anything bad happen to them, to have only wonderful experiences, and to be great blessings for You. But, of course, in this side of eternity, that is not always how it works. So please, Lord, bless those who have blessed me. Take care of them. And whatever You allow and provide for them in the rest of their years here, keep them close to You, keep their faith strong, and provide for

them in all their needs. Continue to use them to be a blessing in whatever new place You call them. Let them hear You talking to them as they dream of You and Your will and bring them safely to You in joy on the other side of eternity (even if it is not in a fiery chariot).

Electric encouragement
Support, loving and effective
Joy and satisfaction for those who go on


Acts 21

4 After looking up the disciples, we stayed there seven days; and they kept telling Paul through the Spirit not to set foot in Jerusalem.
Avoid trouble. Stay away from hostile situations. I can understand that desire! And yet, You blessed Paul with good results following his lack of concern for his personal well-being. "The courage to change the things I can." Give me wisdom to know when to ignore personal safety, when to walk directly toward difficulties and problems. Grant that I focus, not on the danger, but on loving and serving You even in opportunities that have dark clouds and lightning. And if serenity with walking away is what You want, please Lord give me confidence in that part of Your will. Show me Your will, and whatever it is, give me faithfulness in following You.

13,14 Then Paul answered, "What are you doing, weeping and breaking my heart? For I am ready not only to be bound, but even to die at Jerusalem for the name of the Lord Jesus." And since he would not be persuaded, we fell silent, remarking, "The will of the Lord be done!"
It was clearly not their will for Paul to walk into trouble. I have some definite ideas about what I want. I want to have money to eat and enough to give to those who are hungry. I want my team to win the World Series once more in my lifetime (though the Cubbies were very satisfying, Lord,

thank You). I want people I love not to have suffering or problems. And 32 or 167 others. Yet, grant that I loosen my grip and let You steer, Lord. You really are very good at that, Lord! Since I know that Your will is the best blessing possible, what I really want is for Your will to be done. Help me to remember that, in all my prayers for myself, for my loved ones, for people in need, and even in $9^{th}$ inning situations.

22 What, then, is *to be done*? They will certainly hear that you have come.
What will old Mrs. _____ say? (Who by the way, as we all know, is a major contributor!) Fear of what other people will think is a real fear. For me, some years it has been more of a destructive fear than others. But it lurks for me and for many Christians in the background. Help us Lord! Help us to be encouraging to other people in what we do if that is in Your will. Let fear not control our lives. You have not called us to please everyone. Let us always please You. Help us to love and accept people who have opinions different from ours. And let fear of unpopularity never keep us from absolute loyalty to You, first, last, always.

Stay on Your path
Your will, always best
Give fear no place


Acts 22

6 But it happened that as I was on my way, approaching Damascus about noontime, a very bright light suddenly flashed from heaven all around me.
I have had that happen, Lord, many times, that I am on my way, and suddenly I realize that I am not on Your way. I have ways that seem good to me, until I check with You and see You frowning. Help me recognize when I am on a way that is very much mine and not Yours. You don't necessarily

have to flash a blinding light on me and advertise my recalcitrant nincompoopery to all those around me. But however You need to reach me, please call me to see Your way. Bring me to You, and set me on Your way, with forgiveness and by the power of Your Spirit. Keep me strong in faith and discernment to stay on Your way.

10 "And I said, 'What shall I do, Lord?' And the Lord said to me, 'Get up and go on into Damascus, and there you will be told of all that has been appointed for you to do.'"
There are surely those times, Lord, when I realize that I have come to the end of whatever wisdom and planning I was using, and I look ahead and don't have a clue. Give me courage and trust in You to boldly ask, in honest humility and repentance, "What shall I do, Lord?" And when I ask, give me confidence to expect You to answer. Help me to listen to You. Grant me discernment, so that I will hear and see Your answer. And then empower me with Your Spirit to obey You, completely and faithfully. (Of course, it would also be terrific, Lord, if by Your grace, I don't necessarily wait until I don't have a clue. It would be ok to check with You on a frequent basis about what I should do.)

15 For you will be a witness for Him to all men of what you have seen and heard.
I have not seen and heard what Paul did, Lord. I have not had visions of heaven. I have not stood before an angry crowd and courageously witnessed for You. But I have seen and heard a lot. I have seen You bless me in ways that were amazing then, and as the years pass by, grow in wonder and awe. I have heard people who have been greatly blessed by You. I have heard You speaking to me in a variety of ways, blessing me, encouraging me, waking me up, comforting me. So, yes, I guess I have things that I have seen and heard. Give me courage, with the right words and the right timing, and show me the right people and places to share those things, so that You will use them to bless others.

My way, only if it is Yours
Ask, listen, and do
Share the seen and heard


Acts 23

10  And as a great dissension was developing, the commander was afraid Paul would be torn to pieces by them and ordered the troops to go down and take him away from them by force, and bring him into the barracks.
Thank You, Lord, for the civil authorities.  Thank you for using them to protect people and bless people.  Please use them today to bless Your people and protect them from evil.  Use civil authorities on highways to keep the peace and help people refrain from going crazy in selfish, hurrying panic.  Keep civil authorities honest.  Grant that civil authorities receive a just compensation to bless them.  And, yes Lord, help me to have an attitude of respect for the civil authorities that You place around me.  Please take control of civil authorities that persecute Your people.  Use Your gracious and almighty power to restrain and destroy all evil that comes from any civil authority against Your people.  Use Your gracious methods to establish civil authority around the world that will be a blessing to people.

11   But on the night *immediately* following, the Lord stood at his side and said, "Take courage; for as you have solemnly witnessed to My cause at Jerusalem, so you must witness at Rome also."
Thank You, Lord, for showing that You had a plan for Paul, and that You were continuing to work to carry it out.  I like the arrangement You had with Paul, that You stood at His side and told him what the plan was.  I would prefer that You would do that with me.  And sometimes I believe You do get me ready overnight for the day to come, by Your special touch and grace.  An email or text would also be ok, of course.  I suspect that more often You use the things that

You allow and prepare to happen to us and in us to guide us by Your Spirit in the plan You have for us. So whatever arrangement You want is ok with me, Lord. Only guide me, and unfold Your plan in me by Your grace and power, to Your glory.

16 But the son of Paul's sister heard of their ambush, and he came and entered the barracks and told Paul.
You find a way to have Your will carried out. It isn't always the way I can imagine. Paul's sister's son, who is articulate and confident. Who would have thought? I can't see what is coming. But You fill me with confidence that no matter what I can see, You will find a way to effect Your will. Right now, You are at work on ways to carry out Your will in my life in everyone's life for next month, next year, off into the future. I am amazed and delighted at how creative and dependable You are, Lord. Even when things look dark from my point of view, You are finding a way, a way to make even that time a blessing. Thank You, Lord. Thank You that I can depend on You to find a way.

Civil authorities, blessed and blessing
Guide me, Your plan
Find a way, thank You


Acts 24

5 For we have found this man a real pest and a fellow who stirs up dissension among all the Jews throughout the world, and a ringleader of the sect of the Nazarenes.
"Stirs up dissension", that was how they viewed Paul. I am concerned, Lord, that I rarely seem different from the world in which I live. In this world I ought to look different from a lot of people. I don't exactly want to cause dissensions wherever I go, but I want to be Your person, and I want to stand up for You. Help me to be different when different glorifies Your name and honors You. Help me get along with

other people and be an uncontentious blessing when that is Your will. Grant that I not be purposefully difficult with other people. Give me wisdom, please, Lord, to represent You well. (And give me courage to cause effective, first class dissension when You want me to.)

10 When the governor had nodded for him to speak, Paul responded:
"Knowing that for many years you have been a judge to this nation, I cheerfully make my defense.
Outrage comes more easily to my heart and lips, Lord, when I feel accused by someone. Help me to see accusations as opportunities to share You and witness. Give me a peaceful, gracious, and generous spirit, so that when I feel accused I can cheerfully make a defense with dependence and confidence in You. Let my words be honest, gracious, and loving. And let them recognize You and Your will. Help me to make defense opportunities a time to cheerfully stand up for You. (And, of course, if I am wrong (can You imagine that!), help me to also cheerfully recognize my error and apologize for my mistake.)

14,15 But this I admit to you, that according to the Way which they call a sect I do serve the God of our fathers, believing everything that is in accordance with the Law and that is written in the Prophets; [15] having a hope in God, which these men cherish themselves, that there shall certainly be a resurrection of both the righteous and the wicked.
Paul admits that he serves, believes, and hopes. I believe, Lord, that that is Your will for me, also. So with confidence I ask You to help me see the opportunities You give me to serve. Grant that in all serving, I serve by Your power through Your Spirit. Open my heart to believe all You say to me in Your word and through Your servants. Increase my faith to believe what I understand and those other things, too. Lift my spirit with hope as I trust You and look ahead to tomorrow and Life beyond all the tomorrows here. Thank You for Your great and wonderful promises of Life with You

in joy and satisfaction. To serve, to believe, to hope, yes, Lord, that is what I want.

Obviously different when You want
Cheerfully, right or wrong
Serve, believe, and hope


Acts 25

5 "Therefore," he said, "let the influential men among you go there with me, and if there is anything wrong about the man, let them prosecute him."
Thank You, Lord, for Your attitude of justice. And thank You for instilling a sense of justice ["if there is anything wrong about the man"] in this public servant. Bless public servants today with that sense of justice so that they will avoid considering someone guilty because they look different or sound different from them. Keep me, also, from putting people who look different in some negative category. (Think about how hard it is for people to accept me!) And most of all, Lord, bless me with Your sense of justice, so that I am never willing to put down others or agree with calumny suggested by other people.

8 ... while Paul said in his own defense, "I have committed no offense either against the Law of the Jews or against the temple or against Caesar."
What a position to be in, Lord. It would be very reasonable for Paul to be shouting, "I have done none of those things, you miserable crums!" No, by Your grace, Paul speaks, instead of shouting, in defending himself. When someone accuses me of something I am so ready to be exasperated. If I am innocent, it is easy to feel self-righteous and indignant. Help me to remember that righteous and indignation are mutually exclusive terms (thank You for Your servant Rev. Arnie Kuntz). Of course, if I am guilty, I am still exasperated and indignant, just also guilty and ashamed (as

You well know). Help me remember that all righteousness comes from You. Bless me in Speaking as I defend myself, with calm confidence and patience in You. And if I am guilty, help me to openly admit my guilt with repentance and contrition and with trust in You for forgiveness.

11 "If, then, I am a wrongdoer and have committed anything worthy of death, I do not refuse to die; but if none of those things is *true* of which these men accuse me, no one can hand me over to them. I appeal to Caesar."
It sounds like You gave Paul suddenly a clear vision that here was the path to accomplishing what You said was coming, that is, witnessing in Rome. I know that You have a good and gracious will for me, Lord. Fill me, Holy Spirit, so that in the things I say and in the choices I make, I may always be going in the direction of Your good and gracious will. Let me always be aware that You have a blessed direction for me—in my thinking, in my speaking, in reading I do, in caring about people, in things I avoid. Let all my yeses and noes honor You, be inside Your gracious will, and be going in Your loving direction.

May I put down put downs
Peaceful, humble defense
Going Your way, always


Acts 26

14 And when we had all fallen to the ground, I heard a voice saying to me in the Hebrew dialect, 'Saul, Saul, why are you persecuting Me? It is hard for you to kick against the goads.'
I know You are in charge, Lord. If I might make a request, please recognize all those who are persecuting You today, and let them have it, Pow! Wham! Zap! OK, perhaps I overstate this request. Please, Lord, speak to those who attack Your people, to those who stuff their ears with anything they can find so that they don't have to hear You, to

those who live in a world they have constructed without You and try to bring others into their world, to those who deny the right to worship You, to those who would adulterate the Gospel by making Life depend on something besides You and Your grace. Speak to them in a language that they really understand. Speak to them, and in the miracle of Your grace bring them to You. Use them to be a blessing as You did Saul, even today. (That'll teach them!) (Sorry.)

18 [I have appeared to you, to appoint you a minister and a witness]… to open their eyes so that they may turn from darkness to light and from the dominion of Satan to God, that they may receive forgiveness of sins and an inheritance among those who have been sanctified by faith in Me.'
Who, Lord, may I pray for? For those people I know, those I have met, those that live where I live, those in authority, those who are poor, homeless, powerless, lonely, those in other nations, those who dedicate their lives to gods that are not You? Many of them are not citizens of heaven. Many of them are in the dominion of Satan. There are, after all, only those two choices. Reach those who do not know that they do not know You. Turn them around, open their eyes, set them free from that dominion, grant them forgiveness and faith, that they may be made holy by Your Spirit, live Life now, and rejoice in the gift of the eternal inheritance You give.

23 [I stand to this day testifying]… that the Christ was to suffer, *and* that by reason of *His* resurrection from the dead He would be the first to proclaim light both to the *Jewish* people and to the Gentiles."
When You spoke, Light came into people who heard You. They could see life for the Life that it is. You are the first and only One to proclaim Light from personal experience.
Proclaim Light to all who have not heard Your gracious word. Proclaim Light to me—in Your word, in worship, in meditation and reading, through other people. Fill Jewish people today with Light from You. Use them to be a blessing

to all the Gentiles in the world. Proclaim Light to people in our country. Light up our nation, and cast out darkness. Let us be people of Light and grant that we reject and flee from all darkness.

Persecution to service
Blind eyes to see
Shine, Jesus, now


Acts 27

9 When considerable time had passed and the voyage was now dangerous, since even the fast was already over, Paul *began* to admonish them.
You use a variety of means still today to admonish. I have heard You give admonishments about eating too much, drinking too much (caffeine, alcohol, sugar, some sugar substitutes…), smoking, too much TV, too much sitting, putting myself first, and spending time in fear, to mention a few. You let me know that going down these roads will lead to problems, negative consequences, unnecessary expenses, and in general, a sticky end. Thank You for Your admonishments. It must be very frustrating to You when I don't listen. Help me to listen. Help me to be a good steward of everything You have given me. Help me not to have to gain wisdom by my dumb experiences, but by listening to You. And if I don't happen to listen to You the first time, please don't give up on me. Give me another chance to listen and to receive Your counsel and advice.

24 [An angel … stood before me] saying, 'Do not be afraid, Paul; you must stand before Caesar; and behold, God has granted you all those who are sailing with you.'
You really are willing to bless in some amazing ways to accomplish Your purposes. Certainly Your purpose with Paul was a great blessing to people today. But You still have purposes for each person You bring into Your family.

You give us Your gifts through Your Spirit.  And You have purposes You want fulfilled through Your people today.  It must be awfully complicated what You are doing right now to work through people to accomplish Your purposes of blessing.  Thank You, Lord.  Help me not to get in the way of Your purpose for me.  Keep me going in the right direction not only for Your purpose for me, but also for Your purposes for the people around me.

35,36 Having said this, he took bread and gave thanks to God in the presence of all, and he broke it and began to eat. 36 All of them were encouraged and they themselves also took food.

It wasn't enough for Paul to believe You.  He had to give an example of believing You.  By his actions, You touched the lives of the people around him.  I believe You, Lord.  I believe Your promises.  What may I do?  There are people around me who only see the storm, the waves, the frailty of the ship.  Help me to put that belief into action every day, so that people who cannot see what I believe  (and who may, actually, not care), will see something through me that will lead them closer to You, to receive Your blessings and to live Life in You.

Listen to admonishments, the first time
Not in the way, but on the way
Exemplary belief


Acts 28

9 After this had happened, the rest of the people on the island who had diseases were coming to him and getting cured.

There they were, the residents of Malta.  A fierce storm was battering the island.  And You blew in grace—grace that they had never imagined.  Not exactly what they were expecting from one of those storms.  I suppose I am playing with words a little, Lord, but maybe not. There are storms in my life. And I really don't expect anything good to blow in. I would really like it though, whenever there are those storms that try me and require endurance, that You would please, also, make those times of blessing. Blow in Your grace. I probably won't have any idea how You manage it, but that's fine. I know You are good at that. Thank You, Lord.

15 And the brethren, when they heard about us, came from there as far as the Market of Appius and Three Inns to meet us; and when Paul saw them, he thanked God and took courage.
It had indeed been a difficult trip. I think of a difficult trip, Lord, as when the plane is late or there is turbulence. But Paul really had expended a lot of physical and spiritual strength. Then You provided Christians to encourage him. Thank You for the Christians around me, Lord, that You use to encourage me. Thank You for my church family. Thank You for people I meet in traveling. Thank You for people demonstrating faith in You by what they wear in clothes and jewelry. Thank You for people who remind me that You are good, all the time. You give me encouragement and courage for living each day. Please help me, also, to be a person of encouragement to those people I see each day. Speak encouragement and grace through me (words, a cross, actions, a smile built by You, not just with my mouth but with my eyes as well).

24,28 Some were being persuaded by the things spoken, but others would not believe. "Therefore let it be known to you that this salvation of God has been sent to the Gentiles; they will also listen."
You have graciously arranged Your word, so that when it is spoken, some believe. Thank You, Lord, for the power and effectiveness of Your word. Thank You that some believe. It is tempting to focus on those who do not believe, who are not persuaded, and try to think of ways to humanly push and shove so they will be persuaded also. Not my job! Help me

to remember, Lord Holy Spirit, that is Your job, so I don't get in the way. Speaking as a Gentile, Lord, thank You for sending Your salvation to us. We are not Your chosen people, and yet You have graciously chosen from us also. Thank You for Gentile people listening. Grant that Gentile people will take in Your grace and salvation which You freely give (besides Jewish people). Keep bringing people to Life today as surely as You did in Paul's time.

Blow Your grace this way
Encourage encouragers
Receive that which is sent

# Romans

Romans 1

5 …through whom we have received grace and apostleship to bring about *the* obedience of faith among all the Gentiles for His name's sake…
Thank You Lord for giving Your grace to Paul and the other apostles and writers of the New Testament so that they wrote in the power of Your Spirit to bless me and all people today. Please grant me Your grace through Your word and in other ways so that I may be obedient to You. Obey has gotten bad press in my generation, Lord. Let me know You and let me live in You and with You so that I have no hesitation about wanting to obey You always. Show me the areas of my life where I am not so good (ok, where I am really rotten) at obeying You. Forgive me, touch me and heal me. I want to honor Your name. I want Your name to be known and honored by all the people around me. Let me live in obedience so clearly that others will be drawn to know and obey You in their lives. Help me to trust You and obey You in all things, throughout this day.

16, 17 For I am not ashamed of the gospel, for it is the power of God for salvation to everyone who believes, to the Jew first and also to the Greek. ¹⁷ For in it *the* righteousness of God is revealed from faith to faith; as it is written, "BUT THE RIGHTEOUS *man* SHALL LIVE BY FAITH."
Thank You, Father for the good news that You have sent Jesus, Your Son, to be my Savior. Thank You for forgiving me for my sins by Jesus' sacrifice. Thank You for giving me new Life in Jesus by the power of Your Spirit. You have revealed this to me through Your gift of faith. Grant that I use the faith You have given and trust You always, that I recognize Your righteousness, that I believe that Jesus is my

Savior and that He is with me today. Grant that I live in all humility in the righteousness You have given me, by faith, in joy today.

20 For since the creation of the world His invisible attributes, His eternal power and divine nature, have been clearly seen, being understood through what has been made, so that they are without excuse.

Yes, Lord! Clearly seen! When I look at flowers (how varied, how creative, how infinitely geometrical, how perfect, how individual, how inspiring, how peaceful) I recognize Your creating hand, Your eternal power. When I see the mountains, the landscapes, the deserts in their beauty and grandeur, I recognize You and Your love, faithfulness, glory, awe. Grant that I take in a clear vision of You and Your awesome nature when I look around every day. When I see the sky, the sunshine, the stars, moon, and planets. Grant that I recognize Your grace in Your willingness to provide so much that testifies to You in each day. Grant that I even see You in the gifts and abilities You have given people to build homes, towns, cities and transportation. Grant that I see Your love in the things I use that have batteries in them or plugs on them (I rather like that stuff). And by Your grace, let all the other people that see all Your wonderful creations every day also see You, clearly, loving them, calling them to Life more than life.

By grace: Obey You
Live using faith always
Looking around: Seeing You


Romans 2

4 Or do you think lightly of the riches of His kindness and tolerance and patience, not knowing that the kindness of God leads you to repentance?

What patience You have with me, Lord! You have led me and corrected me repeatedly with patience and forgiveness, and yet some of those pitfalls I still fall into. Thank You, Lord, for Your kindness to me in my life. You have opened doors for me. You have taken care of me. You have been tolerant and pulled me back to the path You have for me when I start chasing some wild turkey! You have been patient with me through the years, and last week, and yesterday. Lead me to repentance, Gracious Lord. Let me recognize wild turkeys for what they are. (Nothing against turkeys. But they are turkeys.) Let me remember Your kindness, tolerance, and patience. And grant that forgiven by Your grace in Jesus, I Live faithfully, following You, not judging others, but greatly desiring Your will in my life always.

10 ...but [there will be] glory and honor and peace to everyone who does good, to the Jew first and also to the Greek.
No one does good except You, Lord. So I depend on You absolutely for there to be good that I can do today. It is only by You Living in me, that I can do good. Live in me, Gracious Lord. Let there be glory to You from what You do through me. Let there be honor to You from what I think and say, by Your grace. And as You give me opportunities to do good, as You Live in me, use me to be a blessing, so that others may receive Your peace in forgiveness knowing You, and so that I may receive Your peace. For living in peace with You, trusting You, serving You—this is joy in life for me.

29 But he is a Jew who is one inwardly; and circumcision is that which is of the heart, by the Spirit, not by the letter; and his praise is not from men, but from God.
Holy Spirit, You can see my heart. You can see the dark stuff stuck on or seeping in. Create in me a clean heart, O God. Circumcise my heart. Only You can do this operation. (Not included in Medicare or BCBS for sure.) I would like to use my heart in a healthy, blessed way in all I think and say

and do. And I know, sometimes I let stuff creep in and find a resting place in my heart that is truly yucky! I would like to say that if You would just fix it today, I'll manage to keep it healthy from now on, but You know that's beyond me. So, please, Lord, let me begin this day with my heart cleansed by You. Keep me safe from heart-slowing, heart-attacking crud. Grant that I use my heart well through this day. And yes, before I start every new day (sigh!), do it again.

Your kindness. Your will. No turkeys.
Peace: Good through me, glory to You
A healthy heart: Spirit cleansed


Romans 3

21, 22 But now apart from the Law *the* righteousness of God has been manifested, being witnessed by the Law and the Prophets, <sup>22</sup> even *the* righteousness of God through faith in Jesus Christ for all those who believe; for there is no distinction…
When I think about how righteous You are, Gracious Lord, it is scary. You have perfect integrity, virtue, purity. You are right and correct in all thinking, feeling, and acting. But now all of Your righteousness has been made clear, not to frighten me to death, but rather for my blessing. Make Your righteousness a blessing to me as I use the faith You have given me. I believe in Jesus, Your Son, my Lord. So now by faith, give me the ability to see You in Your righteousness. Grant that I can see You witnessed in Your word. Grant that I can see You, even as You are righteous, loving me. Grant that I can see that part of Your righteousness is that You love me so much that You have allowed me to see You through Jesus, by faith. Grant that today I recognize You, not only as terrific and wonderful beyond my wildest dreams, but also as my loving Father I know by faith in Jesus.

23, 24  ...for all have sinned and fall short of the glory of God, <sup>24</sup> being justified as a gift by His grace through the redemption which is in Christ Jesus.

Thank You, Father for Your gift, justifying me. I recognize that I am a sinner. I am nowhere near being like You in Your glory. Yet You have graciously declared me to be the person I ought to be. Grant that I live as one who is justified as a gift. I have received many wonderful gifts in my life. But this gift from You is certainly the greatest! Thank You, Father! Thank You for sending Jesus. Thank You, Jesus, for redeeming me. I do not in any way deserve Your gift. Let me Live today with my mind and heart full of the joy and memory of being gifted by You. Grant that all I do and say shows Your gift. Let others see me not as the snooty person with the really terrific gift, but as a sinner, graciously redeemed from sin and death, made just by Your gift—the person I ought to be by Your grace, living humbly in thanksgiving to You.

28  For we maintain that a man is justified by faith apart from works of the Law.

It is such a temptation, Lord, to allow that voice inside to be saying, "Boy now I did something! What do You think, Lord, does this get me up the ladder of closeness to You?" Remind me in those times, Lord, that being the person I ought to be doesn't come from doing good stuff. Help me to remember that if I try to use the Law to say I'm pretty good, all I get is shown how far I am from Your perfect will. Help me to recognize the Law as an expression of Your will, and grant that I obey You and do good things only because You have changed me; only because You have made me a new person. I believe You are here, with me, today, Lord. I believe You have declared me to be the person You want me to be. Grant that in this day I will depend on You continuously and act like the person You have declared me to be—Your justified servant.

Recognize You by faith:  Great and loving

Living humbly and gifted
Just. By faith. Not me.


Romans 4

4, 5 Now to the one who works, his wage is not credited as a favor, but as what is due. [5] But to the one who does not work, but believes in Him who justifies the ungodly, his faith is credited as righteousness.

There are often a lot of forms I have to fill out in order to qualify for something. You know, Lord, the forms that ask about income, or education, or experience. But it is awfully easy to qualify for Your blessing—I just need to be a sinner, part of the group of ungodly (we are a large group). My income, education (I keep learning willing or not), and experience change. But here I am, a sinner, still, Lord. Yet I believe in You, that because of Jesus, You make me the person I should be. You declare me to be just and righteous. Thank You Lord! Grant that I live in humility, knowing that You credit me with righteousness because of Your gift of faith that You let me use. And grant that I live in joy and satisfaction—in certainty that I am justified by Your gracious love.

16 For this reason *it is* by faith, in order that *it may be* in accordance with grace, so that the promise will be guaranteed to all the descendants, not only to those who are of the Law, but also to those who are of the faith of Abraham, who is the father of us all…

There are so many guarantees I have, Lord. You know that cabinet where I stuff them all. And of course I keep them because I can't possibly remember all that fine print; so if I ever need one, I have to read the fine print for that one to make sure it actually applies. Your guarantee is unique. No fine print! It is so satisfying to hear Your promise of Life through Jesus. Thank You for the faith You have given me. Grant that I Live in faith today, always rejoicing that by Your grace I believe You and Your promise to me. Grant that I live in joy that Your promise is good, guaranteed today, with no hidden clauses. Terrific, Lord!

17 ...(as it is written, "A FATHER OF MANY NATIONS HAVE I MADE YOU") in the presence of Him whom he believed, *even* God, who gives life to the dead and calls into being that which does not exist.
I think of Your promise to give Life to me even after I die, and I am greatly comforted and blessed. But truth be told, that isn't the great event. The real miracle was that You gave Life to me when I was dead and separated from You. You called my Life with You into existence by grace when it did not exist. As I look ahead, between the Life You have given me and ahead to the Life You will give me, there are years when I often don't see clearly where the path is going ahead. So, please, Lord, call into being the path ahead today. Even if I can't see it clearly, let me step out in faith that this is not a problem for You. Call into being the blessings, joy, and strength You want for today.

Comfort: Justified
Satisfaction: Guaranteed
Life today: Called into being


Romans 5

1 Therefore, having been justified by faith, we have peace with God through our Lord Jesus Christ.
OK, Lord, it is true that I really like Agatha Christie. And Charlie Chan. So it might be from those that I can imagine You spying on me (like You aren't here seeing everything anyway). And there are things You see and hear that, well, if I were You, I'd be frowning and thinking, "OK, Michael, see how you do on your own today!" Thank You for none of that happening. Thank You for peace. Not, certainly, because I deserve it, but because You have justified me by faith

through Jesus. Grant that I live in a continual awareness that I have peace with You. Grant that I live relaxed, without fear. And grant that enjoying the peace I have with You, I choose what I say and do, satisfied that, in this day again, You and I are together.

5  And hope does not disappoint, because the love of God has been poured out within our hearts through the Holy Spirit who was given to us.
I have hoped for things all my life, Lord. Some of them (as I look back) were really awful (thank You for "disappointing" me in those hopes). Some were pretty good, and You have blessed me with them, and a lot of blessings I never dared to hope for. You are gracious beyond my imagination. So when I hope for a relationship with You, where You don't cringe when You think of me, and I don't tremble when I think of You, You have not disappointed me. Thank You for Your love that You have poured generously into my heart. I know You love me—thank You Lord! Holy Spirit thank You for coming into me. Let me recognize the love of God, let me rejoice in Your love in my heart, and let that love flow through me in all I do and say to the people around me. Thank You that Your love is plenty for all of us to share with each other.

21  ... so that, as sin reigned in death, even so grace would reign through righteousness to eternal life through Jesus Christ our Lord.
Yes, it is true, I have occasionally said (or sung) "If I were king!..." Appropriately subjunctive because of course, I am not. And those times I think it would be nice to be king, I am afraid it is because I want to straighten something (or someone) out. Your plan is wonderfully better. Grace reigning. That way I don't have to be daily afraid of being straightened out. It's hard to see, just walking around outside, or watching TV!, or listening to others—it's hard to see that grace is reigning through righteousness. So grant me eyes filled with faith, so that I see You Jesus, and I see

Your righteousness that You give to me and others, and I see grace reigning today, even here where I live. And grant me joy and confidence of Your grace reigning as I look ahead through all the days You have coming, all the way to eternal life.

Peace with You:  Living peacefully
For sure:  Love enough for all
Grace in charge:  what consequences!


Romans 6

4  Therefore we have been buried with Him through baptism into death, so that as Christ was raised from the dead through the glory of the Father, so we too might walk in newness of life.
Thank You, Lord, for my baptism!  Thank You for giving me the benefit of Your death in my baptism.  And on Easter, people, especially the disciples, were amazed at You rising from the dead!  What a miracle!  How gracious You are, Father!  Let me realize the amazing newness that You intend for me.  I don't have to stay in the same old mold.
Sometimes I have felt like, "What an adventure, if I could just take a trip and go somewhere absolutely new!"  Show me, Lord, the newness that You have for me today.  Open me to the adventure in newness of Life that You have prepared for me today.  I don't have to take a trip, today is the adventure!  Make today the amazing new adventure that You want it to be, to Your glory, gracious Father.

11  Even so consider yourselves to be dead to sin, but alive to God in Christ Jesus.
It is easy to think of sin as part of the family—just the normal place where I live; and it's harder to think of walking with You, Lord.  The problems that were here yesterday are still here.  So I thank You for this power-filled calling that You give me at the beginning of this day:  Consider myself!

Dead!  Alive!  When I look in the mirror, I am not looking at me.  I'm looking at my appearance (trying to arrange it so other people (like my wife) will not cringe, but feel pleasantly disposed to me).  Help me to look in Your gracious mirror where I can see that a change has happened to ME.  I can look at my actual self by Your grace.  Help me to see the change—that I am dead to sin.  I am not its slave.  Sin is no longer "normal".  Help me to see the change—that I am now alive to You!  You are not a long way off.  Let me see You right here with me!  Let me see You smiling and ready to walk with me today.  Let me remember to consider my *self* Alive, open to You, rejoicing with You, delighting in You, Living with You in every part of this day.

23  For the wages of sin is death, but the free gift of God is eternal life in Christ Jesus our Lord.
I have spent so much of my life focusing on wages, on earning, and only occasionally thinking about gifts that it really takes some doing, Lord, for me to turn around to Your way of operating.  Get good grades, then I am qualified for … .  Take the right courses, then I am entitled to … .  Have the right degree or the right training, and then I get to … .  And here You are Zap!  Cutting right through all that with Your knock on the door of my heart and there You are smiling, giving me Your free gift.  What a strange, different, wonderful way You have to touch me and my life!  Help me to get my brain and heart muscles disconnected from the rails of do, get, do, get.  Open me to see that You and Your grace and Your gift in Jesus are real.  And real for me!  In the midst of the doing that I am busy with today, let me see the Life I have in You today because of Your gift.  Let me see eternal Life open in front of me that does not stop or even pause at the moment my body stops working.  Let me live in the joy of Your wonderful gift, of eternal Living, with You, even today!  Yes!

New:  The adventure today
"Self, Alive!":  Joy in You

Living!: Your gift, now

Romans 7

4 Therefore, my brethren, you also were made to die to the Law through the body of Christ, so that you might be joined to another, to Him who was raised from the dead, in order that we might bear fruit for God.

It was a blessed and amazing event, Father, that You arranged to bless me. In Jesus dying, I no longer have to try to earn Your favor through obeying the Law. And now thank You that You have joined me to Jesus. Let me see the time You give me as time with Jesus Who is alive and here and with me. Let me see living as an adventure with Jesus in Living joyfully, desiring always to bear fruit for You. Thank You for productive Life with Jesus. Some days (when I look back with tired eyes) don't seem as productive as I would like. Not many items have been crossed off the list. But grant that I may hand each day over to You, Father, in the certainty that joined with Jesus I have, by Your grace, been fruitful, whether I can see it or not. Awake or asleep, Lord Jesus, Life is a fruitful adventure with You.

6 But now we have been released from the Law, having died to that by which we were bound, so that we serve in newness of the Spirit and not in oldness of the letter.

I do enjoy going to museums, Lord. It's fun to see the beginnings. Thank You for blessing people in those centuries in which I cannot imagine surviving. I also have a personal museum of oldness. I don't enjoy it as much as the others. When I am bold enough to creak open the door (which I always keep locked) I am amazed at the pictures, the sound tracks, the darkness in the dioramas. Thank You Holy Spirit that I don't have to live there. I know I still sometimes contribute days to the museum, but lead me and empower me to serve my Lord in Your newness with light and joy and love and wonder.  Let today be a non-museum, New day with You.

24, 25  Wretched man that I am! Who will set me free from the body of this death? $^{25}$ Thanks be to God through Jesus Christ our Lord! So then, on the one hand I myself with my mind am serving the law of God, but on the other, with my flesh the law of sin.
I remember my grandmother, when watching a mystery on TV, saying later that it had seemed such a mixed up affair.  I guess that's what I see, too, when I look at the minutes of a day gone by.  It was a mixed up affair.  Selfish, loving, annoyed, grateful, arrogantly angry, humbly caring.  OK.  That's me, Lord.  Thank You, Gracious Lord, for setting me free from the death that inhabits my flesh.  Thank You that I can serve You in Your will.  Clarify my mixture, Lord.  Set me free today so that I will Live freely, with my mind and heart filled with listening to You, using Your grace in faith to be a blessing in the time You give.  Keep my flesh from getting in the way of my Living single-mindedly with You, serving You faithfully.

Fruitful adventuring with You
Spirit-powered newness
Living freely and unmixed


Romans 8

5, 6  For those who are according to the flesh set their minds on the things of the flesh, but those who are according to the Spirit, the things of the Spirit. $^6$ For the mind set on the flesh is death, but the mind set on the Spirit is life and peace.
It is almost like the whole world is divided into two groups, those with striped foreheads and those with checkered foreheads.  My being either is according to the flesh or according to the Spirit—no other choices.  Thank You Gracious Lord that my being, by Your grace, is according to

the Spirit. And now You give me the privilege of setting my mind. When I get a new clock (and it is amazing how many gizmos with batteries or plugs have clocks—like I really want to know the time that much!) I have to set it. But I don't often think of setting my mind. Of course, I can see that when it is not set it wanders around rather without point or limit. That does sound dumb, dangerous, and unproductive. So thank You, Lord, that by Your grace I may set my mind. Help me to set it again today (it seems to unset itself on a regular basis). Help me to set my mind on You, Lord and Spirit, and on the things that are Yours. And then grant that in this day I will rejoice in You in Life and peace.

26 In the same way the Spirit also helps our weakness; for we do not know how to pray as we should, but the Spirit Himself intercedes for *us* with groanings too deep for words.
It is difficult to know how to pray, Lord. You can see the eternal powers of good and evil in me, around me, swirling, sunshine and storm. While to me it seems rather quiet today. When I pray I think of needs, wants, fears, people I love, people I have promised to pray for, problems, sorrows, griefs. But You, Lord Holy Spirit, can really see me. You know what is most important to pray for. You know exactly what my Father wants to give me to bless me and to use me to His glory. So, yes, Holy Spirit, please intercede for me. Ask for that which is good and important for me. So that I will praise God in the way I should and would like to and don't. Sing through my heart and bring my spirit to the Lord humbly in worship and joy and thanksgiving.

28 And we know that God causes all things to work together for good to those who love God, to those who are called according to *His* purpose.
I'm really glad You are in charge of that, Lord. I start things. I write things on the to-do list. I listen to requests (and spouse-fervent directives). I make plans. I coordinate calendar events. I keep (wonderful) spreadsheets. Does it all work together with results that all the stake-holders would

join me in saying are good? Beats me. Make it work, Lord, please. Thank You for calling me according to Your purpose. Let Your purpose be effective in my life. Fill my life with purposeful Life. And pick up all the ends of things that I touch and start with love and well-meaning, and which I leave hanging. Bring them into a pattern of love and joy and honor and glory to You and blessing to others (and yes, to me). It's way beyond me, so thank You for causing all things to work actually together and really result in good (whether I see it or not).

Mind: Spirit-set
Prayer: Spirit-spoken
Your purpose: Make it all work


Romans 9

25 As He says also in Hosea,
"I WILL CALL THOSE WHO WERE NOT MY PEOPLE, 'MY PEOPLE,' AND HER WHO WAS NOT BELOVED, 'BELOVED.'"
You make it happen, Lord, just by renaming! When I rename a file, it zaps into another alphabetical place. And You are rich in mercy and so gracious and powerful, that You see me and Your people today, and You have made us who we are by just mercifully calling us Your people. It is Jesus' death and resurrection that You use, of course, being merciful. Your plan in Jesus' sacrifice includes renaming me and us. Thank You Lord. Help me to zap to the appropriate place of thanksgiving and joy and worship and service by the power of Your merciful, gracious, calling me one of Your people. And help me to stay there without slipping out of place. Thank You, Lord.

30 What shall we say then? That Gentiles, who did not pursue righteousness, attained righteousness, even the righteousness which is by faith.

I admit, it wasn't my idea. Without You, Lord, my life goals had education, money, family, reading eclectically—but not attaining righteousness. And then You made me Your own and gave me faith in You. Wow! You have shown me so much more in Life than life. Thank You for blessing me through faith in Jesus with Your gifts of forgiveness and eternal Life. Thank You that I can want righteousness in my Life. Please help me to pursue righteousness. It is Your gift. Help me to recognize it, be thankful for it, appreciate it, and want my being to dwell in You and Your righteousness through Jesus today and every day. Strengthen my faith; help me to use it effectively. I trust You, Lord, I depend on You. Let me Live in righteousness today.

33 …just as it is written,
"BEHOLD, I LAY IN ZION A STONE OF STUMBLING AND A ROCK OF OFFENSE,
AND HE WHO BELIEVES IN HIM WILL NOT BE DISAPPOINTED."
There are indeed a lot of ways to be disappointed. Buying stock in what looks like a sure-fire, exploding, new enterprise. Taking a course with a great sounding title. Depending on myself to plan an effective day of blessing without You. And in the original promise, "a stone of stumbling and a rock of offense" sounds unprepossessing to be sure. And yet it was Jesus, Your Son, my Lord, Gracious Father. And now I have seen Him, and You have blessed me with faith in Him. Lord Jesus, when temptations to depend on something else come blowing into my life, help me to remember I have not been disappointed because I trust in You. Let that belief fill my life with Life, so that it is not just a church thing, not just a prayer thing, not just an "Oops, I am in serious trouble!" thing. Let my belief in You be part of every breath I take, part of every thought I think, part of everything I do. I know, Gracious Lord, I will not be disappointed.

Renamed and re-placed
Righteousness: Valued and faithfully appreciated

No disappointment in Jesus

Romans 10

4 For Christ is the end of the law for righteousness to everyone who believes.
I live in a people of reruns, Lord. Old TV and radio shows come "back" to a generation that never saw them or heard them the first time. Art, music, forms of government come back again. And ideas come back. It would be terrific, Lord, if only good, wonderful, blessing things come back. Unfortunately, it doesn't seem to work that way. So it is a great blessing that there is an end to the plan, idea, belief that obeying the law is what makes people righteous and acceptable to You. You, Lord Jesus, are the end. The "do-it-yourself plan" stops with You. Grant that every time I look back and see my sin and think, "I need to get better, or God won't talk to me or like me" I remember: You are the end. No more "do better" to get You to like me. No more "fix it" and then I can have hope. Whew! I really knew that wasn't working, so thank You Lord for relieving me of that nonsense. Please, let people know that You are the end.

10 For with the heart a person believes, resulting in righteousness, and with the mouth he confesses, resulting in salvation.
Thank You, Jesus, that I may believe that You are my Savior. Thank You, Jesus, that I may confess by what I say that You are my risen Lord. Keep me strong in my faith and let my confession be clear. Grant that I rejoice every day in the salvation You give. Look at the people who live around me, Lord. Look at the people I meet. I know You look at them and love them, Lord. Open their hearts to believe in You so that there is no one on the throne in their hearts, but You. Give them speech and thoughts that confess You as their Savior and Lord. Grant them Your blessed result: salvation.

17  So faith *comes* from hearing, and hearing by the word of Christ.
Even if we need hearing aids to hear clearly, it is easy to hear an awful lot of stuff today, Lord.  I remember those five channels on TV.  (Three of them were even pretty clear.)  It seemed easier to choose to hear or not hear.  Now it seems very difficult, Lord.  And with all that coming at people today, there is Your still, small voice, Your powerful, eternal voice, Your speaking to people in Your word.  Spread Your word, Lord.  Make it available to all people, Gracious Lord.  Use all the technologies, use Your people, use me—let Your word be heard, even in the midst of the vast, overwhelming noise.  Let people hear the word that shows You, Lord Jesus.  Use Your word, also today, to create faith through the power of Your Spirit.  Let Your word not return to You empty and ineffective.  Grant that it will accomplish what You desire and succeed in the matter for which You send it.  (Is. 55.11)

Praise to You, the end
Joy: hearts believing, mouths confessing
Your word:  Accomplishing, succeeding


Romans 11

12  Now if their transgression is riches for the world and their failure is riches for the Gentiles, how much more will their fulfillment be!
Thank You for the many generations of faithful Jewish people who trusted You through the centuries, Lord.  Thank You for all the people in Your ancestry, Lord Jesus.  Thank You that because of Your coming as a fulfillment of the promises that were made through the Old Testament, Your gift of grace, forgiveness and Life have come even to me.  There are so many Jewish people today, Lord, who do not appear to have the blessing of Your fulfillment of the promises.  Please reach them, Lord.  Please include them in

Your family. Please bring the blessing to me and the rest of Your family that You have said we will receive, when Your family includes also all the people from Your great heritage. Bring us together to You in Life now and forever.

15 For if their rejection is the reconciliation of the world, what will *their* acceptance be but life from the dead?
There are a lot of things to do. It is possible to participate in many ways in helping other people. But as You look at Jewish people, at Your heritage, Lord Jesus, there are a lot of people who care about others, who do really great things, who don't enjoy Life in their living. Bless them Lord. Give Life to Your people, Lord. Bring them from the death of living without You to the Life of forgiveness and grace and joy in You. Thank You for giving me forgiveness and grace through Your sacrifice, Lord Jesus. Reach Your people with the good news of Life with You now and Life past dying in joy forever with You.

32 For God has shut up all in disobedience so that He may show mercy to all.
The sun is shining, the birds are singing, there is a job to do, a paycheck is coming regularly, there is extra for special occasions, everyone in the family loves and respects each other. OK, rarely, except a few times on "Father Knows Best" (which I did enjoy). So in Your grace, Lord, You help people to see that their life is not perfect. And in particular, You work hard to show people how they have disobeyed You and Your will, how they have messed up their lives and others, and how the consequences for that are really terrible. And the point is not because You enjoy people suffering, but that until people see the problem, they are not very interested in Your gracious help in Jesus. Please let us all see how we have separated ourselves from You. Show us the times we choose to walk our path instead of Yours. And bless all people with the desire for Your help in Jesus. Bring people to Your mercy, Lord, and mercifully bring people to

Life in You. Thank You for the bad news so that we can truly enjoy Your good news!

Gentiles and Jews alive in You
Life in living for Your people
Lead from bad news to Good


Romans 12

1 Therefore I urge you, brethren, by the mercies of God, to present your bodies a living and holy sacrifice, acceptable to God, *which is* your spiritual service of worship.
I really find this difficult, Lord. It is so easy to think of a sacrifice today as giving something extra to a charity. Or giving up some food once in a while. Or going to an extra church service. You are asking a lot. And, yes, Lord, You have every right to ask a lot. You have been merciful to me. You are merciful to me today. You forgive me for all of my sins. You don't bring things up from the past. So yes, Lord, I want to present my body to You. I really need help to do that. Grant me wisdom and strength, courage and perseverance to think and act sexually with purity, to eat and drink with respect for my body, for my health, for my desire to have my body working well for a long time (even, especially in the evening when I am watching TV and I hear snacks calling me; even thinking about salt, oil, fat, and whether I am actually hungry). Grant me wisdom and perseverance in exercising in a way that is good for me. Thank You for the medicine that helps me be healthy, and help me to accept responsibility for being well instead of looking for a pill to fix everything. Help me to put in effort, energy, and creativity when You give me something to do. And help me to listen to You telling me when to stop and rest. You know, Lord, that I have kind of given up at various times in these areas. (OK, that's an understatement!) Grant me consistency and faithfulness in presenting my body to You, by Your grace and mercy. Even, also, tomorrow, too.

2 And do not be conformed to this world, but be transformed by the renewing of your mind, so that you may prove what the will of God is, that which is good and acceptable and perfect.

I remember Silly Putty or something like that. It conformed amazingly. And there is a process of education going on around me that says there are fewer bumps in the road for the person who conforms to the world. (Right, the wide path that leads to destruction, You said.) So, please, Lord transform me. Make my mind new in Your gracious will. Help me to see and understand what is happening in my life and in the joys and messes in the world around me through Your eyes. You said there would be problems, turmoil, and disasters. And You promised joy and strength to all faithfully trusting You and Your promises. Let my mind use a faith operating system, and grant that it demonstrates indeed what is good and acceptable and perfect.

6-8 Since we have gifts that differ according to the grace given to us, *each of us is to exercise them accordingly*: if prophecy, according to the proportion of his faith; [7] if service, in his serving; or he who teaches, in his teaching; [8] or he who exhorts, in his exhortation; he who gives, with liberality; he who leads, with diligence; he who shows mercy, with cheerfulness.

You have given people gifts, Gracious Lord Holy Spirit. And they sure are different. When I see how wonderfully and differently Your servants serve You I am amazed and thankful, Lord. Help me to discern what gift or gifts You have given me for this part of my life. There are times in my life when I felt clear about what gift You wanted me to use. Then things change as time goes by. Let me know how You want me to use the gifts You have given me. Grant that I enter every day faithfully depending on You, with joy and satisfaction, first and foremost, in serving You. In the work You give me to do, in the times of relaxation, in times of recreation let me use Your gifts in ways that honor You and that are a blessing to others. Thank You Lord for Your gifts and Your grace and faith to use them. All praise and honor to You—it's You, not me.

Yes, even my body
Mind: Transformed to Your new
Your gifts: Blessing, today


Romans 13

8 Owe nothing to anyone except to love one another; for he who loves his neighbor has fulfilled *the* law.
Thank You for Your love to me, Lord. Thank You for including me in Your family. I don't deserve any of Your grace and kindness. Thank You for the privilege of sharing Your love, by loving my neighbors. They come in quite a variety. Some are loving, some responsible, some less responsible. And all of them I can love by Your grace. Not because they are loveable, but because You are loving. Thank You that the law, which I never manage to fulfill, You count fulfilled by my using the privilege You give me to love others. Bless the people around me, Lord. Help me to care about them, their property, their enjoyment of life. Let my smile and greeting share the sunshine of Your love to everyone, every time I see them, every day.

12 The night is almost gone, and the day is near. Therefore let us lay aside the deeds of darkness and put on the armor of light.
I tend to look at the temperature first when I think about what to put on, Lord. Then color and pattern for the season or the day's activities. What a practical priority You give in choosing what to put on. I do not live in the darkness of ignorance and sin, but in Your grace and forgiveness and joy. The day I live today is between the darkness and the Day which is coming. And yes, the Day is coming soon. Your signs of the end are all around. And besides that, I

keep getting older (some days faster than others). "Therefore", yes, those are reasons enough—put on the armor of light. Grant that in this day I use the armor You have given. Thank You that while I wait for the Light of Day, I can wear Your gift of the armor of light now. With that armor, chase away all darkness that tries to invade my day, let me see with Your light so that I live in Your joy today. Grant that I keep going forward in the direction You have chosen holding Your armor firmly by faith, with nothing ever piercing through to darken my Living for You and with You.

14 But put on the Lord Jesus Christ, and make no provision for the flesh in regard to *its* lusts.
Yes, I know what others want, whether it is my boss or the people I am with or the pernicious, pushy ads on some media. When do I get what I want? There is that voice inside me. On a good day, I recognize it to be a very selfish voice. Then there are days when I let that voice make sense to me. And, of course, what it wants is not always (translate: hardly ever) what is good and wonderful and gracious and in Your will. Make no provision, You say. OK, please satisfy me with what is good. Grant that I spend no time on making provision for my selfishly voiced, darkly desired wants. Let me know that You are all satisfaction and joy. Let me put You on, Lord Jesus. On my mind and heart, on all my being. Grant that I look forward to a great and enjoyable day today, not because I am selfishly satisfied, but because I am eternally and right now satisfied, by Your grace, having put You on.

Shine. Your love. Every neighbor.
Light armor: all day
Wearing You and satisfied


Romans 14

8  For if we live, we live for the Lord, or if we die, we die for the Lord; therefore whether we live or die, we are the Lord's.
One of the great problems for school students, Lord, as You know is for them to figure out why they are doing all that hard work.  It started off, in the shadowy mists of youth as fun.  But as years pass, ever more quickly (while there should be fun, too) it appears to include hard work.  Are they doing it for Grandma and Grandpa?  For Mom and Dad?  For the teacher?  Or (help them to get to this point) for themselves and for You.  And for those no longer students, help us to get straight (by Your wonderful grace) why we live.  Why do we get up, move quickly, work hard, help others?  Why do we enjoy life, enjoy the beautiful world, sing?  Help me, help us, Lord, to know for sure that it is for You.  Grant that we enjoy blessings with You, accept even hurts and sufferings with joy in You, and use every gift and ability from You to honor and glorify You. (And thank You, Lord, that through life, through death, we are still Yours.)

17  For the kingdom of God is not eating and drinking, but righteousness and peace and joy in the Holy Spirit.
I can hear a small voice back somewhere, Lord, saying, "Are You sure it's not eating and drinking?"  Sheesh!  It's just that there is a lot of eating and drinking in celebrations both then and now.  But there is only so much time I can spend eating and drinking (I would like to be healthy!).  So thank You, Lord, that all the time I can enjoy Your gifts of righteousness, peace and joy.  Please, Holy Spirit, Gracious Lord, open my eyes to see the righteousness I have in Jesus.  Let me live in peace, even when righteous indignation lurks close at hand.  Let peace flow through me in what I say and do with others.  And let me be alive in the joy of Living with You and for You every moment.

19  So then we pursue the things which make for peace and the building up of one another.
Pursuing has a history in America, getting a lot of press for "pursuit of happiness".  And You have given us the blessing

of working, Lord. Thank You. We have pursued money and success in that part of our lives. Please bless me and us that we think with heart and spirit about what we pursue. Grant that we make time amidst other (second class) pursuits for this important and blessed pursuit that You put in our Living. Show us how to aim at peace. Help us to pursue peace well with others in family, community, and our country, also. And help me and us to get our focus off ourselves and building ourselves up. Grant that we rejoice in the grace and power and opportunities that You give us to build up one another. Use us effectively in our thoughts, words, and deeds so that those around us are blessed and built up in heart and joy and wonder Living with You and for You.

Live or die: Yours
Enjoying kingdom Life
Pursuing peace together


Romans 15

1 Now we who are strong ought to bear the weaknesses of those without strength and not *just* please ourselves.
Paul was indeed strong in faith. Thank You, Lord, for calling him and using him to be a blessing to us today. I thank You, Lord, that there have been times in my life when You have given me strong faith in the face of some storm in life. There has been a temptation, then, to assume that all around me are in the same faith place. Help me to have patience with others when that is not true. And when I find myself in the other group, Lord, and fears gang up on me, grant that those who are strong in faith around me will have patience with me and help me through the fears that attack. Grant that I will avoid the temptation to see faith as a tool You give me to please myself, in worship, in work, in relationships. Grant that I always use Your gift of faith with thanksgiving and a caring attitude toward Your servants around me.

**5, 6** Now may the God who gives perseverance and encouragement grant you to be of the same mind with one another according to Christ Jesus, [6] so that with one accord you may with one voice glorify the God and Father of our Lord Jesus Christ.

Perhaps I have watched and read too much science fiction, Lord, but it does sound a little scary to "be of the same mind". OK, I mean it's fine if we can all agree to be of the same mind with my mind. (Not what You had in mind(!), right.) Since it is Your encouragement You give, I know Your plan will be a blessing. (Thank You, I still get to enjoy vegan food, Mozart, and photography.) So yes, Lord, bless Your people, bless us to be of the same mind according to Christ Jesus in Whom we have grace, forgiveness, and all Life. Let all of us Christians with one accord, with one voice, glorify You, our Gracious Father. With the same mind in Jesus, let us in all our different ways, in different places, in different languages have this in common now and forever, Lord, that our hearts sing glory to You!

**13** Now may the God of hope fill you with all joy and peace in believing, so that you will abound in hope by the power of the Holy Spirit.

I read the weather forecast most days and I dress accordingly. I enjoy statistics, Lord. And when there is a probability of rain that is more than 50%, then I look forward to that happening (even though I know there is a significant probability of it not happening.) Yet You (Who graciously (from my satisfied point of view) invented mathematics and probability and statistics) take action completely ignoring all of those lovely numbers and percentages. And when I take an honest look at myself, I'm really glad You do. Not by probability comes hope, but by the joy and peace that You give with faith. Grant me that as You bless me graciously with believing You and trusting You today, You will also take action in my heart, Lord Holy Spirit, filling me with joy in my Savior and with peace in the acceptance and love of my

Father, so that I will abound in hope throughout this day (and please let my face look like it).

Faith strong or weak: Always patience
One voice praising You
Sunshine or clouds: Abundant hope


Romans 16

1, 2 I commend to you our sister Phoebe, who is a servant of the church which is at Cenchrea; 2 that you receive her in the Lord in a manner worthy of the saints, and that you help her in whatever matter she may have need of you; for she herself has also been a helper of many, and of myself as well.
Thank You, Lord, that You send Your servants to many churches to share what You are doing in other places. Bless Your traveling servants with strength and good health, joy and Your Spirit so they will communicate to Your people the way that people are being blessed by Your Gospel and helped by the caring love of Your people. When we, Your people, have an opportunity to help Your servants or participate in Your ministries give us open and generous hearts. Help us to see how You have blessed us so that we may be a blessing to others. Use us, Your people, to effectively support the gracious work which You are doing around the world. Grant that as we take the opportunity to participate in Your work, we will rejoice in each day and support the work of Your servants with our prayers as well as with our loving and giving. Bless all Your ministries in the world with all You want them to have to effectively reach people with Your gospel and Your love.

16 Greet one another with a holy kiss. All the churches of Christ greet you.
So maybe kissing is not exactly what You have in mind for us in our churches in this culture and time. But hugging

might be a blessing. I know, Your people come in quite a variety. Some are huggers and well, some not so much. Bless us in our Christian communities that whatever form we use, we let each other know that we love each other and care about each other. Help us to be open to help each other in any need. Thank You for the help You give us through each other. Give us in our Christian communities a real and wonderful awareness that all (nice word, all) the churches You have created are sending us their hugs. Wow! Makes a person feel really hugged! Let our attitude toward our sisters and brothers in Christ always be one of "The Lord bless you—hugs available!"

19 For the report of your obedience has reached to all; therefore I am rejoicing over you, but I want you to be wise in what is good and innocent in what is evil.
Your grace has blessed us, Gracious Lord. You have given us the privilege of Living in You and with You and obeying You. Grant that we continue to become wiser in what is good. Help us to learn more and more about how to follow Your will and be a blessing to others. Grant that in knowledge and experience we will get good at what is good. On the other hand, there are many opportunities we have to know about and get experience in evil. Help us resist all getting good at evil. Keep us in our knowing, away from knowing evil or knowing about evil. Grant us clear insight into choosing paths that avoid evil (no matter how attractive the paths look) and that aim always to the good that You desire. Fill us with Your Spirit and help us to be a blessing to each other so that we will all grow in wisdom in good, while staying innocent in evil.

Your ministries: Opportunities to bless
Hugs for the Family
Wisely getting wise

# 1 Corinthians

1 Corinthians 1

10  Now I exhort you, brethren, by the name of our Lord Jesus Christ, that you all agree and that there be no divisions among you, but that you be made complete in the same mind and in the same judgment.
Only in You, Lord Jesus can we, Your people, have no divisions. We come from different countries, different experiences. We read Your word and we want to serve You. We rejoice in Your forgiveness and the gift You give of Life eternal. And then—we have difficulty agreeing with each other. Please forgive us, Lord. Please fill Your people anew with Your Holy Spirit. Grant that we be repaired from assumptions and judgements about each other that we have held onto. Equip us with joy and power together in Your Gospel so that we will be Your effective tool to demonstrate Your love. Bring people to You through us, Lord. Make us what we ought to be. Make us, Your people, each and all, complete in You so that we may be different and yet without divisions before You or before the world that You want to reach. May we be of one mind and one Spirit in You.

18  For the word of the cross is foolishness to those who are perishing, but to us who are being saved it is the power of God.
I can hear someone saying, "Let me get this straight. You want me to have my entire life changed by an itinerant Jewish preacher from some 2000 years ago, and you want me to accept and believe that he is God and that he wants to give me life that lasts forever in wonderful joy (as yet mostly unspecified) free of charge, and this is because he thinks I am a sinner that needs to be saved. And you want me to have this strange idea change not only my Sunday mornings (which you do know is my only day to sleep in!) but also

every other day as well. And then you want me to live completely dedicated to him so that I drag other people into this same lifestyle. And you tell me I can hear him talking to me in the words of a book that was written by a large variety of different people (before the printing press was invented!) who all were inspired to tell of the coming of this preacher and then to tell about him after his coming. Is that right?!" To which, of course, Lord, the answer is, "Yes." Make my life that "Yes," today.

30, 31  But by His doing you are in Christ Jesus, who became to us wisdom from God, and righteousness and sanctification, and redemption, [31] so that, just as it is written, "LET HIM WHO BOASTS, BOAST IN THE LORD."
So what do I put in my resume? Born in ..., educated at ..., job experience at ..., and by God's grace, wise, righteous, sanctified, and redeemed. I suspect, Lord, that a lot of people reading that would go on to the next applicant. And yet, Lord, thank You that I may boast in You. You have brought me into Christ Jesus, my Savior. You have given me Your Spirit and wisdom that is very different from philosophers that are world-renowned. You have forgiven me for my sins, thank You Gracious Lord! You have redeemed me from the forces of evil outside me and inside me. You have given me righteousness so that I wear the robe that Jesus gives me by His death and resurrection. And You have made me holy by Your sanctifying power through faith. So if I put all that on a resume, Lord, it is because I am boasting about You. And even without a resume, help me to Live in great joy each day, satisfied in boasting, not about children or grandchildren (who are really very wonderful, thank You), not about possessions (which all came from Your gracious hand, anyway), not about my spouse (who is Your great blessing to me and who will be perfect with just a tiny bit of tweaking), but let me daily boast in You. Only by You am I alive, Living, and filled with hope and joy each day.

Unite us in You
Living "Yes," in Jesus
What a Lord!


1 Corinthians 2

5 ...so that your faith would not rest on the wisdom of men, but on the power of God.
It is so tempting, Lord, to just look for some scientific principle to explain why. There was a lot of wisdom of men to choose from in Corinth, and there certainly is today. But You told the story of depending on shifting sand. And learning, thought, wisdom all fluctuates from area to area, from century to century. The solid rock for our faith is what You have done, Lord, with Your power. You made this beautiful world and gave it to us to take care of. You healed the sick and brought people back from death to life. You changed an angry, narrow minded, religious lawyer into a humble and power-filled servant to bless people through the ages. Grant that I trust You, Lord. Not *as much as* I trust science and reason. Not *more than* I trust science and reason. Grant that I trust and depend on You *alone* (and thank You for science, reason, thought, wisdom—let them be tools to show the wonder of Your love and power).

12 Now we have received, not the spirit of the world, but the Spirit who is from God, so that we may know the things freely given to us by God.
Thank You, Lord, that we receive Your Spirit. It seems like every morning when I get up, there is the spirit of the world, a gray, rapacious smudge in the fabric of reality, eager to have me put it on as I get ready for the day. It never gives up. But it is a consuming desire for things that do not satisfy. It continually whispers, "More!" By Your grace we, Your people, receive Your Spirit. Please Holy Spirit, show us again today all the wonderful riches that we have from You: Appreciation of the world You have made, fellowship with

You and Your people, opportunity to serve You and be a blessing. Desires for being the best servant of Yours that we can be in the place and time and callings that You have given us. Joy, love, wonder, satisfaction in You. Protection from evil using the armor You have given (Ephesians 6). And faith, trusting You so that we can have an attitude of confidence and joy, Living with You in each day.

15  But he who is spiritual appraises all things, yet he himself is appraised by no one.
Ok, Lord, there was that time I got the house appraised. And to my amazement this expert thought it was worth a whole lot less than I did. I'm not sure what made that person an expert. But You tell me that I am an expert at deciding worth, because You have made me alive spiritually in You. You are the One Who decides my worth, based on the sacrifice of Jesus my Lord. And now I can consider the worth of every thing, every event, every idea, every book, every TV show, every... (wow, this could keep me busy for a very long time!). I am the expert appraiser, by Your grace, in the power of Your Spirit. Grant me Your wisdom, and clear vision, so that I will be accurate in all my appraisals. Grant that I will not use my appraisals to hit people over the head or hurt anyone, but to Live faithfully with You. Help me to participate only in things that I can discern are of value. Let me show Your love and Your light for the world, by the appraisals I demonstrate to those around me, by Your grace, to Your glory.

Faith, powered by You
Seeing your gifts
Enjoying: Appraised and worthy


1 Corinthians 3

10, 11  According to the grace of God which was given to me, like a wise master builder I laid a foundation, and

another is building on it. But each man must be careful how he builds on it. [11] For no man can lay a foundation other than the one which is laid, which is Jesus Christ.
Thank You, Gracious Lord Jesus, for being my foundation. Thank You for being the foundation for all Your people. We want to grow in You. Please grant that I am careful how I build on You, my Foundation. Everything I buy I have to bring home and put somewhere. Everything I take in with my spirit I have to put somewhere on You, my Foundation. So it matters what I take in(!). Let my thinking be filled with wisdom. Let my heart take in only joy and all that pleases You. If there is some feeling I have that has no place on You, my Foundation, grant me Your grace and power to reject it, get rid of it, throw it out in the trash. If there is some idea that comes to me that has no place on You, grant that I do not delay, trying to fix it to make it better. Grant that I just get rid of it. Grant that I take in nothing that I have no place for, and grant that I do not give to anyone else anything that they should have no place for, building on You. (Help me to know better than that!)

18 Let no man deceive himself. If any man among you thinks that he is wise in this age, he must become foolish, so that he may become wise.
In doctors' offices there are often the diplomas earned. Teachers try to let their students know who they are by putting them up (truly, in general, a lost cause—students really don't care how much teachers know until they know how much their teachers care). Please, Lord Jesus, as people spend time and money to get a good education, grant that they also grow in their understanding of their need for You. With every increase in knowledge, let there be an increase in humility before You. Let us all every day, start with the honest humility that we become wise only by Your grace. So, whether it is a question of our opening our mouth and saying something or just choosing what to do, let it always be with Your wisdom. Let Your cross on the wall remind us that You are the source of all true wisdom.

21 – 23 So then let no one boast in men. For all things belong to you, <sup>22</sup> whether Paul or Apollos or Cephas or the world or life or death or things present or things to come; all things belong to you, <sup>23</sup> and you belong to Christ; and Christ belongs to God.

By Your grace, Lord, I am a member of Your family, a Christian. It is easy to think of myself as a Christian of some denomination, or a Christian who came to faith in some country. It is easy to consider myself a Christian from this century (rather than other centuries which, from my point of view, had more problems). How parochial! (And snooty!) Help me, Lord, to recognize that we Christians are all one. And all that You have made You made to be a blessing for us (thank You, Lord!). Grant me unity and joyous fellowship with all Christians from every age, knowing that I and we are Yours. Help me to live today, not as a narrow here, now, today Christian, but as a Christian, gifted, blessed, part of a large and varied family, and above all, Yours.

Taking in:  Selectively
Wisdom:  From the cross
Christian by grace:  And Yours


1 Corinthians 4

7  For who regards you as superior? What do you have that you did not receive? And if you did receive it, why do you boast as if you had not received it?

We like people to think that we are somebody! That's a goal that a lot of people have—being somebody. Superior. Perhaps everyone could be superior. Like Lake Woebegone where all the children are above average. You have blessed people so much, Lord. I'm sorry for the times when my inclination has been toward being superior rather than a servant. And having stuff is a tempting way to feel superior (remember, Lord, when I had that Encyclopedia Britannica from 1900! Of course two volumes were missing, but still!). All the things I have, came from You. Thank You, Lord. Help me to enjoy them without making my personal worth depend on them. And please grant, Lord, that I do not need to be superior. Grant satisfaction and joy in serving and encouraging. Rather than being better than others, Lord, what I would really like is to enjoy what You have given and be better than I was yesterday, please.

12 ...and we toil, working with our own hands; when we are reviled, we bless; when we are persecuted, we endure.
Easy for Paul to say. Well, not exactly, Lord. But he depended on You, and by Your grace, He was able to live in a way different from all the people around him. So, here goes, Lord. When You give me something to do, grant that I do it well, honoring You, blessing other people with my work, and being responsible to receive Your provisions, Lord, using the means You give me. On those rare occasions when someone says something to me, trying to put me down, grant that I will lay aside the angry words and actions that spring readily to my mind and heart. Grant that I will reach out with blessing with my words and actions. And when I feel persecuted or I'm tempted to feel sorry for myself because things have turned out differently from the way I imagined (blue skies, balmy breezes, great place to live, loving family (who all think I do everything right!—can You imagine?), and enough money to do all the (wonderful and good) things that I can imagine)—well, when I'm tempted to feel sorry for myself, grant that I depend on You. Grant that I recognize Your love and provision and guidance. Grant that I endure whatever frustration or tragedy or crisis attacks. Be with me. Keep my eyes focused on You. Fill me with Your comfort and peace. Grant that I endure into the joy that You have prepared for me, whether it is here or there.

16 Therefore I exhort you, be imitators of me.
So when I explain how to factor a quadratic equation, I can see that being something to imitate. (Although there are

ways to do it that I haven't thought of, that some students come up with—good for them!) But would it be ok, Lord, if I say, "Please imitate me, but only in the following areas, under these certain conditions." And there would be that caveat, "Don't make any life changing decisions without first consulting your ..." Imitate me. What an amazing, strong, bold invitation. I would like people to imitate me, Lord. I would like to be the person You want me to be, so that others can imitate me. There are several things that need to be cleaned up before that could happen, it seems to me. Help me Lord to be imitate-able. To be the person that others could imitate and be blessed. Cleanse me from crud that I wouldn't want others to copy. Create in me a clean heart, fill me with Your Spirit, Lord. When other people look at me, let them see what You want for their lives, not because I am perfect, but because I am Yours by Your grace. Above all, let me imitate You in everything, always.

Superior in serving
Work, bless, endure joyfully
Worthy of imitation

1 Corinthians 5

5 ...to deliver such a one to Satan for the destruction of his flesh, so that his spirit may be saved in the day of the Lord Jesus.
You have a single-minded desire for us, Lord. Thank You. I think about strength for today, good stewardship so there is enough money, being healthy to enjoy life, things that have to do with physical living. But You make it clear that all of that is worthless if when Jesus comes back, I am not trusting Him for Life beyond this life. Help me to keep Your perspective, Lord. Bless all in our church, and all Your people, so that nothing gets in the way of Life with You. If there are people who are being drawn away from You Father, by lifestyles that are sinful and insulting to Your grace, please do whatever You have to do so that when

Jesus comes back, they may come home with You to Life. And, yes, Lord, if there is anything in my life that I can't see is drawing me from You, cut it out (of course, I prefer an anesthetic first, but that's up to You). I give You permission to do whatever You have to do to separate me from evil so that I may rejoice in Life with You now and forever.

7   Clean out the old leaven so that you may be a new lump, just as you are *in fact* unleavened. For Christ our Passover also has been sacrificed.

The old leaven of sin is so pervasive, Lord. It is so sticky. Even though I have listened to Your loving, gracious word, there is sin in me that keeps trying to spread throughout my being. I want to be a blessing to my family. I want to be a blessing to others. And yet, when I make decisions about what to do right now, often selfishness creeps in. Jesus You have died for me and forgiven me. I am a new person in You. Help me to recognize myself as Yours alone, even if I still look like what I look like in the mirror. In You, Lord Jesus, I am new and alive, separated from sin. Grant me clear vision and ruthless willingness to look, so that I will recognize the old leaven of sin wherever it tries to sneak into my thoughts, my words, my being, and what I do. It sounds strange to say my goal for today is to be a "new lump", but that's it—You know what I mean.

10   [...not to associate with immoral people;] I *did* not at all *mean* with the immoral people of this world, or with the covetous and swindlers, or with idolaters, for then you would have to go out of the world.

We have to associate with the people of this world. And it's true, Lord, the world is a mess. Not Your fault. It's like a swarm of flies, they seem to be everywhere a person looks. So many books and books of laws. All in some way saying, "No, not that. Whoa! Don't go that way! Of course You can't! Not that, either." It must be very difficult to be a lawyer, to have to know all the "no's". When I look out at the sunlit world, it is beautiful. People are scurrying about in very purposeful ways. It really looks good. Thank You for Your people. Thank You, Lord, for the blessings You have provided. Bless Your people with staying away from all that is outside Your will, all the sticky, selfish, and immoral. Bless Your people with living in joy and faithfulness to You, worshiping You, shining with Your light, even in the midst of hurt and crime and greed and idols of money, success and power dressed up for a new century. Help us, Lord, to live in this world, but never to be mistaken for being part of it.

Whatever it takes to be Alive
A new lump for the Lord
No thank you, only visiting


1 Corinthians 6

4  So if you have law courts dealing with matters of this life, do you appoint them as judges who are of no account in the church?
Well, of course, we do actually, Lord. And to various other elected offices. I think how wonderful it would be if for every office there would be a highly qualified Christian that could be elected. But politics is such a sloppy, yucky, swamp, what Christian in her or his right mind, ..., I'm sorry, Lord, we have had some great Christian leaders. And the way to improve the swamp is probably for Christians to step up. Please, Lord, call Your people to public office. Please grant them dedicated honesty and faithfulness to You, no matter what. Please bless our electorate with wisdom and Your guidance to elect the people You have chosen to serve You in positions of leadership across our country. Please give me wisdom also, to listen to You in every election, and to glorify You in voting.

11  Such were some of you; but you were washed, but you were sanctified, but you were justified in the name of the Lord Jesus Christ and in the Spirit of our God.

What a list of sins and sinners in verses 9 and 10, Lord! And it is easy for me to think of that as a description of people so very different from me. But, You know, Lord, that it isn't so very different. "Such were some of you." Yes. Before I tell You how good I am and different from that publican over there, help me to see myself through Your clear sight. It is not because I am a wonderful person that I am blessed by You. Before I think of any group of people as hopelessly separated from You, help me see clearly that only by Your grace I am here. Only by Your washing in the blood of Christ my Savior am I here. Only by Jesus am I justified. Only by Your Spirit am I made holy to be here, now. Only by Your name Jesus; only by Your grace, Holy Spirit. As I look at the varied landscape of people in the world today, let me remember my place of origin without You, and let me pray fervently for all people to receive Your grace, washing, justification and sanctification to come to Life with You.

19, 20  Or do you not know that your body is a temple of the Holy Spirit who is in you, whom you have from God, and that you are not your own? [20] For you have been bought with a price: therefore glorify God in your body.
I remember hearing, "If I had known how long I was going to live I would have taken better care of me." True. More exercise, Lord, more regularly. (Vegan thirty years earlier.) But, here we are, Lord, You and I. Thank You, that I have choices now that were not here those years before. Give me wisdom to choose wisely what I put in my mouth. Grant that in the adventure of living, I still use Your wisdom in what I choose to read. Grant me wisdom and courageous discipline to choose what I watch on TV or in movies (even if I haven't a clue concerning what terribly popular show people around me are talking about). Help me to listen to others with care and concern, and still help me not to take in anything that doesn't belong to me (especially putdowns). In my sexual attitudes toward myself and others help me to always glorify You, Lord. Give me wisdom in medicines I use. And above all, let me listen to You every day. Let me

take in Your gracious love.  Take away memories of crud from the past, and let me rejoice in Your word and Your company with me as I enjoy this day You have given me.

Honoring You with votes
Graciously reach all people
Faithful steward, physically


1 Corinthians 7

3  The husband must fulfill his duty to his wife, and likewise also the wife to her husband.
This really sounded easy before we got married, Lord!  My "Yes!" was unequivocal and enthusiastic.  Upon further reflection, now that we are down the road a ways, it doesn't seem quite so easy.  Help me, Gracious Lord, to love my wife with all my heart and to let her know that daily.  Grant that I appreciate my wife and all she is and all she does and let her know that, also.  Help me to be sexually satisfying to my wife and help me not to let anything (like eating too much or drinking too much or being too tired) get in the way of satisfying her (and my) sexual needs.  Help me to stand up for what is right and give leadership with my wife as You show me (and us) Your will.  Grant that I listen to my wife, giving her my full attention, with respect and openness to her ideas (even if they are (can You imagine, Lord!?) different from mine).  Let me always be respectful and gracious to my wife in public (and at home), and grant that my attitude toward other women be respectful, without lust, and without any appearance of sexual openness.  And above all, grant that I clearly and transparently enjoy walking with my wife with You with joy and satisfaction in every day You give us.

14  For the unbelieving husband is sanctified through his wife, and the unbelieving wife is sanctified through her believing husband; for otherwise your children are unclean, but now they are holy.

When Paul wrote that, one person of a couple might come to You, Lord, and the other didn't. Today there are couples that seem to have chosen to be married where one is a Christian and the other isn't. Bless them, Lord. Bless all Christian people that they live Your Gospel message of forgiveness and joy and Life in You every day. Let them Live invitingly so that their spouse is drawn to You in the power of Your Holy Spirit. Protect Christians in marriage from being drawn away from You by their spouses. Let Your presence grow stronger every day in couples for the blessing of a currently unbelieving spouse and for the benefit of the couple's children. Let the Life of the believer powerfully touch their children, so that they will come to joyous Life in You also. Cast darkness and evil out of every marriage, and use families to be the foundation for our country and this world by Your grace and power.

35 This I say for your own benefit; not to put a restraint upon you, but to promote what is appropriate and *to secure* undistracted devotion to the Lord.
So there were distractions then, too, Lord! There certainly seem to be a lot now. In all that married couples do, Lord, working to provide for their families, helping out at school, helping out at church, finishing education or getting more education, taking children to dance class, tutoring, athletic practice, music lessons, and all that other stuff—please, Lord, let devotion to You be the clear priority of Life for every married couple and family. A lot of possible distractions (and those are only some of the "good" ones!). Please exclude from their lives all evil and all that draws children and couples away from You and away from each other. Limit all the supposed good things so that they don't pull families apart from You or each other. Bless single parents with wisdom, strength, faith and great resistance to the idea that they have to do everything to make it up to their children. Grant all of us, Your people, the power and guidance of Your Spirit to practice undistracted devotion to You, morning, day-long, and at close of day, every day, in what we choose, in

what we omit, in what we read, in what we say, in prayers, in attitudes—always with joy and confidence in You.

Loving my spouse. Also today.
Faith: Powerfully infectious in families
Real undistracted devotion to You.


1 Corinthians 8

1 Now concerning things sacrificed to idols, we know that we all have knowledge. Knowledge makes arrogant, but love edifies.
It sounds, Lord, like there was the group of people who said, "I know that meat is sacrificed to idols before it is offered for sale to the public, and so I know it is wrong to eat it." And there was the group who said, "I know that, and I know there are no gods but One God, so idols are not real, so I know it is right to eat the meat." Help me Lord, to enjoy learning, without ever thinking that what I know makes me better than other people. By Your grace, mix love with everything I know so that I may use things I learn to be a blessing and not to be an opportunity for arrogance. And when someone wants to tell me what they know, please help me to avoid jumping in trying to show that I know more. Rather grant that I listen with love and caring, seeing, by Your grace, what the person is saying from her or his point of view and not just from mine (as wonderful as I think mine is—sorry, Lord, looks like I need some humility in my listening, please, also).

6 ...yet for us there is *but* one God, the Father, from whom are all things and we *exist* for Him; and one Lord, Jesus Christ, by whom are all things, and we *exist* through Him. From You, Father—all these blessings are Your idea. Thank You, Lord! What great ideas You have! And they all come to us who live here, now by Your gracious hand, Lord Jesus. Thank You, Jesus. The sunrises, sunsets, hills, mountains, valleys, rivers, lakes, plains, oceans. The varieties of

architecture and materials for building. The mixture of historic and modern. The ability to enjoy being with a person for a day or a lifetime and the ability to remember it. Music and art, dance, theater, choirs and opera (ok, selectively). Ideas and interesting ways of expressing them. Gifts to us, Lord, thank You for them all. Help us, Gracious Lord, to not only appreciate all that You have given us, but help us to hold onto fiercely, as central to our being, that we enjoy things, people, ideas and life, all good coming from You, always Living for You, Father, through You, Jesus, inspired daily by You, Spirit, to Live to Your glory, alone.

9  But take care that this liberty of yours does not somehow become a stumbling block to the weak.
There are things that I can do that are helpful to me that would not be helpful for someone else, is that it Lord? There is a bell inside me that rings when I think about that. You mean all the things that I think are good are not universally good for every person? What a strange idea! (Actually bordering on arrogance and very isolated living.) I have been blessed in so many ways. And I find it so easy to just recommend all those things for everyone else. Help me to be sensitive to other people and their wants, enjoyments, goals, and ideas. Help me to listen. Help me not to impose my ideas of "terrific" on others. And in particular, keep me from suggesting something that has been a blessing to me, to others, for whom it would be hurtful. Gracious Lord, let me never speak or act in a way that draws anyone away from You and Your grace and love. Grant that I use the liberty You have given me, always to be a blessing to others.

Knowledge--always with love
Graciously enjoying purposefully
Liberty, and loving care


1 Corinthians 9

12 If others share the right over you, do we not more? Nevertheless, we did not use this right, but we endure all things so that we will cause no hindrance to the gospel of Christ.

Not at all a popular concept, Lord, giving up my rights. There are all those laws, constitutions, and the Bill of Rights. And the Patient's Bill of Rights. And the right to privacy (like someone would care about my gall bladder being either in or out). But some of the rights I have might get in the way of Your gospel reaching people—that's what I hear You saying. Help me to see what I have a right to, that would get in the way of Your blessing people with Your gospel, Lord Holy Spirit. Show me attitudes I have that might put people off from being drawn to You. Show me words I say that might be taken wrongly to push people away from You. Give me such satisfaction in Your love and grace that I do not need or want to demand any right that gets in Your way, Gracious Spirit. Let me be a channel of Your love without any self-centered hindrances.

14 So also the Lord directed those who proclaim the gospel to get their living from the gospel.

Thank You, Lord, for providing for those who proclaim the gospel to me and to all Your people. It appears that some of the people in Corinth had some trouble with that. And, truth be told, there are congregations today that have difficulty being willing to provide their pastors with a living from their ministry. Bless all Your servants, Lord, and provide the living that You want them to have from their work. Bless congregations so that they will graciously and generously provide for Your servants that proclaim Your gospel to them. Bless Your servants who receive their living from serving churches with wisdom in using what You give well, and grant them satisfaction with all Your provisions. And please bless me and all Christians so that we not only give offerings to our churches to help support Your servants, but that we also pray regularly, frequently, fervently, lovingly for those servants whom You have sent to bless us. Give them joy and satisfaction in serving You and us.

22 To the weak I became weak, that I might win the weak; I have become all things to all men, so that I may by all means save some.
It took a long time for some of us to get to the point where we are now, Lord. If we are flexible in the way we relate to various people, how will we manage to stay true to ourselves? But that's not the point, I hear You saying. The point is staying true to You. Grant me and all Your people, the ability and willingness to listen to other people, to relate to other people (particularly those who have not yet come into Your family), to reach out to people where they are in their education, employment, finances, family structure, and spiritual growth. Help us not to demand that everyone first be like us in order to come to You. Grant that in whatever situation we find ourselves that we reach out to others and rejoice together in becoming like You.

Rights surrendered to bless
Supporting Your servants well
Loving with listening, flexibility


1 Corinthians 10

4 ...and all drank the same spiritual drink, for they were drinking from a spiritual rock which followed them; and the rock was Christ.
I feel like I am on a journey, Lord. You have talked about Your people as those on a pilgrimage [ Psalm 84.5 ]. Please be there with me, Lord Jesus. Be the rock, the spiritual rock with me. In parts of the world, there are rocks that stand magnificently withstanding erosion. Thank You, Lord, Christ, Messiah, for being the Rock that never erodes. There are so many changes in life as the years go by. Thank You that You are the same—yesterday, today, and forever. Be

spiritual nourishment for me whatever turns there are in the path You choose for me. Give me the confidence that I may depend on You, listen to You, talk to You, trust You. Let nothing else be first in my life, Lord. If anything gets close to being most important instead of You, cut it off. Remove it from my life. Whether You lead me on a path lush with flowers and streams or through the desert, thank You, Lord, that I may drink from You, my Rock and my Redeemer.

13  No temptation has overtaken you but such as is common to man; and God is faithful, who will not allow you to be tempted beyond what you are able, but with the temptation will provide the way of escape also, so that you will be able to endure it.
Thank You, Lord, for Your promise. Not tempted beyond what I am able. Of course, the first thing that comes to my mind is someone offering me seventy three jillion dollars to reject You, and I can imagine taking a moment and then nobly saying that I'd rather have You than anything else. What You are talking about, Lord, I rather think, are the small denials that are so much easier. The times when I don't sound like I am Yours. The times when it is easier to choose justice for myself (because I deserve it!) rather than mercy toward others. Help me to see all the temptations that come to me, not with despair, but with the confidence that You provide me strength and wisdom to endure and to be faithful to You. Grant that in every temptation to despair because of worry or physical suffering I will look in confidence for Your way of escape and endurance—in Your grace, Your strength, Your love, Your joy, Your presence, Faithful Lord.

31  Whether, then, you eat or drink or whatever you do, do all to the glory of God.
It is easier, to be sure, to imagine worshiping You to Your glory, singing to Your glory, praying to Your glory, reading Your word to Your glory—those all seem to fit in with what is glorious to You. Eating? Drinking? You really know how to

get personal, Lord! Eating is more something I do to satisfy my hunger—that sounds good doesn't it Lord? Of course, what I really mean is that eating is something I do to satisfy my wants. (Which, depending on the day and how much fat, sugar, and salt are available can be vastly different from hunger.) So, yes, there is some room for improvement in my attitudes about eating and drinking. Thank You for the amazing number of choices I have when I go to the grocery store. Help me to remember people who have so many fewer choices or have no grocery stores or have no money to buy food. Help me to remember that just because something is available and is delicious, that doesn't exactly make it a blessing to me at this moment. Please grant me wisdom in what I eat and drink. Please grant that I am thankful for all the food and drink that You make available to me. And when I participate in food and drink that are luxurious in fat, sugar, and salt (and calories, etc.) (do church potlucks count?) help me to be satisfied with what is good for me. Please help me to have the same moderation and wisdom and fellowship with You in all the rest of "whatever you do" as well.

Drink from the Rock
Resist, endure, escape
Eat, drink, do—all for You


1 Corinthians 11

2  Now I praise you because you remember me in everything and hold firmly to the traditions, just as I delivered them to you.
Tradition today, Lord, seems like a mixed bag. There are traditions people have in families that have been a blessing. And some Christians enjoy worshiping You in ways that are not so traditional. But I hear You saying something different. There were the traditions of the elders which got in the way of Your gracious message. And there were the traditions

that Paul delivered to people that kept them close to You in the midst of a tumultuous world. Help Your people today to perceive clearly (in what surely is also a tumultuous world) the traditions that keep us close to You. Show us how to receive the traditions You deliver to us in Your word and through people whom we respect, and yet live in the newness of Your gospel applied to people today. Thank You for Your word, for worship of You, for prayer, listening to You and talking to You. Thank You for opportunities to Live for You in each day You give us. Thank You for opportunities to give to others, to be a blessing. Use Your traditions to keep us close to You no matter which way a wind happens to be blowing around us.

28  But a man must examine himself, and in so doing he is to eat of the bread and drink of the cup.
Before I eat and drink of the meal that You have given to Your people, Lord, give me clear vision to examine myself. There have been times in my life when I was so busy I seemed to be struggling to hold onto all the preparations I had made and there was no room for anything more that I could take in. Not good, I admit, Lord. If I am going to receive Your blessing, I first have to want it. And to want it, what really helps is if I recognize how much I need Your blessing. So help me to examine myself and see the gaping holes, the wounds still bleeding, the memories of hurtful words (spoken or imagined) dripping with venom, the stinking selfishness, the excruciatingly silly bubbles of "I can do it myself". Help me to see my many, intense needs for Your grace and Your forgiveness and Your presence in my life, so that I am indeed ready, hungry, open, consciously empty and greatly desiring Your blessings.

24, 25  …and when He had given thanks, He broke it and said, "This is My body, which is for you; do this in remembrance of Me." [25] In the same way *He took* the cup also after supper, saying, "This cup is the new covenant in

My blood; do this, as often as you drink *it*, in remembrance of Me."

When I receive Your body and the new covenant in Your blood be in my body, mind, heart, and spirit so that I receive Your blessings of forgiveness and Life in remembrance of You.  Help me to remember You, not with the attitude of the man whose wife told him to remember when the pot boils as she left, and then when she got back, he said it was about an hour ago, but rather with thoughts, words, and actions that show You and Your love in every moment.  Let remembering not be a sitting down event, but a getting up rejoicing and blessing others event.  Let people see the Light You put in my eyes and let them rejoice with me.  Let me remember after Your gracious meal, that You are with me, and I can remember You in all I do.  And if the joy I carry pushes some people away, let me also remember You as Someone Who was not exactly popular with everyone(!).

Traditions:  Close to You
Empty, repentant, ready
Remembering as loving, faith-filled action


1 Corinthians 12

7  But to each one is given the manifestation of the Spirit for the common good.

To me!  I know people who certainly appear to be gifted, Lord.  But that I should be in the company of those gifted—that's a great blessing.  And as I look around at the great variety of Your people, it is a wonder and a humbling awareness, that we each are given a spiritual gift by You, Lord Holy Spirit.  Thank You, Lord for manifesting Yourself to each of Your people.  Thank You that as I live today, that You are in me.  I feel sometimes, Lord, as if I am on the edge of Your people.  What can I do for the common good of Your people?  Yet, You promise that You are in me working for the common good, for the purposes of divine blessing that You want around me. I'm torn between asking You to show me what good I am doing and what gift I have, and on the other hand asking You to keep up the good work without letting me know so I won't be self-conscious. You know what is best, Lord. Show me what I need to know; help me to desire prayerfully to use the manifestation of a gift that You have given me, Lord God, Holy Spirit. Keep me from thinking too highly of myself (and from thinking too lowly of myself). Use me (and all Your people) today as You will.

11 But one and the same Spirit works all these things, distributing to each one individually just as He wills.
That's really a good idea, Lord. As if I could look over Your gifts that You use to bless Your people and pick what I think I would like! You are really good at this, Lord. With the Corinthians I might pick out something flashy (or what seems flashy to me) like going around healing people. The temptation to use Your gift to have people like me and think well of me would be easy to fall into. Thank You for being in charge. Thank You that in all of Your people, no matter what calling You give us, no matter what gift You want us to use, all the gifts come from You. We can depend on You to be working in and through each of us, all of us. When I gather with Your people, what a wonder as I look out—Gifted people! What a great group to be with! (Even if sometimes in a gathering it seems difficult to see the unity we have—help us Lord!) What a scary thought that when others are looking at me they are thinking the same thing and have high expectations of me, also! Grant me faith to trust You in using the gift You give me, effectively, to Your glory, every day.

24, 25 ...But God has *so* composed the body, giving more abundant honor to that *member* which lacked, [25] so that there may be no division in the body, but *that* the members may have the same care for one another.
How can we do that, Lord? Help me to get over the idea that everyone should look the way I do in my thoughts,

understandings, worship life. Grant that I will look around the world at the varieties of peoples who are part of Your family and see the unity that You see. We, Your people, love You, Lord. We thank You for bringing us to You and to Life. Grant that we rejoice together in You. Grant that we truly care for one another. Help us to see those members of Your family who need to be cared for in some way (whether they are neighbors, fellow church members, or those who live at some distance). Let differences of appearance not get in the way. Grant that we look with Your eyes to see those who need our caring help. Grant that we remember them in prayer and help in any way You want. And put upon our hearts whatever You want us to do to care for others, whether it is to pick out a group (or some groups) that we care for with prayers and financial help regularly or listen to You speaking through appeals throughout the year to discern where You want us to apply special care. Thank You for caring for us. Help us to care, with love, effectively, by Your grace.

Your gift, through me, blessing
Effective in Your choosing
Caring for each other


1 Corinthians 13

4  Love is patient, love is kind *and* is not jealous; love does not brag *and* is not arrogant.
Has patience always been one of the very difficult parts of love, Lord? It certainly is difficult now. It is difficult to imagine selfless, patient love, except when it is shown by someone else. Mother Teresa comes to my mind. But more particularly, You, Lord Jesus. Crowds and crowds of people came to You. Some of the people were selfish, some wanted a political fixer, some liked getting off work and hearing something new, some loved You and rejoiced in You as their Messiah. And You were patient and loved them all.

Help me, Lord, to be patient and kind with people. Especially when the temptation to be frustrated is intense, when someone doesn't say things the way I think would make sense, when someone doesn't appreciate what I think is wonderful, when someone is fervent about something I have difficulty with. Work through me, Lord, so that I can love with Your love with patience and kindness. (And, by the way, help my dear wife to love me with patience and kindness on those rare occasions (Ha!) when I might possibly (Agh!) be difficult to put up with(!).)

5 ...does not act unbecomingly; it does not seek its own, is not provoked, does not take into account a wrong *suffered*. I'm really good at letting people know, Lord, that I forgive them. If someone asks for forgiveness, I make sure I tell them, "I forgive you". Even if they don't specifically ask, I forgive them. The trouble is, later, when I talk to that person, sometimes I let my feelings and thoughts be colored by remembering the wrong I suffered. You are so good at letting go of my sins, Lord. Thank You for loving me today without holding on to any of the crud which I have perpetrated in various yesterdays. Help me, Lord. Grant that I let go of every hurt. Grant that when I forgive, You surgically remove every attachment of the hurt from my feelings and memory. Grant that I never go back and rehearse any time of hurt in my thinking or talking. Grant that I love people with a joyous relationship that only grows with wonder in Your love, every succeeding day.

8 Love never fails; but if *there are gifts of* prophecy, they will be done away; if *there are* tongues, they will cease; if *there is* knowledge, it will be done away.
You have shown me, and all Your people, Lord, that You are almighty, that You have power to start this world and to end it. It is only because You have shown us also that You are loving, always, that we can know You without despair and fear. Thank You that Your love never fails. Thank You for forgiving me in Jesus. Thank You for revealing Yourself in

Your word. Help me to know You, to grow in knowledge of You, to grow in faith by Your grace. But most of all, Lord, grant that I depend on Your love, above and beyond all knowing about You. Fill me so with Your gracious love, that my love for my family and my love for other people will never fail. Whether I understand others or not, whether I share commonalities in values and culture with other people or not, whether I disagree with others' actions or praise them, grant that by Your grace I will always love people, wanting Your love to flow through me.

Following You: Love, patient and kind
Following You: Excellence in forgetting
Following You: Love beyond all else


1 Corinthians 14

1,3 Pursue love, yet desire earnestly spiritual *gifts*, but especially that you may prophesy. 3 But one who prophesies speaks to men for edification and exhortation and consolation.
Thank You, Lord Jesus, that Your people may pursue love. Help us to pursue love, not that we be loved, but that we be loving. And in love for other people, grant that we proclaim You, proclaim Who You are, proclaim Your word. Grant that we proclaim You by the choices we make, by the things we buy, by the groups we support. Help us to proclaim You when we are filled with joy, but also when we are disgruntled, frustrated, and tired. Grant that we proclaim You in a way that gives people consolation in the midst of the challenges and difficulties that they experience. Thank You for proclaiming Your love to us, consoling us in every sorrow.

12 So also you, since you are zealous of spiritual *gifts*, seek to abound for the edification of the church.

Thank You Gracious Lord for the beautiful, inspiring church buildings that You have provided for us. Please grant that every time we see one of those buildings we remember with joy Your calling to build up the Church. It is easier by far to see the needs for physical buildings and repairs. Help us to see the ways You give us to build up Your Church. It is surely Your Spirit that builds Your Church, thank You for using us in Your building work. Bless us that we use the gifts You give us so that they all promote the building up of Your Church. When we look at the picture of the new church building we are sometimes filled with enthusiasm to participate in the building fund. Give us enthusiasm to continually delight, not just in our own satisfaction in what we get from our local churches, but in the Church, Your body here on earth, and in the joy and wonder that we share together in You. Show us, please, Lord, how we may participate in building up Your Church today.

24, 25 But if all prophesy, and an unbeliever or an ungifted man enters, he is convicted by all, he is called to account by all; [25] the secrets of his heart are disclosed; and so he will fall on his face and worship God, declaring that God is certainly among you.

OK, Lord, yes, that is definitely what we, Your people, want. Even though sometimes it looks like what we want is better potlucks, more money in the treasury, ministers who agree with us (in whatever enthusiasm we are enjoying at the moment), and youth groups that solve all the problems we think our youth have (which their parents have not been able to figure out!). Get our focus where it needs to be, Lord. Grant that we welcome, not just people from other churches who we think would make a nice addition to our fellowship, but unbelievers, those who are living separate from You, people in trouble who need help, even that cranky neighbor who makes churlish remarks about us. And when people who need You arrive, grant that they experience Your word of law, showing them their great need, and Your word of Gospel, showing them their great Savior. Let us proclaim

You, in all we say and do, to Your glory, and to the eternal blessing of all who enter.

Lovingly proclaiming You
Gifted, edifying
Welcoming to fellowship with You


1 Corinthians 15

10  But by the grace of God I am what I am, and His grace toward me did not prove vain; but I labored even more than all of them, yet not I, but the grace of God with me.
I have indeed tried to do things by myself, Lord.  What a mess!  There are those times when I worry before I do something.  And then I realize that there You are standing next to me, asking me, "Are you sure you want to do this by yourself, Michael?"  How arrogant I am!  That I think I can do things by myself.  How egocentric that I think I should do things by myself.  I'm sorry, Lord.  Please forgive me.  Whatever You give me the privilege of doing, Lord, grant that I do not forge ahead without You.  Grant that whatever I do, I do by Your grace.  Let Your grace flow through my thinking, speaking, and doing.  By Your grace I am what I am today.  What a terrific plan You have, Lord!  Thank You!

22, 23, 42  For as in Adam all die, so also in Christ all will be made alive.  [23] But each in his own order: Christ the first fruits, after that those who are Christ's at His coming.  42  So also is the resurrection of the dead. It is sown a perishable *body*, it is raised an imperishable *body*.
I remember, Lord, when I went to that retirement seminar.  Retirement, of course, was a ways off, but it seemed like a good thing to know something about.  And the presenter said that after retiring, the next big thing was dying.  What I hear You saying is that the next big thing after retiring is being made alive.  Dying is a small thing along the way.  The really big thing is when You make me alive again.  At Jesus'

coming, I get to have new Life in You. Thank You, Lord. And Life with an imperishable body. Now that sounds terrific. I like my body, Lord. I appreciate the medicines You have arranged for the parts of my body that don't operate quite according to Your original owner's manual. But to be alive and imperishable—nothing will ever stop working, nothing will ever slow down, nothing will ever need replacing. What a deal! Thank You, Lord! I am really looking forward to that! Thank You for now. And thank You that even now I can look forward to Then!

58 Therefore, my beloved brethren, be steadfast, immovable, always abounding in the work of the Lord, knowing that your toil is not *in* vain in the Lord.
I really appreciate Your telling me this, Lord. Because sometimes it is really hard to tell if my working in the opportunities You give is really doing any good. I suppose there is a part of me that would like a bell to go off (with a flashing light in rainbow colors would be nice) when I do something that helps someone, or when I do something that will eventually be a blessing. (Not that others would see, just for me would be nice.) Right, a trifle self-centered and vain. OK. So, here is the bell. Here is the rainbow of lights in Your "therefore". Therefore, because of Your rising and promise to bring Your people to Life eternally with You in joy and satisfaction, therefore, I can be steadfast, immovable, effective in serving You. Help me to be steadfast. Grant that I serve immovably next to You. Grant that I abound in working for You. And thank You for the certainty that in all You give me to do (wherever and whenever) Living in You, my living and working is not in vain. Keep me in You. Accomplish what You want through me, Gracious Lord. Thank You!

Living by grace today!
Coming soon! Imperishable Life!
Effective Living: Happening now.

# 1 Corinthians 16

**1, 2** Now concerning the collection for the saints, as I directed the churches of Galatia, so do you also. ² On the first day of every week each one of you is to put aside and save, as he may prosper, so that no collections be made when I come.

Thank You, Lord, that You give us the opportunity to participate in Your ministry to people in need. Bless Your people so that we will work together. Grant that we recognize those in Your family who are in need. Help us to organize our desire to minister to people with love, so that we are effective in helping people. Gracious Spirit, motivate all Your people so that we will be generous with our giving. Help us to see that all that we have, prospering in each day, comes from You. Grant that we recognize that You have made us stewards of what You have given us. Bless us that we may practice faith-filled stewardship in giving, knowing that You give us what we need so that we are able to give to others in their need. Please bless all the ministries which distribute gifts to those in need. Bless them with wisdom, fill them with the joy of serving You, and populate them with Your servants gifted with love and administration to Your glory. Bless them and the people they serve with our generous giving (inspired and enabled by You).

**9** ...for a wide door for effective *service* has opened to me, and there are many adversaries.

Thank You, Gracious Lord, for opening doors for reaching people in this day. Bless Your people with recognizing the open doors that You provide. Bless Your churches with sending Your servants to work with the people You want to reach. Let them be effective by the power of Your Holy Spirit. Grant that Your workers will have what they need in the ministries You provide. And since change is still threatening to people today, protect Your servants in ministry from the adversaries that resist change and in particular resist You and Your grace. Take away the power they try to use against Your grace and ministries. Grant protection from Satan and all evil. Be present in Your ministries and grant Your eternal Light and Life. And keep us, Your people, faithful in our prayer support of all Your gracious, Life-giving work.

18  For they have refreshed my spirit and yours. Therefore acknowledge such men.
Yes, Lord, thank You!  Thank You for those many people who have refreshed my spirit.  Thank You for my parents and those who encouraged me as a child.  Thank You for those who brought me close to You with Your word.  Thank You for those I name in my heart.  Help me to remember them—Your wonderful servants who spoke a word when I needed it, who led seminars that inspired me, who simply said, "No", when to say, "Oh, all right" would have been so much easier.  Thank You for Your servants who have written and inspired me.  Bless others through them. (Especially C. S. Lewis, G. K. Chesterton, Hannah Hurnard, Oswald Chambers, and Peter Kreeft—thank You.)  I have lost contact with many people who, by Your grace, have refreshed me—if they are still serving You here, please bless them with great joy and satisfaction in serving You.  If they are with You, please grant that their work keeps multiplying in grace through the people whom they have touched with Your love and joy.  And grant that I refresh someone's spirit today.

Together, giving, for those in need
Effective gracious work with protection
Spirit refreshers:  Bless them!

# 2 Corinthians

2 Corinthians 1

4 ...who comforts us in all our affliction so that we will be able to comfort those who are in any affliction with the comfort with which we ourselves are comforted by God.
Your presence is comfort above all, Lord. Thank You, Jesus, for loving us and recognizing when we are burdened with sorrow, depression, fear, turmoil, loneliness, sickness, pain, or disappointment. Sometimes it isn't so clear to us. It seems easier to feel angry, to lash out at someone else around us. Help us to recognize the times when we are going through affliction. Grant that we recognize Your comforting words and presence with us. Send us family or friends to bring Your comfort. And help us to grow strong through every affliction, so that we can recognize other people going through afflictions. Use us, Gracious Lord, to bring Your comfort to them as we love them, care for them, share the comfort You have given us, and spend time with them. Thank You, Lord, for using even yucky times in our lives to grow into blessings.

9 ...indeed, we had the sentence of death within ourselves so that we would not trust in ourselves, but in God who raises the dead.
It would be terrific, Lord, if there were an easier way. Perhaps we could just be aware of things happening to other people that bring the threat of death to them, perhaps we could learn from that. But I hear You saying that is not nearly as effective as when it happens to us personally. Right. I suppose You're right. Nothing like personal experience. So please help me to notice clearly when I am scared to death, when there is some sickness, or weight of sorrow that tempts me to despair—help me to see clearly that NOW! is the time to recognize absolutely that I cannot

trust in myself. There is nothing I can do. There is no set of carefully planned objectives that will lead out of the mess. There is only You. You Who give all life and all Life, let me focus on You. Let me depend only on You. Let me trust You alone, knowing for sure, that as You raise the dead, You can and will lead me through the valley of the shadow of death to more Life with You, either here or there.

20 For as many as are the promises of God, in Him they are yes; therefore also through Him is our Amen to the glory of God through us.

There are so many wonderful guarantees, Lord. Everything I buy has a guarantee. Of course, they are written at great length in small print with a terrible lot of exclusionary circumstances. And the directions to follow to claim help from the guarantees assume that I have a lot of time, a complete packaging center, and the funds to ship the thing to some place that, from the name, I seriously question exists. Your promises are so different. They are yes. Just yes. Grant that when I read Your word or hear your word, I take in all Your promises. Grant that I depend on them in Your grace. And grant that I also recognize all the times You keep Your promises. There are so many promises You make to me that You have kept, loving me, providing for me, opening opportunities for me with Your blessing, blessing my family, helping us through every difficulty. Give me a heart ready with a fervent "Amen!" for every promise You keep. I could be very busy Amen-ing. And thank You Lord, that's just fine.

Comforted to comfort
In life, through death, trusting You
Blessed indeed! Amen!


2 Corinthians 2

4  For out of much affliction and anguish of heart I wrote to you with many tears; not so that you would be made sorrowful, but that you might know the love which I have especially for you.

I remember, Lord, when people wrote letters! I guess that makes me old. I don't, of course, mean business letters, but social letters. Not just the Christmas ones. Now there are so many ways to communicate. And yet, You show this picture of Paul writing from his heart, concerned about the people in Corinth, and his purpose in writing was to let them know the love he had for them. There actually is writing that I do now, Lord. You have given me the privilege of texting and there are varieties of social media. Help me to write purposefully so that no matter what I am communicating, I communicate the love that I have for the people to whom I am writing. That will certainly color the way I write (that is, text or whatever). Please, Gracious Lord, color all my communications with the love You have for me and the love I have for others.

10, 11  But one whom you forgive anything, I *forgive* also; for indeed what I have forgiven, if I have forgiven anything, *I did it* for your sakes in the presence of Christ, [11] so that no advantage would be taken of us by Satan, for we are not ignorant of his schemes.

Thank You, Lord, that I don't have to be afraid of Satan. I know he is powerful and a great enemy. But by Your grace, I may know of his schemes. Help me to be cognizant of every scheme of his and give me wisdom and strength by Your grace, to avoid or resist all of them. In particular, help me to recognize my need to forgive people. I wouldn't leave the door of my home standing open overnight, inviting burglars to come in. Please grant me grace always to forgive so that I never leave the way open for Satan to take advantage of me in my allowing an unforgiving spirit, in my holding on to something someone has done with resentment or constant rehearsal in my mind and heart. Grant that by Your Spirit and grace, I forgive, let go of, and work hard to forget everything that anyone has ever done to me or others. Please, fill that wound in my spirit with Your healing peace and joy, Gracious Lord.

14  But thanks be to God, who always leads us in triumph in Christ, and manifests through us the sweet aroma of the knowledge of Him in every place.
I remember that time I was in a small parade with some young people with crowds of people looking at us. I felt rather self-conscious, Lord. So here You say I am always in a parade, on display. Thanks be to You, people are not looking at me, but at Your triumph in Christ in me. Help me to be honest, always, with other people, so that I never claim to be self-reliant, good, never in need—as if I didn't need a Savior. Let people see You in me, Lord. Yes, it's ok to show every one of Your triumphs in me, even if that means showing how very much I needed You and still need You. Even if it means showing dark and yucky moments from which You rescued me. Whatever You want to show that helps manifest the wonderful aroma of the knowledge of Jesus, my Savior. All my triumph is in You, Lord Jesus. So show Your triumph through me, in every place You lead me. My joy is to celebrate knowledge of You and Your gracious triumph, even in me.

Communication:  Love colored
Forgiveness:  Closing doors to evil
Your triumph:  Even in me


2 Corinthians 3

5, 6  Not that we are adequate in ourselves to consider anything as *coming* from ourselves, but our adequacy is from God, 6  who also made us adequate *as* servants of a new covenant, not of the letter but of the Spirit; for the letter kills, but the Spirit gives life.

I'm glad, Lord, that I don't have to pretend that I understand completely everything You say to me or that I am capable to do all that You give me to do. That would be arrogant and pretty dumb. I admit, the terrible thing is, sometimes I think good things come from me (without You). Please forgive me, Lord. Thank You for making me adequate as one of Your servants. Give me, please, all I need to serve You in the new covenant of the Spirit. Grant that Life comes to people through my serving You. You are the One Who gives Life, please use me to bless people with the adequacy You give, not because of who I am or what I have done, but because of Who You are and what You have done.

12 Therefore having such a hope, we use great boldness in *our* speech.
If You are the One who works through us in all we do, if You have chosen and equipped us as Your servants, then we can be bold in speech, not because we are terrific, very educated, absolutely faithful servants of Yours, but because You have given us and all people eternal hope in You. Because You give us Life, because our hope that sustains us holds onto Your promises of Life with You in joy forever, we can be bold in our speech. Give us boldness in what we say to people. If eternal grace from You is a reality now in our lives, grant that we recognize Your love and the wonder of Your creation as we talk with people. Grant that we speak of You as the One Who has given us Life without end. Grant that we speak Your name, Jesus, in our conversation, giving You thanks and credit for Your creation and for Your care and love to us. Grant that we mention You as we part from people with, "Jesus bless you!" or "Jesus take care of you!" Show us how to speak Your name in blessing in our conversations, and fill us with Your Spirit so that we will speak with the boldness You give.

18 But we all, with unveiled face, beholding as in a mirror the glory of the Lord, are being transformed into the same image from glory to glory, just as from the Lord, the Spirit.

I see the descriptions of You and Your grace, love, and glory, Lord Jesus, and I see my reflection in a mirror, and I know there is a lot of difference. Thank You Lord, Holy Spirit, for transforming me into the image with glory from You that You want. It helps to recognize, Lord, that I am a work in progress. The transforming is still going on. Please grant that I do not slip away from Your gracious transforming. Help me not to wander. Help me not to resist. Keep changing me, Lord, in the way You want. Use the nourishment of Your word and grace to keep the transformation going. And help the people around me to be patient with me, recognizing that You are not finished with me yet. (And help me recognize that You are not finished with them yet, either. Also, help me (and them) to resist giving You suggestions on what needs to be improved!)

Spirit adequacy for Life
From hope: Bold speech
During transformation: Patience, thanks


2 Corinthians 4

2 ...but we have renounced the things hidden because of shame, not walking in craftiness or adulterating the word of God, but by the manifestation of truth commending ourselves to every man's conscience in the sight of God. Yes, Lord, there have been times when I have been tempted to slightly bend (!) Your word to make it apply today in a way that fits what I want. Terrible! I'm sorry, Lord. Grant that I daily renounce things hidden because of shame and never adulterate Your word. Please let Your truth show in my life. Help me to show Your truth to people I meet commending myself to them, not by any power or greatness in myself, but that the surpassing greatness of Your power [v7] show through in all I say to people and in all I do. Thank You for being willing to manifest Your truth in me, a sinner, an earthen vessel [v7]. Help me to remember every day, that I

don't have to be clever or eloquent to serve You. I don't have to be dramatic by my design. Serving You does not depend on my attractively packaging Your love and truth. Help me to serve You, depending only on You with faith in You and trust that You and Your truth showing in me are not only enough, but the great and only value that I have to offer.

16  Therefore we do not lose heart, but though our outer man is decaying, yet our inner man is being renewed day by day.
Thank You, Lord, I really need Your gracious assurance. As the years go by my outer physical and even mental personness keeps having stuff happen. (Imagine! Eating pizza crust was hazardous to my (now broken) tooth!) When I was 20, this verse did not have nearly as much meaning as it does now—thank You for the continued assurance of Your presence. Even if there are things in my body that don't work as well as they used to, and even if I have a few replacement parts, I don't have to lose heart. Thank You, Lord, that more candles on my birthday cake don't have to be discouraging. (Of course, I do think I am past the fire department's published limit now.) Thank You for renewing my inner person, for my being with You and in You, for my Life which You have given me—thank You for renewing me every day. I may have a new ache when I get up every morning, but by Your grace, thank You that I always have new Life with You, a closer walk with You. Thank You that my Life with You never gets old. Draw me closer to You, please, Gracious Lord, every day.

18  ...while we look not at the things which are seen, but at the things which are not seen; for the things which are seen are temporal, but the things which are not seen are eternal.
I really do like things I see, Lord. I like seeing people I love. I like seeing the beautiful mountains, the flowers, the cityscape, and the many other wonders You have put around me. Thank You, that although they are all going away, there will be much more wonderful things to see at home with You.

So, while I enjoy seeing things now, help me to look with joy and great satisfaction at the things that are not seen physically now. Help me to see Your fruit, Lord Holy Spirit, flowing in the hearts and minds of Your people: Love, joy, peace, patience, kindness, goodness, faithfulness, gentleness, self-control. Thank You for the eternal that You bring into this world. When I am perplexed and tempted to despair, help me to see and rejoice in Your invisible eternal gifts that You graciously make visible to us here, now.

Truly showing Jesus
Made new today!
Looking at Your eternal gifts


2 Corinthians 5

4  For indeed while we are in this tent, we groan, being burdened, because we do not want to be unclothed but to be clothed, so that what is mortal will be swallowed up by life. When some part of my body doesn't work the way I want it to, Lord, I feel with Paul's idea of being unclothed. I really don't want my body to stop working. I feel very attached to my body. So thank You, Lord for lifting my vision beyond my physical living now, to the wonderful Life that You have prepared for me. All the things that seem so big to me now, all the things for which I spend time and money and visits to doctors—all of them by Your gracious plan are so small they will be swallowed up by the Life You have prepared for Your people. I still enjoy feeling good and living now, and yet, keep me focused, Lord, on the Life enormous beyond all life. In the living and breathing that You allow me to enjoy now, let me always recognize my enjoyment as coming from the joy of going through this life to Life that swallows up every mortal part of now—Life that will give me joy eternal with You.

14, 15 For the love of Christ controls us, having concluded this, that one died for all, therefore all died; [15] and He died for all, so that they who live might no longer live for themselves, but for Him who died and rose again on their behalf.
To wake up and remember that Life has no end—this is Your gift of beginning each day, Lord. Thank You. And because You have died for us, Your people, we are Alive in You and Your love controls us. Take over our lives, Lord. Be in control. Lead us and empower us in the choices and decisions we make. Help us to see how we may Live for You in all that we do. Show us how to Live for You in starting the day, with beginning preparations, attitudes and conversation shared with others. Bless us in Living for You in what You have given us to do in the day. If we are alone, help us to give the time and activity to You Who are with us. If we are with other people, help us to Live for You with them in all we think and say and do. In the chores, in helping family or friends, in choosing end of the day entertainment, reading, loving, caring—let us do these for You, Lord. And as we end our day, let us entrust our day to You to use for blessing and ourselves to You to care for us and refresh us with sleep. In all we are and do, Gracious Lord, let us Live for You, Who have died and risen, Who love us and care for us, Who are with us in every moment. Thank You, Lord, that we may Live for You today!

20 Therefore, we are ambassadors for Christ, as though God were making an appeal through us; we beg you on behalf of Christ, be reconciled to God.
To be an ambassador sounds glamourous and exciting. Living in a foreign country, representing my country. Being recognized as a person of importance. Ah, but there is that—recognized. So people are looking at me, Lord, and expecting everything I am and do to look like it comes from You. That is challenging. OK. Thank You for making me Your ambassador, but stay close, Lord. Grant that when others look at me they see Your caring love. When I am with other people and You want to make an appeal to them

through me, help me to get out of the way, so Your appeal comes through clearly.  Grant that I focus time, prayer, and attention to being reconciled to You.  Help me to recognize my sin, that I will repent and by Your grace receive Your forgiveness so that I may be Your ambassador of forgiveness.  And about living in a foreign country, Lord, help me to rejoice in You and Live in joy in the midst of a people whose focus tends to be hampered by frustration, fear, sorrow, disappointment, worry, confusion, loneliness, and selfishness.  In my life, Lord, help me to keep the Light on, for those looking for Light in darkness.

Joy in life from Life
Living for You:  all the time
Ambassador:  You through me


2 Corinthians 6

12, 13  You are not restrained by us, but you are restrained in your own affections.  [13] Now in a like exchange—I speak as to children—open wide *to us* also.
It's not that I hold back purposefully, Lord.  I don't think I exactly realize that I am holding back.  I guess my experience is to have a basic level of protection, by not being completely open with everyone, and then when I do open up, I have trouble doing it.  I think I am open, when I am half closed, just because my grip is so tight.  Help me to be open with You, Lord.  Help me to see when I am holding back.  Show me the things I am holding onto that I don't want to see.  Fill me completely, so that there is nothing between us.  Grant that by faith I will Live without fear, with joy in Your presence, open to listen to You, open to have You clean my house with Your gracious power and forgiveness.  If there are any times when I should practice some being closed, (social media, times of tactfulness), show me how to do that without pulling away from complete

openness to You. Thank You for being open to me in Jesus through Your Spirit!

17 "Therefore, COME OUT FROM THEIR MIDST AND BE SEPARATE," says the Lord.
"AND DO NOT TOUCH WHAT IS UNCLEAN;
And I will welcome you."
There were people then, Lord, who put idols and other things first in their lives. It was really important for Your people to come from their midst and be separate. Sometimes I am tempted to think that I live in a very different time. Fat chance! Putting things first instead of You is widespread if not rampant around me. I cannot leave the planet, but I ask You to do Your security sweep of my attitudes every morning. Grant that I enter every day separate and united with You. Keep me separate from every priority that takes me away from You. Give me clear vision to recognize when I am not separate, when I am following the herd. Grant that without fear of other people, I stay away from all that is unclean, and rejoice only in being separate and together with You. As You give me opportunity to be with other people, Lord, help me to stay graciously separate, with Your other people (not obnoxious, uppity, or arrogant) and help me to Live as a loving invitation to being separate, together with You.

18 "And I will be a father to you,
And you shall be sons and daughters to Me,"
Says the Lord Almighty.
You honor me so much, Lord. You have blessed me with forgiveness and new Life in You. You call me to serve You. And You even make me Your child. I forget who I am sometimes, Lord. Help me remember. Help me remember when I hear what has happened in the world every day. Help me to remember I am Your child. Help me to remember when I am doing mundane chores. Help me to remember with thanksgiving and gratitude when I have the opportunity to care about and love someone. Help me to

remember when someone says something that hurts, when I have to listen to anger, when someone shares their frustrations and discouragements. Help me to remember and Live as Your child speaking Your words, sharing Your love, encouraging with Your Spirit. When people get to know me, let them recognize Who my Father is.

Always, everywhere, open to You
Separate, loving, with You
My Father's child


2 Corinthians 7

1 Therefore, having these promises, beloved, let us cleanse ourselves from all defilement of flesh and spirit, perfecting holiness in the fear of God.
You have promised us, Lord, to be our Father and that we shall be Your sons and daughters. Thank You Lord for Your wonderful promises. Please bless us, Your people, that we will be washed clean by Your forgiveness from all the physical and spiritual things that contaminate us and pull us from You. Please give us discernment, strength, and self-control so that we will avoid things that try to fill us with priorities that are not Yours, whether they are in entertainment, food, beverage, reading, socialization, or attitudes. Keep us strong so that we delight in holiness not because we think we have to, but because we hold in our hearts a sense of great awe at Your presence with us, whether we are working, eating, drinking, relaxing, reading, watching television or other entertainment. Let us make choices that honor You. Keep us in Your gift of holiness, rejoicing in Your presence.

6, 7 But God, who comforts the depressed, comforted us by the coming of Titus; [7] and not only by his coming, but also by the comfort with which he was comforted in you, as he reported to us your longing, your mourning, your zeal for me; so that I rejoiced even more.

There are times, Lord, when You have seen our depression, our discouragement, the difficulty we had finding a reason to get up in the morning. And You have touched our lives with someone to bless us. Thank You, Lord. Please lift up our hearts and spirits today with the gifts You give us, with the opportunities You open to us to serve You today, and with the people around us. Let us see You with us today, Gracious Lord. And You give us people whose spirits we may lift. Give us the right words and actions, Lord, so that whether it is a text we send, an email, a letter (can You imagine, Lord?!), a gift, a visit—grant that by Your power we may show others that we miss them, that we care about them, and that they are in our thoughts and prayers. Please use us to lift spirits today, Gracious Lord.

10 For the sorrow that is according to *the will of* God produces a repentance without regret, *leading* to salvation, but the sorrow of the world produces death.

If I pay attention, Lord, there is a lot of sorrow in the world. I'm afraid that I don't always pay attention. The sorrow I see in the world, whether it is anger between people, accidents, family or personal tragedies, crime, selfishness, or abject stupidity—the result is depression, hopelessness, bitterness, pessimism (generally hidden in a cloak of "having a sense of reality"), broken relationships, broken families, and a lot of other experiences of death touching life here. So I have tuned that out a lot, Lord. Help me to care for people as You give me opportunity without being overwhelmed by the sorrow of the world. Please bless all people who suffer in this world, Gracious Lord, with hope and joy in You. And when it comes to the sorrow I experience about my failures and the disobedience and disrespect I have shown You and my failures to listen to You, please help me to go on to repentance. Help me not to get stuck in sorrow. Lead me to change of mind and heart and spirit, by Your grace, so that the sorrow I experience leads me to closer Life with You.

Holy choosing, walking with You
Comforted to comfort
Sorrow, repentance, change, Life


2 Corinthians 8

4, 5  …begging us with much urging for the favor of participation in the support of the saints, [5] and *this*, not as we had expected, but they first gave themselves to the Lord and to us by the will of God.
Thank You, Lord, for the example of the people in Macedonia. Please fill Your people with this spirit of desire today. Can You imagine, Lord, if all the people who go shopping at midnight or early in the morning on the Friday after Thanksgiving, would line up at churches and charities at those times begging for the favor of participation in the fundraising You have in process to be a blessing to people? I know You can imagine it, Lord. I have some trouble with that. But by Your grace it is possible. Help us, Your people, by Your grace, filled with Your Spirit, to give ourselves first to You, Lord, so that we are filled with joy, anticipation, and enthusiasm for giving to You for people whom You want to bless. Amen! Make it happen, Lord!

9  For you know the grace of our Lord Jesus Christ, that though He was rich, yet for your sake He became poor, so that you through His poverty might become rich.
There are so many get rich books available, Lord! Just follow these 7 (15, 25…) steps and blah, blah. So then when a person looks at rich people it might be expected that they are all satisfied, enjoying life, blessed and wonderful people. (And, of course, You have blessed some of them that way, Lord.) But most of them don't seem to be there. Grant us, Your people, the joy of recognizing real riches in You, Lord Jesus. You have joy, Life without end, wonder, awe, real satisfaction in Living. And by Your sacrifice of

Yourself and all You had, You give us riches beyond our imagination, not accessible through money or hard work. Thank You, Lord. Help us to realize how rich we are. Grant that we Live in satisfaction in You. Let no fears of living get in the way of satisfaction in Life in You. And bless those people who are on the blah, blah 7 or so step plans who may not know You—bless them with eyes opened to the riches of Your sacrifice, Your love, and Your gift of Life and joy unending.

21 ...for we have regard for what is honorable, not only in the sight of the Lord, but also in the sight of men.
You have graciously given me the opportunity to serve You in the days You give me, Lord. You change the plan from time to time, in Your gracious will. And You give me strength for each day. Grant me wisdom and skill so that I will not only follow You faithfully, but give the appearance to others of Your love and grace in Life. Bless me that my words not only carry meaning to me in my dependence on You, but that they are clear and not misleading to my family and others who hear me. Help me not to sound like something I don't mean. Let my loving words and actions never sound hurtful or mean. And bless Your Church and all Your churches and charities so that all money is handled in a way that honors You, also in the appearance that is given to people who might observe the administration of those funds.

Enthusiastic generosity
Rich and satisfied
Visible faithfulness


2 Corinthians 9

7 Each one *must do* just as he has purposed in his heart, not grudgingly or under compulsion, for God loves a cheerful giver.

Bless my purposing, Lord. I set a purpose with my heart, and sometimes it fades over time. Or something comes up and it gets pushed aside. There are times, too, when fear locks up my heart, so that I find it very difficult to set a blessed purpose in my heart of what I really want to do that is important and honors You. Grant me Your grace and power to purpose well. In particular help me to rejoice in all You have given and grant that I decide to give from what I have received, that I willingly give, and that I effectively carry out giving with a joyful spirit. Help me to give not just because I am convinced that a person or a charity is wonderful and in Your will, not just because I am convinced that the need is important and urgent, but because I love You, and You provide the opportunity to give to one of Your ministries. Let me trust You completely and give cheerfully.

8 And God is able to make all grace abound to you, so that always having all sufficiency in everything, you may have an abundance for every good deed.
Thank You, Lord! What a promise! Sufficiency in everything! OK, I am just a little iffy on "everything". My suspicion is that You are thinking of what I need, and I am thinking of what I want. I've got to adjust my thinking, I suppose, Lord. Right. Help me to see how You graciously provide for what I need. Help me to see the blessings You give. And grant me satisfaction in Your blessings. Remind me (I really do know this, surely by now!) that I never get satisfied with wants. When I let them lead, they, all of a sudden, multiply. "Why, there is this, and this, and that, and I forgot about those…" So help me Lord to see the abundance that You give me so that I can rejoice (and take in satisfaction) in giving for all the good that You give me to do. Lead me, Lord—satisfaction in receiving and satisfaction in giving.

13 Because of the proof given by this ministry, they will glorify God for *your* obedience to your confession of the

gospel of Christ and for the liberality of your contribution to them and to all.
So, Lord, when I give in the power of Your Spirit with liberality, You are holding that up as proof to the world that Your gospel is real, powerful, and full of Life-giving power. That's really amazing, that You do all that, just with my giving. Certainly it is Your gospel that shows me Jesus my Savior. And knowing Jesus (and being known by Him in grace and love!) changes my life of existence to Life lived with You. So thank You, Lord, for the privilege of such consequences to the Holy Spirit moving me to give with liberality and joy. It's not me, it's You and Your grace. Wave the flag of Your grace being effective. Stir people to praise You and give glory to You. Help me to recognize every opportunity You give me to give, without hesitation, without fear. Let me share in the joy of giving glory to You, by my giving and by all Your people giving. Praise and glory to You for multiplying Your provisions, motivating Your people with Your grace, and shining the light of Your love through loving liberality.

Purposeful joyful giving
Satisfaction: Receiving and giving
Grace. Giving. Glory to You.


2 Corinthians 10

5 *We are* destroying speculations and every lofty thing raised up against the knowledge of God, and *we are* taking every thought captive to the obedience of Christ.
Thoughts. Now that sounds difficult, Lord. I sometimes think I do pretty well in my words and actions (which is a delusion, Lord, I'm sorry—it's just that I do better at them than at my thinking). Help me, Lord, to put all my words and actions under Your guidance and direction. Be in control, and in Your grace, keep me out of Your way. And when it comes to thoughts, Lord, take them captive. Keep them in

obedience to You.  When fear, selfishness, wool-gathering, worry, thoughts about preparing to deal with evil that has not happened yet—when they try to push into my thoughts, Lord, let Your Spirit guard me and send those back where they came from (certainly not from You).  Bring me into the habit of passing every thought through Your evil detector.  Make my every thought captive to obedience to You, Gracious Lord Jesus.

12, 13  For we are not bold to class or compare ourselves with some of those who commend themselves; but when they measure themselves by themselves and compare themselves with themselves, they are without understanding. [13] But we will not boast beyond *our* measure, but within the measure of the sphere which God apportioned to us as a measure, to reach even as far as you.
It starts in school, I think, Lord.  Comparing ourselves to others.  How well we fit into the boxes of expectations along with the other students around us.  Then we are compared when we apply for a scholarship, a school, a job, a promotion.  Not Your plan.  You have given each of us, Your people, a place, a calling, a sphere.  Since we seem to want to analyze, help us to analyze where we are in Your calling.  Help us to recognize the direction in which You are calling us.  Help me not to compare myself with other people, with other Christians, with others in the opportunities You have given me.  Let my desire be to follow You, in the place where You have put me, in the sphere where You call me to serve.  Help me measure the direction of my compass to line it up with Yours.  Help me to use the full zeal You give me in Living, without settling for anything less.  Let my analysis always be filled with Your hope, joy, clear vision, and the power of Your gospel to follow You faithfully.

17  But HE WHO BOASTS IS TO BOAST IN THE LORD.
I remember the story, Lord, of the man who had pictures (slides in the old story!) of the Jonestown flood.  He used to show them to audiences, far and wide.  Then after he died,

he offered to show them in heaven to a gathering there, and You told him that was fine. Then on the evening in question, You reminded him that Noah was in the audience. I can think of things that I have boasted of, if only to myself. But real, valuable, wonderful, healthy, and encouraging boasting is always in You. I have so much to boast of in You, Lord. You have given me Your word, so powerful that You use it to bring me to Life and to joy, wonder, awe, and satisfaction in You. You have given me people who care about me and who have blessed me. You work through Your people to shine Your Light to peoples around the world, bringing people to You and Life. Even though we, Your people, are sinners, You love us, provide for us, give us faith to depend on You, in our Savior, Jesus. You prepare a place for us where we will have eternal joy with You. You stand by us in every need. And while we are here, You provide beauty and wonder and awe for us to enjoy. In You we can boast, honestly and with enthusiasm. You are great and greatly to be praised. Thank You for the privilege of boasting about You. Thank You for You.

Every thought: Captive to You
More strength to serve available
Joy: Boasting in You


2 Corinthians 11

3 But I am afraid that, as the serpent deceived Eve by his craftiness, your minds will be led astray from the simplicity and purity *of devotion* to Christ.
Thank You, Lord Jesus, for loving me, extending Your grace to me through Your Holy Spirit, and giving me Life with You now and forever. There are a lot of opportunities to rejoice in that good news in every congregation. There are study groups, service groups, social groups, administrative groups, and others. And the temptation comes to me and others to stray from the simplicity and purity of devotion to You as we

participate in various different activities.  Please help me and all Your people, Lord, to rejoice in all the opportunities You give to bless each other and other people.  But help us to do that always clear in mind and heart that our devotion is to You, personally, Jesus, our Savior and Lord.  Grant that we may socialize devoting ourselves and all our relationships to You.  Grant that we may serve always clear that we are serving You.  Grant that we may study and learn, always looking for You and listening to You.  Grant that we may worship in whatever forms we use always clear that we are worshiping You.  In all we are and do, inside and outside our parishes, bless us with devotion to You alone.

9  …and when I was present with you and was in need, I was not a burden to anyone; for when the brethren came from Macedonia they fully supplied my need, and in everything I kept myself from being a burden to you, and will continue to do so.
You have called Your chosen servants to bring Your gospel to people in many places in many ways around the world, Lord.  Thank You for proclaiming Your good news to people.  Thank You for calling people to You, also now in my lifetime.  Bless Your Church so that Your people fully supply the needs of all those servants of Yours.  Bless us so that we recognize Your ministries.  Bless us so that we trust You to provide for us and through us for them.  Bless all Your missionaries with effective ministry through the power of Your Holy Spirit.  Help them so that they have no cause for worry about their needs being supplied.  There seem to be so many ministries You have, Lord.  Sometimes I feel such a desire to help them all.  I know that isn't Your plan.  So show me and all Your people which of Your ministries You want us to support, and help us to be generous in our gifts.  And arrange (what a job!) the gifts of Your people so that all Your ministries are fully supplied, by all of us Your people trusting You and giving sacrificially and generously, trusting You and rejoicing in Your ministries of grace.

13  For such men are false apostles, deceitful workers, disguising themselves as apostles of Christ.

Lord, they're still here! "Find your harmonic center. Peace and harmony in thought. Follow Jesus the Great Teacher and you will succeed." And other similar dribble that claims to solve all problems and lead people to complete satisfied living. They use words that sound positive. But they leave out Christ and Him crucified and are therefore demonic, pure and simple. Please help us recognize false apostles and representatives of the evil one for what they are. Help us to distinguish good and kind from great and gracious. Help us never mix "modern thought" or "clarified thinking" with the gospel You have given or with the faith in Jesus our Savior by which You keep us close to You now and forever. Help us to recognize good sounding evil without fear. You have overcome the world! Thank You Jesus! Give us wisdom and strength to live in the world but not of it, always keeping our eyes on You, our Perfect Light, our Gracious Lord, and our Eternal Life.

Devotion to You: In everything
Fully supported ministries
Only You: Jesus, Savior, Lord


2 Corinthians 12

9  And He has said to me, "My grace is sufficient for you, for power is perfected in weakness." Most gladly, therefore, I will rather boast about my weaknesses, so that the power of Christ may dwell in me.

Thank You, Lord. I qualify for Your help if what is needed is weakness. As days go along smoothly, my opinion of myself is rather satisfied. And then I hit a wall where it appears that I am not as confident, loving, caring, or considerate as I thought I was. I am not sufficient for living a life of respect and consideration for the people around me. Selfishness and fear and thoughtlessness creep in awfully quickly, Lord.

Please forgive me. Thank You for Your grace being sufficient for me, Lord Jesus. Work with Your power through me in every weakness of mine, please. Let Your grace flow in the desert of my weaknesses and failures. Let Your power work through me to bless people. Thank You for stepping in, Lord. You are great at this! Help me to keep an honest assessment of myself with great confidence in Your sufficient grace and power.

10  Therefore I am well content with weaknesses, with insults, with distresses, with persecutions, with difficulties, for Christ's sake; for when I am weak, then I am strong.
Since You give me strength when I feel weak, Lord, I don't have to feel destroyed, depressed, or disgusted with myself. Thank You, Lord. The temptation to despair or self-pity when I see my weaknesses is really very strong. Thank You that I can be honest about myself, and when I recognize my weaknesses and the challenges that come to me, I can recognize Your strength at work. Thank You that I have had opportunities to bless people. It's pretty clear Who is responsible for the strength and effectiveness of any blessings in those times. Thank You for being with me. Grant that I approach the opportunities that come to me each day without fear, but with contentment. Grant me contentment in You, Lord. Truly You give the strength for every day. Shine Your light throughout this day, and let no darkness of discouragement or spiritual lethargy get in the way of Your wonderful lighting up this day.

19  All this time you have been thinking that we are defending ourselves to you. *Actually*, it is in the sight of God that we have been speaking in Christ; and all for your upbuilding, beloved.
It's true, Lord, that when I read Your word, there are times when I feel guilty (thank You for helping me to recognize my sins, Lord). Sometimes it seems that Your word paints one of the Old Testament or New Testament saints in stunning glowing colors that seems really different from me. Help me

to always hear Your gospel in Your word, Lord. Help me to receive the power of Your Holy Spirit building me up. It's not just that I have parts of my spirit that seem to sag sometimes (although there are some parts that do, Lord). I need Your building project to continue through every day. If I am not being built up, I am slipping into decay, Lord. Only by You am I built strong and able for the day ahead. So keep building, Lord. Let me never complain about the architecture. You know what is coming and the reason You are building me the way You are. I'll work very hard to keep any architecturally critical comments to myself. Praise to You, Lord—keep on building!

Sufficiency: Only from You
Contentment: Weakness depending on Your strength
Keep building: Your style


2 Corinthians 13

5 Test yourselves *to see* if you are in the faith; examine yourselves! Or do you not recognize this about yourselves, that Jesus Christ is in you—unless indeed you fail the test? I remember being nervous about tests, Lord. There weren't enough in school, there had to be more tests for getting jobs, and more applying for special programs. And I remember a time when I thought self-tests were the best, until I realized that I was the harshest grader I knew. Thank You for the privilege of examining myself to see if I am in the faith. I find that I am a sinner. I find that the variety of sin that I participate in seems to grow through the years. But I find You, also, Lord. Thank You for living in me. Thank You for my baptism. Thank You for Your gift of faith, to hear and depend on You in the gospel that You speak to me. Help me, Lord, to remember and enjoy that You are in me, throughout the day so that all I am and want and choose and say and do are all with You and by Your grace.

11 Finally, brethren, rejoice, be made complete, be comforted, be like-minded, live in peace; and the God of love and peace will be with you.

Thank You, Lord, for Your gracious will that we Your people be blessed with these blessings. Make us complete with growing in You through Your Spirit, through Your word, and through the fellowship we have together. Bless us with comfort by Your gracious presence with us in every time of trouble. Help us to be like-minded. We tend to resist that. Forgive us and make us new every day with a clean heart and a new spirit so that we may have the mind of Jesus. Thank You for the peace You give; help us live in that peace, conscious of Your gift in every moment. Be with us every day. When You are with us, then we are truly complete and comforted, then we are drawn to one mind in You. Then we live in Your peace that passes all our understanding, and our hearts and minds are kept in You. Praises to You, Gracious Lord!

14 The grace of the Lord Jesus Christ, and the love of God, and the fellowship of the Holy Spirit, be with you all.

I am not Alive without Your grace, Lord. Let me live with Your grace. Without any merit in me, You have blessed me. So by Your grace I know Your love. Grant that I am never frightened by Your presence, knowing that You love me, Father, so much that You have sent Jesus to be my Savior. So let me live in the wonder, the awe, the satisfaction, and the inspiration of Your love. By grace, shine Your love through me today and every day. And throughout this day let me live in Your fellowship, Lord Holy Spirit. By Your fellowship I know I am never alone. By Your fellowship I can depend on Your guidance, Your wisdom. By Your fellowship I can live wherever You lead me. Bless all Your people with Your grace, Your love, and Your fellowship, and with Your blessings make us blessings to the people You bring into our lives.

You in me: Faith-full

Peace: You with us
Fellowship, by grace, with love

# Galatians

Galatians 1

3 Grace to you and peace from God our Father and the Lord Jesus Christ.
So I go to the mailbox to see if I got any actual mail among the plethora of junk and ads. And there is a really fancy envelope, parchment with terrific handwritten address, with Your return address, God, Heaven. Now I, being the sinner I am, might reasonably expect the letter to start off with, "Now Michael, there are some things we have to talk about..." But no! When You write to me You start off, "Grace to you and peace…" Wow! I am blessed and amazed that You can write also to me that way. (Of course Paul had some negative things to say later, and You, reasonably point out to me things that are wrong, but You come to me in a Spirit of blessing.) I truly desire Your grace in Jesus, in order to live, Lord. And living, I really want to live in peace today and every day. Since peace doesn't grow on trees (or occur naturally on the streets of my city) thank You for peace coming from You. Let me Live by Your grace in Your gift of peace in this day that You have given. Thank You for Your terrific letter, Lord!

11 For I would have you know, brethren, that the gospel which was preached by me is not according to man. <sup>12</sup> For I neither received it from man, nor was I taught it, but *I received it* through a revelation of Jesus Christ.
People really have tried to come up with their own gospel, haven't they, Lord. It seems like in every century, almost every generation, someone has come up with The Plan for living that doesn't depend on You and Your grace and forgiveness. OK, when I honestly look very closely, there have been a few times when I have tried making a Plan. I have tried to adjust Your Gospel to fit better into my

circumstances. Surely You want me to think this through and be reasonable. (And then I hear You saying, "Not.") Thank You for continuously reaching me with Your Gospel Good News of Life in Jesus. Thank You Holy Spirit for washing me with Your grace every day and turning me to Jesus. Thank You Jesus for showing me Your gift of Life through Your sacrifice for me. Your Gospel—let me Live by Your Gospel. Grant that by the wonder and awe of Your forgiveness in Jesus, Lord, that I will follow You faithfully throughout this day. Thank You for Your Plan (sure works better than mine!).

24 And they were glorifying God because of me.
Thank you, Lord, for Paul. Glory be to You for Your grace to him who was heading the other way as fast as he could go. It's not just the Word which You gave through him, but also the hope You give to me that when I head the wrong way, You are there putting up obstacles, and using a variety of methods to turn me around and bring me back. Thank You, Lord. Glory to You for the inspiration that You have given through more recent gracious turned around servants of Yours: G. K. Chesterton who tried to found a heresy of his own and found that it was *Orthodoxy*. C. S. Lewis and his writings stir my faith wonderfully (I cry in heart and soul and body at *The Lion, the Witch, and the Wardrobe.* Thank You also for *Screwtape Letters* among many others.) To hear Lewis talk about where he came from and how You relentlessly pursued him (also using G. K. Chesterton's *Eternal Man*) and turned him around is truly a blessing to me and many. Glory and praise to You, Lord, for all whom You have reached, for the many that You have turned around and used as Your servants, and for the joy and inspiration that You have brought to Your people through them.

Grace and peace, from You, now and always
Life, in Your Gospel, alone
Inspiration through Your servants

Galatians 2

4,5 But *it was* because of the false brethren secretly brought in, who had sneaked in to spy out our liberty which we have in Christ Jesus, in order to bring us into bondage. ⁵ But we did not yield in subjection to them for even an hour, so that the truth of the gospel would remain with you.
Thank You, Lord, for the freedom that I enjoy in this country where I live. And thank You for the longer lasting freedom that I have in You, Jesus. There are still times when I take in messages from myself that I am not good enough. When I do something dumb. Again. And I promised I was going to watch my tongue and what I did. But Your gospel is true separate from me. Thank You for liberty by Your action, Jesus, by Your sacrifice, death and resurrection. Thank You that I am free to be alive in You today. Grant that I live in the fresh air and sunshine of Your gift of liberty, no matter what the weather is and no matter what is happening around me today.

16 Nevertheless knowing that a man is not justified by the works of the Law but through faith in Christ Jesus, even we have believed in Christ Jesus, so that we may be justified by faith in Christ and not by the works of the Law; since by the works of the Law no flesh will be justified.
Nothing I do makes me right with You, Lord. I can look back and think, "Boy that was really a good thing to do!" But no matter what it was, what came from me was imperfect. So thank You for the gift of faith that You give me, Lord, Holy Spirit. Thank You that I can believe the good news that I have forgiveness and New Life in Jesus, my Savior. You have been sent, Lord Jesus, to atone for my sins as the Christ, the Messiah. Grant that I Live justified today. Not proud in myself. But proud of You, Father, that I am made just in a right relationship with You by Jesus. You are terrific, Lord! Let the smile on my face today, show that.

20  I have been crucified with Christ; and it is no longer I who live, but Christ lives in me; and the *life* which I now live in the flesh I live by faith in the Son of God, who loved me and gave Himself up for me.
Lord Jesus, You have given me the benefit of Your crucifixion.  You have graciously included me.  So in the moments I have today, I am not just me, alive, heart beating, doing stuff.  You Live in me.  What a different view of this day!  This life today, Lord, let me see is Living by faith in You.  In every joy I see, in every difficulty I face, in every time of thinking or speaking or doing—Live in me, Lord Jesus.  What a wonder today is, Lord Jesus, with You Living in me.  I get to Live by faith in You.  In small things and large, it's You, Lord—You make living truly Life.

Liberty in Jesus, today!
With smile and faith, proud of You
With You, I live Life


Galatians 3

11  Now that no one is justified by the Law before God is evident; for, "THE RIGHTEOUS MAN SHALL LIVE BY FAITH."
Thank You, Lord for faith.  Thank You for forgiveness in You Lord Jesus, that I receive by faith in You.  Sometimes it seems as if faith were a fancy garment to take out on Sunday when I go to church.  I don't want to get it dirty by using it too much, so I save it for special occasions.  Ha!  Not Your plan at all!  Use it every day!  What a plan!  OK, so, please help me Lord today to take faith with me wherever I go and whatever I do.  Grant that I trust You, depend on You, recognize You with me, and Live faithfully through each moment.  "Never leave home without it" could certainly apply well.  Thank You Lord that no matter how much I use the faith You give me it never wears out or gets old.  In fact it appears to glow and become more useful by Your grace the

more I use it. (And help me remember, Lord, to use it first, not after I try some other plan of mine.)

14 ...in order that in Christ Jesus the blessing of Abraham might come to the Gentiles, so that we would receive the promise of the Spirit through faith.
You have promised Your Spirit to all who believe in You, Lord Jesus. Fill me with Your Spirit today. Let me see things from Your point of view. Let fear have no place in my heart in this day. Remind me through Your Spirit of all You have said to me, and of all the blessings You have given me. Empower me to be the blessing You want me to be through Your Spirit. Grant that I trust You, Lord Holy Spirit, to be present in me. Grant that I depend on You. Stir the faith You have given me, so that I never live alone, but always leaning on You. Thank You for coming into my life and my heart. I rejoice in You, Great Promise Fulfilled!

29 And if you belong to Christ, then you are Abraham's descendants, heirs according to promise.
There are some great stories written, Lord, about someone who inherits an island, a castle, a secret mine, or some other dream treasure. But a lot of those stories have sticky ends that are not part of the dream. I am so blessed, Lord Jesus, that I belong to You. Thank You. And to be brought into Abraham's descendants is a wonder in itself. But then to be an heir according to Your ancient and new promise brings joy to me that fills my heart and lights up the future. Please keep the wonder and awe of that inheritance fresh in my mind and heart. Grant that I live, not in arrogance as if I were responsible for the riches in my life, but in humility, confidence, and satisfaction in Your light of promise today and in every tomorrow, brightly lit with Your promise fulfilled.

Use faith unstintingly
Reminded, empowered, alive
An heir with a future!

Galatians 4

4 But when the fullness of the time came, God sent forth His Son, born of a woman, born under the Law.
Thank You Father for the fullness of time having come. Your people trusted that You would fulfill Your promise of Messiah to come. Thank You that I get to trust and believe that You have already sent Jesus, Your Son. That waiting must have been very difficult as centuries went by. When I have to wait a couple weeks, it seems like a long time! Thank You, Jesus, for coming and for being born of Your mother Mary. When I talk to You I know I am talking to a person, like me, but perfect. Truly human. And at the same time, You are the Son of God my Father. What a wonderful Gift You are! And I don't have to wait for my birthday or some other special day. The time has come. You have been sent. You are here and I can talk to You. Thank You for taking on the position of being under the Law as I am, so that I know You know exactly what it is like. Grant that I recognize You with me and Live joyously in Your company throughout today.

5 ...so that He might redeem those who were under the Law, that we might receive the adoption as sons.
OK, Lord, if I were in charge of the script, I probably would have a great and wonderful scene with Jesus arranging for me (and us) to be able to come into Eternal Life. But to have us come as Your adopted children is beyond my wildest imagination! It's like a time machine of grace that brings me back to the beginning. I get to have a relationship with You as You first intended, as one of Your children. What an amazing blessing! Thank You, Father, for bringing me to You as Your child. Grant that today I live as Your child. Not with my nose stuck up, expecting others to bow, expecting cars to stop and let me pass as I walk in town (not going to happen!). Rather grant that I live as Your child, recognizing other people as Your children, together celebrating You as our Father, and living with Your love and joy!

6 Because you are sons, God has sent forth the Spirit of His Son into our hearts, crying, "Abba! Father!"

As Your child, Father, I get to have the Holy Spirit, the Spirit of Jesus, in my heart! Is my heart big enough? My view of who I am just got bigger, Lord! Thank You Holy Spirit for being in me. Thank You for leading me and opening my heart and my mouth to be able to call my Father, "Abba!"—"Dad", "Dear Father"! My temptation is to put You, Dad, my Father, on a distant cloud, with lightening around You. Talking to You as Dad Who cares about me, Who wants to listen to me, Who loves me more than I can comprehend—that is a really new experience for me even, again, today. Gracious Lord, Father, Dad, let me know that You are present with me today and every day and that I can talk to You in every part of living. And please help me to want more than anything else to live to honor and please You, loving You in all that I am and do.

Thank You, Father, for Jesus, now
Living as my Father's child
Talking to my Dad


Galatians 5

1 It was for freedom that Christ set us free; therefore keep standing firm and do not be subject again to a yoke of slavery.

You have turned the lock. You have opened the prison door. You have set me free. Without You I am locked up by my sin and guilt with no hope of living Life as You intended now or in any forever coming. Thank You for setting me free! But You have done more than that, Lord. You have set me free with a purpose. As I come out of sin and guilt by Your gift of forgiveness, You give me a purpose in life, a vocation to which You are calling me. Help me to live for freedom. Grant that I do not turn around and head back to wanting to earn Your favor by things I do, by following the law, by obeying You. In the new Life You give me, grant that I obey You and do things freely, not to get something from You, but just in freedom, loving You, Living in new joy. Help me not to live in spiritual bartering or spiritual capitalism. But rather grant that I live open-heartedly, Living and giving freely.

13  For you were called to freedom, brethren; only *do* not *turn* your freedom into an opportunity for the flesh, but through love serve one another.
There are so many paths open ahead, Lord. The prison of trying (without any possibility of success) to earn Your favor by trying to pay for my sins by doing good stuff is behind me and ahead there are so many possibilities. Thank You for lighting up the paths. Keep me on the paths where I love others. Where I love my brothers and sisters in the faith. Where I love all people I meet. Where I love people who do not appear to fit into my categories of "nice", "good", or "positive". Guide me and empower me in the freedom You have given me so that I serve others as You want me to. Even if my serving does not seem reasonable or analytically explicable. Keep me free, loving, and serving.

22,23  But the fruit of the Spirit is love, joy, peace, patience, kindness, goodness, faithfulness, [23] gentleness, self-control; against such things there is no law.
OK, Lord, this is a terrific list. I really like this list. I want these in my life. The trouble I have is that some of these seem to exclude some other things that I have trouble letting go of. Does joy mean I can't grumble and kick furniture? (Probably, yes.) Does patience mean I can't remonstrate severely with customer service representatives who have trouble spelling customer service? (Yeah, that's probably a yes, too, isn't it?) Does gentleness mean I have to stop imagining bad things that might happen and live with muscles tensed, just in case? (I think I heard Your, "Right on!") And self-control. I would much rather control other people than myself, probably because it seems easier. OK,

Holy Spirit, since these are fruit that You grow by the grace of God in the climate of forgiveness that I have in Jesus, let it happen! Put away all those other things that get in the way, and grow Your Fruit! Not even just tomorrow, but today, please.

Live freed freely
Light paths of loving service
Let Your fruit grow!


Galatians 6

1,2 Brethren, even if anyone is caught in any trespass, you who are spiritual, restore such a one in a spirit of gentleness; *each one* looking to yourself, so that you too will not be tempted. ² Bear one another's burdens, and thereby fulfill the law of Christ.
Lord, do you watch those shows where people buy older homes and then spend $100,000 or so to "restore" them. Of course they never looked that good when they were new. Restoring is expensive. When You give me, and all of Your people, the calling to restore a person who has sinned, first I hear You saying that You would like me to avoid saying (if only to myself) "serves him right, to be involved in that nonsense!" (I'm sorry I have slipped into that sometimes, Lord!) Second, thank You Lord that You have paid for the restoration. Restoration of a person is expensive, but You have paid the price through Your sacrifice on the cross. So cost is not the object. Please help me to be a blessing to whomever You want me to help. Work through me to mend that which is broken, to repair what isn't working, to help a person receive the equipment You give, and by Your grace work through me to complete whatever is lacking. Help me to participate in restoration projects with love and gentleness. And before I complain about what a lot of work it is, help me to realize how much work You are doing through others restoring me. Thank You for that, Lord.

10  So then, while we have opportunity, let us do good to all people, and especially to those who are of the household of the faith.
Opportunity is such a positive sounding word, Lord.  You have given me many opportunities in my life, and You give other people great and wonderful opportunities, too.  Some people don't seem to have many, though.  So it is wonderful that there are times when You give to me and to each of Your people, opportunities to do good to others.  You don't care about race, gender, or any of the other divisive categories people from time to time use.  Thank You for the opportunities You give.  Help me always to see them.  Grant that I trust You for all I need to do good to all people.  Thank You that I can be a blessing to others in Your family.  Show me good that I can do for someone or for several someone's today, for those in my family, for those in Your family of grace, or for strangers that I meet.  Thank You for Your Opportunities!

18  The grace of our Lord Jesus Christ be with your spirit, brethren. Amen.
I don't deserve Your love and mercy, Lord.  And You know that.  So Your grace is such a wonderful, let the sunshine in, lift up my spirit, gift.  You know, better than I do, how much I need Your love, Your mercy, Your undeserved favor.  By Your grace that You give me, let me be the person that You want me to be.  Shine through my spirit with the Light of Your presence and Your love so that others are blessed.  Not so they recognize me, but that they might recognize You and Your grace.  Of course Your grace shines brightest in me when I have fallen down and need help getting up again.  I would prefer not to stumble so much, Lord.  But whatever You want, let Your grace be with my spirit, gracious, merciful Savior and Lord.

Bless restorations, mine and others
See and use "good" opportunities
Your grace, my spirit's companion

# Ephesians

Ephesians 1

3 Blessed *be* the God and Father of our Lord Jesus Christ, who has blessed us with every spiritual blessing in the heavenly *places* in Christ.
Thank You, Gracious Father, for Your wonderful blessings. I admit that when I think of blessings, it is easier for me to think of things that can be wrapped or that can be found on Amazon.com, Best Buy, or Barnes and Noble. (You know, Lord, my candy stores of choice.)  But when I am facing discouragement, fear, temptation, or other storms I depend on Your spiritual blessings.  Grant that I recognize Your blessings for my spirit, Lord.  Grant that I recognize them as more wonderful and enjoyable than anything (!) at the aforementioned locations.  Grant that I use them well, knowing that they are not just pretty to look at, but greatly useful and effective in every need.  Help me to use them also in what I remember, and in the joys and times of satisfaction that I experience.  Let me feel joy and satisfaction only in You, with a real sense of Your gracious presence.

17 [I pray] … that the God of our Lord Jesus Christ, the Father of glory, may give to you a spirit of wisdom and of revelation in the knowledge of Him.
Every once in a while I think of all the courses I didn't take at school.  You know, Lord, the ones that didn't seem important at the time.  Like auto mechanics (I really wish I had taken that!), sewing, cooking.  And I wish I had found a course on fixing copiers—that would have been really useful!  But You have a much more interesting and valuable course of knowledge that is available to me—knowledge of Jesus, eternal, human, living in Your will, not giving in to temptation, caring about me and all people.  Grant, Lord, that I may

continue to grow in knowledge of Him (even if I have trouble knowing everything about smart phones). And grant that in coming to know my Savior better and better I will have Your gifts of wisdom and revelation to use and depend on by Your grace in all the times when I am fearful, uncertain, and frustrated. What a course, Lord, no tests (at least not on paper) and the older I get, the more interesting and more applicable the course! And the benefits of wisdom and revelation keep growing in importance and usefulness. (Thank You, Jesus, for paying my tuition!)

18, 19 *I pray that* the eyes of your heart may be enlightened, so that you will know what is the hope of His calling, what are the riches of the glory of His inheritance in the saints, [19] and what is the surpassing greatness of His power toward us who believe. *These are* in accordance with the working of the strength of His might.
I can remember both "Queen for a day" (now, of course, on YouTube) and "If I were king!" Hope, riches, power—a dizzying and regal combination. And You say I can just open my eyes and see them! OK, Lord, let the eyes of my heart be enlightened. Let me see, and know inside, the hope You give so every day I can feel the warmth of Your sunshine (clouds or not). Grant that hope be so much a part of me that I see no limit, no glass or concrete ceiling, no end point, no dark hole, only opportunity, possibility, joy, and wonder opening ahead without end by Your grace. Grant that I appreciate how awesomely rich I am in You, with wealth more valuable than any monetary measure. And thank You for Your power at work in me and all Your people. Use it through us to let people see Your glory and love. Use it to bless people with healing, comfort, encouragement, satisfaction, and wonder in Your grace today. Let me be Your humble servant, and let Your regal blessings flow through me.

Spiritual blessings: Wonderful and useful
Wisdom and revelation in Jesus

Hope, riches, power: Seen, working

Ephesians 2

4, 5 But God, being rich in mercy, because of His great love with which He loved us, ⁵ even when we were dead in our transgressions, made us alive together with Christ (by grace you have been saved)...
Loneliness is a real enemy to satisfied living, Lord. For people who live alone and for people who live in the midst of a bunch of family, loneliness can still strike. Thank You for Your grace by which You have reached me and Your people. Thank You for bringing us from death and loneliness (living only in and for ourselves) to Life with You. Let me and all of us Live in the joy that we are alive together with You, Jesus our Lord and Savior. Grant that we enjoy blessings today together with You. Grant that we make choices today together with You. And grant that no matter what storm or attack comes against us, we face it in Your company, Gracious Jesus. Let all of our life today be Living together with You.

6, 7 ...and raised us up with Him, and seated us with Him in the heavenly *places* in Christ Jesus, ⁷ so that in the ages to come He might show the surpassing riches of His grace in kindness toward us in Christ Jesus.
I enjoy museums, Lord. It's wonderful to see artifacts that remind me of great events in the past. I enjoyed Night at the Museum, but I haven't actually wanted to live in a museum. But You graciously have an open, living museum planned. Thank You for Your grace Lord in raising me with Jesus and giving me a place with Him in the heavenly places. Use me and all of Your people now to show the amazing, surpassing riches of Your grace in the way You are kind and loving toward us in Jesus in this day. Let Your light reflect from us to those around so that they can experience Your open,

living museum that shows off Your grace and love, and be drawn to You and Life.

10  For we are His workmanship, created in Christ Jesus for good works, which God prepared beforehand so that we would walk in them.
OK, I have tried planning ahead, Lord. I have made wonderful lists (and (!) lists of lists so I could keep track of lists). You have Your own list of good for me to do. Thank You for making a list and then providing all I need to carry out Your will. Just the list would be awfully daunting, Lord. Thank You for Your great and wonderful preparations. Since You have made the preparations, I know they will be great and effective. Show me what You want me to do, Lord. Please forgive me for those that I have missed. Grant that I do not bypass any wonderful opportunity that You have prepared for me to do. What a joy! I can look into this day and know that even though I cannot see them now, You have great stuff lined up, prepared and ready. OK, by Your grace, here we go!

Living with You
Show off Your grace
Created, prepared, walking in good


Ephesians 3

11, 12  *This was* in accordance with the eternal purpose which He carried out in Christ Jesus our Lord, [12] in whom we have boldness and confident access through faith in Him.
"Do you think He would be interested in these little things?" Yes, I've thought about prayer and wondered with others if maybe what I was wondering about was really a subject to talk to You about, Lord. Thank You for Your openness. Thank You that we can talk. I remember growing up learning that there were categories of prayer. But You just tell me that I can have boldness and confident access to You

through faith in Jesus. Please grant that I talk to You in conversations through the day, not just with lists of things I want or that other people need, but just "Wow, look at that! What do You suppose she meant? Do You think it's a good idea to help him? Help me to be patient, Lord! What a mess! Do You suppose You might just take all this trash and instantly make it appear stuck to the people who dropped it here?" Some of my conversations are not spiritual and I do let frustrations show a little (!). Thank You, Lord, that I don't have to wait for access to You until Sunday or worship or a particular place. Grant that I remember I have access (better than texting!) to boldly come to You in every moment today. Help me sort through the feelings and ideas I have so I can Live in love and wisdom and joy (and let You take care of things that are none of my business).

16, 17 ...that He [the Father] would grant you, according to the riches of His glory, to be strengthened with power through His Spirit in the inner man, [17] so that Christ may dwell in your hearts through faith;...
I remember someone telling me some (!) years ago that exercise is really a good thing, Lord. And of course, it is a way to strengthen my outer man. I have been somewhat hit and miss in that area. Help me Father that I will be strengthened more regularly through the Holy Spirit inside. You have given me faith. Help me use it to trust Jesus completely. Grant that I live using inner (strengthened, well-developed) muscles as I enjoy this day. Please, Jesus, dwell in my heart. Not just at Advent and Christmas when I think about preparing a place for You and having You dwell in me. Dwell in my heart in every day, in every moment. Occupy my heart so completely that my inner person rejoices in Your Spirit's strengthening and so that there is no room in my heart for anything that would distract me from focusing on You, listening to You, following You—no room for anything but You.

17 – 19  ...*and* that you, being rooted and grounded in love, [18] may be able to comprehend with all the saints what is the breadth and length and height and depth, [19] and to know the love of Christ which surpasses knowledge, that you may be filled up to all the fullness of God.

Comprehending three dimensional objects, for me, takes thought, pictures, and sometimes holding the object. And although I like looking at a tetrahedron, there are a limited number of things to know about it. Open my knowing, Lord. Help me to see how small everything is that I know. The knowing which I have done has been based on reading, listening, and experience. But knowing Your love, Jesus, comes from the love that You have given me. Keep that love strong in my heart, Lord. Use the love that You have given me to enable me to see You and Your love in all the dimensions that fit into this world, and in all the dimensions that fit into Life forever with You. Grant that I know—more than the appearance of Your love—the experience of Your love. And grant that I may then look at people and opportunities during the moments of this day through the newness of Living in Your love.

Available! Boldly conversing
Strengthened. Jesus please dwell.
Rooted, comprehending, knowing Love


Ephesians 4

1-3 Therefore I, the prisoner of the Lord, implore you to walk in a manner worthy of the calling with which you have been called, [2] with all humility and gentleness, with patience, showing tolerance for one another in love, [3] being diligent to preserve the unity of the Spirit in the bond of peace.

Thank You, Lord, for the calling with which I have been called. In Your grace You have brought me to a new Life—to Life lived with You. Help me not to be concerned about being worthy of Your calling only once or twice a year or once a week or while I am talking to You. Grant that I desire to Live inside the grace and direction and love of Your calling each moment in a way that is worthy of Your calling. At home, at work, with family, with friends, with co-workers, with strangers, alone. Let my attitude toward others be a clear window into my heart where, by Your grace, there is real humility, where I have a desire to be gentle always, where patience dwells (grown by Your love through every adversity), where it is ok for people to be different from me. Let my thoughts, words, and actions show my desire to preserve the unity You give us, Lord Holy Spirit. Connect all of us, Your people, Gracious Lord in the peace we receive from Jesus which goes way beyond our understanding. Make it the healing power to end all fretting and fear on our faces and in our hearts, minds, words and actions.

11, 12 And He gave some *as* apostles, and some *as* prophets, and some *as* evangelists, and some *as* pastors and teachers, $^{12}$ for the equipping of the saints for the work of service, to the building up of the body of Christ.
Thank You for giving Your servants so that I (with all Your people) may be equipped and ready. There are wonderful technical schools today where it is possible for a person to learn and be equipped to do a lot of jobs serving people in important ways: Plumber, car mechanic, copy machine repair, Information Technology (so companies can take my money in an effective and efficient way), and many more. But Your equipping is much more practical on a daily basis. Grant that I recognize Your equipping and as You give me opportunities to be a blessing grant that I use the equipping You have given me—let me use it well and to Your glory. And please grant that every work of service I have the opportunity to do may build up Your body of believers here. Thank You for the equipping that does not require a belt or case full of tools. (But please help me remember to take Your equipping with me wherever I go.)

26, 27  BE ANGRY, AND *yet* DO NOT SIN; do not let the sun go down on your anger, ²⁷ and do not give the devil an opportunity.
Now, see, there You go.  Not what I expect.  "Be angry."  Of course, You obviously know what You are doing.  Because if I try to just close my eyes and push the steam inside of me—well, You know, that's pretty much the road to ulcers.  (Not at all nice.)  So I appreciate Your understanding of the way You built me and of the world in which I live.  There is that other extreme; and yes, I have dumbly gone down that road.  Holding on to anger.  It starts off pretty simply, Lord.  I just hang on to anger, but then it gets harder and harder to let go.  I keep finding justifications for holding on, people are such unjust, hurtful, miserable sinners.  (Other people, of course.)  Right.  Help me to allow myself to realize that I am angry, to be angry in an appropriate way, to use language that is honest, but not intentionally hurtful.  And at the end of the day, whether the situation is fixed or not, whether the other people understand what they have done or not, whether they accept responsibility or not, whether they are sorry or not—grant that I let go.  Grant that I do not provide any garden of anger for the devil to use for planting evil in my heart.  Forgive me my sins (please don't hold onto them or remember them) as I forgive others (with likewise and ditto).

Looking like Your servant
Have equipment, use me
Lovingly angry


Ephesians 5

1  Therefore be imitators of God, as beloved children.
I never gave it much thought growing up, Lord.  You remember when people would say I was like my father.  And my mother said I was like her, enjoying language.  It wasn't planned, it just happened.  Planning to imitate has a bad

connotation today. But You tell me I can have both. You certainly have shown me You love me. Help me to naturally Live as Your beloved child. But more than that, grant that I see You loving people, accepting people, helping people and grant that I imitate Your gracious love. Grant that I see the joy You have in Your people being alive in You, and grant that I imitate that joy, rejoicing in being alive in You. Help me to be a real, excellent, blessed imitator of You in all I am and do today.

8-10 ...for you were formerly darkness, but now you are Light in the Lord; walk as children of Light [9] (for the fruit of the Light *consists* in all goodness and righteousness and truth), [10] trying to learn what is pleasing to the Lord.
As a sinner, I can understand being called darkness, Lord. Listening to You, being loved by You, coming to know You is like walking into brighter and brighter days. Thank You for being all Light. Thank You for bringing Light into my life. Some days my list is busier than others, but no matter what is in my day, please grant that I may honor You. Help me to learn what is pleasing to You. The sound of "goodness, righteousness, and truth" is a blessed sound to me. Let me see how they apply in ways that are pleasing to You in the conversations I have with people today, in the choices I make, in the attitudes I choose, in the thoughts I think. Oh, what fun it is to … please You.

18, 19 And do not get drunk with wine, for that is dissipation, but be filled with the Spirit, [19] speaking to one another in psalms and hymns and spiritual songs, singing and making melody with your heart to the Lord.
There was a time when I memorized some psalms and hymns. It's been a while, Lord. At least, Lord, help me to speak to people with the joy and fervor of the psalms and hymns when I talk to people about how thankful I am for all You are and all the ways You have blessed me. OK, now I do like to sing. I prefer to sing in tune and on key, although I suspect the people around me in church just put up with me

a lot.  Give me singing in my heart to You that is in Your tune and on Your key.  Grant that I make melody with my heart to You, Lord all through this day in such a way that neither You nor anyone else who happens to hear me cringes.  Make the songful joy in my heart pleasing to You and uplifting and catching to others.

Excellent imitator
Satisfaction: Pleasing You
All day, a catchy melody


Ephesians 6

13 – 15  Therefore, take up the full armor of God, so that you will be able to resist in the evil day, and having done everything, to stand firm.  [14] Stand firm therefore, HAVING GIRDED YOUR LOINS WITH TRUTH, and HAVING PUT ON THE BREASTPLATE OF RIGHTEOUSNESS, [15] and having shod YOUR FEET WITH THE PREPARATION OF THE GOSPEL OF PEACE…
It would be nice if when You bring us to Life we would live in sunshine and flower lined pathways (hypoallergenic, of course) with birds singing all the time.  But You have plainly said the days are evil.  So thank You for giving me and all Your people the armor we need for every day.  Yes, I know, there have been days when I have been in a hurry (and figured I could get through the day just fine, thank You very much) and not put on the armor.  Yeech!  What a dumb idea that was!  Grant that I remember Your truth that Your love and forgiveness and Your calling me to follow You are more important that any philosophy, laws of motion, quadratic formulas, or any other truth I may come by (although I am rather fond of quadratic formulas, Lord).  So, Your way, Lord.  Grant that I put on the armor You give me, every day.  Grant that I depend on Your righteousness, not on my niceness, goodness, or practiced glibness.  And grant that I stand firm every day with Your armor, and with my way determined by

Your good news of Jesus Who gives us peace through every evil day.

17  And take THE HELMET OF SALVATION, and the sword of the Spirit, which is the word of God.
I remember once, when I had the opportunity to take a course on fencing. It seemed silly (although Errol Flynn was truly terrific). And yet, You are putting a sword in my hands. Thank You for Your word. Grant that throughout my life I grow in Your word. Grant that I remember Your word, so that I may have it available when I need to use it (I admit the picture of a light saber comes to my mind readily!). And most of all, help me to use Your sword, Holy Spirit, faithfully and responsibly—not as a club to hit people over the head, not as a prop to hold up things I like to think, but as a weapon for Your gracious truth and against evil. Let me use it to protect my Life and others' Lives by Your power and direction. Let me use it to cut through balderdash and nonsense. And let me use it never with anger or hurtfulness, but only with love and joy and thanksgiving.

18  With all prayer and petition pray at all times in the Spirit, and with this in view, be on the alert with all perseverance and petition for all the saints.
Yes, the world seems very large. While it is smaller because news travels faster, the difficulties and enormous challenges that are apparent in many places around the world, makes it seem larger and more complicated. So it feels more comfortable to just pray for concerns right here where I am, Lord, but I know my sisters and brothers face a lot more challenges than I do. Bless them, Lord. Bless Your people whose lives are threatened by their faith. Bless Your people who suffer physically for their faith. Bless Your people who live in the midst of people who are fierce in their rejection of You. And bless Your people who have no problems or enemies and are in danger of falling asleep in their faith. Grant that we all rejoice in You today, that we Live for You and serve You as You desire, that we reflect Your love and

grace so others are attracted to You. And help me to remember faithfully to include all the rest of my family in You in my daily conversations with You.

Your armor: Don't start the day without it
Your sword: Lovingly swash and buckle
Your people: My family to pray for

# Philippians

Philippians 1

9, 10 And this I pray, that your love may abound still more and more in real knowledge and all discernment, [10] so that you may approve the things that are excellent, in order to be sincere and blameless until the day of Christ.
Your servant Oswald Chambers *(My Utmost for His Highest)* made it clear that the greatest enemy of the excellent is the good. Please grant, Gracious Lord, that love fill my heart to the exclusion of all annoyance and that the love in my heart will continue to grow each day. Grant that I can know what I am seeing and feeling clearly from Your gracious, eternal point of view. Grant that I will discern what is good, what is bad, what is run away ugly, and what is excellent above all in Your desire and blessing. Let my words and face and actions show that I approve what You consider excellent with sincerity (that is without any cere—crud, selfishness, ambiguousness—watering it down.) Thank You that You provide that which is excellent for me to discern—may I rejoice in those blessings today.

21 For to me, to live is Christ and to die is gain.
Some mornings it seems very complicated to get up. There seem like a lot of things to think about and a lot of things to do. But You have made this very clear, Lord. There is a day ahead. I may live or I may die. Only two possibilities. If I have the privilege of living, then please grant to me also that all of living in this day be Christ. Grant that I make choices during this day knowing that I want all of my living to be Christ. Grant that I rejoice and give thanks today, wanting all of my living to be Christ. Grant that I recognize challenges and storms with faith and confidence, wanting all of my living to be Christ. And if I have the privilege of dying, make it

clear to me, body, soul, and spirit, that to die, by Your grace and wonderful eternal blessing, is gain, being with Christ.

27 Only conduct yourselves in a manner worthy of the gospel of Christ, so that whether I come and see you or remain absent, I will hear of you that you are standing firm in one spirit, with one mind striving together for the faith of the gospel.
I remember people in the wedding party being told when standing firm, bend your knees (or you will faint from lack of blood flow). So keep my blood flowing by Your grace and Your power Holy Spirit, so that I may stand firm. And, yes, it is to all of us, Your people, that You are talking. So grant that *we* stand firm. It is so easy for us to think of each other by denominational names. It is easy for us to box each other with complaints about what we don't like about each other. Yuck! Grant that we show mercy toward one another. Grant that we rejoice with each other in the joy we have in You, Lord Jesus. Grant that we recognize we are one family in Your love and grace, Heavenly Father. And grant that we stand firm with united joy and effort striving for the faith of the gospel, so that all can see You are the One Who gives Life in Jesus, now and forever.

Excellent: With discernment and approval
Living or dying: For Jesus
Standing firmly: One family in Jesus


Philippians 2

1, 2 Therefore if there is any encouragement in Christ, if there is any consolation of love, if there is any fellowship of the Spirit, if any affection and compassion, 2 make my joy complete by being of the same mind, maintaining the same love, united in spirit, intent on one purpose.
Thank You, Jesus, for being encouragement to me throughout each day. How could I hope to serve You and be

a blessing without Your forgiveness, Your love, and Your guidance?  Grant that we Your people will have our minds tuned to Your encouragement.  Grant that on full days and empty days we will rejoice in the consolation of Your love and maintain an attitude of love toward all.  Grant that we will enjoy the fellowship we have in You Lord, Holy Spirit, and that our fellowship with You will unite us here in the swirl of changes and storms.  And grant that our one purpose as Your people will always be to serve You—living for You, with You, by Your grace, to Your glory—now and forever.

12, 13  So then, my beloved, just as you have always obeyed, not as in my presence only, but now much more in my absence, work out your salvation with fear and trembling; [13] for it is God who is at work in you, both to will and to work for *His* good pleasure.
Thank You for Your gift of salvation, Gracious Lord.  Thank You that Your gift is not just a doodad to put on a shelf or in a vault, but a joy and power to make each day new and a blessing.  Grant that we, Your people, will rejoice in Your gift of salvation having results in our attitudes today, in our words of care and love for others, in peace which we share with others.  We live in the midst of a sinful world as sinners, and there is fear and trembling that pushes on our spirits.  Thank You that You are at work in us, not from a distance of time or space, but right now inside us, willing and working for our lives to please You.  Keep us out of the way!  Take charge!  Let Your gift of salvation have blessed results in our Lives today!

14, 15  Do all things without grumbling or disputing; [15] so that you will prove yourselves to be blameless and innocent, children of God above reproach in the midst of a crooked and perverse generation, among whom you appear as lights in the world.
When I think of lights in the world, Lord, there are those who get great press.  I remember J. S. Bach, Mozart, Katherine Hepburn, Myrna Loy, Bing Crosby.  Each generation has

308

those that are considered lights.  More to the point I think of Pope Francis, Billy Graham, C. S. Lewis, G. K. Chesterton.  It's hard, Lord to think of myself as a light.  And, of course, I have a fair amount of practice in grumbling if not necessarily in disputing.  Help me stay in Your program, Lord.  Grant that I let go of grumbling and turn all the inclinations of my heart that lead toward disputations over to You.  By Your grace, make me blameless and innocent in the righteousness of Jesus.  And yes, truly it isn't hard to see this generation as crooked and perverse.  If You want me to appear as a light let Your Light flow through me.  Shine with Your love and joy through all I am and do.  Let all Your people be the lights You want us to be, and use us to bring people from darkness to Your Light.

Serving.  Encouraged, loved, befriended.
Saved.  With wonderful consequences.
Lights.  From Your Light


Philippians 3

3 For we are the *true* circumcision, who worship in the Spirit of God and glory in Christ Jesus and put no confidence in the flesh.
Thank You, Lord, for bringing us into Your family now.  It is a pleasure every morning to get up with most of my flesh and blood working.  As You know, we have had conversations about some parts that need Your caring improvement— please Lord, in Your grace.  But even with all Your blessings thank You that I do not have to depend on my physical flesh and blood to have confidence for today.  Grant that we, Your family, worship You in Spirit and in truth.  Holy Spirit inform us through Your word.  Keep us faithful to You in our worship throughout every season of the year.  Grant that we teach young people effectively so that they also enjoy lives filled with worship and joy in You.  And grant that we glorify Jesus our Lord in worship each day, in our attitudes and emotions

about what is important in life, and in the way that we rejoice together with the people around us at home, at work, at play, in relaxation. You are great and greatly to be praised, Gracious Jesus our Savior and Lord!

12 – 14 Not that I have already obtained *it* or have already become perfect, but I press on so that I may lay hold of that for which also I was laid hold of by Christ Jesus. [13] Brethren, I do not regard myself as having laid hold of *it* yet; but one thing *I do*: forgetting what *lies* behind and reaching forward to what *lies* ahead, [14] I press on toward the goal for the prize of the upward call of God in Christ Jesus.
It is nice to get done with a job. A good feeling when the project is finished and turned in. Yet there is an ongoing mission on which You send me. I know that I, with Paul, am far from perfect. So help me to press on through every day You give me. You have a continuing purpose for me. Grant that I do not forget Your purpose for me in the midst of stuff going on and things being finished. Grant that I continue through this day to press on to lay hold of that which You have prepared for me. One of the challenges, Lord, as You know, is that my generation is very big on remembering. Whether it's bread being a quarter (which I do actually remember, Lord—what happened to that!), or all that I have done and said, relatives I have, pictures I have taken…it's a long list. But pressing on means there are things I need to forget. Help me not to hold onto anything that is dragging me down or keeping me from pressing on toward the goal You have for me in Jesus. Help me to get good at forgetting the right stuff, and pressing on in each day, unhindered, toward the call, Lord, that You give me in Jesus, that has no end.

20, 21 For our citizenship is in heaven, from which also we eagerly wait for a Savior, the Lord Jesus Christ; [21] who will transform the body of our humble state into conformity with the body of His glory, by the exertion of the power that He has even to subject all things to Himself.

Talk about difficult, Lord! I live in a time when people not only can't wait for a letter to be sent through the post office. They can't even wait for email! Texting, skyping, facetime—that's where it's at! Sheesh! Well, You did say eagerly. So yes we, Your people, eagerly wait for You, Lord Jesus to come. Help us to wait well. Knowing some of what is coming helps with the waiting, Lord, thank You. Keep us focused on You and Who You are and Your love and grace while we are waiting, Lord Jesus. Thank You for Your promise that You will change our bodies so that they will fit in the wonderful, amazing Life that is coming. (You are going to do something about my funny looking (really wide) feet, right, Lord?) (Unless other people's feet need to catch up with mine…I'm glad You're in charge, Lord.) So waiting. OK. Grant that we, Your people, will live in eager waiting, that we will show our eager waiting in the priorities we choose, and that we will wait in the confidence You give us in word and sacraments. Come soon, Lord!

Worshiping Jesus, Glorious Lord
Forget. Press on. The upward call.
Waiting well. Eagerly. Confidently.


Philippians 4

4, 5 Rejoice in the Lord always; again I will say, rejoice! ⁵ Let your gentle *spirit* be known to all men. The Lord is near. When I receive Your invitation to rejoice, Lord, the temptation I have is to translate that to mean "Have fun" or "Be happy". And as I listen to You, I realize that's pretty silly. What a combination: Fierce, resounding, symphonic joy and a gentle and gracious spirit. Because, You are near. You are close to me. (Thank You for Brother Lawrence and his *The Practice of the Presence of God.*) It's the "always" that makes me think of "fierce". Help me to rejoice in You, Lord. Grant that I be aware of Your presence. Let joy fill my spirit, no matter what I am doing. And combine that with gentleness. Not that I have a gentle spirit by nature, Lord. But You mean the gentle spirit You have given me. Let others see the joy and the gentleness in my spirit today. So fill my being with joy in You and gentleness toward others that there is no room for anything else (crankiness, discouragement, selfishness, billowing exasperation, or depressing darkness). What a joy! You are near, with me, and I rejoice in You, Gracious Lord!

6, 7 Be anxious for nothing, but in everything by prayer and supplication with thanksgiving let your requests be made known to God. [7] And the peace of God, which surpasses all comprehension, will guard your hearts and your minds in Christ Jesus.
Now, Lord, just think of all the medicine companies that would go out of business if we all were anxious for nothing! (Yeah! Help them with alternate career training!) It is easy to come up with "But what about...!"s. It's like there is a dark and evil spirit that likes to reside in me and feels very threatened by Your gracious words. (Please kick it out, Lord!) So, without exception!, in everything I can turn to You with prayer, supplication, and thanksgiving. Keep me from just prayer with whining. Grant me strong faith, Lord Holy Spirit, so that I pray with supplication trusting You to take care of every need. And please grant that I always remember in praying to You, Lord, to thank You for answering my prayer—I know that You listen, I know You care, I know You are able, and I know You are willing to bless me. So Thank You for answering my prayers. Let Your peace protect my heart and mind in Jesus my Savior. And bless all of us, Your people, in Living without anxiety, but with prayer, supplication, thanksgiving and Your wonderful, beyond our imagination, peace.

8 Finally, brethren, whatever is true, whatever is honorable, whatever is right, whatever is pure, whatever is lovely, whatever is of good repute, if there is any excellence and if anything worthy of praise, dwell on these things.

You know me so well, Lord. There I am, while I am supposed to be accomplishing something, or I am supposed to be thoughtfully figuring something out. And what am I doing? Dwelling on problems, nonsense, old baggage, hasty words, frustrations, desires for things that I have not exactly talked to You about (because I have a pretty good idea what You would say), and other assorted crud and corruption. The good news, Lord, is that I am, of course, very good at dwelling on things. It's just that I really need Your help in what I dwell on. Sweep my memory registers clean of crud. Ring Your "Wool gathering again, Michael!" bell when I just stand or sit and dwell on stuff. And show me what to dwell on. Open my eyes and ears to see, read, hear and listen to that around me now that is honorable, right, pure, lovely, of good repute, excellent, and worthy of praise. You have created that which is good and beautiful in the world where I live. Let me see all that is good. And fill my heart and mind with good so much that when I pause to dwell on something… good, excellent, and wonderful just pop out and fill my thoughts, to Your praise and glory, Gracious Lord.

Full of joy, sharing gentleness
Peace replacing anxiety through prayer
Hmmm ! Good, excellent, praise-worthy!

# Colossians

Colossians 1

9, 10  For this reason also, since the day we heard *of it*, we have not ceased to pray for you and to ask that you may be filled with the knowledge of His will in all spiritual wisdom and understanding, <sup>10</sup> so that you will walk in a manner worthy of the Lord, to please *Him* in all respects, bearing fruit in every good work and increasing in the knowledge of God...
I do feel good, Lord, when I have some fix-it problem come up in the house which I have done before.  The experience and wisdom I acquired the first time (that is, remembering what not to do) make me more confident the next time.  But although there is a lot of instruction offered online and in practical courses, living as Your servant, living worthy of You, my Lord, does not come from practical capsules of wisdom.  Fill me with spiritual wisdom, Gracious Lord, and understanding of Your will so that in important things I will be Your worthy servant (things like getting up in the morning, opening my mouth, putting my thinking in gear, worshiping You in all I do, and caring about people).  Grant that with Your spiritual wisdom and understanding, I will bear fruit to Your glory in all I am and say and do.

11, 12  ...strengthened with all power, according to His glorious might, for the attaining of all steadfastness and patience; joyously <sup>12</sup> giving thanks to the Father, who has qualified us to share in the inheritance of the saints in Light.  Remember, Lord, when I was 20 and pretty much thought I was immortal?  Just show me a challenge!  Here I come!  And (somewhat arrogant) stuff like that.  Thank You, Lord, that while I have less confidence in my body and mind doing whatever I want it to do, I have a lot more confidence in You and Your wonderful power.  Grant me strength in this day,

Lord, to use the physical and mental abilities You have given me with Your power in my spirit so that I may live for You. At home, work, and in the other times let me have steadfastness in my attitudes, words, and actions demonstrating clearly that I am depending on You. And yes, grant that I not only talk about how wonderful patience is, but actually use it in dealing with stuff (like computers whizzing at what seems a slow speed), and dealing with myself and other people. Thank You, Father, for strength to live in steadfastness and patience now and Your grace opening the way ahead to live with the saints in Light.

17   He is before all things, and in Him all things hold together.
I like lists, Lord. I admit it—I am a list person. I can see how someone might decide to put together an encyclopedia of stuff. (A really big list with comments.) When I have taken courses, it seems there is always a list of categories and specifics that go with that topic. Psychology and philosophy have wonderful lists. Mechanics and engineering have really good lists. Theology has terrific lists. And all (what a marvelous concept!) is held together in You. Wow! Whatever good there is in each item, in each concept, in each understanding—all is held in Your hand. Thank You for organizing the "all" that is around me by Your grace. Thank You, that no matter how much the "all" seems to expand, no matter how big it gets, no matter who is pushing or pulling on the "all"—You are in charge, You have the "all" safely in Your hand. Some of the "all" seems really crummy, Lord, please scrunch it out of existence. Some of the "all" needs clarification and help to be useful, Lord, please guide it and direct it to greatness. And some of the "all" is beautiful and awesome. Thank You, Lord. Grant that we human persons spend our time, efforts, imagination, and enjoyment in that part of the "all" by Your grace and to Your glory.

Spiritual wisdom:  Honoring You
Your strength:  Steadfast. Patient. Light.

The universe, in good Hands. Thank You.

Colossians 2

2, 3 [I want you to know how great a struggle I have] ...that their hearts may be encouraged, having been knit together in love, and *attaining* to all the wealth that comes from the full assurance of understanding, *resulting* in a true knowledge of God's mystery, *that is*, Christ *Himself*, ³ in whom are hidden all the treasures of wisdom and knowledge.
You have blessed me so much, Lord. Yes, my heart is encouraged. You give me joy in each day. You have made Your people a fellowship in You with Your love. Open me and all of Your people to the understanding You want us to have. More than an understanding of the Church through the ages. More than an understanding of forms of worship which are a blessing. Grant us that understanding that gives full assurance in every moment, because we know Your mystery, Father, which is Jesus. Grant that we, Your people, come to understand Your amazing love, promising Your Messiah, sending Your Son, Jesus, human and divine, giving us new Life in Christ Jesus, our Savior and Lord. Grant that we rejoice in Who Jesus is, and Live in the confidence and wisdom of Your eternal grace through Him.

6, 7 Therefore as you have received Christ Jesus the Lord, *so* walk in Him, ⁷ having been firmly rooted *and now* being built up in Him and established in your faith, just as you were instructed, *and* overflowing with gratitude.
Christmas and birthdays mainly, I think of receiving gifts. Thank You, Gracious Lord, for Your gift of Jesus. Thank You that I have received Him. Keep me firmly rooted in my faith in Him, by Your grace. Let Your instruction which I receive from Your word and Your people be a continuing blessing to me. Let my establishment in faith overflow into my living. In all the walking I do let me walk in You. I suppose that includes the way I use my mouth (it is so easy

to open it and words just kind of spill out, and then when I hear a growl from across the room, I look back and wish I had chosen different words (or kept my mouth in a more closed position)). Grant, Lord, that all the words I speak grow from faith, love, and gratitude to You (then I can relax my jaw muscles and not worry about spills).

8, 9  See to it that no one takes you captive through philosophy and empty deception, according to the tradition of men, according to the elementary principles of the world, rather than according to Christ. [9] For in Him all the fullness of Deity dwells in bodily form.
If all the bad guys had a sign stuck to their foreheads that said, "Evil", life would be a lot easier, Lord. And books, and TV programs. But, of course, then, truth be told, when I looked in the mirror, well, it might be scary. The grain is mixed with the tares. Right. So give me Your gracious insight, Jesus. In You is the fullness of God. No mixture with anything bad. Help me to see wisely, hear wisely, read wisely. Protect me from love of wisdom that includes accepting and promoting taking any path but Yours. Protect me from scams and deceptions. Not just the (incredible!) stuff in emails, but some invitations to participate in events and entertainment and fellowship. Help me to separate tradition that is a blessing from that which is from the other side. Grant that, by Your grace and power, I never give up the freedom of Living in You and with You to any captivity or enslavement. Thank You, Gracious Lord, for Your protection and deliverance.

Assurance:  Understanding, knowing Christ
Rooted, growing, walking, speaking
Deliverance from every attractive captivity


Colossians 3

12 So, as those who have been chosen of God, holy and beloved, put on a heart of compassion, kindness, humility, gentleness and patience.

What a blessing! You have graciously chosen us, Your people; You have made us holy in Jesus' sacrifice; You have loved us who were not lovable. And as a result we can put on a new and different heart designed by You. Grant that we put on that new heart today, Gracious Lord. Let us come alive around the world in all the places and situations in which You have placed us. With a new heart grant that we will have compassion toward those around us. Grant that our words and actions show kindness to others. Let us be gentle in every contact we have with other people and with the world You have given us. Let us be patient with things that don't work the way we want them to and with people who are different from us. And, of course, while it would be easy to think what terrific people we are (compassionate, kind, gentle, and patient—not bad!), grant that we recognize we get no credit from You in using our new heart and that therefore we should give ourselves no credit either. Rather, grant that we live in the satisfaction of being Your faithful servants.

15 Let the peace of Christ rule in your hearts, to which indeed you were called in one body; and be thankful.

Who should I let give the answer in class today? The girl who is always right, the student who is often wrong but has enormous (and loud) enthusiasm, or the one sitting quietly, paying attention faithfully, over on the side? There are a lot of (loud) voices that want to rule in our hearts, Lord. The voice of "I know what's right" (emphasis on "I"). The voice that sounds a lot like the murmur of voices outside. The voice "I deserve justice, retribution, and revenge." They seem so close, Lord every day. Help us to let, allow, and encourage the peace we have in Jesus our Savior and Lord to be in charge today, right from the beginning, and right to the end. Thank You, Lord, for calling us to peace in You, again, today.

23, 24 Whatever you do, do your work heartily, as for the Lord rather than for men, [24] knowing that from the Lord you will receive the reward of the inheritance. It is the Lord Christ whom you serve.

There are things that I like to do each day, Lord. And some I don't like so much (getting up is occasionally one of them). Also there are some things that are awfully routine (and mostly boring). But when I say that, I realize I am saying they are like that, to me. They are like that if I am focused on myself. And they vary depending on how I feel on any given day (wonderful!, ok, or creaking along). So please grant Lord, that I get my focus off me and onto You. Grant that I do (great, mediocre, and routine) for You, not for me. Getting up, taking medicines, working, reading, studying, caring for others, listening, following directions, thinking creatively, balancing the budget, washing dishes, loving, enjoying, and all that other stuff—grant that I do all I do, heartily, with enthusiasm, for You, Lord. Then Your peace and joy and satisfaction is part of everything I do, all through this day. Thank You, Jesus, for letting me live for You today!

Using the new heart, humbly
Your peace ruling, again
In all, living for You today


Colossians 4

2 Devote yourselves to prayer, keeping alert in it with *an attitude of* thanksgiving…

Thank You, Gracious Lord, for inviting us to talk to You in prayer. Thank You for Your grace, letting us know that You are willing to listen to us. Lead us in consciously devoting ourselves to prayer at particular times of the day and in the busy, quiet, exciting, boring, social, alone, contributing, receiving times of the day. Help us to talk to You with forms that others prepare or that we prepare. Help us to use formats if they are a blessing (thank You for ACTS (Adoration, Confession, Thanksgiving, Supplication) and ACTSIS (adding Intercession and Submission)). Help us to converse with You as we notice things during the day (with "Wow! You are really good at that, Lord!" or "Thanks!" or "Please help him or her" or "Yipe! Please fix that, Lord"). Keep our hearts and minds open to experiencing and living each day along with You. Thank You, Lord, that You are with us to talk to and to share with (and to listen to) throughout each day.

[http://www.dictionaryofchristianese.com/acts-adoration-confession-thanksgiving-supplication/ is a history of ACTS]

3, 4 ...praying at the same time for us as well, that God will open up to us a door for the word, so that we may speak forth the mystery of Christ, for which I have also been imprisoned; [4] that I may make it clear in the way I ought to speak.

Thank You Lord for sending workers into Your harvest. Please, Father, send more and more so that all of Your family may be brought to You. Open doors for Your saving Gospel word to reach people in the place where I live, in the country where I live, in countries and places where Your Gospel has been proclaimed but where people have lost their first love and enthusiasm for You, in countries and places where You and Your Gospel are publicly hated and rejected by some people, in places where Your Gospel has not yet been translated into the popular written language, and in places where there is yet no written language. Open doors for Your Gospel to reach those who are blind and deaf (and thank You for the "Faith Comes By Hearing" ministry in serving those needs). Grant that all missionaries may proclaim Your word clearly and effectively. And create new congregations enjoying Your Gospel in places where they are needed. (And if I may be of use in spreading Your word, please use me.)

5, 6  Conduct yourselves with wisdom toward outsiders, making the most of the opportunity. ⁶ Let your speech always be with grace, *as though* seasoned with salt, so that you will know how you should respond to each person.

You sound a little bit, Lord, like You are talking about people from another planet. But, of course, in a major sense, You are. Outsiders. It is easy sometimes to think of this as a Christian nation and people I see (who are friendly and kind and helpful) as all part of Your family. But a brief time watching prime time TV or reading "popular" books or watching the news and new movies can convince a person that there are a significant number of Outsiders around. You have given us, Your people, this day today. Tomorrow is a possibility, but since today is a sure thing, please help us to make the most of the opportunities You give us today. Fill our speech with Your grace and love and caring for other people. And season our speaking so that we will also keep our mouths shut at those times when that is appropriate and loving, and open them when, in Your will, that is gracious, important and loving.

Lifetime Conversational Partner
Reach people with Your word, everywhere
Today, speak through us

# 1 Thessalonians

1 Thessalonians 1

3 ...constantly bearing in mind your work of faith and labor of love and steadfastness of hope in our Lord Jesus Christ in the presence of our God and Father...
Thank You, Gracious Lord, for the privilege of being employed by You here. Our work is faith and love and hope. Grant that we rejoice every morning as we get up in the employment You have given us. I admit there are some jobs (like sorting through piles of stuff that have built up) that I do not approach with joy and eagerness. But to believe in You, to trust You, to listen to You—these are my delight. Bless us that nothing intrudes into our faith, into our trusting You, into our depending on You. Especially keep us from depending on ourselves. Thank You that we get to love with the love You have given us. Please continue to let Your love flow through us in what we say and how we speak. Speak to us and show us ways to love people, and grant that we listen to You and follow Your will with joy and enthusiasm. Thank You that we may always Live in hope in You, Jesus. Children and parents and friends and weather may be sometimes iffy, but help us to be steadfast in hoping in You. And walking with You, grant that we will be dependable and loving—whether as parent, child, friend or spouse (without any iffyness).

5 ...for our gospel did not come to you in word only, but also in power and in the Holy Spirit and with full conviction; just as you know what kind of men we proved to be among you for your sake.
Thank You, Lord. I really need that. You have given me some mountain top experiences, Lord. And there are days that seem to be in deep valleys. Make Your word consistent in me in power, in You, Lord Holy Spirit, and with full

conviction, so that I will demonstrate also the result of Your effective word in my life among other people. And then, Lord, You know that in congregations (yes, like the one I am in) there are some people who have been blessed by You, and then they have seemed to fade away. They don't appear to be actively part of the family, just now. Bless them, Lord. They have received Your word. You have touched them. There was power in the word You gave them. Use that power, Lord. Light Your fire in them, Spirit of Life. Let conviction of joy and blessing and wonder in You bubble up again in their hearts and lives. Make them so Alive in You that it shines brightly in all of their living. Let them be part of the proof You give to the world that You are here and Your word with power and Spirit is still available and giving Life today.

9, 10 For they themselves report about us what kind of a reception we had with you, and how you turned to God from idols to serve a living and true God, [10] and to wait for His Son from heaven, whom He raised from the dead, *that is* Jesus, who rescues us from the wrath to come.

It isn't quite so obvious today, Lord, turning from idols. No strange looking statues to get rid of. Unfortunately it is harder to get rid of the idols we do have today. Please help all of us today to recognize the idols that attract us. If we are still keeping an idol or two in our (heart's) closet, help us to admit that and get rid of them. Thank You for friends and family. Thank You for the beauty of the world You have made. Help us to keep all of them in their proper place in relationship to You. Let no thing and no idea, no cause and no person take first place in our life instead of You. Thank You for the privilege of serving You, Gracious Lord and God. Grant us wisdom and power and satisfaction in that serving. Grant that we will be effective as You desire. And grant that as we serve, we are always aware of waiting, of keeping one eye on the horizon, on the edge of living. Let the anticipation of Your coming fill us with confidence, joy, and enthusiasm for Living and serving while we wait.

Enjoying full employment
Your word: Hidden, bubbling
Waiting with one Number One


1 Thessalonians 2

8 Having so fond an affection for you, we were well-pleased to impart to you not only the gospel of God but also our own lives, because you had become very dear to us.
We, Your people, Lord, really want to share the wonderful good news of the Gospel with all people. We want all people to come to the truth, to You, and to Life. I'm afraid, sometimes, the motivation we have is a little tainted. I suspect, we would like to share the Gospel with others and have them come into Your kingdom so that You can fix them and they won't be such a problem for us anymore. (Is it as bad as (cringe!) we want You to make them as wonderful as we are?! I hope not.) Help us, Gracious Lord, to see people as You do. Help us to care about people. Grant that we love the people around us, whether they are in our families, our workplace, our travel companions, or just those who live around us. Help us to have a fond affection for people. Stir our hearts so that people will be dear to us. Grant that by Your grace, we share our lives with the people around us. Open our hearts so that we give love with our lives so that we can bless people, because people are dear to us, in Your grace. Thank You for the people who loved us and shared their lives and Your love with us.

11, 12 ...just as you know how we *were* exhorting and encouraging and imploring each one of you as a father *would* his own children, [12] so that you would walk in a manner worthy of the God who calls you into His own kingdom and glory.
Before I can exhort others to walk worthy of You, Lord, I need to take in Your exhortation, encouragement, and

imploring myself. Help me to hear You exhorting me. You are so gracious to encourage me, grant that I see Your encouragement and take it in. And as I waver on the edge of selfishness, waywardness, and evil, help me to hear You imploring me to come away and follow You. Grant that by Your grace at work in me today I will recognize You. Help me to see the calling You give me into Your very kingdom, which You have prepared so generously. You are so glorious, beyond my imagination, Lord. Grant that I walk today with the joy of Your calling, with the wonder of Your exhorting even me, with the power of Your gracious encouragement. Grant that I look worthy of You today to those who see me, so that they will look around and see You, Gracious and Glorious Lord, and receive their own calling from You.

13 For this reason we also constantly thank God that when you received the word of God which you heard from us, you accepted *it* not *as* the word of men, but *for* what it really is, the word of God, which also performs its work in you who believe.

There are so many voices that claim authority today, Lord. "Have you read the new article …? Did you hear about that best seller book that explains … ? There is now confirming evidence that the recent find of the ancient … !" Help us Lord to hear You. You have graciously given us Your word. Help us to cut through all the fog that floats around and accept the word You have given us as the word of God, You speaking to us. We, Your people, need to be in Your word each day. It is easy to feel as if we have been inoculated, since we are blessed with faith from You, and to feel as if we don't need any booster shots. Forgive us, Lord. Bless all of us with daily walking with You in the power of Your Spirit. Open us, inform us, connect us with Your love, with the power of Your forgiveness, so that we Live by Your power, listening to You. And please bless people who need to receive Your gift of Life with reading, listening to, receiving Your word as a letter of love from You. Let them listen to

You and come to know You and Your love in Your word. Grant that Your word will do its work in us and in all whom it touches so that we may be strong in faith and rejoice in Life now and forever, together with You.

Giving our lives and love
Walking graciously worthy
Your word, still working, please


1 Thessalonians 3

8 ...for now we *really* live, if you stand firm in the Lord.
How difficult it is to be at peace and satisfied, Lord, not knowing if the ones we brought to You are still steadfast in the faith You have given them. Whether it is children or friends that we love, we want them to grow in their faith, Lord. Bless them, Lord. Keep them close to You. Make them strong in their faith. In their walk with You, grant them the great joy of bringing others to You. It would be a blessing to hear reports from some modern Timothy that all is well with the people we care about. Help us to remain firm in prayer support for them. Help us to trust You in Your care for them. As we are able, let us give Spirit powered effective encouragement to them. And thank You for those who cared about us and brought us to You. Thank You for their words and caring and sacrifices. Bless them with joy and satisfaction in all they had the privilege to do by Your grace. And let us honor them and You by our living in fellowship with You—Alive and healthy in our Living, by Your grace and mercy, by Your love and Your power.

11 Now may our God and Father Himself and Jesus our Lord direct our way to you.
It is so easy to think of the day ahead as something that I need to plan carefully, with balance of important and urgent, using appropriate electronic devices to remind me of the plan (or in extreme need, 3x5 cards!), including

psychologically appropriate breathing time and physical discipline of exercise. But, really! Direct my way, Lord! Show me how to be a blessing to those I love and care about. Show me how to be a blessing to those others You love and care about that I will meet in this day. I think of a map of all the airlines that are going to fly today, and realize that it is nothing compared to Your plans, directing Your people today. Guide and direct all of us, Lord. Help us to take with us all that You want us to carry (and none of the fearfully claimed "Don't You think I might need this, Lord?" stuff). Help us to be patient with the time, Lord, trusting You to direct our way to be a blessing to those we love, in Your right and gracious time. You know the temptation we have to go back and try to micromanage people's lives with what we think is best. Help us to Live whole-heartedly in the direction You give us today, trusting You to do far better than any (possibly arrogant) micromanagement that we would consider doing. Thank You that we get to walk with You today, Lord. Let all of our joy and satisfaction be inside Your gracious directing.

12  ...and may the Lord cause you to increase and abound in love for one another, and for all people, just as we also *do* for you.
What a wonderful prayer, Lord! Thank You! So now please bless all of Your people to be heartfelt in their prayers for all the groups of Christians around the world. Bless us, Your people, in praying for our congregations and all the gatherings of Your people, without limiting our love or desire by anything other than Your great love for Your people. Bless Your people, in small groups, in families, in congregations, in church bodies, in national groupings—cause each and all of us to increase and abound in love for one another. Grant that we abound in love in our groups and reaching out to the others in our communities, extending our prayers and love to the many we have not seen and have not heard of. Cause us each and all to increase and abound in love for all people—the nice ones we know, the

ones we know whom we have much too easily categorized as "not nice", and people who are strangers to us including those whom we may meet only once before we join them in eternal joy. Thank You for those who love us (including some You appointed, whom we may never meet in this life). Thank You for being loved and for the privilege of loving others.

Loved ones: Healthy in faith
Your direction, for us and them
Loving all, even each other


1 Thessalonians 4

1  Finally then, brethren, we request and exhort you in the Lord Jesus, that as you received from us *instruction* as to how you ought to walk and please God (just as you actually do walk), that you excel still more.
When I first heard Your instruction it sounded great and then it took some maturity until I realized how far from walking that way I was. Thank You for Your forgiveness. Thank You that I may use Your power and guidance each day to follow You. Thank You that I actually do walk in Your will (in a limited way, by Your grace). Help me to see the times I sidestep Your will, or hop over places where You want me to walk. Keep me from all vanity of thinking that I've got this made (and don't need Your help all the time, only when I call!). As I listen to You and honestly look at my daily walk, I know I have a lot of room for more faithfulness. Please help me, Lord, to excel still more. Fill me with Your Spirit so that I will rejoice in You always and live in this day close to You. Let my fellowship with You in every step be clear, so that others can see You with me.

11, 12  ...and to make it your ambition to lead a quiet life and attend to your own business and work with your hands, just as we commanded you, ¹² so that you will behave properly toward outsiders and not be in any need.

You realize, Lord, that "ambition" is often today used in a very different context. Thank You for shining Your light on the reality in which we live today, and showing us a good place for ambition. If we live in a cabin in the mountains, it can be a quiet life, but in other places, it can seem anything but quiet. Help us deal with all that tries to disturb the quiet that we enjoy with You. Give us excellent hearing when it comes to Your voice, and deaf ears when it comes to voices that try to disturb us, mislead us, or push us into depression and despair. Give us joyful and sincere hearts to attend to the work You have given us to do. Grant that we only involve ourselves with others and their work in order to encourage them and their work, to Your glory. Please use the work You give us to do so that we may have what we need and so that we may give to those You want us to help. Let the attitude that You give us, of rejoicing in You in peace, in a quiet life, be a blessing to those we meet today.

13, 14  But we do not want you to be uninformed, brethren, about those who are asleep, so that you will not grieve as do the rest who have no hope. ¹⁴ For if we believe that Jesus died and rose again, even so God will bring with Him those who have fallen asleep in Jesus.

Thank You for hope, Lord, when someone we love dies and goes home to be with You. It is true that I miss those I have loved, those who have been a great blessing to me. Thank You that I can remember them and celebrate the blessings we enjoyed together. As I look through the family albums (shows how old I am!) I find relatives from generations before I was born. Thank You for the joy that I will get to meet the faithful ancestors when You come back. (Some of the pictures look rather forbiddingly serious, but I suspect You will have arranged a joyous smile by the time I see them.) Keep me faithful and close to You, Gracious Lord. And keep me in the joy and wonder of Your promise of bringing all Your family with You when You return. Grant that the joy of waiting for the reunion fill my living with wonder and satisfaction as I finish the days You give me, in Your grace and mercy and love.

Improving my walk
Working quietly: Selective listening
Reunion joy coming


1 Thessalonians 5

4 – 6 But you, brethren, are not in darkness, that the day would overtake you like a thief; ⁵ for you are all sons of light and sons of day. We are not of night nor of darkness; ⁶ so then let us not sleep as others do, but let us be alert and sober.
It is certainly possible, Lord, to see some people stumbling around finding enjoyment in things that appear with Your light to be dangerous, destructive, and leading to evil. You have graciously given us Your light, so that we may see the landscape of evil that surrounds us. Help us to live in Your light, without joining into any part of life in darkness. Grant that we will be alert and notice when something tries to appeal to us from the darkness like selfishness, pornography, trying to take the control of our lives away from You, worry, fear, idolatry of putting some person or thing first before You. Grant us clear judgement about choices we make in spending time and money. Help us never to give in to any intoxicating influence of sin, but to confess our sins daily and live in the Light of Your forgiveness. Since we know the end of darkness is coming, help us keep our faces turned always to Your Light.

8  But since we are of *the* day, let us be sober, having put on the breastplate of faith and love, and as a helmet, the hope of salvation.
You have graciously given us wonderful defensive gifts for living in this present time, Lord. Help us to use faith today,

not because we are visibly under attack (although we certainly are continuously attacked by the forces of evil). But because we want to keep in fellowship walking with You, trusting You to be with us, to guide us, to provide for us, to protect us. Grant that we use Your gift of love, so that our lives will be so filled with loving and caring for other people that there is no room for the enemy to squeeze in. And grant that we use hope in this day, the certainty that You have provided us. We hope for Your blessing through us to others and we know You are doing that, whether we see it or not. We hope for Your blessings to us today, and we know that You are indeed using the moments of this day to touch us with Your blessings. And we hope for the eternal joy of Living with You, loving You, in wonder and awe and satisfaction. For You are preparing a place for us, and leading us to Yourself, even through this day. Thank You and praises to You, Gracious Lord of faith, love, and hope!

11 Therefore encourage one another and build up one another, just as you also are doing.
Way to go, Lord! You have truly blessed me with people encouraging me. (OK, I admit, there were one or two times when I felt unencouraged, but thank You that I can be aware of many times when You have blessed me through those around me with encouragement.) Thank You for people building me up in faith by their faith, in wisdom by their teaching, in joy by their Life attitudes of rejoicing. I hear You saying that it is definitely my turn. There are times when I feel discouraged, please, Lord, do not let those get in the way of my serving You. Pull me (yank if necessary!) out of the self-pity, and blahs that I sometimes slip into. Grant that I use every opportunity to encourage those around me (whether I know them or not). Use me to build up other people in faith, by my trusting You and depending on You, in wisdom, by my sharing what I have received from You, and in joy, by seeing You walking with me, by looking for Your blessings every day, and by Spirit-led purposeful rejoicing today and every day. Grant that people whose lives I have

the privilege to touch be aware of being encouraged and built up by You, Gracious Lord of Life.

Living in Your Light
Filled, overflowing with faith, love, hope
Encouraging, building up:  Our calling

# 2 Thessalonians

2 Thessalonians 1

6 – 8  For after all it is *only* just for God to repay with affliction those who afflict you, <sup>7</sup> and *to give* relief to you who are afflicted and to us as well when the Lord Jesus will be revealed from heaven with His mighty angels in flaming fire, <sup>8</sup> dealing out retribution to those who do not know God and to those who do not obey the gospel of our Lord Jesus.
We don't face the same persecution and afflictions that the people suffered then, Lord.  In comparison, we live a very blessed life.  Instead of direct opposition to our faith and Life in You, we have had many decades of encouragement from our culture.  We seem to have come to a different climate now.  But perhaps people have said that for centuries, I don't know, Lord.  It's not that we suffer persecution.  It's that there seems to be a growing indifference to us and to You.  We seem to be ignored, as not part of current reality (unless we can be used to elect someone).  Help us not to slide away from fervent, faithful Living with You and following You.  Grant that we recognize that the time is coming when those physical, mental, and spiritual afflictions that do beset us from time to time will come to an end.  Keep us from desiring (no offense James and John) fire to come down from heaven and zap people who seem so different from us and so opposed to You and us.  Help us to lean on Your mercy for ourselves and please allow Your mercy time to reach them as well.  Grant that we live in the hope and satisfaction of Your company and that we leave the fire and cleaning up to You in Your good time.

10  …when He comes to be glorified in His saints on that day, and to be marveled at among all who have believed— for our testimony to you was believed.

The day is coming, thank You Lord, when You will come. We want very much to glorify You, Lord Jesus. Guide us, direct us, empower us with Your Spirit so that we may Live using the gifts You have given, so that we may touch people with Your love, so that we may serve You in such a way that when You come You receive glory from us. We do believe You, Lord. We believe You are here with us. We believe You love us and walk with us today. We believe that we can depend on You in every need. We believe that You have made this beautiful world in which we get to live. And yet with all that, You assure us that we will marvel at You, at seeing You, at being with You in unending joy. OK, Lord, I am really looking forward to that day. Lift up my vision, so that I can recognize in a growing way now how wonderful and great and gracious You are. Let the joy of Who You are shine from my eyes and heart, from my words and actions in this time of waiting for the great marvel of actually standing there with You, in the new and eternal presence You are preparing.

11, 12  To this end also we pray for you always, that our God will count you worthy of your calling, and fulfill every desire for goodness and the work of faith with power, $^{12}$ so that the name of our Lord Jesus will be glorified in you, and you in Him, according to the grace of our God and *the* Lord Jesus Christ.

Please grant also for us, Lord, that You make us worthy of our calling. The calling You have given us to be Your people and to serve You sharing Your love and joy daily is a high and challenging calling. Show us Your vision of every goodness, and grant that our desires reach to You for exactly those blessings (and none of the stuff from shadow or darkness). Grant us wisdom and discernment daily to know the difference. Let the faith You have given us be effective. Let it grow daily in the power and grace of Your Spirit and Your word. Grant that we use the faith You give us to trust You in stepping into each day putting our faith to work with Your power in Your Spirit. Grant that all of our

Living—thinking and feeling, speaking and doing—glorify You, Lord Jesus. Praise to You Lord Father for Your wonderful and abundant grace and the gift of our Savior Jesus, Your Son. Make clear the vision today: Your calling to Live to Your glory by Your presence and grace and power.

Steadfast in waiting now
Shining with joy. Expecting more.
Life purpose: Glorify You.


2 Thessalonians 2

1, 2 Now we request you, brethren, with regard to the coming of our Lord Jesus Christ and our gathering together to Him, ² that you not be quickly shaken from your composure or be disturbed either by a spirit or a message or a letter as if from us, to the effect that the day of the Lord has come.
There are groups, also today, that say and claim outrageous things. Help us to remember all You have said to us. Keep our faith strong. Keep our focus on what is not seen, rather than on those who would defame You and Your grace and Your presence with us. Keep Your people safe and secure in Your hands Gracious Father. You have given us peace in You, Lord, and assured us that nothing can take it away. Grant that we don't leave it behind or give it away by fascination with the new, the modern views, the emerging discoveries. Thank You that we may live in a composure of peace and joy no matter what happens. When we feel threatened, grant that we do not sink into fear or uncertainty. Grant that we remember and rejoice in You and all You have given us and all You have said to us. You have told us that You will let us know when You come back. Grant us undisturbed, productive days now, while we are waiting. We look forward to Your return, Lord Jesus! Thank You for being with us now!

13, 14  But we should always give thanks to God for you, brethren beloved by the Lord, because God has chosen you from the beginning for salvation through sanctification by the Spirit and faith in the truth. ¹⁴ It was for this He called you through our gospel, that you may gain the glory of our Lord Jesus Christ.
It is easy, Lord, to somehow fall into the trap of thinking that I am saved because of what I have done.  There is so much emphasis, especially in this culture, on earning what a person has.  And yet You are very clear that all the joy I have in You, Father, is because of Your actions.  You have made me holy by the work of Your Spirit.  You have given me faith to believe the truth about Jesus, Your Son and our Lord.  You have reached me with the good news of the Gospel and called me to Life in You.  Help me not to be in any way vain or prideful as if Your wonderful blessings were my doing.  (I know, there is that little voice inside, "Well don't I get credit for at least being a pretty nice person?  Huh?"  Forgive me, Lord.  Grant that I look for no credit, that I desire no praise for me, but only for You.)  Grant that a spirit of thankfulness for Your grace abide alone in my heart without contradiction from selfishness.  And let that spirit of thankfulness be visible so that others see in me, not pride in myself, but only pride and thankfulness in You.  To You be the glory.

16, 17  Now may our Lord Jesus Christ Himself and God our Father, who has loved us and given us eternal comfort and good hope by grace, ¹⁷ comfort and strengthen your hearts in every good work and word.
Yes, Lord, thank You for loving us.  Thank You for giving us, here in this box of time in which we live today, blessings so great that they are vastly bigger than the box of time in which we find ourselves.  Thank You for eternal comfort and encouragement.  Show us again today, the comfort we have because You are our Savior.  Touch us again with the encouragement that You are our Lord, in charge with love, even in these passing moments.  And You have given us

such expectation, such hope! When a student starts a course of study she hopes to finish in the plan she has made, but she still knows that her interests and abilities may lead her to other goals along the way. The hope You give us is such an eternal certainty that You fill us with joy and confidence for Living now, in the light of what we know is coming by Your grace. Let that hope, certainty, joy, and confidence show in every work we do and in every word we speak. Let our thinking and feeling be so filled with that hope that the melody of Your eternal blessings reach the hearts of those we meet today.

Through every storm: peace
Proud of You, Lord!
Confidence for now from Your gracious then


2 Thessalonians 3

1, 2 Finally, brethren, pray for us that the word of the Lord will spread rapidly and be glorified, just as *it did* also with you; ² and that we will be rescued from perverse and evil men; for not all have faith.
Gracious Lord, thank You for Your word. Thank You for those who followed Paul in spreading the word so that it has reached even me. Thank You for the availability of Your word in many formats, print and electronic. Bless all those who are working to spread Your word today. Grant that they will be blessed by Your Spirit, and Your word will spread rapidly and be recognized as indeed Your word of Life for all. Protect all those who are working to spread Your word. Keep them safe from those people who are separate from You and going their own, different, direction. Protect them from evil attacking body, mind or spirit. Give them strength for all the great work You have given them. Give them audiences ready and willing and open to hear and receive Your word of Life. Bless all Your people that we will continue to support the work of spreading Your word, in our

homes, in our communities, in our countries, and throughout the world to all people. (Bless especially Faith Comes By Hearing in all the work they do to reach people with Your gracious, Life-saving good news.) Thank You for all those organizations that are at work to reach people with Your gospel. Make their work effective to Your glory.

5 May the Lord direct your hearts into the love of God and into the steadfastness of Christ.
St Augustine said clearly, "Our hearts are restless until they find their rest in You." Left on our own, our hearts keep jumping from one attempt to find a solid, satisfying place to live to another and to another. People have tried to find satisfaction in getting riches, in giving riches away (some with twisted motives of being liked by other people or by You), in collecting the most of something (electronic toys (I'm sorry, Lord, I have a soft spot in my heart for those folks), bells, statues, dolls, baseball memorabilia, historic memorabilia, art, and countless other things). Help us to enjoy the things You give us here, and at the same time grant that we recognize that our satisfaction comes from You. Please Lord direct our hearts away from satisfaction in money, houses, toys, or other things. Direct them into Your love. Grant that we take in and drink deeply the real satisfaction of being loved by You. Grant that we take satisfaction in the steadfastness of Christ Jesus our Savior and Lord, and in Living in fellowship with You, Father, Jesus, and Holy Spirit. Thank You that we don't have to keep trying new things to find satisfaction. Grant that we begin this day and every day with our hearts resting in satisfaction in You.

7, 16 For you yourselves know how you ought to follow our example, because we did not act in an undisciplined manner among you. [16] Now may the Lord of peace Himself continually grant you peace in every circumstance. The Lord be with you all!
Thank You, Lord for giving the opportunity to work, so that we can live in Your discipline of earning what we need by

Your grace. Bless those people who are having trouble finding work—grant that they will find the work that You want them to do. Bless those people who are having trouble wanting to work. Grant them a desire to provide for themselves and their families, depending on You for ability and wisdom. Bless all those people who are working each day with the satisfaction of serving You in what they are doing. Bless all of us with joy in You so that when we get up at the beginning of our day we will rejoice in Your presence and enter into the work You give us to do with joy, thanksgiving, a desire to do what we do well, and to Your glory, and a desire to be a blessing in whatever You give us to do. Throughout this discipline, grant us peace in every circumstance. Help us to remember that all peace comes from You, our Lord of Peace. Grant that we walk in Your presence and peace in all we do today, Gracious Lord.

Spread Your word to all
Direct our hearts: Satisfaction
Working for You, in peace

# 1 Timothy

1 Timothy 1

2 To Timothy, *my* true child in *the* faith: Grace, mercy *and* peace from God the Father and Christ Jesus our Lord.
Lord, I hear You saying this to me, too, if that's ok with You. I know it was Paul's greeting to Timothy, but it's still You. And You haven't changed. From You comes all grace, mercy, and peace. Thank You, Lord. There are people who don't value these highly. Please bless them, Lord. Help them to see their needs. I know I need Your grace, Lord. Nothing in my hand I bring to You. Reach me with Your grace again today. Wash me in Your mercy with forgiveness of my sins. And grant me peace. There are such opportunities to worry, to fear, to take in the load of brokenness from the world. Grant that I take in only peace from You, so that I may, in faith, reject worry and fear, and reach out with Your grace, mercy and peace to people experiencing the brokenness of this world. Let Your peace flow through me.

5 But the goal of our instruction is love from a pure heart and a good conscience and a sincere faith.
That almost sounds like a chemistry formula, Lord. Take a pure heart, a good conscience, and a sincere faith and out comes love. Your effective, gracious plan. So please grant me a pure heart, Lord. It's hard for me to see all the impurities (and if I looked to take them out, I might have trouble tearing some out—I'm sorry I have gotten attached to a few), so please tear them all out. You give me confidence that when they are gone, there will still be me, remaining. With Your forgiveness, Lord, grant me a good conscience. Keep my conscience healthy in Your will, Lord. Use it to help me recognize paths of evil and scams and "free lunches" so attractively packaged by evil. Help me with my

conscience to see the wonderful open doors that You provide for me to live with You and serve You, in joy and satisfaction.  And strengthen my faith every day.  Make it sincere—without any fillers that take away from the power of Your gift of trusting in You (like, perhaps I should worry just a little or think about a back-up plan just in case You don't provide for me the way I want—yuck!).  Then mix it well, Lord, and let love flow out today and every day!

18  This command I entrust to you, Timothy, *my* son, in accordance with the prophecies previously made concerning you, that by them you fight the good fight.
It's not that You want me to go around with a chip on my shoulder, looking for a fight.  Thank You, Lord.  I'm not interested in looking for opportunities to win some fight with people.  But there is a good fight that You set before me each day.  Help me not to turn away.  Grant that I never turn back in the face of the enemy.  In Your word You have made plain that we, Your people, have enemies.  Grant that I may grow in Your word, be instructed by Your word, be empowered by Your Spirit through Your word, so that I am prepared always to fight as You desire.  In particular, help me to recognize when to stand up for You and Your way of grace and blessing.  Help me not to be pulled into evil by a desire to be like other people or a desire not to disturb other people.  Sometimes evil looks so quiet, mild-mannered, in need of compassion.  Let me see with Your eyes, Lord.  Grant that I never be misled by a desire to be compassionate into going over any Rubicon line away from You.  Grant that I use the sword of the Spirit fearlessly, effectively, and with tough love in Your gracious will to protect myself and others and to follow You faithfully.

Your peace, through me
Mixed well to love
Battling with Your word

## 1 Timothy 2

**1, 2** First of all, then, I urge that entreaties *and* prayers, petitions *and* thanksgivings, be made on behalf of all men, ² for kings and all who are in authority, so that we may lead a tranquil and quiet life in all godliness and dignity.

Thank You Lord, for Your encouragement to us to pray. I know there are some people who really want to be in charge, in authority, the one to make decisions for the city, state or country (or world). I can't imagine wanting to do that. Please call people to positions of authority whom You have chosen to be a blessing in these offices. Please bless people who have authority with the gifts You want them to have. Bless them with wisdom and insight and with a discerning spirit to listen to You and follow Your will. Protect them from all evil that would hurt them or lead them into selfishness or perversity. Provide for them wise counselors and faith-filled staff. Help them to follow Your will for blessing people whether their decisions will be popular or not. Grant that the people over whom they have authority appreciate them and their faithful hard work and support them in their exercise of wisdom and their faithfulness to You. Work through all those in authority to bless people with peace, tranquility, and the freedom to live, honoring You with all their lives.

**3, 4** This is good and acceptable in the sight of God our Savior, ⁴ who desires all men to be saved and to come to the knowledge of the truth.

There are a lot of people on this planet at the moment. And You care about each one. Thank You, Lord. I know it was hard for Your people in the Old Testament to believe You cared about those Other people. And I suppose it's hard for some of Your people now to believe Your love extends to people with vastly different life experiences, to people who seem angry and antagonistic all the time, to people who think You don't exist and are living only for the brief time they are alive, here. Bless them all, Lord. It's true that I wouldn't want to walk down a dark alley with some of them or even listen to what seems like gobble-gook from others. Bless them, reach them, use Your people to love them (even me, yes, Lord). Turn them from waywardness, despair, self-satisfaction, and idolatry, to You. Bring them to the knowledge of the truth of grace and forgiveness in Jesus, and the gift of Life forever with You.

8  Therefore I want the men in every place to pray, lifting up holy hands, without wrath and dissension.
People can have such friendly discussions with disagreements included. But when Your people decide on a way of saying what Your will is, we have a habit of holding onto our words with clenched fist and a wrathful disposition toward anyone who dares to disagree with us. Not at all Your way of loving and blessing. Forgive me for times when I have participated in that, Lord. Grant Your Spirit to Your people so that we can, in every place where You have called us and put us, pray (hands folded or lifted up without rules about how to fold them or how high to lift them!), with an attitude of gratitude for all our sisters and brothers. Grant that our conversations be in faith with You, without aspersions cast about other Christians who are in some way different. Grant that our prayers be united in dependence on You, in honoring You, in seeking Your will, in rejoicing in Your blessings, in desiring to follow You, Living in Jesus, and serving You faithfully, always.

Authority: With wisdom, faithfulness, and blessing
Reach, invite, bless all
Praying: United in Jesus


1 Timothy 3

2, 3  An overseer, then, must be above reproach, the husband of one wife, temperate, prudent, respectable, hospitable, able to teach, [3] not addicted to wine or pugnacious, but gentle, peaceable, free from the love of money.

You have graciously called and provided people to help us, guide us, and support us in our faith, Lord. Thank You! So, since You have really high expectations of those people, I hear You saying that it is the responsibility of Your people to pray for them. Bless them, Lord. All those You have given us to bless us. When reproach comes knocking at their door, send it packing by the power of Your Spirit. Help them not to be extreme in attitudes. Bless them with prudence, good judgement, good management, self-discipline. Make them worthy of respect without greatly desiring it. Let them be open to welcome all people to You. Give them ability to teach well. Keep them from problems with alcohol or a pugnacious spirit. Grant that they demonstrate gentleness and peace. Provide for them with such blessings that they never slip into loving money and stuff. And grant that we, Your people, will not be problematic for them, but rather, always be a blessing to them.

8, 9 Deacons likewise *must be* men of dignity, not double-tongued, or addicted to much wine or fond of sordid gain, [9] *but* holding to the mystery of the faith with a clear conscience.

You have provided Your servants whom You have called to various offices of ministry, also to give us examples of how we may live for You. Help us to emulate all the good qualities we see in them. In particular, help us, Your people, to enjoy daily life as we are enjoying Your gift of Life, to appreciate Your blessings, and to do that without demeaning You or Your grace. Grant that we live in joy, not in a stuffy way, but with dignity as Your servants. Help us never to be deceitful. Let us speak truly, and show people faithfulness to You. Keep us from unhealthy addictions, whether to alcohol, drugs, pain-killers, books (!), money, one-up-man ship, or anything else that would take us away from You. And grant that we rejoice in the mystery of Your gracious love in sending Your Son, Jesus, to live here, to die, suffering what we deserve, and to rise again, giving us Life with You now and forever.  Grant that we hold this mystery clearly, by faith, and as dearly as Life.

15  ...but in case I am delayed, *I write* so that you will know how one ought to conduct himself in the household of God, which is the church of the living God, the pillar and support of the truth.
There are interesting quizzes online that are true/false in nature.  And there is the expanding truth we get to know about Your wonderful creation as science works as Your tool to show us Your glory and Your handiwork.  There is the partial truth we know about ourselves (which You know a lot better than we do—thank You for not insisting that we face all that truth all the time—I'm afraid, sinner that I am, it would be too much).  But the great truth is the truth You reveal about You and Your grace and Your love and mercy.  Grant that Your Church always clearly, joyously be faithful in showing and proclaiming this truth.  Make Your household of faith, the Church a solid pillar supporting Your truth.  Fill us with Your Spirit, Lord, so that when people look at Your Church they see the gracious truth You give and are drawn to Life in You.

Protect, bless, use overseers
Hold the Mystery throughout life
Inviting, accurate truth


1 Timothy 4

7, 8  But have nothing to do with worldly fables fit only for old women. On the other hand, discipline yourself for the purpose of godliness; ⁸ for bodily discipline is only of little profit, but godliness is profitable for all things, since it holds promise for the present life and *also* for the *life* to come.
Going to the gym.  Getting out early in the morning to exercise.  Thoughtful choosing of foods that fit with a training

program. There are some people who faithfully do those things. But they mostly seem to feel constrained to do them; it's not because they like them. So the discipline that You want in us is still discipline, but it has a permanent benefit, not just temporary. And it's possible to actually like discipline for godliness. Help us, Your people, and those You are inviting, to be as rigorous in our training: Talking to You to begin each day. Listening to You in Your word to begin each day. Consciously asking You to direct our thinking throughout each day, whether it is enjoying Your creation and gifts, solving problems, looking for direction, limiting unprofitable woolgathering, thoughtfully caring about other people, working diligently. Help us to enjoy the rigors of continuous training for godliness, Lord, aware of Your gracious and powerful presence with us. (Do you suppose You could keep my muscles in tone as a side benefit of reading Your word, Lord? So I could avoid all the sweating? Right. Keep exercising. Ok, Lord.)

12 Let no one look down on your youthfulness, but *rather* in speech, conduct, love, faith *and* purity, show yourself an example of those who believe.
Thank You, Lord, for Timothy and his work of ministry. Your desire for him was to show himself an example of those who believe. So if that is an example for us to follow, help us to follow it, Lord. If this is what people are supposed to see when they look at us, help us to show it. Grant each of us a loving heart that is visible in everything we say and all we do. Help me not be satisfied with 70% or some such nonsense. Keep our faith strong and growing, Lord, with Your word and Spirit. Help us to show our faith, not by spouting quotes of doctrine but by demonstrating that we are trusting You in times of joy and times of sorrow, times of plenty and times of need, times of peace and times of anxiety. And please give us purity that shows in our attitude toward people of the other gender, in the way we talk to them, in the way we look at them. Help us to be pure in our language and our thoughts as well as our actions. Help us to show purity in

our thinking about You, unmixed with selfishness or hurtful desiring of things, or a prideful attitude that implies that we don't need You.  Let our example, by Your grace and power (no matter what age we are) lead people to You.

13 – 15  Until I come, give attention to the *public* reading *of Scripture*, to exhortation and teaching.  [14] Do not neglect the spiritual gift within you, which was bestowed on you through prophetic utterance with the laying on of hands by the presbytery.  [15] Take pains with these things; be *absorbed* in them, so that your progress will be evident to all.
Thank You, Lord, for Your servants whom You have called to bless us with Scripture, exhortation and teaching.  We, Your people, in one way or another, have given them a lot to do.  Help us to respect them and the time You give them, so that we do not make demands on them that take them away from the main thing.  You have told them to pay attention carefully to Scripture, exhortation, and teaching, to really care about them.  Help us not to pull them away from that priority.  Bless them through Your Holy Spirit to not only take time to prepare Your word for us, but also to take time to read Your word and listen to You for themselves as well.  Bless them in their preparation and communicating to us, that they will get out of Your way and let Your Spirit use them to bless us, inspire us, and empower us for service to You.  And bless them in their knowledge of You and Your will and their knowledge of us and how we learn so that they will teach us well and effectively, to Your glory and our blessing.

Daylong disciplining to enjoy
Me:  Your visible example!
Your servants:  Blessed to bless us


1 Timothy 5

5 Now she who is a widow indeed and who has been left alone, has fixed her hope on God and continues in entreaties and prayers night and day.

Gracious Lord, bless people who are alone. Bless those who feel lonely with Your presence and with friends who will extend Your love to them. Bless those who are alone and helpless, who do not have the means to provide for their shelter, food, and necessities. Provide for them through Your people and through groups that share Your loving help. Bless those people who are not alone, who are surrounded by other people, who are busy, and yet are lonely. Give them relationships with You through people who care about others. Bless those who are alone and yet have plenty. Grant that they feel satisfaction in Your blessings and a desire to be a blessing to others who need their help. Bless those who are alone and satisfied and thankful for Your blessings—let Your light shine through them to bless all those who see them or meet them or know them.

17 The elders who rule well are to be considered worthy of double honor, especially those who work hard at preaching and teaching.

You have graciously given wisdom with experience to some of Your servants, Lord. Thank You! Grant Your Holy Spirit to all those who are in authority in Your Church. Grant that they rule well in every opportunity You give. Bless those who proclaim Your word with closeness to You, with power and knowledge and wisdom in Your word. Grant that they proclaim effectively, inspiring us and empowering us for following You. Bless Your servants that teach us, Your people. Give them insight in and through Your word. Grant them effective means to reach us and bless us with knowledge, joy, and strength for faithfully following You. And please grant that we, Your people, will respect and honor Your servants whom You have sent to bless us. Grant that we will honor them with our words, thoughts, prayers, and actions, to Your glory.

23 No longer drink water *exclusively*, but use a little wine for the sake of your stomach and your frequent ailments.
OK. So for Timothy a little wine was going to be helpful to him and lead him to good health. Today, Lord, You have given a veritable plethora of medicines, herbs, and good foods to bless us in our health. Help us to recognize when we need to make a change and seek something to help us. Help us to be willing to make adjustments so that we can be good stewards of our bodies. I don't know how Timothy felt about wine, but there are some medicines that I like better than others. Give us willingness to take the medicines that You want to be a blessing to us. Give us wisdom to recognize when we go past "a little" and get stuck on wanting bunches of medicines (more than are good for us or with a desire to never feel any ache or pain ever). And please, Gracious Lord, give us joy and satisfaction in You, so that our attitudes are safe from anxiety and harmful stress, and rather filled with peace and gratitude in You, to our good health, and to Your glory.

With You, never lonely
Honoring Your servants
Healthy choices in You


1 Timothy 6

6 But godliness *actually* is a means of great gain when accompanied by contentment.
I want to follow Your will, Lord. You have been gracious and merciful to me, and I want to follow You faithfully. So You tell me that there is a benefit that comes with godliness—that there is great gain to me in following Your will and wanting to be the person You want me to be. It comes when I also include in my life—and that's where I start to splutter a little. There is the "c" word. You know, Lord, if a person watches much television or looks at advertisements, contentment is something that comes only when a person has more. More

stuff, more education, more love, more adulation, more square feet in the house, more houses in more beautiful locations, more people who give more respect, ... . Help me, Lord, to believe You, that contentment is possible in Your grace. Grant that I do not resist Your gift of contentment by continually looking for greener grass, better work, more appreciation of me and my abilities. Thank You for giving me opportunities to advance during life, but please grant me contentment at every place along the way. Help me to see Your love and all Your gifts (including Your gifts of worship and praise), and help me resist the swirling call to contentment only if I get "more". Grant that I live content in You here, now, today.

12  Fight the good fight of faith; take hold of the eternal life to which you were called, and you made the good confession in the presence of many witnesses.
It is a battle, Lord. There are some things I want to hold onto. There have been disappointments, hurts, insults, betrayals, my personal stupidity, and I remember them! And I find myself holding on to them. It's so hard to let go! I say I forgive people, but I feel Your pain and sorrow when I pull out hurts from the past and rehearse them and ask You to feel sorry for me again. If I am going to take hold of eternal life, I have trouble holding onto the hurts that I like to rehearse. Right. I hear You saying, that's the point. I have to let go of everything to take hold of the eternal life to which You call me. Help me then, Lord, to let go. Help me not to keep wanting You to feel sorry for me because things have happened to me or because people have done things to me. Help me to let go, knowing You love those people, too. Help me to use all the weapons You give me of faith, salvation, and Your word, and grant that I fight every temptation to go back, every temptation to feel sorry for myself, every temptation to ask You to go back to old hurts with me, every temptation to let evil in with self-pity. Grant that I fight the good fight with Your power today, and letting go of

everything else, grant that I take hold of the eternal life You give me today and every day.

17  Instruct those who are rich in this present world not to be conceited or to fix their hope on the uncertainty of riches, but on God, who richly supplies us with all things to enjoy.
I have tried some other places to put hope.  I have tried hoping that if I were really nice to people life would be pleasant and satisfying.  I have tried hoping that working hard and learning lots will always lead me to success.  Perhaps I could put hope on a couple things besides You, Lord.  Only really positive blessings that You have given.  How would that be?  Right.  I get one choice.  Everything around, as really good as it looks, bottom line is uncertain, right?  There is only one Certainty, and that is You.  So, I know You are right, and loving, and gracious—help me to fix, to attach my hope onto You.  Not with removable tape, not with a list of conditions (I hope in You, Lord, as long as the following are taken care of—I'm sorry it's a pretty long list), not as long as the people around me agree with me, not with a one year adjustment option.  Help me to fix my hope on You, now, by Your grace, by the power of Your Holy Spirit, with all my heart, for times of sunshine, for times of storms, in times of plenty and in times of need, for now, for tomorrow, for all of my life, forever.

Contentment along the way
Letting go to take hold
Certain hope:  Only in You

# 2 Timothy

2 Timothy 1

7  For God has not given us a spirit of timidity, but of power and love and discipline.

Open me, Gracious Lord, to Your blessings that You give. Sometimes it is like getting a package and wondering what it is, and whether if I open the package will this add to what I am doing or will it change my direction, my activities, my life. That's what it's like getting Your blessings, Lord. I have this feeling, "Am I ready for this?!" While I do not like to think of myself as timid, Lord, power, love and discipline seem (at least first thing in the morning) like a lot to receive and use. Yes, there is the question, in my very human heart—how will I use this?  So with this wonderful blessing, please Lord, give me confidence in You, that You will enable me to use these blessings that You give me.  Help me to use Your power graciously.  Help me to do that with the love You provide, caring about people and not selfishly or egotistically.  And I can see that in order to do that, I need to use Your gift of discipline.  (Even though, You do understand, discipline is not exactly my all-time favorite activity—there are several others that would rather come ahead of discipline.)  So operate on me, open me, change me, Lord, that I may live in You and for You in discipline, as Your disciple, following You faithfully.  Make me a blessing using Your gifts of power, love, and yes, even, especially, discipline.

9, 10  ...who has saved us and called us with a holy calling, not according to our works, but according to His own purpose and grace which was granted us in Christ Jesus from all eternity, [10] but now has been revealed by the appearing of our Savior Christ Jesus, who abolished death and brought life and immortality to light through the gospel.

Thank You, Lord for having a purpose for me. You have created a world that is beautiful and interesting. And I can spend a lot of years learning, enjoying, appreciating Your creation and the people here. Now there does come the time (just a small piece of time between activity A and activity B) when I see a glimpse of emptiness for just an instant before I recover and move on. But life is not just a bunch of activities lined up with a jump across yawning empty space between. You have given me a purpose that has no emptiness in it. By Your grace You have revealed Life that is continuous in Jesus. Thank You Lord for Your gospel. Thank You for shining Your eternal light on Life that is lived for You now and forever. Grant, Lord, that I Live that blessed Life by Living in Your light, rejoicing in Your grace, walking with Jesus my Lord, wanting to honor You and serve You continuously, in every moment that You give me here and now, and then with You forever.

14 Guard, through the Holy Spirit who dwells in us, the treasure which has been entrusted to *you*.
Talk about alarm systems! There are some very fancy ones available, You know, Lord. Someone touches the car, sirens blare. Pry open the door and not only is there a warning sound, cameras record the intrusion, agencies spring into action, security forces are mobilized, … and all that. And that to protect stuff. So it makes sense that for the real Treasure that You have entrusted to me, You have also provided real protection. Grant that I recognize the treasure of Your grace, of faith in you trusting You for Life now and forever in Jesus my Savior. Grant that I listen to the Holy Spirit Whom You have given me, so I don't ignore His warnings when He sees things that can pull me and lead me away from You. Lord, Holy Spirit, guide me, direct me, take control of my life in Your grace. Let nothing infect me with the poison of the enemy. Help me to see clearly so that I recognize the good and wonderful around me with thanksgiving and praise, and so that I recognize the evil and destructive around me and use the weapons You give me

with Your presence, the shield of faith, helmet of salvation, breastplate of the gift of righteousness from Jesus, and the sword of Your word—help me to use them well, by Your power. Keep the treasure that You have given me, secure, Living, and overflowing with joy today and every day.

A blessed spirit of power
Continuous Life, on purpose
Treasure guarding: Spirit powered


2 Timothy 2

1 You therefore, my son, be strong in the grace that is in Christ Jesus.
Thank You, Lord Jesus, that You have strength for us. We want our children to be strong. Thank You for the encouragements to exercise, to get up off the couch and be active. Bless children with healthy activities (and for that matter, adults, too) so that we can be good stewards of our bodies. But real strength is not in muscles. Help me and all Your adults to give a good example of strength. Our strength does not depend on us or anything we do. Help us to see that all our strength comes from grace in You, Lord Jesus. We do not deserve to be strong in the face of trials, temptations, and suffering. Help us not to depend on ourselves. Show us daily the strength we have from Your gracious love and forgiveness. What really makes us weak is the weight of our sins and the memory of our sins. Cleanse us, Lord. Wash us clean by Your grace. Grant that we lean completely on You for Life and health and every good—including the strength to be doing what You give us to do each day. As we depend on You, give us strength to battle against all temptations and strength for whatever cross we carry. Grant that we use the strength You give, by Your grace, to honor and glorify You in all we think, say, and do.

7  Consider what I say, for the Lord will give you understanding in everything.
I want to understand everything You put in my life. I want to understand Your will. I want to understand Your word and how it applies to me and to people today. Thank You, Lord for giving understanding. Sometimes I try approaching Your will or Your word with analysis and tools of learning. Help me not to forget that understanding comes from You, not from me gritting my teeth and creating steam in my thinking. Help me to take time every day to consider what You say to me in Your word, Lord. Use my mind and heart to be open to what You want to communicate to me. Grant me understanding that is more than cognitive. Grant me understanding that changes my heart, my mind, my attitudes. Grant that understanding You, I will enter this day on fire with the joy of Your love so that I shine with Your light and share Your love with all the people You bring into my day.

22  Now flee from youthful lusts and pursue righteousness, faith, love *and* peace, with those who call on the Lord from a pure heart.
You never seem to talk about sitting around, Lord. Every day is a pilgrimage, a pursuit of Your blessings. And in order to be going somewhere, I suppose it makes sense that I have to leave somewhere. Grant me Your fire in my spirit today, that I do not just meander along, wanting to be in the right direction, but that I flee from all that pulls me away from You and particularly from lusts. Burning with wanting, whether it is impure sexual wanting or selfish lusting for things, for wealth, for power or anything else that tries to replace You—all of it is a destructive lust. Keep me from this Gracious Lord. Help me to see those things and flee with all the strength You give me. And help me to pursue with conscious intent Your great blessings of righteousness in Jesus, faith, filled with Your Spirit, love, the great gift from Your loving heart, and peace that gives a solid, joyful place to Live with You. No matter how busy today seems, help me

consistently to be fleeing and pursuing in whatever else I do, by Your grace. Even if I feel tired, Lord, help me never to give up faithfully fleeing and pursuing, with Your strength. Thank You, Lord!

From You:  Strength for the day
Power filled Light for the way
Never sitting:  Fleeing and pursuing


2 Timothy 3

5  ... holding to a form of godliness, although they have denied its power; Avoid such men as these.
What a horrible list of personal attributes!  Avoid them?  Like finding an old dead body and purposefully running away!  Having said that, Lord, it certainly is possible to see a lot of those characteristics in people today.  Some of them appear in people who seem to want to be famous at any cost.
Some of them in people who without hesitation demonstrate that accumulating things is most important to them.  First, Lord, help me never to be in those groups.  If any of those traits try to plant themselves in me, hit me up the side of the head with a two by four, or something, to get my attention and rescue me.  And while it is impossible to not live in the world, grant me a sensitive spiritual nose to recognize these blights when they are near and to steer clear of them, to not participate in them, to go Your direction away from them, and to not appear in any way to give them any support or encouragement.

14  You, however, continue in the things you have learned and become convinced of, knowing from whom you have learned *them*.
Where did you get that idea?  A lot of times people don't exactly know where they got the ideas they hold onto dearly.  Perhaps a relative, a respected teacher, a really good advertising campaign?  But we know where we have gotten

the blessings, the understanding of Your grace, the confidence to Live every day of life with You, the sending to serve people in Your name with love and joy in our hearts, the certain hope of Life beyond life with You.  We know—we got them from You.  Help us to be convinced by Your Spirit of all that You want us to learn, remember, and Live by.  Grant that we recognize Your presence with us as we Live by what we have learned and received from You.  And grant that as we show what we have been convinced of, other people will also recognize that it comes from You, and receive Your eternal blessings with certainty in their hearts that they came not from us, but graciously, from You.

16, 17  All Scripture is inspired by God and profitable for teaching, for reproof, for correction, for training in righteousness; [17] so that the man of God may be adequate, equipped for every good work.
With Your inspired word, Lord, You make us complete— adequately equipped.  To be a professional person, like a teacher, it seems that there is a course of study, a degree or two that are necessary.  And then there is an endless set of other, additional, important, currently necessary, applicable to students today, seminars, courses, lectures, DVD's, workshops, … .  You, Lord, have graciously managed to pack into Your word, which You have inspired for our benefit, all that is necessary for us to be complete and fully equipped for every one of the good things that You have prepared for us to do.  Help us to rejoice in having and reading and studying Your word.  Open Your word to us, Lord Holy Spirit as we read it and listen to it.  And grant that we use what You have given us, effectively, to be about the work You give us to do today.  Help us to never be finished listening to You in Your word.  And help us to never put off doing Your work from lack of confidence.  Fill us with faith that we have what we need, and that You will continue to give us more along the way as we need it.

Avoiding all rotten

Because You said so
Complete. Doing. Listening.


2 Timothy 4

2 …preach the word; be ready in season *and* out of season; reprove, rebuke, exhort, with great patience and instruction.
"What are you going to do in the off-season?" That's the question baseball players get asked, Lord. And football players, and … . But not Christians, right? There is no off-season. Not summers. Not weekdays. Not vacations. Not during office hours. Not before and after work. Not even when we are alone. Still in season. So help us, Lord, with Your strength to never give up. Fill us with Your Spirit, so that we may live in wisdom and shine with the light of Christ Jesus wherever we are. Bless us with faithfully following You when other people agree with us and when they don't, when we feel healthy and when we feel under attack (i.e. lousy), when resources are plentiful and when they are not, when we feel confident and when fear lurks at every corner. Grant that by Your grace we love You, worship You, depend on You, rejoice in You, and serve You consistently no matter what the season around us may be. Your love and joy, forgiveness and power are always in season! Praise to You!

8 …in the future there is laid up for me the crown of righteousness, which the Lord, the righteous Judge, will award to me on that day; and not only to me, but also to all who have loved His appearing.
The greatest day! When You appeared once, here on earth, to people. And the days You appeared to me in my life. Like driving a car in the desert and running low on gas in the middle of nowhere. And then a stranger appearing with directions to a gas station close by! Saved! Like driving along and suddenly passing out, the passenger trying to steer with the driver slumped over the wheel, unable to stop the car, and an angel bringing the car to the side to a stop

with no injuries. (Thank You, Lord!) Yes, Lord I have loved Your appearing. I have loved Your appearing with grace in my life, forgiving my sins, opening me to Your Light and Joy and Life. Bless my family, my friends, all the people I know—bless them with loving Your appearing. And grant us Your crown of righteousness through Jesus our Savior and Lord.

16, 17  At my first defense no one supported me, but all deserted me; may it not be counted against them. [17] But the Lord stood with me and strengthened me, so that through me the proclamation might be fully accomplished, and that all the Gentiles might hear; and I was rescued out of the lion's mouth.
How can I keep going, Lord?   How can I withstand the evil, the pessimism, the selfishness, the hatred?  When it comes from my sinful self it is hard to put up with.  When it comes from outside, from other people, from assumptions that come blaring from media and "entertainment", it is also hard to put up with.  Stand with me, Lord.  Let me never pull away from Your help or be afraid of Your presence.  Grant that I will speak and act in a way that demonstrates my love and faithfulness as Your servant, even when I am with people who are different, even when I am subjected to "entertainment" that I don't think You like (and I shouldn't either!).  Let me feel Your loving strength and Your joy of Living.  Strengthen me to give witness to You always.  Let Your Light show in the choices I make.  Grant that I am always willing to be recognized as the one standing with You.

Ready with love:  Always in season
Rejoicing in Your appearing
Standing together, please, Lord

# Titus

Titus 1

1 Paul, a bond-servant of God and an apostle of Jesus Christ, for the faith of those chosen of God and the knowledge of the truth which is according to godliness…
You went to a lot of work to choose, reach, change, and send Paul as apostle, Lord. Thank You! He recognized that he was Your servant and the one You sent so that Your people would have faith. Give Your gift of faith, Gracious Lord, to people now. It is not by reasoning out what You have done for us that we are blessed, but by believing what You tell us. Grant that we believe and trust You early in the morning, through the day, still at the end of the day, when we have a moment to meditate and when we are inundated with pressing matters. And bless us with knowledge of Your truth—Who You graciously are and how You have brought us to You. Bless us with faith and knowledge that show up in the way we live. When people look at us let them see, not people who want to be noticed as good, but You and Your love and grace reaching out to them.

8 …but hospitable, loving what is good, sensible, just, devout, self-controlled…
You have given elders, spiritual leaders, in our congregations so that we might emulate Your gracious will. Thank You, Lord. Help us then to be hospitable. Help us to care about how others are blessed and their needs met. Let us be open to help people who are traveling. Grant that we will welcome visitors to our communities with the joy and caring hearts that You give. Help us to love what is good. It is easy to love what we think is good for us or makes us look good. Help us to use our senses and our thinking to recognize what is good by Your blessing and what is just, more than what is justice. Help us to be devout in our living,

devoted to You, enjoying Living with You in the time You give us, without being uppity, without appearing to want others to think we are somehow holy. And before we try to control the direction of the world and the lives and attitudes of other people, grant that we use Your power and grace to control ourselves first.

9 ...holding fast the faithful word which is in accordance with the teaching, so that he will be able both to exhort in sound doctrine and to refute those who contradict.
The teaching You graciously give us is connected to Your word, thank You, Lord. And the word that You give us is connected to the teaching You provide, thank You, Lord. Open our eyes and hearts and minds to receive Your teaching and word. Let us recognize those whom You have provided to lead us in our understanding by the power of Your Holy Spirit. Grant that what we receive and know, believe and trust is effective so that we can share Your gracious love with others (not with "I know more than you do", but with "Isn't God great, rejoice with me in this"). And give us wisdom and love so that we clearly recognize that which is opposed to Your grace and love, that which is contrary to Your word, that which is hurtful to the faith You have given. Grant that we reject those things, not with hatred of people, not with violence, but with love and faithfulness, offering and showing truth in our Lives, words, and attitudes, depending always on You and the power of Your Holy Spirit.

Trusting and believing You
Controlling ourselves to love Your good
Saying "Yes" and "No" faithfully


Titus 2

2  Older men are to be temperate, dignified, sensible, sound in faith, in love, in perseverance.  ³ Older women likewise are

to be reverent in their behavior, not malicious gossips nor enslaved to much wine, teaching what is good.

I wonder what "older" meant to Paul, Lord. I have a high degree of certainty that I am included, no matter where he drew the line. People in my culture tend to think of themselves as young for quite a while, then as middle age for a longer period, and older only when other people are extremely polite but don't listen very much. (OK, maybe I'm just being sensitive. Sorry, Lord.) Help us, who are to be examples to those who are younger to be sensible in the sense of self-controlled. The temptation is to get to a point when we would rather just forget conventions and other people's expectations. Help us to be dignified with joy, and without any stuffiness. Let our behavior show reverence for You in all we are and do. Grant that we be sound in our examples and teaching, helping others to trust You, to enjoy and share Your love, and to persevere through time and difficulties. (And if we are going to drink wine, help us to focus on quality and not on quantity.)

9, 10 *Urge* bondslaves to be subject to their own masters in everything, to be well-pleasing, not argumentative, [10] not pilfering, but showing all good faith so that they will adorn the doctrine of God our Savior in every respect.

While outright slavery does not seem to exist in this country, I hear You talking about the work that we do. Help us, Lord, to do the work that You give us to do, well and with respect for those in charge over us. Grant that whether we think they are wonderful people or not, we do our best, and encourage them, expressing our creative (and obviously wonderful) ideas with respect and without argument. Keep us from the temptation to steal time, money, or things in our workplace. And grant, Lord, that we will show faithfulness to You in our life and work. Make us a blessing to those in authority above us, to our fellow workers, and to anyone we supervise. Let us clearly show that we represent You, not with arrogance, but with humility and love, always demonstrating our trust in You, our Lord and Savior.

11 – 13  For the grace of God has appeared, bringing salvation to all men, [12] instructing us to deny ungodliness and worldly desires and to live sensibly, righteously and godly in the present age, [13] looking for the blessed hope and the appearing of the glory of our great God and Savior, Christ Jesus.

In Your grace, Lord, appearing in Jesus, you have instructions for us whom You have redeemed.  Thank You for showing us Your will.  Bless us in denying, living, and looking.  Some of what is around us is obviously ungodly and easier to identify.  Grant that we give it no room in us.  The worldly desires are a little harder.  Keep us in the world but not of it.  Even when they appear plausible as part of the "modern way of life in our advanced century", help us to see through the flummery, keep us safe from all that tries to draw us away from You.  Give us strength and wisdom to control ourselves and to Live by Your grace, showing Your righteousness and our love for You.  And keep us looking, Lord.  Grant that we clearly appear to be looking for Your awesome and blessed appearing, Lord Jesus.  When people look at us, help them to see You reflected in our eyes, our hope, our words, our yearning for the great homecoming You are preparing.

Teaching by example
Working hard:  Appearing faithful
Denying, Living, and looking


Titus 3

1  Remind them to be subject to rulers, to authorities, to be obedient, to be ready for every good deed…
It's easy to say, "I didn't vote for that person!"  Hardly the point.  Please help Your people to have respect for our rulers.  Bless us with obedience to authorities (in Your will), demonstrating that we are being faithful to You as we do

that. Now You go on saying to be ready for every good deed as if our attitude toward authorities and our obedience leads us to be ready. I admit, that has not been obvious to me. Help us to not let political opinions or selfish angers get in the way of being ready. Grant us Your Holy Spirit so that we will be ready with faith in You, joy in Living with You, and love for people. And grant that we recognize opportunities to do something good when we see them. Bless us with readiness, willingness, and, by Your grace, ability to step in and be a blessing in every opportunity You give us.

2 ...to malign no one, to be peaceable, gentle, showing every consideration for all men.
We look around at people, and the temptation is to think we know what is in people's hearts. You have said to leave that up to You, so help us not to let that get in the way of our attitudes toward others. And then, of course, there is the fact that the things that really bother us about other people is often (if not usually) what we don't like in ourselves. So thank You, Lord for being peaceable, gentle, and considerate toward us. Help us to be clear about Your grace and forgiveness before we start forming attitudes about others. And then using Your gracious power following our being forgiven, let us reach out to other people without desire to malign them. Grant that we will reach out with peace. Grant that we will be gentle in words and actions. And grant that we will show to people and make clear an attitude of loving consideration toward every person (with no "except, of course", "but You don't really mean ...", or "only if they smile"). Help us to be considerate with full awareness and memory of Your consideration toward us.

5 – 8 He saved us, not on the basis of deeds which we have done in righteousness, but according to His mercy, by the washing of regeneration and renewing by the Holy Spirit, [6] whom He poured out upon us richly through Jesus Christ our Savior, [7] so that being justified by His grace we would be made heirs according to *the* hope of eternal life. [8] This is a

trustworthy statement; and concerning these things I want you to speak confidently, so that those who have believed God will be careful to engage in good deeds. These things are good and profitable for men.

Wow, Lord, what You have done! Bless all those whom You have appointed to speak good news to us, so that they will speak confidently concerning these things, so that they will pass along repeatedly insights through Your Holy Spirit regarding these trustworthy statements. The washing of regeneration and renewal in the Holy Spirit! Make them a blessing to us and through us today. And when we receive the encouragement of Your wonderful and abundant grace, help us to take it in (this will require that we stay awake, so feel free to have Your angels give us a knock on the head if indicated). Grant that we take in the nourishing words You provide and let them be productive of good deeds. Grow fruit of blessing, goodness, caring, encouraging, and helping from the power of Your nourishment through us.

Ready for Your opportunities
Considerate: From being forgiven
Hear Life: Live fruitfully

# Philemon

6 ...*and I pray* that the fellowship of your faith may become effective through the knowledge of every good thing which is in you for Christ's sake.
You have created people to need people, Lord. Thank You. Fellowship with others is a blessing. People have used a lot of different foundations for fellowship with others. Living on the same street, graduating from the same school, liking the same sport, speaking the same language, delighting in the same trivia (Star Wars!), watching the same soap opera. Thank You for a more excellent basis for fellowship. Grant that we, Your people, will have fellowship based on what good we see in ourselves and others, which You have given us. Let us recognize in other people the good which honors Jesus Christ our Lord. Grant that we celebrate that good, celebrate Jesus, and rejoice in fellowship together, now and without end.

14 ...but without your consent I did not want to do anything, so that your goodness would not be, in effect, by compulsion but of your own free will.
There is a lot of good done in the world, thank You Lord. Now if it were all done for the right reasons, then we would have something. Ouch! As I have grown up, Lord, I have learned many reasons for doing something good. To survive, to get good grades, to please people I like, to please people I don't actually like but want to impress, to be dutiful as a citizen, to not get in trouble, and stuff like that. Here, You make it clear, Lord, that good that is good is not done because I am under compulsion. Real good is from my heart moved by Your grace. I can only want good, when I know Your love. Fill my heart with Your grace, so that I can earnestly want to do that which good in Your gracious will. When I am tempted to do good for the wrong reason, Lord, ring that "wake up, Michael" bell, and grant that I do that

which is good with a full heart, willingly, joyfully, and with humble satisfaction in You and Your grace.

20  Yes, brother, let me benefit from you in the Lord; refresh my heart in Christ.
It is easy to look back and think of people whose hearts I would like to have refreshed more. Please forgive me for missing opportunities that You have given me in the past. Help me to focus on today and the todays You give me. Open my eyes to see ways to refresh the hearts of people around me.  Fill me with joy and willingness to give benefit from Your grace and love to others.  Grant that without hesitation I touch people by refreshing their hearts in You, Lord Jesus.  What a privilege, Lord!  There are a lot of people who appear to need their hearts refreshed.  Use me (more powerful than uncola, real things, right generation or noting the time of 10, 2, and 4), by Your grace, as You will, to bring great (and, if appropriate, fizzy) refreshment.

Celebrate the fellowship of gracious good
Doing good, by fervent desire
Sent to refresh hearts

# Hebrews

Hebrews 1

2 [God]... in these last days has spoken to us in His Son, whom He appointed heir of all things, through whom also He made the world.
Father, You spoke to some of Your servants like Moses and Paul in a direct way. And at Mount Sinai when You spoke, the people became very frightened. Thank You for speaking to me through Jesus, Your Son. It wasn't just at the time of the apostles that You spoke through Jesus. I have come to know Jesus through Your word, through Your sacraments, through Your people witnessing by word and action. Keep speaking to me through Jesus. Let me hear You speaking to me personally. Whether it is when I wake up in the morning, when I am considering the plan for the day, when I am with other people, or when I am alone let me hear You. Let me hear You when I am confused or troubled or joyous. Keep me close to Jesus so that I may always hear You speaking to me through Him.

3 And He is the radiance of His glory and the exact representation of His nature, and upholds all things by the word of His power. When He had made purification of sins, He sat down at the right hand of the Majesty on high.
What are You like God? How do you feel about the beauties of this world? How do you feel about the things I see and hear? You tell me that Jesus is the exact representation of Your nature. So I can imagine what Jesus is like as I read and hear His word, and I know what You are like—loving, wise, troubled by the consequences of sin, having compassion for me and other people today also. You made the world through Jesus, and You really liked what You had made, so as I see beautiful landscapes, mountains, seas and flowers, You like them even more than I do. You would

be taking beautiful pictures of flowers, mountains, and family and friends, too, if You didn't have such a perfect memory for everything. And there are places and events and actions and a variety of things today that make You uncomfortable, I'm sure. Help me to enjoy getting to know You through Jesus. Help me to enjoy what You enjoy. And help me to feel uncomfortable where You feel uncomfortable.

14 Are they not all ministering spirits, sent out to render service for the sake of those who will inherit salvation? Thank You for Your angels, those wonderful ministering spirits of Yours. Thank you for Your ministry through them— guiding me, protecting me from evil, opening my eyes to situations where I can help someone, helping me to enjoy Your beautiful creation. Thank You, Lord, that I may know that right now, You have provided an angel who is working to protect me and to bless me. I'm sorry that if angels get together for conferences, my angel has every right to use me as an example of recalcitrance and laziness. Help me cooperate with Your wonderful servant. Grant that I serve You, obey You, and enjoy Your gifts, so that I may gladden the heart of my angel. And help me to remember to thank You for my angel and thank my angel for his ministry on a regular basis (if it's ok with You).

In Jesus let me hear You
Recognize You and enjoy with You
Bless Your angels


Hebrews 2

1 For this reason we must pay much closer attention to what we have heard, so that we do not drift away *from it*.
It is, it seems to me, Lord, so very hard in the stream of life to stay in exactly the same place. Either I am growing closer to You or I am drifting away. And with one thing and another (work, spouse, children, time for me, helping out at …, caring

for family, keeping up with communications (in whatever flavor I am using today)) it seems so easy to drift. It is not that I don't want to pay much closer attention to what I have heard from You. It is easy to tell myself there isn't time right now, but surely later will be better. Show me, Lord, how to use the time You give me (the same number of hours that You gave to Mary, to Paul, to Augustine) so that I can and will pay much closer attention to Your gracious communication to me. Keep me drawing nearer to You. And if I start drifting or am in danger of drifting away from You, ring my drift bell loudly and effectively.

15 ...and might free those who through fear of death were subject to slavery all their lives.
That's what my fears are really about, Lord, aren't they. Death is separation. I have feared the end of blessings. I have feared separation from loved ones. I have feared not being good enough. I have feared not doing enough. And it is hard for me to see that is slavery. Until You speak Your word of Gospel, of freedom, and You shine a light on my fears and chains. Wow! What a miserable sight! Let me begin this day and each day seeing with the light of Your gracious freedom. Let me recognize when I am doing something or thinking something because of some fear. Whenever fear attacks me and tries to enslave me, remind me that I am free in You and Your grace. And then shine the light of Your freeing grace so brightly that darkness and fear flee from my landscape.

18 For since He Himself was tempted in that which He has suffered, He is able to come to the aid of those who are tempted.
Of course, in order for me to receive Your aid, in order for me to ask you for Your aid, I need to recognize that I am tempted. Seems obvious, I know, but sometimes they seem like options or invitations or opportunities. Give me clear sight so that I recognize temptation. Give me instant aversion to temptation by Your help. Come to my aid and

grant that I resist temptations. Especially help me resist temptation when I am angry, tired, or discouraged. Or when I really like the temptation. (Particularly rehearsing some unfairness or painful experience.) Yuck! Thank You for being here with me and coming to my aid!

Attention my heart:  Drift no more
Free from fear
Aversion to temptation


Hebrews 3

6 but Christ *was faithful* as a Son over His house—whose house we are, if we hold fast our confidence and the boast of our hope firm until the end.
Thank You Lord Jesus for blessing us and making us the house of God's children with Your gifts. You have been faithful and blessed me by giving me faith through Your Holy Spirit. Grant that I live with faith, (confidently). You have given me hope to hold onto. What a hope! Let me see You today, blessing people, shining through others. Grant that I focus on Your eternal blessings that stretch through this day and come from Your grace and power. People talk about hopes, and they often mean things they wish for. But You have given a certain hope—not a wish, but a blessing of Life with You now and forever, that I can hold onto without anything taking it away. It lasts throughout life and past the end of my life into Life. Thank You, Lord. Keep me strong in that faith and certainty.

13 But encourage one another day after day, as long as it is *still* called "Today," so that none of you will be hardened by the deceitfulness of sin.
Thank You, Lord, for Christians around me. We certainly need encouragement. If sin always wore a covering of fluorescent, flashing puce that had a sound of an off-key whistle it would be easier to avoid. But deceitful it is. Grant

me encouragement through those around me.  And grant that I may be an encouragement to others, now, today, in the time when it is needed.  Help me not to put off encouraging words—help me to sense the urgency of the need for encouragement:  Today.

14  For we have become partakers of Christ, if we hold fast the beginning of our assurance firm until the end.
You have given me the assurance that begins in You, Lord.  Thank You that the assurance I depend on each day does not begin with me.  There would be some days Lord when my assurance would be a 10.8 and some days a negative 32.  (On a scale of 1 to 10.)  With the assurance You give me, I know I have become a partaker of You, Lord Christ.  Show me what that means in the living of this day.  Let me be a partaker of You in conversations I have today, in entertainment I choose, in what I want, in my thinking and feeling.  Let me be a partaker of You in the wonders I recognize around me and the joy I take in from Your love and Your gifts.  Let me be a partaker of You in word and sacrament.  And let me live in joy, assured by Your grace, being a partaker of You in every part of this day.

With faith, certain hope
Encouragement, today
Partake of You, living Life in life


Hebrews 4

2,3  For indeed we have had good news preached to us, just as they also; but the word they heard did not profit them, because it was not united by faith in those who heard.  ³ For we who have believed enter that rest…
That sounds so good, Lord!  I talk about rest.  And there are a lot of ads on television about places to go to rest (like spend half a million on a place near the ocean where there are lots of things to do, to visit a few times a year)—they

don't sound very restful. Even vacations that are less expensive seem to get planned, keeping busy with things to do that are not part of ordinary days. And there are days, I come home and flop on the bed and take a nap. But to come into Your rest, that sounds really wonderful! The colorful brochures for Your rest are included in the good news You speak to me. Well, You know, if You had a prophet with a background in advertising today, he might do that. The thing is, none of us can get there from here by car, bus, train, plane, or ... transporter. Help me to believe Your wonderful good news of forgiveness in Jesus and new and eternal Life by faith in Him. Grant that I enter Your rest, living with You now. Grant that I enter Your rest, wanting Life with You above all. Grant that I enter Your rest when this part of life is over, never to be outside of Your rest again.

14,15 Therefore, since we have a great high priest who has passed through the heavens, Jesus the Son of God, let us hold fast our confession. [15] For we do not have a high priest who cannot sympathize with our weaknesses, but One who has been tempted in all things as *we are, yet* without sin. Sometimes, Lord, it feels like "holding fast our confession" is like holding onto a tree in a raging storm with so much of the world blowing past with gale force winds. But You know that, Jesus. You were tempted. The world was going a different direction from Your direction, all Your life. Help me to recognize the solid ground on which You stand. Keep me there with You, no matter what news, tragedy, invention, electronic global event, or financial struggle happens by. Remind me it is not with my white knuckles that I hold on, it is not with repeating the right prayer every day (nothing against prayers or prayers that are meaningful to me), but with the confidence of faith in You (which is a lot stronger than any grip I have).

16 Therefore let us draw near with confidence to the throne of grace, so that we may receive mercy and find grace to help in time of need.

Let me come again, today, Lord, to Your throne of grace. I come not with goodness in me (no matter how much I practice a confident smile in the mirror). My confidence is in Jesus. You have told me that I may come because Jesus brought me into Your family. As I begin this day I need Your mercy. (The story still rings true for me, Lord, that I have done really well today, nothing has gone wrong, I have not said anything harsh. I have not experienced doubt or fear or discouragement. But now I am going to get out of bed, and I'll be needing Your help.) Right. Grant that, since You offer me Your mercy, I take what You give me. Thank You, Lord. Only in Your mercy can I enter this day. And whether I am consciously searching or not, grant that I come upon Your grace at just the times when I am opening my mouth or heart and want to particularly Live in You, wherever I am, whoever I am with. Thank You for knowing just the right time and giving me Your mercy and grace.

Life in Your rest
Stand with You on solid ground
Mercy and grace and the right time


Hebrews 5

9,10. And having been made perfect, He became to all those who obey Him the source of eternal salvation, [10] being designated by God as a high priest according to the order of Melchizedek.
Thank You, Lord Jesus, for being The source of eternal salvation. In reading about other people it appears that a lot of people have tried some other plan. Some try philosophy, some magic, some idols, some being good. And while I have difficulty imagining anyone doing those things, I realize that I lose focus sometimes, too. You are the high priest designated by God to be the source of eternal salvation for me. Grant that I live being thankful for all the good things that You have given without trying to misuse any of them as

the source of being eternally saved. Saved I am, thank You, Jesus, only through You. From You alone comes my salvation. Morning, noon, and night let me recognize You and rejoice in You my Savior.

11  Concerning him we have much to say, and *it is* hard to explain, since you have become dull of hearing.
Ouch! A difficult letter to receive! Not that my ears don't work, but that I have them tuned out. I get so busy listening to what I like to hear (echoes in my mind of successes and satisfactions and compliments) that I can't hear anything that might require me to think or change my life. Help me to listen to You always. Give me sharp hearing to take in exactly what You are saying in Your word or some other way. Let me listen to You when You say things I like to hear and (even) when You say things I find difficult. I would rather listen to You, no matter what You say, than have to have You send me a letter saying I am dull of hearing. Open the ears of my heart.

14  But solid food is for the mature, who because of practice have their senses trained to discern good and evil.
So what I hear You saying, Lord, is that the way You arrange for me to become mature is by practicing what You have taught me, so that I learn to discern good and evil. It is true, Lord, that I have chosen some things that I thought were good, and eventually they turned out to be hurtful, destructive, and evil. Remind me to talk to You when I am deciding, and ask You to show me Your will (instead of later on giving You one of my asides, "That'll be ok, right, Lord?") If I were going to play a sport, I would be conscious of practicing. Just living, I forget that I am practicing Living with You and for You, according to Your word, and by Your grace every day. Help me remember that right now, and always, I am practicing Living with You and for You. May it be with discernment and to Your glory.

Jesus, Source, Savior

Sharp hearing
Practice Living


Hebrews 6

10  For God is not unjust so as to forget your work and the love which you have shown toward His name, in having ministered and in still ministering to the saints.
I love You Lord.  Thank You for giving me the opportunity to show that love.  Saying, "I love You" is made visible in ministering to Your people.  Show me where You have called me to minister.  Open the way for me to use gifts You have given me to be a blessing to Your people.  And use me as You desire to minister to the saints.  Help me with courage and confidence in You to get past every suspicion that attacks me from inside that I am not good enough (of course I'm not, but You are) or capable (right, only with Your grace) to do anything to bless others.  Help me see in all I do, an opportunity to do it well, by Your grace and power, to Your glory, and to be a blessing.

12  ...so that you will not be sluggish, but imitators of those who through faith and patience inherit the promises.
Faith and patience sound so quiet, Lord.  They sound like things that You want me to do sitting down somewhere, quietly, thoughtfully.  But what I hear You saying is that they are the opposite of sluggishness.  They are anything but quiet.  Believing is muscle work when what I see doesn't look like what I believe.  Patience is using muscles for perseverance, keeping at what You want me to be and do—over a long period of time.  In a tug of war, pulling on the rope steadfastly in Your direction without giving up, until the end of the event.  In a time when someone has been thoughtless or hurt me, standing next to them, having in my hand a pie pan filled with blueberries topped with shaving cream and using every muscle I have resisting throwing it.  Help me Lord to actively work hard believing, and to

strenuously work hard being patient, persevering and resisting any tendencies toward being an avenging angel.

18-20 ...so that by two unchangeable things in which it is impossible for God to lie, we who have taken refuge would have strong encouragement to take hold of the hope set before us. [19] This hope we have as an anchor of the soul, a *hope* both sure and steadfast and one which enters within the veil, [20] where Jesus has entered as a forerunner for us, having become a high priest forever according to the order of Melchizedek.

Thank You, Lord, that I may take refuge in You. It is wonderful that I can take refuge in You as I am walking along, watching cars almost hit each other, or listening to people shout at each other, or when I am with someone I care about and I don't know what to say to help. (Or when I bang into someone else's life with hurtful or insensitive words or actions and greatly desire their forgiveness.) In every moment of life let me by faith, through Your grace, take hold of the rope that You put in my life. How wonderful that I may take hold of the rope of certain hope that is anchored in the holiest place in heaven where You, Jesus, have entered with Your sacrifice to give me absolute forgiveness that I can count on for sure, now and always. Let me see the hope every day. And grant me a firm grip as I take hold of the hope You give.

Visible love
Strenuous patience
Your hope firmly gripped


Hebrews 7

19 (for the Law made nothing perfect), and on the other hand there is a bringing in of a better hope, through which we draw near to God.

If all You had given me were a set of really great rules, Lord, I would be discouraged all the time. The law gives a beautiful vision of perfect, but keeps letting me know I'm not there, not getting any closer to being there, and probably won't ever get there. So hope in Jesus is music to my ears, so to speak. Instead of depression and going further away, I experience drawing nearer to You. Thank You, Lord, for hope. Thank You Jesus for being the source of hope that lights up my day each day. There are days when everywhere I look I see brokenness. "They ought to do something about that!" But then I rejoice that no matter what it looks like around me, You are graciously drawing me closer to You. Let me experience that hope and let me draw closer to You each day. (And if I am in some sense "they", grant me courage and ability to do something about whatever it is they should do something about.)

24,25 ...but Jesus, on the other hand, because He continues forever, holds His priesthood permanently.
[25] Therefore He is able also to save forever those who draw near to God through Him, since He always lives to make intercession for them.
I have had some really good days, Lord, with experiences of being close to You. It seemed like You were right there with me. I looked out into the day, and if it wasn't exactly like walking off into the sunset (thank You for Richard Burton and Jean Simmons in *The Robe*), at least You and I were walking together and the sun was glorious, the flowers and landscape beautiful. But of course most of the time it isn't quite like that. So I really appreciate Your letting me know, Jesus, that Your priesthood is permanent. You save me not on those mountain top days, but every day, forever. There is never a day when You are not interceding for me. You always are making intercession for me. Thank You! When the day is not so bright with sunshine in my heart, remind me that You are still available and I can absolutely depend on You. And when the sun is shining brightly in my heart, give my soul voice to sing Your praise.

26,27  For it was fitting for us to have such a high priest, holy, innocent, undefiled, separated from sinners and exalted above the heavens; $^{27}$ who does not need daily, like those high priests, to offer up sacrifices, first for His own sins and then for the *sins* of the people, because this He did once for all when He offered up Himself.

You have made The sacrifice for my sins, Lord Jesus. How great is that? Sometimes I forget how great that is. Thank You that You have done that. Thank You that now I get to live new life in You. Help me to look ahead at each moment considering how I may follow You and be a blessing, rather than how I may make it up to You for my thoughts, words, and deeds so that I can get to the point of walking with You. Remind me that I walk with You now, today, because You have sacrificed Yourself, forgiven my sins, and given me Life with You.

With hope, drawing near
Depend on Your intercession, always
Your sacrifice, new life


Hebrews 8

1  Now the main point in what has been said *is this*: we have such a high priest, who has taken His seat at the right hand of the throne of the Majesty in the heavens.

It is so easy, Lord, to think that what I need is Someone to provide more money, to rescue me from my dumbness, to protect me from bad things happening; there that would take care of what I need, right?  But You know, what I really need is a high priest. I, a sinner, need a way to come close to You, my perfect Creator and gracious God.  What I need is You, Jesus, to intercede for me. I need You to bring me out of death into Life. I know, Hebrews was written to, well, Hebrew people. But the surprise for them, and certainly for me as a Gentile, is that I, also, have a high priest in You,

Jesus. You, Who sit on the right hand of the throne of Your Father in heaven, also care about me. You intercede for me. Thank You, gracious Lord. Help me to live in that confidence that without any doubt, I have what I need—I have You.

10 "For this is the covenant that I will make with the house of Israel
After those days, says the Lord:
I will put My laws into their minds,
And I will write them on their hearts.
And I will be their God,
And they shall be My people.
Thank You, Lord, for sharing this covenant that You first mentioned in Jeremiah 31.33 and 34, not only with Your chosen people, but also with even me, these many years later, here and now. Your decisive love and grace are the blessing I need. As You know, I go up and down in my attitudes. Some days I feel strongly that I belong to Your people, and some days I look back at the end of the day and just wonder. Thank You for Your gracious love in reaching me in Jesus and giving me this enduring hope and confidence: You have chosen to be my God and graciously include me as one of Your people. Help me to live daily in that confidence, and by Your grace to act like it.

12 "For I will be merciful to their iniquities,
And I will remember their sins no more."
What wonderful mercy You have, Lord, toward me. Personally I remember too well many of my sins. Years later, now, I have memories come to me of dumb and hurtful things that I said and did. Sheesh! Remember no more sounds awfully good! And You have a better view than I do of how I have stumbled and fallen through the years, way beyond what I am aware of. And still, graciously You decide by Jesus' sacrifice to be merciful to me and remember all that stuff no more. Thank You, gracious Lord! Help me today to remember how wonderfully You have chosen to

forget, so that I may live in newness, not plagued by old memories, but dwelling in the mercy and hope You give me for looking ahead and walking with You (in merciful forgetfulness).

Satisfy my need—You
Live as Yours
Gracious forgetting, strength to Live


Hebrews 9

12 ...and not through the blood of goats and calves, but through His own blood, He entered the holy place once for all, having obtained eternal redemption.

I can imagine walking by the store with the dyfragal sysquestomat. I could see it in the window with its long-lasting batteries and colorful led lights, with its blue-tooth connect-ability to practically everything everywhere. But the price was immensely beyond anything I had. There was no way to obtain it. That's the way it was before You came, Lord Jesus. I could see the wonderful blessing of Life with God. I could want it, desire it, wish for it. But there was no way for me to obtain it. But You came and sacrificed Yourself, taking the blood of Your sacrifice into the heavenly holy place once for all time, for all people, and You obtained what I could only dream about and wish for. You obtained eternal redemption for me. Thank You, Lord. Of course, the words are not enough. Let me Live my life as a thank you to You. Let the words of my mouth and the meditation of my heart, the work of my hands, the direction of my steps, all I am, on a daily basis be thanks and praise to You, now and forever.

14 How much more will the blood of Christ, who through the eternal Spirit offered Himself without blemish to God, cleanse your conscience from dead works to serve the living God?

Clean is very in right now, Lord. I live in a time of great cleanliness. And most of me is pretty easy to clean, what with 23,427 kinds of soaps, cleansers, shampoos, etc. The part of me that is hard to clean is inside me. My conscience and memory hold onto the most appalling stuff. And when they keep hitting me over the head for earlier today and yesterday and all yesterday's yesterdays I have trouble getting on to serve You faithfully. Cleanse my conscience and heal my memory again today, Lord Jesus by Your sacrifice through the Holy Spirit that I may leave behind doing things that have no Life in them and get on to living Life in You and with You and serve the Living God, by Your grace. May I serve You, Lord, unhindered by dead stuff and filled with new Life in Jesus.

28  So Christ also, having been offered once to bear the sins of many, will appear a second time for salvation without *reference to* sin, to those who eagerly await Him.
Thank You Jesus, for bearing my sins, for forgiveness, for new Life with You. I do wait for Your second coming. Can we talk, just a little, about eagerly. I really do want You to come and take me home. It's just that the sun is shining, it's a beautiful day, there are a lot of books I haven't read yet, I love my family, and You (just like Adam's excuse) have given me some wonderful things to do—so could I eagerly wait for You to come just a little later. There are the trip and the graduation and the wedding coming. OK, I admit, that's pretty much nonsense compared to how much I really do eagerly wait for Your coming. And of course, there are days when the sun is not shining, when I look around and everything I see is some problem that needs to be fixed. The world seems to creak with brokenness more each year. And I really look forward to Your coming to take me where there is nothing broken. Help me to enjoy what You have given me now, to do my best in Your grace to serve You and be a blessing, and still to eagerly wait for You to come now, five minutes from now, tomorrow, whenever You come. Thank You that I can look forward to Your coming!

Live praising for eternal redemption
Move from dead works to living Life
Wait filled Living


Hebrews 10

9,10 Then He said, "BEHOLD, I HAVE COME TO DO YOUR WILL." He takes away the first in order to establish the second. ¹⁰ By this will we have been sanctified through the offering of the body of Jesus Christ once for all.
I think of St. Peter or St. Paul coming into the room and of my being amazed to be with one of Your holy servants, Lord. It's hard to wrap my mind around the fact that You have sanctified me through the sacrifice of Jesus. You have made me holy. Not just a retouch job, patching up some of the more glaring holes, but actually made me holy. I don't feel very holy. So in order for me to live as Your holy servant now, please remind me as I begin this day, as I live in this day, as I finish this day that Jesus has once for all time accomplished making me holy, and that when You look at me, You see the holiness that He gave me. Grant that I live, not stuffy or puffed up, but walking with You in thanksgiving and praise and wonder every moment.

14 For by one offering He has perfected for all time those who are sanctified.
Ok, we both know, Lord, that I am not perfect. But You tell me that You have perfected me. Not that You practiced first and then You got it right. But You have taken care of all the things that are missing in me. When I finish each day, if I honestly look back I see holes where I wish I had said one more thing (or one less thing). I wish I had used different priorities. I wish I had tried harder and actually accomplished what I think You wanted. You graciously make the day that is slipping away a blessing. Finishing is up to You, not to me. And there are all those people I meet

today, and if perchance I happen to think that something they said was incomplete or less than perfect, lo and behold, there You are in charge of filling in all that was missing and finishing all the blessings You work through them. Help me to live in confidence that You are perfecting, not just for a limited engagement, but for all time, to the end, until You come back, Lord Jesus. Yes! What a Lord!

24 And let us consider how to stimulate one another to love and good deeds.
I've got the other part down pat, Lord. The part about stimulating other people to frustration and hurt. No problem there. I do need some help on this one, though. (Like a lot!) Grant me a clean heart, O Lord, so that from the very inside, my thoughts, words, and actions start in You. And, of course, it is easier to help someone than it is to help someone to help someone else. Whether it is in parenting, grand-parenting, (or uncle-ing, aunt-ing, etc.) help me to stimulate to love and good deeds. And even with friends and people I meet, use me to encourage loving and doing good, by Your grace. Please, take anything in me that is an obstacle, out of the way!

Holy and very thankful!
Satisfied, living with perfected people
Stimulating to multiply good


Hebrews 11

1 Now faith is the assurance of *things* hoped for, the conviction of things not seen.
Thank You Jesus, for Your gift of faith. I really appreciate the blessings You have given me: The place to live, family, food and clothes. But many of the blessings You have given, I can't see. Strengthen my faith so that I see with the eyes of faith. Your love, love from my family, ability to think and reason for another day, desire to live with You and for

You, joy in You no matter what is happening. These are not seen. With Your gift of faith, I have assurance of these. Thank You that I may have conviction of really important blessings. Whether my home is full of things that are blessings or appears empty, grant me clear sight of the love and promises and hope You give. Grant me conviction to recognize the well-worn armor leaning against the wall ready to use at a moment's notice. Grant me the certainty that the ticks of the clock are not leading to times of fear or anxiety, for by Your grace I am assured, convicted, certain in mind and heart, that You and joy and wonder, strength and power and endurance may be unseen, but are certainly here. I am assured that I can hope for the very best—Living with You now and forever.

8,10 By faith Abraham, when he was called, obeyed by going out to a place which he was to receive for an inheritance; and he went out, not knowing where he was going. ... [10] for he was looking for the city which has foundations, whose architect and builder is God.
It used to be that before I was willing to leave home, I wanted a paper map that showed exactly where I was going, Lord. Of course, now You have arranged for all that to be on my "phone". (Very difficult to come up with an excuse for getting lost anymore.) But You call me every day to walk out into the day telling me to follow You, without exactly specifying where we are going. I have some general ideas from other days, but You bring new things, new situations, new challenges, new blessings, new people, new visions into each day. I am definitely looking for that eternal city which has permanent, solid foundation in You, where You have designed everything and every moment to be a blessing. Help me to live trusting You with the faith You have given me, so that while I can't see the map for today, I can be sure You know where we are going. When something new comes up, keep me close to You and Your direction through faith. Through faith give me certainty that today also will be a day's march nearer home.

29 By faith they passed through the Red Sea as though *they were passing* through dry land; and the Egyptians, when they attempted it, were drowned.

I always knew You gave me faith. I just didn't think I would have to use it this much, Lord. Some of the things that happen seem like attacks. You want me to do what, Lord?! They seem impossible. I can see the very real possibility that I am not going to make it through this. So whenever that happens, please grant that I remember that You gave me what I need for this. You have given me faith that is stronger than any well-made plan that I could come up with. You have given me the tool I need to use in every difficulty. You have provided me with faith that really works in impossible situations and in every experience of being under attack. Grant that I use Your gift of faith without doubt, without whining, with joy and satisfaction in You. I know that by faith I can pass through every raging storm, dry and unscathed because You have made faith exactly the powerful connection to Your limitless love and power that I need. Help me to remember, Lord, that if I take faith, I don't need a lot of luggage to travel into today. Thank You, Lord.

Enjoy blessings not seen, by faith
Faith along the way going home
Wherever You lead, faith works


Hebrews 12

1,2 Therefore, since we have so great a cloud of witnesses surrounding us, let us also lay aside every encumbrance and the sin which so easily entangles us, and let us run with endurance the race that is set before us, ² fixing our eyes on Jesus, the author and perfecter of faith, who for the joy set before Him endured the cross, despising the shame, and has sat down at the right hand of the throne of God.

Thank You, Lord for all the saints. Thank You for their witness, for their encouragement. Sometimes I forget to listen to Your cheer squad. It is easier to get used to encumbrances and sin, "Yes it is clinging to me, but, of course, it always does that." Give me a break! Help me to lay it aside, to tear it off! In the wonder of seeing You, Lord Jesus, in the satisfaction of faith which You have given and perfected, I want to have all those things that cling to me removed. Please, Lord, even if it hurts me, take them off. Grant that unencumbered I may run the race that You have set before me. Grant that I use the faith You have given, that I keep my vision focused on You, and that I see the path ahead not as a stroll, or an opportunity to meander on various side paths, but as a race with urgency. Let the cheers and encouragement of Your witnesses ring in my ears and grant that I keep pace with You every day, right to the end of my race.

10,11 For they disciplined us for a short time as seemed best to them, but He *disciplines us* for *our* good, so that we may share His holiness. [11] All discipline for the moment seems not to be joyful, but sorrowful; yet to those who have been trained by it, afterwards it yields the peaceful fruit of righteousness.

Discipline just doesn't sound like a very positive word, Lord. It sounds like limits. It sounds like I don't get what I want. It sounds like I have to do things that someone else wants me to do. So I really appreciate Your putting it this way. You discipline me for my good. Well, of course, it still doesn't sound great, but I believe You, that it will be a blessing. (Sounds like a painful one, though.) I'm sorry, Lord. I give up. I know that You know me and know what blessings You want to give me. And Your blessings are wonderful! So lead me with discipline so that I may have the peaceful fruit of righteousness. (Now it has been some years, Lord. Have we gotten there yet? OK. Still more coming.) In today, keep me in Your discipline. Keep me in Your training program. Grant more and more peace from the righteousness that You give to me as a result. Mother Teresa did say that there is time to rest at the end. Thank You, Lord.

28 Therefore, since we receive a kingdom which cannot be shaken, let us show gratitude, by which we may offer to God an acceptable service with reverence and awe.
History seems to be the story of a whole lot of shaking that has been going on for a very long time, Lord. There are so many things around that I wish were stable and solid. But then every day there is news about something thought to be solid that has shaken. (Where would newspapers be, Lord, if everything stayed solid? Newspapers in heaven must be very different!) So, therefore, since You have given us, that is me, a kingdom, a Life with You, which nothing can shake, I really have a lot of reason to rejoice, Lord. Thank You, Lord, that in a shaky landscape, You have provided a solid foundation in You and Your love and Your forgiveness. Grant that I will show You gratitude in what I do today. Grant that I enjoy Living with You today with an attitude of reverence and awe, recognizing You, serving You, loving people, showing joy—all on the solid Foundation that You have given me, the solid Foundation that You are.

Unencumbered running, with You
In Your discipline, blessing, peace
Gratitude on the Rock


Hebrews 13

7 Remember those who led you, who spoke the word of God to you; and considering the result of their conduct, imitate their faith.
Imitate has gotten bad press, Lord, in my day. It sounds like something not real imitating something real. But You are leading me to imitate and be real. Please grant that I value with thanksgiving all those who have spoken Your word to

me. Pastor Kreidt comes to my mind and heart quickly, besides, of course, John, Paul and all Your other Biblical proclaimers together with saints like Saint Francis. Grant that I recognize their lives, their faith, the results of their faith filled lives as that real history that matters for me. Help me to remember them. And grant that I imitate their faith with real Living, real faith, real trusting You, real choosing those things that are real blessings, and real communication with other people that shows Life Lived faith first.

8,9 Jesus Christ *is* the same yesterday and today and forever. [9] Do not be carried away by varied and strange teachings; for it is good for the heart to be strengthened by grace, not by foods, through which those who were so occupied were not benefited.
The new food pyramid or the old one…hmm. Your pyramid of nourishment, Lord is very simple: Strengthened by grace. Just as there are a lot of different diets and food plans, there are varied and strange teachings that claim to sustain people today. Give me clear vision, Lord, to see through all that gobbledygook so that I am not carried away from You or even pulled away. You, Jesus, are the same—then, now, and forever, so I don't need a new plan for my spiritual strength and sustenance. Your grace was effective then, and it is exactly what I need to Live today. Grant me Your grace in Your word and sacraments. Sustain me daily with Your grace. Grant that I never step out into the day treading on the ephemeral mist of self-reliance or personal character, but only, always, in word and deed on Your grace. The same today, yes, thank You, Jesus.

20,21 Now the God of peace, who brought up from the dead the great Shepherd of the sheep through the blood of the eternal covenant, *even* Jesus our Lord, [21] equip you in every good thing to do His will, working in us that which is pleasing in His sight, through Jesus Christ, to whom *be* the glory forever and ever. Amen.

I really like the blessing You have arranged here, Lord. You are the God of peace. I have difficulty imagining or experiencing peace sitting watching television. Sometimes Your peace is very real when I read. Or when I walk in the mountains and look over the valleys below. And from You comes this blessing, yes, please Lord: Equip me in every good thing to do Your will. Thank You for the imagination You have given me. Sometimes I forget to imagine inside Your will. You have a terrific, wonderful, and good will! All that is good—comes from You. Grant that all my imagination, all my creativity be inside Your will. Grant that I use the equipment You have given me so that I will do good, and be pleasing to You, through Jesus Christ, Your Son, my Lord. Glory to You, Lord, Father, Jesus, Holy Spirit. Amen.

Real, blessed, imitation faith
Nourished by the same, new old grace
Equipped for Your good and Your glory

# James

James 1

2-4 Consider it all joy, my brethren, when you encounter various trials, ³ knowing that the testing of your faith produces endurance. ⁴ And let endurance have *its* perfect result, so that you may be perfect and complete, lacking in nothing.

When I consider the trials that people faced in the time of James, Lord, it is very difficult to complain. And yet there are times when I need endurance. I suppose this is like asking You to give me really great muscles, Lord, but if it's all the same to You, I'd rather not have to use them. I would like to be good at endurance. But, truth be told, I don't exactly want things I have to endure, just the ability will be fine, Lord. Right. I hear You saying it doesn't work that way. And there have been trials. And You have graciously blessed me through those experiences. Please use the result of those experiences so that I will be complete, made ready and able to Live by Your grace, without fear. For You stand with me in every trial. Help me to use the endurance You have produced without whining, and with great joy, knowing that You are with me.

5 But if any of you lacks wisdom, let him ask of God, who gives to all generously and without reproach, and it will be given to him.

Thank You for Your gracious promise Lord. I admit that there are times when I would like You to give me wisdom later, after I have done what I want to do first. But, I'm sorry, Lord, I know that Your wisdom will lead me to blessings that are better than anything I can come up with on my own. So thank You for Your generous promise. Grant me wisdom, now, today. Help me to see Your will, to hear people with Your gracious wisdom and love, to recognize choices that are not obvious without Your wisdom. Grant that I will be a blessing to those around me by the gift of Your wisdom. In Your wisdom is joy and satisfaction. In Your wisdom is everlasting blessing. Let me hear Your bell ring when I try to take a step lacking wisdom, and grant that I choose rather to Live in Your wisdom. In Your grace, let Your wisdom in me look so attractive that others will see it and You (not me) and want their own gift of wisdom from You.

17  Every good thing given and every perfect gift is from above, coming down from the Father of lights, with whom there is no variation or shifting shadow.
"What a sale! I've got to go and stock up at these wonderful prices!" That might be my experience once in a while here. But thank You, gracious Father that You don't operate with sales. No variation in You. Gracious and merciful You are today, so get all I can because who knows what tomorrow will bring?! Never! You bring Your light of joy and mercy and every good and perfect gift into my life today. And I can rest secure and confident that You will be there tomorrow just as loving, still wanting to bring Your light and gifts to me then. Considering how changeable things are here, right now, (and probably always have been) that's really saying something. It's difficult to avoid that "stock up now!" attitude, Lord. Let me relax in peace and confidence in Your unchanging grace, in Your promise of blessings with good things, and in a sense of unhurried satisfaction today in all the wonderful good that You have already given.

Endurance, and willingness to use it
Wisdom, used to Your glory
Unhurried satisfaction today, confidence for tomorrow


James 2

5  Listen, my beloved brethren: did not God choose the poor of this world *to be* rich in faith and heirs of the kingdom which He promised to those who love Him?

Poor, Lord, according to whom?  When I watch people trying to decide whether to buy the seven million dollar island or the ten million dollar island for their weekend home, I feel substantially poor.  But when I consider people who live on three hundred dollars a year, I feel extremely rich.  You have chosen people who are not distracted by riches of wealth, influence, position, honor, or education to receive the riches of Your gifts of faith and eternal inheritance.  So (I feel this as a delicate balance!) I ask You to not let me have distracting amounts of wealth, influence, position, honor, or education.  Put those things in a blessed proportion in my life.  Grant me humble attitudes in each.  And grant me a poverty, an emptiness just right to be filled with the riches of Your promise of faith and eternal inheritance.  I am really glad You are the One doing that.  What a mess if it were up to me!  Thank You, Lord.

8  If, however, you are fulfilling the royal law according to the Scripture, "YOU SHALL LOVE YOUR NEIGHBOR AS YOURSELF," you are doing well.

Thank You, Lord, that You are graciously at work through me.  I would really like to do well at this, Lord.  Grant that I love my neighbors whether I know them well or not, whether we have a lot in common or not, whether I like everything they do or not, whether they are loud or quiet, whether they talk like me or not, whether they are better looking than I am or (wonderful!) like me.  Help me to love people and be open to bless them no matter what.  And, on the other hand, grant that I love myself in a good way, as Your forgiven child, even when I do dumb stuff and my temptation is to be grouchy with myself and to snarl at any person who comes within twenty feet.

22  You see that faith was working with his [Abraham's] works, and as a result of the works, faith was perfected.

What an amazing arrangement You have given me, Lord! You give me faith so that I can trust You. Then You show me opportunities to do good things, which of course are impossible for me to do by my power and abilities. Then You help me to use the faith to trust You so that I can do things that I was pretty sure I couldn't do. Thank You, Lord. And then in the process, You strengthen and perfect the faith You gave me. Help me to recognize this wonderful cycle of blessing that You have given. Help me to see opportunities always with faith, instead of just gasping, "Who? Me!?" Keep my faith healthy through use and through growing by Your grace. And when I lean toward the temptation to say, "Ok, Lord, I've got this one" and try to walk into the day without using Your gift of faith, whack me up the side of the head with a (small, please) two by four, so I remember how this works.

Enough poverty to be rich in You
Loving neighbors, and me
Only faithfully work


James 3

13 Who among you is wise and understanding? Let him show by his good behavior his deeds in the gentleness of wisdom.
You have given me wisdom, Lord Holy Spirit. Thank You. And You have provided me with a very nice closet in my home. It is true that there have been times when I have carefully wrapped the wisdom You gave me, and placed it in a protected place in my closet. Duh! Like I should keep it safe and in good condition and not use it too much! I'm sorry, Lord, that sometimes it comes to me as a shock that You want me use it, too. Daily. Today would be nice. Help me to find all the benefits of the wisdom that You have given me, Lord. In particular, gentleness. During the day, life seems to come at me in waves, high and low, left and right,

bright and dark, loud and quiet. My temptation is to respond in kind. Grant that I use wisdom and Live in gentleness no matter how the waves of life show up. Let me shine with a steady light from Your grace and wisdom. And grant that gentleness from me provides a gracious calm place for the people around me, that we might together praise You for wisdom and gentle Living.

17 But the wisdom from above is first pure, then peaceable, gentle, reasonable, full of mercy and good fruits, unwavering, without hypocrisy.
It is so easy, Lord, to think I am using wisdom when I find things wrong with the way that other people do things. I call it wisdom, but, of course, what it is I suppose is saying other people do things differently from the way that I do them (and naturally my way is after all, right, right? Sheesh!) Not at all merciful from Your way of thinking! You have shown me mercy today and every day, Lord. And You know I really need it. Grant that I use wisdom from You, not to remonstrate with other people, but with mercy (not how much I know, but how much I care, right?). And grant that I reflect Your wisdom without wavering, without hypocrisy. I enjoy humor. I know humor is most helpful when I am laughing at me and what I think and do. Keep me from thinking sarcasm is humor, especially when the sarcasm is aimed at other people. That's where the wide doorway to hypocrisy opens; keep me from that, Lord. Let wisdom from You produce good fruit in me with unwavering caring with mercy.

18 And the seed whose fruit is righteousness is sown in peace by those who make peace.
It is so easy to think, Lord, that I am using wisdom with peace when I am not actually saying anything to hurt anyone (no matter what I think or what my face looks like). Sow Your seeds in peace that comes from me. Let Your peace fill my heart and overflow—that I be not troubled or afraid. Grant that Your wisdom shows in my life with You working

through me to make peace in the spaces I am in. Let Your fruit of righteousness grow abundantly in that peace. Let the peace in which I live be healthy soil for Your fruit. Continue to create life-giving, joyous peace and its fruit of righteousness through me today, Lord.

Wise gentleness in every storm
Wisdom to be honestly merciful
Build peace through me


James 4

6 But He gives a greater grace. Therefore *it* says, "GOD IS OPPOSED TO THE PROUD, BUT GIVES GRACE TO THE HUMBLE."
I have mixed feelings about humility, Lord. I admit that I have a lot to be humble about. When I look back at things I still feel embarrassed about, I realize that I ran ahead, on my own, without waiting for You or asking You. So, yes, I am rightfully humble. It's just that I know I should be humble. And I am. So that's good. And that's where my humility starts slipping a little. I see people who do not appear humble, and I do better than they do at it—see, there I go, off the deep end! Help me to be humble humbly. Not proudly. Help me to be naturally dependent on You with humility, not purposefully waking up in the morning, "Yes, Lord, I will be indubitably humble today!" Rather grant that I Live by Your grace in humility.

8 Draw near to God and He will draw near to you. Cleanse your hands, you sinners; and purify your hearts, you double-minded.
What a wonderful promise, Lord! As I rejoice in You and think about You, I draw near to You. And You promise to draw near to me. Thank You, Lord! Of course, You are right about double-minded. I can start to talk to You, and feel satisfaction in Your blessings, and my mind adds a second track that goes off on its own, flying into some fancy about

how I want other blessings or how I see threats to Your blessings. Sometimes I find it hard to locate the switch to keep on one signal at a time. Please help me to do that, Lord. Keep me from double-mindedness. And If I should slip in that direction, scrunch out every thought and heart-threatening imagination except our conversation, Lord. My mind and heart drawn near to You, filled with Your presence, please grant, Gracious Lord.

15 Instead, *you ought* to say, "If the Lord wills, we will live and also do this or that."
Thank You for Your good and gracious will, Lord. Grant that I listen to You in making all plans and that I entrust all plans to You, to Your gracious will, to Your power to bless them. Forgive me for thinking that there are good and wonderful plans that are just the right thing right now even if they don't appear to be in Your gracious will at this time. Help me to see and trust that there are more than enough great, wonderful, satisfying, blessed plans inside Your gracious will to occupy me and all my abilities and desires for all of today (and all of the other todays You graciously have coming).

Humbly humble in Your grace
Single-mindedly near to You
In Your gracious will always


James 5

8 You too be patient; strengthen your hearts, for the coming of the Lord is near.
Perhaps my clock works faster than Yours, Lord. I've been patient for at least five minutes, now. That should be enough, right? I'm sorry, Lord. When I think of patient, I am using human thinking separate from Yours. Strengthen my heart, Lord. Thank You for Your coming being near. Grant that I use Your strength to be patient with other people (especially the ones close to me, whom I love, and whom I

expect to get with my program!). Grant that I be patient with stuff, including computers that are supposed to be smart enough to do what I want. Grant that I be patient with people whose advertisements say outrageous things and have misspelled words (thank You for spell check!). Grant that I never be patient with evil. And yes, I suppose most of all, truth be told, help me to be patient with me, with dumb things I say, with mistakes I make, with body parts that are not operating smoothly and to my satisfaction—that would probably make it easier for me to be patient with other people. Strengthen my heart in You, by Your grace, so that I will be patient.

11 We count those blessed who endured. You have heard of the endurance of Job and have seen the outcome of the Lord's dealings, that the Lord is full of compassion and *is* merciful.
Thank You Lord for giving me grace to endure things that in Your gracious will You don't want to take away. I suppose this is not my favorite blessing, from all the wonderful blessings You give me. But it is really wonderful to have, as opposed to not being able to endure hurtful, painful, discouraging things. Before I whine, Lord, please help me to remember that You are merciful and full of compassion, that You will help me with Your best blessings, and that along the way You have given me endurance, and good it would be if I go ahead and use it.

15 And the prayer offered in faith will restore the one who is sick, and the Lord will raise him up, and if he has committed sins, they will be forgiven him.
Thank You, Lord that I may pray, using the faith that You have given me, to restore people I love. Please strengthen my faith and answer my prayers, gracious Lord, heavenly Father, for the sake of Jesus, Your Son. Please restore those for whom I pray to a relationship with You of joy and satisfaction. Please restore them to confidence in You and Your love. Please restore them to closeness to You every

day. And please, in Your gracious will, restore them to good health physically with the ability to get around, eat, sleep, and do the things their new Spirit led desires have focused on. Please restore them, raise them up, and give them Your gracious gift of new Life in living this life. Thank You, Lord.

By Your strength, patient, in Your time
Endurance with willingness to use it
Faithfully trusting Your restoration

# 1 Peter

1 Peter 1

3, 4  Blessed be the God and Father of our Lord Jesus Christ, who according to His great mercy has caused us to be born again to a living hope through the resurrection of Jesus Christ from the dead, to *obtain* an inheritance *which is* imperishable and undefiled and will not fade away, reserved in heaven for you.
Thank You, Lord for Your mercy.  I suppose it is a dream of a lot of people, that somewhere there is a rich relative of theirs, and one day they will receive an inheritance that will bring great blessings to their life.  (Like the insurance policies that were sold 70 years ago.  With the proceeds today, you can get a really great meal at a restaurant and a year's subscription to the Wall Street Journal.)  But You have graciously arranged that our inheritance will not fade, perish or become defiled.  Thank you, Lord, that it is reserved specifically for each of us in heaven.  Bless us with directing our hope through all the things that deteriorate, fade, become worthless or unhealthy to the certain joy based on Your great sacrifice for us.  Let us Live in new birth, using Your wonderful blessings now, with a continuing focus on the fulfillment of all our hope.

8  ...and though you have not seen Him, you love Him, and though you do not see Him now, but believe in Him, you greatly rejoice with joy inexpressible and full of glory.
You have graciously let some people see You, Lord Jesus.  For most of us, though, we believe in You without seeing You visibly.  And yet You have given us a new heart to know You, to listen to You, to Live with You, to love You.  Fill us with Your Holy Spirit, Jesus, Lord of Life, so that we will recognize You every day.  So that we will rejoice in Living with You and for You today.  Thank You that we don't have

to see You with our eyes, right now, in order to enjoy Your presence and Your love. Be part of every moment of this day, and strengthen our faith, so that whatever You give us to do or say reflects joy in You and the glory of Your grace.

13  Therefore, prepare your minds for action, keep sober *in spirit*, fix your hope completely on the grace to be brought to you at the revelation of Jesus Christ.
Gracious Lord, grant that we prepare our minds for action also today.  Let our minds be awake to Your loving us, not because we are perfect or good or obedient, but because Jesus, our Savior, has made us new by His death for us and His resurrection.  Grant that we take in the knowledge of You and Your love through Your word, so that our minds will have a foundation for all they need to do.  Train us in thinking, so that all our thinking be based on faith in You, not on ourselves.  Grant that our minds operate smoothly oiled with love from You and love for others.  Use our minds so that we will communicate Your light and Your love in what we say and do.  Use all the experiences in our lives so that we listen to others with our minds and hearts and show Your compassion to others.  Let our minds be sober and unmixed with evil intoxications.  And let us use our minds to show that we are always dependent only on Your grace in Jesus our Lord and coming King.

Hope anchored in the imperishable
Loving You, reflecting joy
Minds graciously prepared and used


1 Peter 2

2  … like newborn babies, long for the pure milk of the word, so that by it you may grow in respect to salvation.
We feel a lot of longings, Lord.  There is a longing to fit in with the group (give us sense and faithfulness to You so that we get past this).  There is the longing to consume sugar

(bless those so driven with moderation and good health). There is the longing for the peace and satisfaction and good and joyful (thank You for that longing that draws us to You throughout life). Grant us this longing, please Lord—to long for Your word, to desire to come close to You and listen to You, to so have our lives filled with Your will and Your grace that there is room for nothing else. In addition, grant that we may keep growing (not in girth, which of course is often too easy). Grant that we keep growing in every day in openness to You, in turning our will over to You, in seeing joy in Living with You now, no matter what we are doing. Grant that we may grow in turning ourselves over to You so that You may make us, indeed, Alive, Joyful, and Eternal.

4, 5 And coming to Him as to a living stone which has been rejected by men, but is choice and precious in the sight of God, ⁵ you also, as living stones, are being built up as a spiritual house for a holy priesthood, to offer up spiritual sacrifices acceptable to God through Jesus Christ.
It sounds so limiting, Lord, to be made into a house. So fixed. No more freedom to go about and do. But You make us living stones, Gracious Chosen Living Stone Divine. Bless us that we be built up as Your spiritual house, where we fit exactly as You desire and where far from coming to the end of our freedom, we come to the beginning of our freedom to Live new open joyful lives in You. Bring us to that beginning so that we may offer up, in each day, the moments of our will with which we are gripping tightly what we want for ourselves. Grant that we offer it up to You freely, with joy and love for You, glad and satisfied to have Your will instead. If that means listening instead of talking, help us Lord. If that means willingly giving in instead of claiming our rights and privileges, help us Lord. If that means focusing all our attention on someone else instead of ourselves, help us Gracious Lord. Help us to see the spiritual sacrifices we may offer up, acceptable and glorious to You, today.

9  But you are A CHOSEN RACE, A royal PRIESTHOOD, A HOLY NATION, A PEOPLE FOR *God's* OWN POSSESSION, so that you may proclaim the excellencies of Him who has called you out of darkness into His marvelous light.
It's true that when we read about the blessings You gave and the close relationship You had with Your people in the Old Testament we, who are not of Your original chosen people, can feel left out.  But now You have also made us, Your people, Your chosen ones.  Thanks and praise to You, Gracious Lord.  As You have made us Your people give us voice to include Your virtues in our conversations.  Grant that in this day and every day we naturally, by Your grace, proclaim in attitudes, words, and deeds Your greatness, Your love, Your kindnesses—Your patience, Your forgiveness, Your joy—and Your desire to bring us all to You with eternal satisfaction in being finally and completely in exactly the right place, the Company of Light, the free and open Life encompassed lovingly by You.

Longing:  To grow through Your word
Longing:  To give to You
Longing:  To proclaim Your Light


1 Peter 3

1-4  In the same way, you wives, be submissive to your own husbands so that even if any *of them* are disobedient to the word, they may be won without a word by the behavior of their wives, ² as they observe your chaste and respectful behavior. ³ Your adornment must not be *merely* external—braiding the hair, and wearing gold jewelry, or putting on dresses; ⁴ but *let it be* the hidden person of the heart, with the imperishable quality of a gentle and quiet spirit, which is precious in the sight of God.
OK, Lord, wives are really nice people.  They put up with a lot.  Thank You for using them to be a blessing.  Please use all Christian wives to be a great blessing to their husbands.

Bless them so that they are witnesses to You showing Your gracious will, showing love and respect to You. A gentle and quiet spirit sounds good. You know, Lord, what each husband needs. Bless wives to be the encouragement to their husbands that they need in their spiritual life, and in their physical life as well. And bless wives with great satisfaction in serving You even if (I suspect a great deal of the time!) they are not shown the appreciation they deserve.

7 You husbands in the same way, live with *your wives* in an understanding way, as with someone weaker, since she is a woman; and show her honor as a fellow heir of the grace of life, so that your prayers will not be hindered.
Help us, who are husbands, Lord, to honor our wives. Grant that we show appreciation for the wonderful people they are. Help us to recognize the witness they give of Your grace and Your love. Grant that we receive the encouragement they give with thanksgiving. Make us blessings to our wives so that we are always encouraging to them. Help us to understand that our wives are often much stronger than we are (physically and in other ways) but to treat them with love, not expecting them to use all their strength for us, but rather wanting to use all our strength to love them, protect them, and provide for them. Thank You for the partnership You give us as fellow heirs of grace. Grant that we will live each day as partners, brought together by You, and together depending on You for all that we need for every challenge and for every opportunity. Grant that we honor and glorify You together throughout our lives, only by Your grace and power, Lord Jesus.

17 For it is better, if God should will it so, that you suffer for doing what is right rather than for doing what is wrong.
There is that (at least, I suspect, American) idea that no one should suffer for doing what is right. But the truth of the matter is that there are a lot of people suffering, right now, for doing what they believe is right and in Your will. If You give me the opportunity to suffer for doing what is right,

please grant that I do not go around complaining and being moody and outraged. Help me to offer to You all those times when I may Live in Your strength while I am hurting or being blamed by others unjustly. Certainly there are times when I suffer for being stupid or selfish or hurtfully angry. Please forgive me for those times, and grant that I suffer willingly with repentance. Keep me from that, Lord. Rather grant me the privilege, if I am to suffer, to suffer for doing what You want, for loving unselfishly, even though others may not be able to recognize my commitment to You.

Wives encouraging in the Lord
Husbands encouraging in the Lord
Suffering in right: willing, joyful


1 Peter 4

7  The end of all things is near; therefore, be of sound judgment and sober *spirit* for the purpose of prayer. "You know that test I told you was coming? Well, it's tomorrow." With those words a teacher brings sober awareness and, in some, great motivation, right Lord? And with Peter's words, You give people an opportunity to wake up and recognize that we are "that close" to the end. Thank You for reminding us that it is important what happens in each day. Grant us sound, accurate, Spirit-filled thinking and judgment so that we will see clearly Your blessings around us and in us, and at the same time see clearly the work of the enemy exposed as that which pulls and leads us away from You. Grant that our being is wide awake and alert as we talk to You frequently, worship You, delight in You, repent to You, rejoice in Your forgiveness, and depend on You. Open our hearts and minds to the priority of talking to You, all the more as we realize in Your grace that our days in this lifetime are limited. Help us to remain close to You here as we approach the time when we will come close to You there.

10 As each one has received a *special* gift, employ it in serving one another as good stewards of the manifold grace of God.

Some people are focused on natural abilities or abilities that are nurtured, Lord, when in fact You graciously touch Your people with the gifts that You want us to have. Help us to recognize the gifts that You give us. Help us to recognize them, not with "Wow, am I good or what!", but with humility and thanksgiving. Grant us a willing spirit to use what You have given us to be a blessing to others. Help us to see the opportunities that You give us to use what You have given to touch others with Your grace and blessing. Help us to step out and serve with absolute confidence that You, Who gave the gifts, are also with us to make them a blessing through us. Let not our selfishness or busy agendas get in the way of serving You. Grant that we enjoy using the gift or gifts You have given us, satisfied, not in ourselves, but in You, Your provision, and the privilege of serving You.

13 ...but to the degree that you share the sufferings of Christ, keep on rejoicing, so that also at the revelation of His glory you may rejoice with exultation.

You remind us, Lord, many times to use what You have given us. If it's all the same to You I would rather use one of Your other blessings rather than sufferings that I share with You. And yet, there are times of suffering. And it is truly a blessing that during those times, I may feel close to You, experiencing Your presence. Whenever times of suffering come, Gracious Lord, help me to see that I am sharing Your sufferings. Not exactly like the people that Peter wrote to whose lives were threatened. But still suffering. Help me to depend on You always, and especially during suffering. And grant that even in those difficult times, I keep on rejoicing by Your strength and grace and the power of Your Holy Spirit. So that when the sufferings are over, and when time passes into the revelation of Your glory, by Your grace, I may truly rejoice with exultation.

Got a moment, Lord?
Joyfully using gifts to bless
Rejoicing through all suffering


1 Peter 5

2 ...shepherd the flock of God among you, exercising oversight not under compulsion, but voluntarily, according to *the will of* God; and not for sordid gain, but with eagerness.
Thank You, Lord, for the elders in the faith, Your servants, whom You have called to lead us and nourish us in Your word and guide us in the Life You have given to us. Bless them, Lord, with joy and wonder walking with You in each day. Give them wisdom to oversee us to our blessing and Your glory. I suppose that after bumping into a lot of smelly sheep day after day, they might get tired or lose some of their initial enthusiasm. Keep their spirits fresh and joyful in You. Give them eagerness to be about the work that You have given them to do. Give them wisdom and power, Lord Holy Spirit, to proclaim Your word faithfully and to our great blessing. And please guide those in charge of provisions for them, so that Your servants will receive bountifully as You have also provided for us (without them having to think about or worry about their provisions). Bless us as Your sheep so that we will be a blessing (smelly as we sometimes are) to the under-shepherds whom You have given us.

6, 7 Therefore humble yourselves under the mighty hand of God, that He may exalt you at the proper time, [7] casting all your anxiety on Him, because He cares for you.
I like humility as much as the next person, Lord. And I can see that it is a really good thing. I suppose I have a little trouble with the idea of wearing humility, so that it is always what I show everyone. You know that there are times when I would really like to be, well, seen as smart and knowledgeable, and ok just a little (not a lot) better than

some other people. You know, when I actually admit that to You, it really sounds miserable. Right. Wearing humility by Your grace as my regular apparel. And then instead of trying to sound like I'm ok and can handle everything (which, of course, is silly) I can recognize the anxiety that attacks and know to cast, throw, forcefully eject and dump all of it on You. You are very gracious to accept all that I cast upon You, Lord. Thank You for caring for me. Thank You for taking all the anxiety and compacting it with Your gracious, divine compactor, and then flicking it off to oblivion. Keep me in that loving, effective plan of Yours: Humility, depending on You, always letting go of all anxiety, rejoicing in Your caring.

8, 9 Be of sober *spirit*, be on the alert. Your adversary, the devil, prowls around like a roaring lion, seeking someone to devour. [9] But resist him, firm in *your* faith, knowing that the same experiences of suffering are being accomplished by your brethren who are in the world.
I have a healthy respect for lions, Lord. In the zoo or in the wild, I enjoy seeing them but am quite satisfied at a distance. But the picture that Peter gives here is truly scary. Thank You for the assurance that Your plan includes dealing with the devil and all his assistants. Bless Your people that we will always be on the alert. It is pretty easy to get lazy in watching our perimeters, daydreaming, advertisements, television, movies, listening to jokes, joining in hurtful attitudes, and a lot more ways the enemy tries to attack. Keep us from being lulled to insensitivity by successes. Keep us from being depressed, discouraged, or afraid because of pain and suffering. Remind us daily that You give us all we need to resist evil and the evil one. Grant that we keep the tools You have given us sharp and in working order with Your word and with faith, consciously, prayerfully depending on You. And grant that we will encourage others in their faithful resisting of evil, also.

Sheep: Care and feeding of elders
Humbly throwing anxiety
Faithfully resisting, even lions

# 2 Peter

2 Peter 1

2, 3 Grace and peace be multiplied to you in the knowledge of God and of Jesus our Lord; ³ seeing that His divine power has granted to us everything pertaining to life and godliness, through the true knowledge of Him who called us by His own glory and excellence.
Thank You, Lord! Show us Your glory and excellence through Your word, Gracious Lord. Call us and grant us true knowledge of You. There are a lot of different ideas of what is really necessary (from 4000+ square foot houses to a backpack with 10 items). Thank You that You know exactly what is essential pertaining to Life and godliness. Keep us in that true knowledge of You, Father, Jesus, Holy Spirit. And I can just see every time we think about You, Lord, every time we consider what we know about You and rejoice in knowing You, Your grace and Your gift of peace pops into our life. It just multiplies again and again through the day. (There it is! Oh, there's some more! And over there! Yes, thank You Lord!) Grant that we recognize with joy the Living we get to do in Your multiplying grace and peace.

10 Therefore, brethren, be all the more diligent to make certain about His calling and choosing you; for as long as you practice these things, you will never stumble.
I remember, Lord, hearing about the famous pianist who in his seventies, was only practicing four hours a day. Yes, I am tempted to think about some things I have practiced when I was young, and now, that's taken care of—I don't have to practice any more. Forgive me, Lord. Help me to be diligent in remembering Your calling. Help me to rejoice again in this day that You have chosen me and brought me to You and to Life. Grant that I practice depending on You and listening to You in every part of my life. Shine Your light

on the way ahead today, Lord. Keep my following muscles and trusting muscles and listening muscles in good shape, so that walking with You in Your light, I may never stumble. Thank You that You give me opportunities to practice today. Grant that (with no whining!) I practice today with diligence, joy, and satisfaction.

19 *So* we have the prophetic word *made* more sure, to which you do well to pay attention as to a lamp shining in a dark place, until the day dawns and the morning star arises in your hearts.

Thank You, Lord, for Peter and his testimony about You speaking through Jesus, our Savior. Thank You for the prophecies that You gave in Your word. Thank You that now we get to see the fulfillments of those prophecies in our Lord Jesus. Although the sun comes up with brightness and heat, there is still a lot of darkness in the way people think. Thank You for Your light shining in this present darkness! In the midst of the clouds and dark mists that float past in this day, help us to pay attention! Help us to think with the benefit of Your light. Grant that we make choices about the way we spend money with the benefit of Your light. Let Your light encourage us so that we Live in hope as we wait for Your day to dawn. It is sure a lot more enjoyable walking in Your light than trying to produce my own light (I've tried, as You know—dim, flickers a lot, strange colors). Thank You for Your people Lord, who reflect Your light wherever they are, what a blessing! Help each of us to face Your light so that we may also reflect Your loving, gracious light for those around us—until You, Lord Jesus, our Morning Star, rise in our hearts on that Day.

Grace and peace abounding
Remembering Your calling with practice
Let Your Son shine in

2 Peter 2

9 ...*then* the Lord knows how to rescue the godly from temptation, and to keep the unrighteous under punishment for the day of judgment.

Previous to this verse, Lord, Peter lists several examples of really bad situations. This generation is not lacking in such examples. Thank You for the example of Your rescuing Your people from the temptation to join in the really rotten things going on. (I can hear that strange voice inside me, "Would it be ok, Lord, if I enjoy the temptation a little without actually falling into it?" Forgive me, Lord!) Please keep us close to You, Lord. Please help us to recognize the evil in our day. Keep us from joining in with any evil that is infesting our time. Keep us from condoning it. Keep us from accepting it. Help us to clearly see the difference between the evil that is present and the people who are participating in it. Grant that our Living is clearly with You even if we suffer ridicule, injustice, or being made outcasts. And use our Living with You to show You and Your Light to the world, effectively inviting people to come from the influence of evil to You and Light and Life.

19 ...promising them freedom while they themselves are slaves of corruption; for by what a man is overcome, by this he is enslaved.

Buy the car with cameras in all directions and automatic protection from running into anything, and you will never have an accident! Well they don't quite say that, but it's close (I'm sure I could still manage to have an accident!). It is so attractive to try to get freedom by buying the right thing, taking the right pill, joining the right group, reading the right book (oops! website). It is very easy, Lord, to see things that other people are overcome by. Not so easy to see what I let overcome me. Help me to see, Lord. Help me to see with Your eyes, before the overcoming begins. While it is a clear and present danger approaching, let me see it, Lord. I am on the lookout for things that look bad, sound bad, and are surrounded by darkness. What I have trouble with is things that really look good. Eating, drinking, sleeping, reading, talking, working—all really good, in moderation. It's seeing the line where I unwittingly, inadvertently pass the edge of moderation heading for the slippery downhill slope—that's the hard part, Lord. Keep me looking, Lord. Grant that I enjoy Your blessings the way You want me to. Let my focusing on You and worshiping You keep me enjoying Your blessings well, and to Your glory.

21 For it would be better for them not to have known the way of righteousness, than having known it, to turn away from the holy commandment handed on to them.
How horrible, Lord! Bless Your people Lord, and keep us close to You. If Your people were faced with having to give their lives for their faith, the decision would be clear. But so often people drift away, very slowly, always thinking that they are still close to You, they just need to turn slightly. Please let people see the slow creeping of separation from You. Fill them Holy Spirit, set them on fire with Your presence and with love for their Savior and Lord. Touch each of us, Your people, Lord, at the beginning of each day. Lead us to check our direction, to reach out for Your hand, to ask Your protection and guidance for the day (even if that means a radical change of plans for the day!). Keep us from the deadly creeping, by daily repentance, forgiveness, joy, love, and worshiping You.

Evil recognized. Spirit-powered avoidance
Enjoying Your blessings, well
Worshiping You: Avoiding creeping.


2 Peter 3

1, 2 This is now, beloved, the second letter I am writing to you in which I am stirring up your sincere mind by way of reminder, ² that you should remember the words spoken beforehand by the holy prophets and the commandment of the Lord and Savior *spoken* by your apostles.

Remembering is a tricky thing, Lord. When I look through photo albums (!) and notes of courses I have taken, there is an enormous amount of stuff. And in one way or another it is stuffed into my memory. But like a terrific computer with a terabyte hard drive, I don't pull all of it up into the currently used operating system of my mind very much. So I hear You saying You want some things to open every time I turn on the operating system. Memory so important that it is part of the thinking system today. OK, Lord, stir my mind, connect my daily use mind to the words You have spoken to me through the prophets, through Your apostles, through the Old and New Testaments. Help me, that my mind may stay stirring and not settle into dusty lethargy at any time. You are the One Who sent Your word and Your prophets and apostles, thank You that my stirred mind may focus on You and rejoice in You. May my mind always be stirred by remembering Your gracious, loving voice.

9  The Lord is not slow about His promise, as some count slowness, but is patient toward you, not wishing for any to perish but for all to come to repentance.

How do I count slowness? Lord, it has changed through the years, as You know. There was a time when days were very long, years were endless expanses of time. What a difference! Yes, it would be terrific if the wonders of Your promised Home and joys of being in Your eternal gracious presence could happen soon (of course, after the D'backs win the world series again and the Packers win the Super Bowl again would be nice (or will that take too long?) Sorry Lord, I know—wrong focus.). Your focus, thank You Lord, is on wanting to include all. Please reach people, Lord. Use Your people to enthusiastically share the joy of Life in You. Grant that we don't just sit around in impatience waiting for You to return (since part of the wait is Your patience also for us!). Grant that we get with Your program, Lord, that we use the time You give us well and to Your glory. And grant that we Live in confidence that You are accomplishing Your return and the fulfillment of Your promise in Your, really good, loving and caring, time.

14 Therefore, beloved, since you look for these things, be diligent to be found by Him in peace, spotless and blameless.
We are looking for Your return, Lord. During every day, it seems like there are times when, if I were really honest, I would say, "Perhaps, not right now, Lord, is the best time." How will You find me? When there is a knock on the door I would like to be able to say, "Come on in!", without a request of "Would You please wait, while I clean up a few things?" Grant that we will be diligent, not just to get up at the right time for whatever is happening today, not just to be ready for the work or task that scheduled for today, not just so that we will be reasonably acceptable in the mores of today. But grant that we will be diligent with mind and heart to be Living in peace toward ourselves and all people. Grant that we be diligent in Living in forgiveness from you for ourselves and extended to all others. Grant that we Live in the washing of our baptisms and Your words of grace, spotless and blameless. Grant that when You knock on the door of our life or our world we will answer with joy and enthusiasm, "Praise to You Lord! Come in!"

Mind stirred by You
Faithfully Living, while enthusiastically waiting
Diligent in peace and sharing You

# 1 John

1 John 1

3 ...what we have seen and heard we proclaim to you also, so that you too may have fellowship with us; and indeed our fellowship is with the Father, and with His Son Jesus Christ. You have given Your word even to us also, now, what seems to me a lot of years later. Thank You, Lord! Thank You for the proclamation of Who You are and Your grace and love in Jesus our Savior. Grant, Gracious Lord, that the growing family of Your people may receive the proclamation of what John and the early Christians saw and heard about You, Lord Jesus. And grant that we may then also be included in fellowship with them and with You. People apply to belong to clubs and honor societies. And if they are accepted they live with a sense of honor and fame (either humbly or the other way). But You graciously include us in the very highest honor there is—fellowship with You. We get to participate in Life with You. Thank You, Lord! Grant that we recognize with great joy (and, yes, humility) the life-changing privilege of fellowship, of participating in Life with You, Lord, not just for a limited number of years now, but through life, through death, and through eternity.

7 ...but if we walk in the Light as He Himself is in the Light, we have fellowship with one another, and the blood of Jesus His Son cleanses us from all sin.
There is darkness around, to be sure. And some people live in that darkness and even write books about how to get along in the best possible way, living in darkness. Incredible, Lord! Whenever we find ourselves living in a cloud of darkness, Lord, grant that we wake up, by the power of Your Holy Spirit, and turn our faces to the Light. Help us to Live in the world, but not in darkness. Let us walk in the Light with You, Lord Jesus, today. Lift up our eyes to

see people walking in Your Light around us. Encourage us by that fellowship we have with them and with You. And grant that we be encouraging to others who are tired of living in darkness. Let them see Your Light, let them see You, in the fellowship of people You have established, that Lives, by Your grace, in Your Light.

9 If we confess our sins, He is faithful and righteous to forgive us our sins and to cleanse us from all unrighteousness.
It is so much easier to pretend they are not there, Lord. To just forget about things we have said and done that have hurt people. As if they were just little pebbles on the path others have to walk over (their problem, not ours!!). What is much harder is to recognize that, though we try really hard to follow You faithfully, we still sin, we still participate in selfishness rather than compassion and love. Help us, Lord, to recognize and rejoice that You are faithful and ready and desire to forgive us and cleanse us from all the yucky, hurtful, willful parts of our lives, so we don't have to work to forget them, we don't have to pretend they are not there. At the beginning of each day (and the end, and in the middle…) here they are, Lord. We bring our brokenness to You, trusting You to be willing and able through Your love and sacrifice and righteousness, to forgive us, cleanse us, make us new, and send us into the time ahead, in thanksgiving, joy, and fellowship with You.

Fellowship: Life with You
Fellowship: With those in Light
Fellowship: Forgiven and cleansed


1 John 2

5, 6 …but whoever keeps His word, in him the love of God has truly been perfected. By this we know that we are in

Him: ⁶ the one who says he abides in Him ought himself to walk in the same manner as He walked.
I want to walk in the same manner as You, Lord Jesus. That has been my commitment for many years. I know that I have failed to do that, Lord. Thank You for Your word. Thank You for showing me my sins. Thank You for the grace to recognize and own my sins with repentance. Thank You for forgiveness and strength and great desire to be faithful in Living as You Lived. Only by Your grace can I take steps each day following in Your footsteps. Help me not to switch directions when I see sacrifice, unselfish loving, self-control, or suffering ahead. I like to think that makes it the wrong path, but certainly You walked that direction. Help me to follow You faithfully, without regard for where Your path takes me, and with confidence that I am in You by Your grace.

20, 21 But you have an anointing from the Holy One, and you all know. ²¹ I have not written to you because you do not know the truth, but because you do know it, and because no lie is of the truth.
There are so many people and groups that want to help me know the "real" truth, newly discovered, modern in outlook and research, more fully enlightening me (and taking me away from You). All the truth I need I receive from You, Lord. You have graciously anointed me with Your Spirit. Thank You, Lord! Even though I do not know all the answers to all questions (other people's or even mine), I know truth is only in You, Lord. Keep me firmly in Your truth. Let me see how Your truth makes sense and applies to me, here in this place, and now in this particular piece of time. Help me not to look for other "truths" that pull me away from You. Your truth grows brighter, clearer, more important, and more applicable as years go by. Protect me from all that is not in Your truth. Grant that I trust Your anointing and Your teaching, always desiring whole-heartedly only to Live confidently knowing You, Who alone are all Life and joy.

24  As for you, let that abide in you which you heard from the beginning. If what you heard from the beginning abides in you, you also will abide in the Son and in the Father.

You have graciously planted Your gospel in me, Lord. There is a temptation to keep redoing my operating system with new versions, that offer better protection from anything bad happening, and give me many, new, cool features that I haven't had before. Help me to resist, O Lord! What I heard from You in the beginning (mine, that is) is what I need to abide in me. Establish it in me with Your everlasting protection so that no attempting updates change Your grace and love to me. Let Your system that You have given me grow, mature, and be productive, so that with joy I may abide in You, no matter what darkness and storms show up, Living in peace and Light and satisfaction.

Wherever Your path leads
Firmly in Your truth
No updates: Abiding in You


1 John 3

13, 14  Do not be surprised, brethren, if the world hates you. ¹⁴ We know that we have passed out of death into life, because we love the brethren. He who does not love abides in death.

I admit, Lord, I am still surprised by what is acceptable to a large number of people. It's easy to feel like I am part of the group where I live. The church, the neighborhood, the city, the have-children group, the married group. There are a lot of groups I feel like I belong to. But I am different, thank You, Lord. You have made me different by bringing me out of death into Life with You. By Your sacrifice, taking my place in death, You have given me forgiveness, Life and the ability to love other people with Your love. Thank You for the privilege of loving my sisters and brothers in You. Help me to remember that it is ok to be fundamentally different from some other people.  Help me to be different lovingly.  And when I see people doing what seems like incredible things to other people, help me not to be surprised, but only recommitted to loving people and grateful for Life in You.

18  Little children, let us not love with word or with tongue, but in deed and truth.
I have learned to say nice things to people.  I thank You for the privilege of speaking Your words of encouragement and caring love to other people.  It is enjoyable to speak kindly to people I see as I walk and go into businesses.  But thank You for jerking me to attention by reminding me that for some people, You want me to do more than just say words of blessing.  Help me recognize those people, Lord.  Grant that I never be too preoccupied to notice people who need deeds of love.  Thank You for the Society of St. Vincent de Paul, the Salvation Army, and other organizations I can use to love in deed and truth.  But let me always be open and ready to help people with deeds personally, here and now, as You give me opportunity.

21, 22  Beloved, if our heart does not condemn us, we have confidence before God; [22] and whatever we ask we receive from Him, because we keep His commandments and do the things that are pleasing in His sight.
Thank You, Lord, for John's ringing confidence in You.  There are times when I ask You for things that later turn out to be silly, in retrospect.  Sometimes I ask You for healing for people or help with emergencies.  I know that Your gracious will is always best and wonderful (even when it seems different from my really terrific and excellent ideas(!)).  Thank You, Lord Holy Spirit, for living in me and enabling me to love the will of my Father.  Grant, Gracious Lord, that I ask well, in Your loving and gracious will, always depending on You.  Grant that I then have that confidence that whatever I ask I receive from You.  You are wonderful to be listening, even to me.  Thank You for finding in each of my prayers, even in Your obviously busy schedule, that which is good,

worthwhile, and a blessing. Everything I ask I turn over to You Who love to answer prayers with Your great and enduring blessings. Use my prayers in the power of Your Spirit to fulfill Your will—to bless Your people, this world, and also me.

Different, ok, and loving
Words And deeds
Asking well. Great answers.


1 John 4

1, 2 Beloved, do not believe every spirit, but test the spirits to see whether they are from God, because many false prophets have gone out into the world. 2 By this you know the Spirit of God: every spirit that confesses that Jesus Christ has come in the flesh is from God.
We do test quite a lot of things, yes, Lord. "Well maybe I'll try it since it's on sale." And if the cereal or whatever passes the test, then it is accepted as a regular menu item. It is possible to subscribe to Consumer Reports that gives the results of tests with recommendations on products. We also like to hear that someone we trust has tried something (so we don't have to be the ones to test it ourselves—it might turn out to be perfectly horrible, after all). But it is easy to just listen to someone give an opinion about You or about how the world works, without actually testing whether that opinion comes from a belief in You, Lord Jesus, You Who have come as a human being, God's gift to us. Help us to be as careful in listening, in taking in thoughts and opinions as we are in what cereal we eat and what car we drive. And before we give an opinion, help us to confer with You, Jesus, since we know that You are fulfilling Your promise to be with us now and always.

15 Whoever confesses that Jesus is the Son of God, God abides in him, and he in God.

I suppose I think of confessing that You are the Son of God, Lord Jesus, as standing on a street corner and telling people how You are wonderfully true man and true God. But that doesn't seem to be Your call to me. Help me to see how I am confessing You as true God in the optimism I feel, think, and speak. In the way I appreciate the world You have made. In the confidence I have that You give us strength through every trial and difficulty. In the openness I have toward other people and the love I share with people in need. Grant that I confess You clearly as my Lord and my God by the way I use time, by the choices I make, by the entertainment I enjoy. And please then, abide in me and grant that I abide in You, today and every day, Gracious Lord and God.

18, 19  There is no fear in love; but perfect love casts out fear, because fear involves punishment, and the one who fears is not perfected in love. [19] We love, because He first loved us.
None of us here likes to admit that we are afraid, Lord. We see ourselves as above that. We can take care of ourselves—that's a popular attitude. At least that is what the world sells. But if people are honest, a lot of people are afraid of health problems, money problems, family problems, being asked to have convictions and stand up for them, and a lot more (especially dying). Thank You for loving us. First. Since without You, we certainly could not love. Fill us with confidence through Your Holy Spirit so that when we have an opportunity to be afraid, we can rejoice that You love us, that You are with us, and that we can take seriously all those times You said in Your word, "Fear not". Help us say "No" to fear. Let not our hearts be troubled, neither let them be afraid, right, Lord? Thank You, Lord. Let Your perfect love cast out all fear from us, and grant that we, loved as we are by You, may so love, fearlessly, by Your grace, that fear is pushed out of other people as well.

Test that thought

Confessing my Lord: Let it show
No to fear, in Your love


1 John 5

11, 12  And the testimony is this, that God has given us eternal life, and this life is in His Son. [12] He who has the Son has the life; he who does not have the Son of God does not have the life.
Thank You Gracious Lord for Your clear testimony through Your Spirit to us that You have given us eternal life, and the eternal life You give us is in Jesus. I feel for people in this world. John said that the world is in the evil one. In his power. There are people who seem to live without caring about You or any Life after life. Please wake these people up, Lord. Use me as You will to help them. There are people who want more than living now and don't know how to find it. Show them Jesus, their Savior and Lord. Use me as You will to help them, Lord. And there are people who really want eternal life and think it is found in a variety of strange places and through people or things other than Jesus. Reach them, Lord. Grab them. Pull them away from all that takes them away from You and Jesus, Your saving Gift to us. Use me as You will Lord, by Your grace, to show Jesus in my life and heart. Grant that people will see the true Light and leave the flickering deadly campfires of human choosing.

14, 15  This is the confidence which we have before Him, that, if we ask anything according to His will, He hears us. [15] And if we know that He hears us *in* whatever we ask, we know that we have the requests which we have asked from Him.
This is indeed the confidence we have in coming to You, Lord. We want to ask always according to Your will. (Well, of course, honestly, we would like Your will to be always according to what we ask. But we know better than to hold

onto that very tightly, because we are definitely looking at things the wrong way around. Help us to get straight in our viewpoint, our attitudes, and our asking.) So, help us always to see Your will. Help us to limit our asking to Your will. But, please, O Lord, help us to expand our asking to Your enormous, gracious, creative, imaginative, loving, beyond our imagination caring and giving—will. Forgive us for asking too little. Open the eyes of our hearts and minds to the great joy You have in listening to us and the wondrous openness You have to bless us. Thank You then for hearing us. Thank You for giving us the certainty that we have received the requests which we have asked of You. What a gift You give us in talking to You, Lord, and asking You for blessings which are in Your enormously large and gracious will!

16 If anyone sees his brother sinning, if the sin is not deadly, he should pray to God and he will give him life. This is only for those whose sin is not deadly. There is such a thing as deadly sin, about which I do not say that you should pray. (NABRE)
I would say, open my eyes to see others sinning, but You know, Lord, that I find it incredibly easy to see other people sinning. (Myself, not so much, sad to say. Help me with that, Lord.) So thank You for this great privilege that You give me. Instead of letting a feeling or thought grow in my heart of "What a nincompoop!" or "How can they do that!" help me to just turn to You immediately asking for Your forgiveness for that person. Yes, I may not ask regarding sin that is deadly. In particular the sin of people telling You, Lord Holy Spirit, to buzz off and leave them alone (how eternally rude, idolatrous, and horrible). Keep me from touching sins that are deadly with prayer. But keep me always loving and open to reach out, without fail, to You every time I see a sister or brother sin, asking You to forgive them, knowing that this is indeed Your will for me and them. Thank You, Gracious Lord.

Your Light:  Eternal life visible
Asking confidently inside Your vast will
Avoiding exasperation:  Asking You to forgive

# 2 John

4 I was very glad to find *some* of your children walking in truth, just as we have received commandment *to do* from the Father.

To meet Your people and experience fellowship with You, Lord, this is truly a joy. Like walking through a desert and finding a previously unseen oasis! (With Vernor's Ginger Ale...) Meeting people who know You and love You and are hospitable with joy to others—what a delightful experience. The world has darkness in it, but You provide people with smiles on their faces, who are gracious and willing to listen to people they meet. You provide people who see the darkness of the world, but who see and reflect Your Light, here and now. Thank You, Lord! How wonderful! So, I guess, having been blessed by these servants of Yours, I ask You, please make me a blessing to others around me, and especially to those of the household of faith. Let me be walking in truth, Living in joy, seeing and reflecting the Light of Your presence with us here and in every now.

9 Anyone who goes too far and does not abide in the teaching of Christ, does not have God; the one who abides in the teaching, he has both the Father and the Son.

Amazingly, there seem to be people who take in Your coming, Lord Jesus. Who are thankful for Your life and death. Who know Your teaching. But they are not satisfied—they want more. You are not enough! How terrible! They go too far. It's like they wave at You in passing, but keep on going. Please help them, Lord. Please help them to see that they have lost everything by not staying with You. Grant that they see the growing darkness in which they live and turn around to see You and Light. And, yes, Lord, help me and all Your people to see when we are in danger of trying to add a little something to what You have told us. Keep us from tidying up places that seem to us not to be organized the way we would choose. May we never fix what You have said or done, because we think we know better. Help us always to listen to You and abide in You and Your teaching with great joy and absolute satisfaction.

10, 11  If anyone comes to you and does not bring this teaching, do not receive him into *your* house, and do not give him a greeting; [11] for the one who gives him a greeting participates in his evil deeds.

Yes, Lord, there are people who come. They come to the door of my home. They come with phone calls. They come with internet sites and internet advertisements. They come in YouTube and social media. They have new(!) and amazing(!) discoveries(!). From this, Gracious Lord, deliver us. I do have a temptation sometimes to try to communicate and straighten them out, help them to get back on the right path to You. But I hear You saying that if a roaring lion comes to my door or approaches me in any other way, it is not time to stand around and talk. Help me to never participate in the evil, but just leave, Lord. Turning away or walking or running—whichever, led by Your Spirit, by Your grace and power, is appropriate.

Joy: Your people of Light
Avoiding tidying up
Roaring lion: Run

# 3 John

2   Beloved, I pray that in all respects you may prosper and be in good health, just as your soul prospers.

It is wonderful and a privilege, Lord, to hear the prayer of John.  I sometimes feel guilty praying for healing for people, or praying that people do well in their financial and other responsibilities, as if these things were so secondary to their spiritual lives that they are not important.  You make it clear here, that our prayers may rightly include the whole person.  So please bless the people I have agreed to pray for, Gracious Lord.  Grant that in all respects they may prosper and use the wonderful blessings You give with thanksgiving and generosity.  Grant that they may all be in good health, and if that requires healing, please grant them the healing they need, in Your wonderful and caring will.  And yes, please bless them all that they may have their souls prosper as well.  In Your grace, Lord, may we prosper according to Your caring and generous will.

6   ...and they have testified to your love before the church.  You will do well to send them on their way in a manner worthy of God.

Thank You Lord for all of Your people who have graciously received me in various places where You have let me dwell, and thank You for their sending me off with Your blessings.  Please let them continue in their loving attitude toward those whom You bring to them.  Let them know how much a blessing they are.  Help me, also, Lord, to show love and a sincere, warm welcome to all who come to my parish.  And while I think everyone should stay that we may continue to grow together in You, I know You call people on in Your wisdom and grace.  Grant that I will share Your love with them as they leave, and if it is Your will, grant that we may continue to enjoy fellowship with You after You call them somewhere else.  Grant us the wonderful anticipation of gathering together with You at home where we never have to leave.

8 Therefore we ought to support such men, so that we may be fellow workers with the truth.

Today, You let Your people know of so many wonderful missions where You are reaching out to bless people with Life, health, and many other physical blessings. In a variety of ways, You bring these to the attention of Your people. Sometimes it seems overwhelming. But Your love and resources are bigger than every need! So bless us that we participate boldly in supporting Your work, with absolute confidence in Your provisions. And grant us the great joy of knowing that as we support Your ministries, we are fellow workers with the truth. It would be wonderful (and challenging and hard work, of course) to go and work in the ministries You have established. Thank You for calling people with the gifts You want in every place. Give us, please, Lord, satisfaction as fellow workers with Your gracious truth, even here in the places where You have called us. May Your truth always keep multiplying in the power of Your Spirit.

In all respects, prosper
Loving, coming, going
Participate with the truth

# Jude

1, 2 Jude, a bond-servant of Jesus Christ, and brother of James,
To those who are the called, beloved in God the Father, and kept for Jesus Christ: ² May mercy and peace and love be multiplied to you.

Thank You, Lord, for Your call, calling us out of the world to Live with You. We, Your people, have been loved by various people, Lord. Sometimes it has been a great and wonderful blessing, sometimes not quite so much. But the very best there is, is to be loved by You, Father! Thank You! As we move around in this world, still, please keep us, Father, for Jesus. Keep us strong in our faith. Grant that we serve You, walking through this world today, without any of it sticking to us. Thank You for the days You give us. As we enter each one, let Your mercy come to us, forgiving us. Let Your peace come to us, no matter what winds are blowing around us. And let Your love be also multiplied to us so that we may Live in Your love and share Your love with our sisters and brothers, and with the residents of the world who have not yet heard Your calling.

3 Beloved, while I was making every effort to write you about our common salvation, I felt the necessity to write to you appealing that you contend earnestly for the faith which was once for all handed down to the saints.

You have graciously given faith to Your people, thank You, Lord! It is true that sometimes I don't think much about that. Faith is something that is a wonderful gift, that is carefully put in a good place, available to use when needed. I don't often think of Your gift of faith as something that I need to contend for. I already have it, why contend for it? But the mood of the world in which I live is like the 8% humidity where I live. It sucks things dry. And the world tries to suck the wonderful, powerful Life out of my faith. Grant that I contend by connecting the faith You have given me to Your gracious word and sacraments frequently.  Grant that I contend by using the faith You have given me regularly so it doesn't get stiff and dry from lack of use.  And grant that I contend by avoiding those things in association, entertainment, reading, listening, seeing, or thinking that I know are contrary to the faith You have given me.  Help me to be willing and enthusiastic to put my heart into contending, so that I do it earnestly by Your grace and to Your glory.

20, 21  But you, beloved, building yourselves up on your most holy faith, praying in the Holy Spirit, [21] keep yourselves in the love of God, waiting anxiously for the mercy of our Lord Jesus Christ to eternal life.
Build on our strengths, our talents and abilities, we are told.  But the solid foundation for all the building in our lives, Lord, is You and Your gift of faith.  As we learn, grow, mature, progress in whatever way You want, let all of it be based on You and on Your gift of faith.  Grant that all the growth and building in our lives be essentially connected to praying in the Holy Spirit.  Grant that we pray in You, Holy Spirit, by asking You to guide our reading of Your word, by asking You to guide our thinking and our wanting—grant that we think clearly by Your grace and that we want well, with Your discerning power.  Grant that our praying for ourselves and others will always depend on You, Lord Holy Spirit, to want well, to ask well, to put wants into Spirit-powered, Spirit-chosen words.  Stir our hearts, Holy Spirit, so that we are never satisfied to Live without talking to You.  Let our conversations with You be a foundation of Living, a joy, and a confidence in You.  Thank You, Lord for Your love and fellowship as we wait for Your return with great joy and anticipation.

In every storm:  Multiplication of peace
Contending earnestly, in every part of living
In everything:  Talking to You

# Revelation

Revelation 1

3 Blessed is he who reads and those who hear the words of the prophecy, and heed the things which are written in it; for the time is near.
Thank You Lord for the words of prophecy, and thank You for the promise with them. Please bless us as we read these words and hear You speaking to us. You were first speaking to people in a radical, threatening time for Your people. This time seems to be quieter. It is possible to follow You without others threatening our lives. Of course, the expectation is that we will at least try to fit in to society—and although quiet, there is the same threat. Help us to read Your word, to hear You speaking, and then also to heed what You say to us. Even today, even in this culture with its quiet and strenuous expectations of us, grant that we heed Your word and commit ourselves daily to following You. For the time is near for us, too. Certainly You are coming again, Lord Jesus. But if You do not come by the end of our lives, You will certainly come then for us. So the time is near. It is not centuries away. It is in this life that we get to listen to You, rejoice in You, and follow You. Grant that we do that faithfully.

4 – 6 John to the seven churches that are in Asia: Grace to you and peace, from Him who is and who was and who is to come, and from the seven Spirits who are before His throne, [5] and from Jesus Christ, the faithful witness, the firstborn of the dead, and the ruler of the kings of the earth. To Him who loves us and released us from our sins by His blood— [6] and He has made us *to be* a kingdom, priests to His God and Father—to Him *be* the glory and the dominion forever and ever. Amen.

Gracious Lord, please grant us that grace and peace that only comes from You. You are eternal and winds and storms in time have no effect on You. Thank You that we have grace and peace from You now in Jesus. Thank You for Your Spirit by Whom we come to know You and peace. Help us to remember the peace we have in You, since Jesus is ruler of all rulers on the earth also today. (Rule us also, as You use the means You desire to choose our earthly rulers—make earthly rulers today a blessing to us and make us, together with them, a blessing, honoring You.) Have dominion over us nationally, in our states and communities, and most of all in our hearts.

17, 18  When I saw Him, I fell at His feet like a dead man. And He placed His right hand on me, saying, "Do not be afraid; I am the first and the last, $^{18}$ and the living One; and I was dead, and behold, I am alive forevermore, and I have the keys of death and of Hades.
Grant Gracious Lord Jesus, that we fall before You in our spirits in this day. Grant that we humbly recognize who we are and Who You are, with awe and wonder and whole-hearted obeisance. As we rise to continue living with the Life You give us here, grant that we do so with complete confidence in You. Take away all fear as we think and love and make choices in these days until the end of our days here. Whenever fear knocks on our door, let us remember You, First, Last, and Present now with us. In Your rising to Life without end, let us receive strength, joy and enthusiasm for Living. As we approach death (no matter how many years ahead), let us be fully Alive in the joy and wonder that You have the keys of death, and that You have graciously unlocked death, making it the door to Life with You forever.

In quietness, in twisted expectations, faithfulness
Have dominion, now
Humbly Alive throughout life

Revelation 2

2 'I know your deeds and your toil and perseverance, and that you cannot tolerate evil men, and you put to the test those who call themselves apostles, and they are not, and you found them *to be* false.'
It seems more complicated today, Lord. Rather than one group in a community, we have several or a lot of groups of Your people. Please bless us that we will recognize You among us. Grant that we first look for good in each other rather than evil. Grant that we use the blessings of Your word to test all those who want to be seen as being sent by You. Give us clear understanding so that we will honor You with what we believe and in the associations that we form. We know there is evil in the world, Lord. The message we receive from the world is that toleration is a basic virtue of humanity. Help us not to get pulled into tolerating evil. Grant that we put You first in our Life, in our words, in our actions, in our choices, and in the fellowship we have with others.

4 But I have *this* against you, that you have left your first love.
I can remember times, as I look back, Lord, when I experienced You sitting next to me, walking with me. I remember talking earnestly to You with relief and great commitment for obedience. I look back at some of the notes I have written through the years, and some of them are really inspiring. I can feel with the people in Ephesus. It's easy to let the brightness and enthusiasm, the joy and fervor fade. And since I know You haven't moved any farther away, I suppose ..., well, help me Lord. Help me to get up in the morning looking for You, instead of just focusing on being busy getting ready. In all the things that I need to be busy doing, grant that I enjoy Your presence. And help me to recognize the things I really don't have to be busy doing. Love, You? Yes, Lord, I love You. OK, my list of things and people I love is a little longer than it used to be. Right, I

haven't gone through it recently to prune it and bring Your light to focus on it clearly. Good idea. Help me to do that, Lord. Give me courage to sweep out unnecessary hangers-on: ideas, stuff, whatever I brought in with love at the time, but which in Your light and company is misplaced. Fill me with Your Spirit so that I will love You with joy and enthusiasm today and every day You give me.

10 Do not fear what you are about to suffer. Behold, the devil is about to cast some of you into prison, so that you will be tested, and you will have tribulation for ten days. Be faithful until death, and I will give you the crown of life.
We don't face exactly the same suffering that the people in Smyrna did. But You have told us that we should expect suffering in our lives no matter what century we live in. Evil still tries to get us to despair, it still tries to pull us away from You. It still tries to get us to think that we have to depend on ourselves. There is still tribulation. You have "not promised skies always blue, flower strewn pathways all our lives through …" (Thank you, Lord for Annie Johnson Flint and her *What God hath promised*.) Grant, Gracious Lord, that we will not face today or any other day with fear. You have given us what we need for today, grant that we use it well. Thank You for the gift of faith. Grant that we depend on You, and Live filled with faith not just for a time when we experience a mountain top with You, not just for youth or until we are successful, but through every day through every tribulation, through every attack of despair—right to the end. By the power of Your Spirit grant that we will be faithful until death. Thank You for Life with You now and for the great, amazing, and wonderful gift You have promised of Life with You then.

Listening for Your voice among the voices
Loving You, now, enthusiastically
Living faithfully—to the end

Revelation 3

3 So remember what you have received and heard; and keep *it*, and repent. Therefore if you do not wake up, I will come like a thief, and you will not know at what hour I will come to you.
I don't like to think of us, Your people, being asleep, and needing Your words of warning. But, are we truly awake, the way You want us to be, Lord? Are we only focused on the buildings and the personnel and creating the right systems for dealing with personal and spiritual growth information accurately and appropriately? Help us remember what we have received from You. Remind us of the ways You want us to care about people. Show us the people that You have sent us to serve. Grant that we take more seriously the needs of the people we are called to serve than our needs for up to date physical worship and education facilities. Let our concern about the physical place where we worship and fellowship be directed to meet the needs of the people You call us to serve. Grant that we repent of any and all selfishness in our planning, thinking, or fellowship. Grant that we continue to grow spiritually so that we may be about serving You effectively as You desire, awake, alert, listening to You, desiring to serve You above all.

8 'I know your deeds. Behold, I have put before you an open door which no one can shut, because you have a little power, and have kept My word, and have not denied My name.'
Thank You, Lord, for being here, with us. We want to serve You, Lord. Keep watch, that we don't just say, but do. Thank You for the open door that You have put before Your people. Thank You, that the opportunity to serve You is as individual as the group of Your people and the gifts You have given them. Thank You for the power You give us to serve You. Keep us strong in using Your power, and not slipping back into relying on ourselves. Keep us in Your word. Grant that we grow in reading and hearing and

studying Your word.  Grant that we never deny Your name.  (It is awfully tempting, Lord, to claim credit for the people involved in the ministry or the congregation.  Help us to remember that all credit is Yours.)  Grant that we don't want, in word of mouth or in advertisements, to be known as the church with the great facility, or the great choir, or the great preacher, or the great worship.  But the church with the great Savior.  In that way, Gracious Savior, may we all be known as we go through the door You open before us.

20  Behold, I stand at the door and knock; if anyone hears My voice and opens the door, I will come in to him and will dine with him, and he with Me.
So, what I hear You saying, Lord, is that, nice it would be if I am listening!  It isn't just the noise of music or television.  There is also a noise in my head.  It's pretty much the noise of selfishness.  "Have I gotten in everything today that I wanted to do?  I've been doing really well in being a help to others, is it time for me yet?"  Or just the noise of thinking about how I could be a great (and recognized!) help to someone, and what wonderful things people will think of me if I do the following great things... .  Help me, Lord to be quiet!  Help me to listen for Your voice.  Grant that I keep my attention off myself.  Grant that I keep part of my attention on others and part, listening for Your knock.  Help me to live in a thought and feeling and physical space that is not so cluttered that there is no room for You to come in.  Grant that when I hear Your voice I will, with joy, open the door, without asking You to wait until I fix something first (that is messy or that I think You would rather not see).  Grant that I will be open and eager for You to come in every day.

Awake. Sent. Serving.
Through the open door, today.
Quiet. Listening. Eager.


Revelation 4

1  After these things I looked, and behold, a door *standing* open in heaven, and the first voice which I had heard, like *the sound* of a trumpet speaking with me, said, "Come up here, and I will show you what must take place after these things."

Thank You Jesus for showing us today, this vision of what is coming.  Let it be a blessing to us, as You intend.  Through the certainty that there is an "after" the now we are living in, grant us encouragement and hope.  Through the necessity of Your "must", let us see Your grace and Your justice and Your love moving through this time when we live, into the open door where time ends.  Keep us from using the words of Your vision in any way selfishly, but only with confidence in You and in Your continuing grace giving us Life through death into that Life which is "after".  Thank You for the privilege of coming up to see the vision of "after" with John.  Open our hearts and minds beyond the categories and limits in which we live, by Your gracious vision, to stretch to Your love and Your almighty will.

8  And the four living creatures, each one of them having six wings, are full of eyes around and within; and day and night they do not cease to say,
"HOLY, HOLY, HOLY *is* THE LORD GOD, THE ALMIGHTY, WHO WAS AND WHO IS AND WHO IS TO COME."

The creatures are a little scary, Lord, but clear with the witness and confession that is fundamental to our Life, by Your grace.  Let their untiring recognition and honor glorifying You echo from our thoughts, our words, our prayers, our loving, our actions, our imagination, our remembering.  And while it doesn't fit very well into our human understanding, Lord, Your being You in the past, always, in the present everywhere, and in the future always is the Light that graciously lights up our present and gives us confidence to live the limited days we have here.  Let our hearts be filled with honoring You and with thanksgiving because there is infinitely more to Life than the finite life and living we enjoy in Your blessing now.

10, 11 ...the twenty-four elders will fall down before Him who sits on the throne, and will worship Him who lives forever and ever, and will cast their crowns before the throne, saying,
[11] "Worthy are You, our Lord and our God, to receive glory and honor and power; for You created all things, and because of Your will they existed, and were created."
Here You show us the depth and fabric of worship: Worship declares You worthy of glory and honor and power. Grant, Gracious Lord, that in these days before we get to the Life then, we will use Your grace and revelation to inform and fill our worship with Spirit-powered recognition and joy and appreciation of You because You are indeed worthy. Grant that in worship each day and in fellowship with other Christians, we will glorify You. You are worthy of glory, Lord. Grant that we will honor You in our thoughts and words and actions with all our hearts. You are worthy of honor, Lord. And grant that we whole-heartedly turn over all power You give us to Your use and purposes. You are worthy of all power, Lord. Worthy are You, Gracious Lord. You have created all things and us and all with which we live. Thank you and praise to You for Your gracious will to create us and make us Your own.

Seeing, opened, stretched
Echoing honor and thanksgiving
Worshiping You Who are Worthy


Revelation 5

5 and one of the elders said to me, "Stop weeping; behold, the Lion that is from the tribe of Judah, the Root of David, has overcome so as to open the book and its seven seals."

There is no roadblock to eternal joy; thank You, Lord. To get to the gate of heaven and find it locked with no one having the key would be the ultimate in horrible. Thank You, Lord, for overcoming. What have You overcome? I suppose besides evil and sin in general, specifically what You have overcome is us. ("What's wrong with the world?" the newspaper asked, and thank You for G. K. Chesterton's answer, "I am.") We have a sinful, self-will that would always like to lead us away from You. Thank You, Gracious Lord, for overcoming us. Please let us recognize You, Lion of the tribe of Judah, today and not think or imagine going any direction but following You. Thank You for C. S. Lewis' *Narnia Tales,* and Aslan. Thank You that we may follow You Who are not tame, not safe, but enormously loving. Please grant that as we Live in this day, we do so with the joy and certainty that You have overcome, You are leading us, and You will open the way, right into eternal joy with You.

9, 10  They sang a new hymn:
"Worthy are you to receive the scroll
   and to break open its seals,
   for you were slain and with your blood you purchased for God those from every tribe and tongue, people and nation.
[10] You made them a kingdom and priests for our God,
   and they will reign on earth."  [NABRE]
Indeed, Lord, You are worthy of all praise from us. Thank You for purchasing us, for redeeming us by Your sacrifice of Yourself. Thank You, Gracious God, that we belong to You. Help us to live today as those who have been redeemed, as those who no longer belong to evil and selfishness, but to You. Even more proudly (and thankfully) than those people who wear shirts emblazoned with the name of the company who has bought their services, may we Live showing Your name as the One Who has bought us. And grant that we Live now serving You in the callings You have given us, by Your power, Holy Spirit. Grant that we Live as Your priests, showing Your sacrifice, showing that You have bought us,

showing Your grace and love, showing our faithfulness to You. Help us to be a people of our King and Savior, Jesus. Let our service and pride in being Yours be the song in our heart every day.

12, 13 ...saying with a loud voice,
"Worthy is the Lamb that was slain to receive power and riches and wisdom and might and honor and glory and blessing."
[13] And every created thing which is in heaven and on the earth and under the earth and on the sea, and all things in them, I heard saying,
"To Him who sits on the throne, and to the Lamb, *be* blessing and honor and glory and dominion forever and ever."
Sometimes, Lord, at the end of our movies with heroes, the hero goes off into the sunset without a lot of fanfare and without much thanks or honor. (Except, of course, Star Wars, which has a pretty good scene of honoring the heroes.) We look forward to You, Lord Jesus, receiving the honor and praise and worship that You deserve. Thank You for showing us the event in heaven when that happens. Of course it used to be, that the good guys always won in movies. Seems like, not so consistently now. Thank You, Lord, that there is no doubt about the outcome of life. There are days when the outcome seems to be shifting back and forth. There are temptations that come to us to wonder if there is a victory at the end. Bless us with certainty in Your victory, Lord Jesus. Bless us with Living in the joy of Your victory on days when it is obvious and on days when it is really difficult to see. Let the wonder and awe of the Hero's welcome with honor, praise, and worship that is coming for You in heaven (let us have a good view and be able to participate in the joyous festivities)—let that coming event lift our spirits and empower us to faithfulness as we have the opportunity to Live with You and for You now.

Overcome. Following You.

Bought by You. Proud of it.
Empowered by Your victory.


Revelation 6

6  And I heard *something* like a voice in the center of the four living creatures saying, "A quart of wheat for a denarius, and three quarts of barley for a denarius; and do not damage the oil and the wine."
What I hear You saying, Lord, is that the time is coming when a lot of very bad stuff is going to happen.  It will be very difficult to get through those times for all people, but certainly for those who are not depending on You.  Help us now, Lord, to learn to depend on You.  There are enough bad things happening now.  Grant that we, Your people, see them and remember in a new and fresh way to talk to You, to repent to You, and to depend on You for getting through each day, recognizing Your presence with us and trusting You.  And during these days, please, Lord, let the bad things that happen wake up other people.  Let them hear You calling them to a faith relationship with You, so that they, too, can depend on You now and in every difficulty and disaster to come.  Touch people now, so that they don't have to try to endure the shaking of life that is coming, by depending on themselves.  Grant, Lord, that we demonstrate by what we say and do, that we are depending, not on ourselves, but on You Who love us, are with us, and care about us.  Make our faithful dependence on You a visible encouragement to others, by Your grace and power.  And with that grant us the encouragement that there is a purpose to our going through challenges and trials now (whether we see it or not).  In every need, grant us joy and satisfaction in You.

10  …and they cried out with a loud voice, saying, "How long, O Lord, holy and true, will You refrain from judging and avenging our blood on those who dwell on the earth?"

There I am, crossing the street with the walk light, and someone facing a red light comes rushing around the corner, just missing me. And there rises in my heart a cry to You for justice. How selfish of me. How amazingly small. There are all those people who have stood up for You to the death. They willingly gave their lives rather than deny You. They, with great reason, would like justice. They would like You to show the world that they were right, that You are the One and Only Savior, God, Lord, and King. Yet they need to wait, You say, for the end to come. Help me not to be so petty, Lord. Help me to recognize that it is important for me not to "sweat the small stuff, and everything is small stuff." (Thank You for Michael Mantell and Richard Carlson and their quotes.) Grant that I focus my time, my energy, my spiritual fervor on listening to You and following You faithfully without concern for having the world see that I am right and they are wrong. Grant that I patiently wait for that until the end. Help me now to be faithful and leave it up to You to use my faithfulness to encourage others and also leave it up to You to straighten other people out. (Keep me clear that I don't have time and energy for both faithfulness and straightening. Straightening other people out is just not my job. How much more time and energy I have if I just leave that up to You! Thank You, Lord!)

16 ...and they said to the mountains and to the rocks, "Fall on us and hide us from the presence of Him who sits on the throne, and from the wrath of the Lamb."
What a striking, scary picture, Lord! You are so Righteous, so Glorious, so Holy, so Powerful! All those people who have ignored You or seen You as good for some people but not for them because they were above such things—all those people who have seen You as a good example, a good teacher—all those people who have known You as the Savior and yet have gradually separated themselves from You—all those people who have hated You because You are Righteous and opposed to what they want—for them, it will be unbearable to see You coming. Grant, Gracious

Lord, that we never stray into those groups of people. Show us that Your coming is our great joy and the beginning of the Life You have prepared for us. Help us to look forward to Your return with enthusiasm and wonder. And help us to be open and visible to others in our earnestly desiring Your return. Grant that we show by our faithful Living that You open a door to all people today, so that they never have to fear Your Holy and Righteous Presence, when time is rolled up, and there is no place for anyone to hide.

Learning to depend on You now
Following now. Justice later.
Joy: Seeing You without hiding.


Revelation 7

9, 10 After these things I looked, and behold, a great multitude which no one could count, from every nation and *all* tribes and peoples and tongues, standing before the throne and before the Lamb, clothed in white robes, and palm branches *were* in their hands; [10] and they cry out with a loud voice, saying,
"Salvation to our God who sits on the throne, and to the Lamb."
It sounds a little like a toast, Lord, to You. You will have gathered us all together in heaven. Without Your guidance most of us will be speechless. And a few might be thinking of saying, "Say, God, nice place You have here." But with Your guidance, we will rejoice in the best thing we have, and that is the salvation You have given us. Help us to prepare now for the celebration. Help us to recognize that the very best we have to celebrate with You, our Lord and God, is not the advancements we have received through the years, and not the amount of stuff, rolling stock, or autographs we have accumulated, not the people we have met or places we have been, but what You have given us: forgiveness of our sins, being saved, and the Life unending we have with You.

Since that is the wonder and subject of our celebration then, please grant us, Lord, that we may keep Living in You now with priorities and values that reflect the great celebration to come, with You in heaven.

11, 12 And all the angels were standing around the throne and *around* the elders and the four living creatures; and they fell on their faces before the throne and worshiped God, 12 saying,
"Amen, blessing and glory and wisdom and thanksgiving and honor and power and might, *be* to our God forever and ever. Amen."
If we move to a new land here, we might have to learn a new language, Lord (like Texas (!), (no offence intended, Texas)). And when we get to heaven You will teach us a new language, in how to talk to You, how to appreciate You, how to be with You. Help us to get ready now, Lord, before we move, by learning to at least recognize these parts of the heavenly language: All blessing, all that is good and touches our lives, blessing us, comes only and alone from You, Lord. All that we think of as glorious can only rightly be glorious if it comes from You, Glorious Lord. Help us to recognize You as the source of all that is real wisdom. Instead of having a few days every year to be really thankful, lead us to recognize thanksgiving as an essential attitude we can have as we think about You. While there are various ways we express honor now, grant that we see You as the One who personally really deserves all honor. And while we think of power and might in terms of lifting, moving, or possibly blowing things up, You demonstrate real power and might by creating from nothing, by making us, and thank You, Lord, by bringing us to Life. Grant that we rejoice in the heavenly language that we can learn and use now.

16, 17 They will hunger no longer, nor thirst anymore; nor will the sun beat down on them, nor any heat; 17 for the Lamb in the center of the throne will be their shepherd, and will guide them to springs of the water of life; and God will wipe every tear from their eyes."

It does sound wonderful, Lord! There are a lot of people who suffer from hunger, and by Your grace, they will never have that problem again. And there are some of us for whom it would be a blessing if we could no longer hunger for things that are not very good for us, like fat and salt. Thank You, Lord, our Shepherd that You will provide for us so that we will not be in want. Bless those people today who are in need. Grant that when Your people reach out and help them, they may also have a vision of Your gracious provision for us in heaven. Bless those people today, Lord, who are suffering and fearful and grieving. Please let them have a taste of that promise of the place where all tears will be wiped away in your grace. Give us, Your people, a sense of urgency in helping those who are suffering, since You have made it clear that You want people to be helped. And when suffering seems unending, please bless people with encouragement and hope by the promise You give of an end to all tears.

Living with heavenly priorities
Learning Your heavenly language
Hoping through suffering: End coming


Revelation 8

1 When the Lamb broke the seventh seal, there was silence in heaven for about half an hour.

You have created the world, beautiful and a blessing, and it will be an awesome and terrible moment when the time comes to begin its destruction. You have graciously given people time to recognize You and Your love and grace. Thank You, Lord. Please make Your good news effective now while there is time, so that people will come to You and receive Your gift of Life. It is awfully easy to be so occupied with stuff that we don't see time passing. Please bless Your people that we will use the time You give us well, to be a blessing to those in need, to Live and proclaim Your gospel that we may Live in joy in You and that others may see Your love and grace and forgiveness. Grant that Your people will Live with a sense of time having a limit and the end coming, and yet rejoicing in Your love and Your power. Grant that other people live with an awareness of time being limited and the end coming. Keep them from despair or from life without caring—grant that they recognize their need for Your blessing of continuing Life. Thank You for coming quickly and at the same time waiting for all to be invited to Life.

4 And the smoke of the incense, with the prayers of the saints, went up before God out of the angel's hand.
Thank You, Gracious Lord, for listening to our prayers. Thank You for desiring and enjoying that people pray to You. As we talk to You, Lord, help us to recognize Your smile as You are listening. Give us the encouragement of Your presence as we talk to You. (I'm sorry to say that sometimes I have said prayers as a form, kind of aiming them at the ceiling, without opening my heart to seek You in my conversations. Please forgive me, Lord.) Grant that we may always converse with You, having confidence that You are listening to us. It is mind-boggling to me thinking of all the people right now talking to You, and You carrying on a conversation with all of us! But, You are You, and so, help us to have peace in our hearts that while it seems amazing to us, it's no problem for You. Receive our prayers, then, Lord, as incense—as a pleasing event to You. Grant that every time we talk to You through the day, in a formal way, in a friendly conversation, in a cry—we may know with satisfaction that You are available (not the "chat time will be available in 5 minutes"!). Grant us confidence that You enjoy us talking to You about things small and large and that You take our requests seriously. Thank you for always working for our blessing in the answers You give and in the timing You choose. Even if some prayers get answered fully right at the end, while the trumpet is blowing.

5  Then the angel took the censer and filled it with the fire of the altar, and threw it to the earth; and there followed peals of thunder and sounds and flashes of lightning and an earthquake.
You have told us many times that the end is coming.  That there is destruction coming.  It's true that we don't like to think about it.  In this time that You have given us, there is living and growth and building.  There are places of prosperity, there are vast tracts of land available, there is water that is available in some areas, and the sun faithfully rises every day (as You spin our earth around—what an amazing event, setting this all in motion!).  As we hear about land being destroyed, commerce being thrown into confusion, water made unusable, and light itself beginning to fail, it is really scary!  All of our living is balanced precariously on Your willingness to keep it going.  Bless us with satisfaction in the days You give us.  Make us effective in witnessing our thanks to You and faith in You.  And when we think of You bringing an end to all that we know here, keep our focus on Your grace, on Your love bringing us to You, on Your gift of Life that has no end.  And on Your presence, You Who are unchanging, Loving Father, Jesus, and Holy Spirit.  Let praise rise from our hearts to You now and always.

Time in short supply!  Using it well.
Talking to You, Who are listening.
In peace, in change, depending on Your unchanging grace.


Revelation 9

2  He opened the bottomless pit, and smoke went up out of the pit, like the smoke of a great furnace; and the sun and the air were darkened by the smoke of the pit.
As You show the picture of the end unfolding, one of the frightening experiences people have is darkness.  Even on

stormy days, we have confidence that light is on the other side of the clouds, and the end of the storm is coming when sunlight will shine again. And yet, with the symbol of darkness, You help us to see the darkness that flows through our world today. There are people who think they are living in light—with education, abilities, busy schedules, and contacts with people—but who cannot see You, cannot see their own need for You. Bless us today with Your Light shining through every darkness that attacks us. Bless us that we always depend on Your Light, no matter how dark any day looks. Blow Your wind of grace through the world so that people may see Your Light and come to You, while there is still time. You are the Light of the world, Jesus, and You have called us to be Light where we are. Grant that we shine brightly, consistently, lovingly, by Your grace. Use us to dispel darkness now before the fearsome darkness comes at the end.

4 They were told not to hurt the grass of the earth, nor any green thing, nor any tree, but only the men who do not have the seal of God on their foreheads.
Thank You Lord, for putting Your seal on us, Your people. Let us rejoice in Your seal, not with arrogance or pride, but with thanksgiving and faith at Your generosity and grace given to us, bringing us to Life. Thank You that we may listen to You now, Lord. Grant that we truly appreciate the time we have now to worship You, to grow in You, to serve You. Grant that we use this time with a sense that the end of this time is coming. Thank You for protecting Your people through the end times as well. Bless us with confidence that whether we go home to You before the end times or live through them, we are in Your gracious hand, in Your protection, and we may depend on You Who have sealed us in the blood of Your sacrifice, Lord Jesus. May we humbly continue to rejoice that we are sealed by Your grace and kept in Your loving care through all the days You give us.

20, 21  The rest of mankind, who were not killed by these plagues, did not repent of the works of their hands, so as not to worship demons, and the idols of gold and of silver and of brass and of stone and of wood, which can neither see nor hear nor walk; [21] and they did not repent of their murders nor of their sorceries nor of their immorality nor of their thefts. They will see destruction all around.  They will know Your wrath poured out in their world.  And they will not repent! Now is the time.  Please, Lord, help us to admit our sins. Help us to see where we have not listened to You.  Help us to see not only the idolatry of putting physical things before You, but the idolatry of putting our ideas, our desires, our depending on ourselves in place of Your will, Your desires for us, and Your grace and strength that You offer us.  Help us to recognize our sins now, every night at the end of the day, every morning as we begin the day, whenever we recognize our will as sneaking away from Yours—help us to repent and desire to Live only in Your will by Your grace in forgiveness of our sins.  Keep us from the sins of murder, sorcery, sexual immorality, and stealing of any kind.  And bless those whose lives touch or delve into any of those so they might see how far they are from You.  Let them desire You and Your forgiveness.  Bring them to repentance now while there is time.

In darkness, Light now
Confidence:  Sealed.  Protected.
Seeing our need.  Repenting.  Now.


Revelation 10

1  I saw another strong angel coming down out of heaven, clothed with a cloud; and the rainbow was upon his head, and his face was like the sun, and his feet like pillars of fire. As You describe Your messenger that You used, to communicate with John, thank You Lord for including the rainbow on his head.  From the time of the flood, You have

used the rainbow to give us confidence that You have a covenant that You make with us of grace. You had the right and the power then to end the world before or after Noah. You had the right to end the world in the time of John. Thank You for Your covenant of grace, by which You reach out also to us, now. You have the reasonable right to reject us for not following You faithfully. Please remind us every day that we have another day, only by Your grace. Grant that we take in every breath with recognition of and thanksgiving for Your undeserved love and mercy, by which You bring us to You and keep us close to You. Certainly rainbows have been used in our culture to sell a variety of things, but grant that we rejoice in Your rainbow, Your covenant of grace and mercy, having no fear of Your angel messengers and no fear of time coming to a screeching halt at Your gracious will.

7 ...but in the days of the voice of the seventh angel, when he is about to sound, then the mystery of God is finished, as He preached to His servants the prophets.
You have been graciously opening Your mystery through Your servants for a very long time. And You have given us a record of their witness in Your word. Thank You, Lord. If we get up and look out the window, the world (our world in which we breathe and touch things and think) seems full and busy, if it is only the water coming down the mountainside or the wind moving around the trees. It's hard to see the world coming to an end, Lord. Help us to see past the beauty and busy-ness of what is visible, to the mystery of Your grace carrying us beyond time to the end, to the goal You have for Your people. Help us to focus in such a way on Your gracious conclusion, that others notice our gaze and take time to wonder about You. Bless people who are not satisfied with the clear awareness of satisfaction in You and Your love and Your grace—they need help recognizing satisfaction. And bless those people who are satisfied without You, with an awareness of Your grace and gifts and a hunger for Your gifts that are so much more satisfying—

both now and into the conclusion which You are even now preparing, as You care about us all.

10, 11 I took the little book out of the angel's hand and ate it, and in my mouth it was sweet as honey; and when I had eaten it, my stomach was made bitter. [11] And they said to me, "You must prophesy again concerning many peoples and nations and tongues and kings."
"Here let me show you how to do that," I have said. And then I realize when I try to show what I know, that I have forgotten exactly how to do it. Most distressing, Lord. So You remind us to take in first what we want to give others. Help us, Lord, to take in Your message of repentance, mercy, forgiveness, and Life. Grant that we don't just hear it, but bring it into our selves, into our living. Before we want to have others receive Your grace from us, help us to daily recognize our sins, our brokenness. Help us to eat Your good news, taking it inside ourselves, applying it to ourselves. Grant that we don't so much plan to package satisfaction in You so that people will receive it, but grant that we rejoice in You and Live in such satisfaction, that people cannot help but notice and stare at us and wonder. Grant that we proclaim You and Your grace every day, in faithful actions and faithful words.

A rainbow: Your promised grace, always
Gazing: Past time, to satisfaction in You
First receiving You. Then showing You.


Revelation 11

1 Then there was given me a measuring rod like a staff; and someone said, "Get up and measure the temple of God and the altar, and those who worship in it.
If John could measure it, there is no doubt that it is real. Thank You, Lord, for the promise of Your presence with us always. Thank You for Your presence with us now. Yes, I

can remember some days that were so stormy and cloudy that it didn't seem possible to see anything around me, and my feeble eyesight needed help to see You there. Bless all Your people with certainty that You are with them. Give us courage and satisfaction that You are with us whether we can see You or not. When there are days when clouds and fogs and storms of confusion and discouragement move in, give us confidence always that You have not moved, just because we find it difficult to see You. Break through the clouds with Your gracious Light. Let us recognize Jesus walking with us. Fill us with the joy of Your presence, Holy Spirit. Grant that we continue to depend on You, with love and caring for other people, especially when there is fog around us. Let our consistent dependence on You shine light into the lives of others where darkness and fog have crept in.

3 And I will grant *authority* to my two witnesses, and they will prophesy for twelve hundred and sixty days, clothed in sackcloth.
You have given Your Church time to witness, thank You, Lord. Bless Your Church with the power of Your Spirit, so that we use the time You give us well. There have been places in the past where Your witness was proclaimed, and then the witness came to an end. It's amazing that with all the joy and power You provided, Holy Spirit, there came a generation that lived separate from You. Help us to see that the time is limited where we Live. Give us fervor and dedication to Live in faith and witness to Your grace and support Your ministries, while You give us time. Help us not to be afraid, seeing places where Your witness came to an end. Only let us be faithful to You. And use the words of our mouths and the meditation of our hearts to be pleasing to You and effective in blessing people around us. Grant time, and effectiveness in that time, so that Your Church will grow, and Your people will be multiplied in number, also here and now.

12  And they heard a loud voice from heaven saying to them, "Come up here." Then they went up into heaven in the cloud, and their enemies watched them.

Sometimes it is not so obvious what the end result of the Church and Your people will be, Lord. We get mixed up with a lot of other people through the day. Our smiles, our encouragements, our words of confidence honoring You might seem small in the busy activity that swirls around us. Thank You for assuring us that the time is coming when it will be obvious. Encourage us with this picture: Your people, Your Church, called to come to be with You, pulled away from all those who deep inside, would rather that You would leave them alone. Knowing that the day of visible victory is coming, let us not weary of following You. Grant, Holy Spirit, that some of the joy of that day will come into our hearts, burning fiercely, glowing brightly, sounding joyously, in Your song, that we sing, now.

Rejoicing in Your presence now
In this time:  Growing in faith
Joy of victory:  Flowing through us now


Revelation 12

4  And his tail swept away a third of the stars of heaven and threw them to the earth. And the dragon stood before the woman who was about to give birth, so that when she gave birth he might devour her child.

The story of Your coming at Christmas, Jesus, is such a joyous, peaceful story. Christmas cards have scenes of snow lightly falling with a light glowing around the manger scene. Actually, Your coming, according to John's account, was anything but peaceful. Thank You Lord, for Your gracious promise of our Savior coming. Thank You for the prophecies of Your grace and love in the Messiah coming. Help us to have a sense of how much Satan would rather have had Your coming, Jesus, be an end to God's grace.

Grant that we recognize the wonder of Your coming against the background of sin and evil, not with fear, but with confidence and satisfaction that You have fulfilled the promise. As we live by grace, help us to recognize that grace has an enemy. Let us rejoice in how precious Your love and forgiveness are. Grant that we treasure the Life that You give to us. Always protect us from allowing the joy and Life we receive in forgiveness, to be buried under layers of busy life or passage of time or attraction of things. Thank You for Your gracious protection.

10  Then I heard a loud voice in heaven, saying, "Now the salvation, and the power, and the kingdom of our God and the authority of His Christ have come, for the accuser of our brethren has been thrown down, he who accuses them before our God day and night.
It's easy to look around and see things that are not right. The struggle of living in a place where evil dwells is ongoing. So thank You, Lord, for the vision of the victory that has happened. (It's easy to get exasperated, Lord, and wonder, "Why can't they see the evil!?") Grant us peace now, knowing that while there is still time ahead during which we struggle, there is no doubt about the end result. Help us to live in the confidence of that victory. Grant that we join in that song in our hearts that Your salvation is clear, Your power is over all, Your kingdom is being created also in our lifetimes, and Your Savior and Messiah has come. Help us to live in the certainty of Your complete and final dealing with our accuser.

17  So the dragon was enraged with the woman, and went off to make war with the rest of her children, who keep the commandments of God and hold to the testimony of Jesus.
So it is not our imagination, we are in a war with evil and the evil one. You have given us weapons to protect ourselves and weapons to take the offensive in this war. It would be nice if the volunteer armed forces would be in charge of fighting this war. Or if there were a draft to pick soldiers to

fight the battle. But You have made it clear, Lord, that no one is left out. We Your children are in the war. So grant that we are not lazy or passive when it comes to resisting evil. Help us not to get used to or comfortable with evil around us. Keep us strong in our faith. Help us to continually delight in spiritual nourishment in Your word and sacraments. Grant that we keep in practice using the weapons and tools You give us so that we keep Your commandments, testify faithfully to You, and consciously enter every day using the energy and resources You give in standing up for You against every evil.

Knowing grace has an enemy, Treasuring Life
Certain of victory, singing Your praise
Fighting the war: Equipped and faithful


Revelation 13

4 ...they worshiped the dragon because he gave his authority to the beast; and they worshiped the beast, saying, "Who is like the beast, and who is able to wage war with him?"
There are people who have no use for worship in their lives, Lord, but You show that everyone worships. Everyone has something that they depend on. Help us to see the worship that is going on now. We want to worship only You, Gracious Lord. So help us to recognize worship of government, as if it were going to solve all problems and provide for everyone. Help us to recognize worship of social systems, as if they were able to bless people without Your grace and love. Help us to recognize worship of education, as if that, without You, were the answer to what is needed in our world today. And while we reject all worship of these systems, thank You for the blessings that You give through them. Keep our focus on You, Lord. Grant that we depend on You for all we are and all we need. And please help us to see Your gracious hand at work to bless people through

government, social systems, and education. Use them Gracious Lord, to make a difference now in this day, not as separate entities, but as Your tools to keep order, to help people use their abilities to be blessings, and to help those people who are in need. Grant that people who are blessed through these systems today, see the blessings coming from You and Your gracious hand. And grant that we all worship (only) You.

10  If anyone *is destined* for captivity, to captivity he goes; if anyone kills with the sword, with the sword he must be killed. Here is the perseverance and the faith of the saints.
Your picture of the time that is coming shows Your people under attack. The need for Your people to persevere will be intense. It is easy to think of those times coming, Lord, as a long time away. "They probably won't be in my lifetime." Help us to see that our time is not that different, Lord. There are so many choices we make, Lord. What will we agree with? What will we support? The choices don't come to us like a legal document to read carefully, to think about, to sign, and to have notarized. The choices seem to come to us in casual remarks by people we are with, when we are asked, "Isn't that so?" And we find ourselves nodding, perhaps not entirely sure what the person exactly means. Help us to see the need we have to persevere. Help us to see the need we have to live by faith. Grant that we hold onto You for dear Life, not just when we vote or sign something (but certainly then, too), but when we choose what we enjoy, when we choose what is funny, when we choose what we agree with, when we get up in the morning and take a deep breath.

17  ...and *he provides* that no one will be able to buy or to sell, except the one who has the mark, *either* the name of the beast or the number of his name.
The attack that is coming, Lord, You show is not at some distant place, not something to watch on CNN, not something to just wonder about and discuss. The attack that

is coming is going to attack Your people at the grocery store, at the drug store, at what used to be called the 5 and dime (now, I suppose, the large general store, the warehouse store, ... the internet). Your people will be attacked by control of money and control of what goods are available for them to purchase. Is it going on now, Lord? The time will come when it will be devastating. Help us to be thankful for being able to use the money You provide for us now. Help us to know that persecution is possible, even in lands where there is, right now, great freedom. There are groups of people who have suffered persecution here, please bless them with an end to that, Lord. Help us to be aware of how we use the finances we have from You. Grant that we purchase wisely, with thanksgiving to You, with an awareness of what our purchases encourage. In all our use of money, help us to prayerfully, always put You first.

Seeing blessings. Knowing they come from You.
Choosing: With perseverance and faith
Giving, buying, saving—faithfully


Revelation 14

4 These are the ones who have not been defiled with women, for they have kept themselves chaste. These *are* the ones who follow the Lamb wherever He goes. These have been purchased from among men as first fruits to God and to the Lamb.
You are keeping Your people holy and undefiled by Your grace and power now, Lord. Praise and thanks to You now and throughout this time You give us. Our time is limited here, but during that time, Lord, help us to recognize Your work of keeping us close to You by Your word and sacraments. Help us to delight in walking with You. As You paint this picture of Your Church, You describe us as "first fruits to God". Help us to see ourselves as an offering to You. Grant that we hold nothing back from Your use. Fill

our hearts so completely, Gracious Spirit, that we desire in and through all that we do each day to offer ourselves for Your use in blessing the people around us, in witnessing to You, in satisfaction of Life at its fullest. Let nothing get in the way of our offering ourselves to You, Lord. Inhabit our desires so completely that nothing draws us from You. Let us prepare now, as those who desire for You to use us, so that we will rejoice then in the company of the saints.

6, 7 And I saw another angel flying in midheaven, having an eternal gospel to preach to those who live on the earth, and to every nation and tribe and tongue and people; 7 and he said with a loud voice, "Fear God, and give Him glory, because the hour of His judgment has come; worship Him who made the heaven and the earth and sea and springs of waters."
You have sent Your gospel to people now, Lord, thanks and praise to You! What good news You bring us that we have forgiveness in You! Continue to make Your gospel effective through the time of our lives and until the end of time. Bring people to You so that we may together recognize You and rejoice in Your presence. Help us to see You now as the One Who loves us. The One Who has sent Your Son to be our Savior. The One Who gives us Life with You now so that we may rejoice in walking with You now no matter what else is going on around us. Help Your people to rejoice in You as Creator. You have graciously made us and all things, and given us this beautiful world in which to live and Live with You. Help us to worship You, Creator, Savior, Lord, King now in our hearts and minds. Grant that we enjoy this time here knowing You as Glorious Creator, Gracious Savior, so that we may whole-heartedly join in the new song of praise to You at the end with all the Church and the hosts of heaven.

13 And I heard a voice from heaven, saying, "Write, 'Blessed are the dead who die in the Lord from now on!'"

"Yes," says the Spirit, "so that they may rest from their labors, for their deeds follow with them."

Thank You for the comfort You give to us, Lord, as we remember those dear to us who have already died. Thank You that they are blessed. Thank You that we may entrust them to Your gracious care. Thank You that they are not forgotten. Remember each of those people who are important and dear to us. Hold them in Your gracious hand, Lord. And then, for me, Lord, I have changing ideas about "rest". There was that time when I had to take a rest, so that I could grow and mature well. There was a time when rest seemed to get in the way—a little bit once in a while was ok, but not something to be overdone. There was "stuff to do". And there is a time when I am a little more ready to rest. Energy doesn't seem to last as long as it used to (imagine that!). I'd still rather not need rest, but I have to admit, it feels good. And now You show a picture of rest that is absolutely satisfying. Help us to use the time well, and use all the energy You give us to serve You and be a blessing in whatever callings You give us. Grant that we use rest responsibly, now, with thankful hearts. And grant that we look ahead to the rest to come, running to meet You just as fast as we can, using all the strength and energy You give us right to the end, sliding into home with You in joy and satisfaction, finally ready for Your gift of rest.

Being used as You desire
Learning to worship and praise You
Using energy well, rest in moderation


Revelation 15

2 And I saw something like a sea of glass mixed with fire, and those who had been victorious over the beast and his image and the number of his name, standing on the sea of glass, holding harps of God.

Victory is a wonderful thing. The trouble is, Lord, that my image of victory is having a winning score at the end of the game. A banner on the website the next day celebrating victory. Wearing the medal the next day for everyone to see. The victory that You show is when I depend on You through every difficulty. Then I face death for what I am holding onto. Then I am conquered and put to death by the enemy, while I am holding onto You. And then there on the glassy sea mixed with fire, I can stand victorious. I suppose You know, that, speaking personally, I prefer my version. Right. Ok, so we, Your people, get to use Your version. So help us to remain faithful through every difficulty (and even through every time of blessing and peace). Grant that we rejoice in Your smile, and don't demand or expect to wear victory medals or get adulation and praise now. The time for recognition is coming later, so help us to be satisfied with Living faithfully with You and for You, here and now, and leave all the results and timing to You.

3 And they sang the song of Moses, the bond-servant of God, and the song of the Lamb, saying,
"Great and marvelous are Your works,
O Lord God, the Almighty;
Righteous and true are Your ways,
King of the nations!"
The song about Your great and marvelous works is a song that we can sing now, thank You Lord. You are gracious and You deliver us from evil that attacks us. Whether it is sickness or grief or needs, You know how to bless us, and in Your mercy, You do touch our lives and bless us. It would be nice if You could just touch our lives with an inoculation against all problems and evils, all sicknesses and frustrations. But then we would, I'm sure, forget You and Your blessing and grace. So You help us to remember by continuing to touch our lives with Your marvelous works so that we can continue to celebrate Your love and mercy. And as You deliver us You continue to send us and point us into the mission You have given to us. So please, Lord, help us

to see Your many graces, Your touches of mercy and deliverance. Help us to see and Live in thankfulness and praise. While we wait for the end of all the suffering, help us to use the mercy You show us as strength for carrying out the mission You have given. Use us effectively as those who have received mercy, to show mercy to others. Use us as those who have seen Your Light and grace, to show Your Light and grace to others. And through all the attacks help us to keep singing, with a song in our hearts celebrating Your great and marvelous works.

7 Then one of the four living creatures gave to the seven angels seven golden bowls full of the wrath of God, who lives forever and ever.

"How was I supposed to know I did something wrong!" In little children, Lord, it is an opportunity to teach Your will and the skill of listening to You through our conscience. In adults, it is close to offensive whining. And so You are prepared to show Your wrath to those who, heretofore, have not been listening to You. Bless those people who have working consciences but have been working hard not to listen to them. Grant that the voice of their conscience will get through the earplugs. (And when I am in that group, Lord, help me also to hear and repent.) Bless those people whose consciences are not working. Send Your Spirit to give them a transplant, with a working conscience. Like using divine hearing aids, let them finally hear You and Your will. Bless them with repentance, and let them hear Your grace and come to faith in You. Bless people who need to see their rejection of Your gracious invitation. Bless them here and now, before Your wrath consumes them and the time for their repentance is over.

Living victoriously, in defeat. Medal later.
Touched with mercy: singing and serving.
Seeing, repenting, believing. Now.

Revelation 16

4 Then the third *angel* poured out his bowl into the rivers and the springs of waters; and they became blood.
Terrible things are happening as we get closer to the end. You will see to it that all people are affected. When people are driving, sometimes after an accident, someone says, "I didn't see any warning sign!" So thank You, Lord, for warning all people that the end is coming and that You mean everything You have said. Help people in this day, when we see problems with basic necessities to recognize that You are communicating to us and to all people, encouraging us to keep alert; the end is coming. There are people on the planet who can feel that problem severely. Help people in our country, even with the blessings that we have, to recognize Your warnings. You have given us such wonderful blessings, it is hard for some to see any problems. Reach even well-to-do people (which, actually, is most of us, compared to other countries). Grant that we change from frustrations about how to manage our blessings, busy schedules, and investments to thankful stewardship managing our time to listen to You, seeing our brokenness, living in repentance and thanksgiving.

15 ("Behold, I am coming like a thief. Blessed is the one who stays awake and keeps his clothes, so that he will not walk about naked and men will not see his shame.")
Break into my schedule, Lord?! This week is really full, I suppose You know! I'm sorry, Lord, it's easy to get full of myself. Like a thief? At any moment. There are times when I feel closer to You than others, Lord. I do know, it's not Your doing. Help me to stay close to You, Lord. Help me to live each moment throughout the day, busy or relaxing, in Your presence and company. You have given me Your righteousness to wear. Thank You, Lord. I admit, fashions change from decade to decade (or day to day). And sometimes I have gone places where wearing Your righteousness was out of fashion. Yup, I was in the wrong

place! Help me to be in the right places. And even though not everyone I meet has the same fashion awareness, help me to wear Your righteousness with thanksgiving, joy, and pride in You and Your wonderful grace. Help me to always be ready for Your coming with that attitude of closeness to You and thanksgiving for Your grace.

17 Then the seventh *angel* poured out his bowl upon the air, and a loud voice came out of the temple from the throne, saying, "It is done."
I suppose You hear each of us say this. "I have a lot more to do. There are places I'd like to see. There are goals I haven't met. I'd like to get over this or past this problem, health issue, difficulty, and then have some time when everything is working. (There are a lot more books (websites) that I would like to look at.) But in my heart, Lord, I really am looking forward to the end, to the end of time, to the end of problems, to the end of frustrations, to the end of temptations (the ones I find easy to resist and the ones I find myself welcoming too much!), to the end of inflation, to the end of misunderstandings, to the end of broken relationships, to the end of my selfishness, to the end of worry (I'm sorry, Lord, help me trust You always). So when Your voice says, "It is done, that's it, the end has come," You give me a rock of hope for every day, now. Help me to hold on, Lord. Grant that I enjoy the time You give now. Grant that I follow You faithfully. Grant that I use the time You give well and to Your glory. And grant that I live in the hope and certainty that by Your grace the day is coming, when You will say, "It is done. Time to come home."

Warned, keeping alert, listening to You
Ready. Dressed well. By Your grace
Hope is growing—end is coming.


Revelation 17

3 And he carried me away in the Spirit into a wilderness; and I saw a woman sitting on a scarlet beast, full of blasphemous names, having seven heads and ten horns.
There is a heavy burden of the enemy, Lord, as we go on in another day of pilgrimage in the desert. It seems like a desert sometimes, because our own sinfulness gets in the way of seeing Your blessings and power. The enemy had the people of Asia Minor involved in things that they put first in their lives. It hasn't changed, Lord. Help us to see how things try to take first place in our lives. Give us discernment and faithfulness to You so that we always put You first. Help us not to give in to any attitudes of "That's just the way politics is," or "You have to accept that in business." Give us sensitive awareness so that bells start to ring in us when we are close to those attitudes. Help us to see how You being first in our hearts and Lives gives guidance and direction and strength to choose how we can Live by Your grace and power in society, in fellowship with other people, in politics, in business, in education—in every part of our living, on the pilgrimage, in the desert.

8 "The beast that you saw was, and is not, and is about to come up out of the abyss and go to destruction. And those who dwell on the earth, whose name has not been written in the book of life from the foundation of the world, will wonder when they see the beast, that he was and is not and will come."
There are a lot of wonders in the world today, Lord. Some of them are the wonders of creation that You have put here for us, so that we recognize Your presence with us. Some are attractive appearances of the enemy among us. Power seems attractive to people. In this time that You give, Lord, help people not to be drawn to flashy, attractive power and away from You and Your love, mercy, peace, and grace. Let people see worldly wonders for what they are. There is no huge amount of money waiting to be transferred into our bank accounts waiting for our personal bank information. Help us also to see that bullying people is not only wrong in

school, it's wrong as a method for fixing the world. Help us to depend on You, Lord, and Your power. Help us to Live in the joy of the wonder that You show in Your love, Your Spirit, and Your word. Let us be faithful in prayer, to bless our world and provide for those in need. Yes, I admit, it would be wonderful for You to zap evil with flashes of lightning, and create blessings for those in need with warm glows of sunlight arriving on clouds from heaven. But until then, keep us faithful in trusting You to answer prayers, even without flash, wonder, awe, and zapping.

14 "These will wage war against the Lamb, and the Lamb will overcome them, because He is Lord of lords and King of kings, and those who are with Him *are the* called and chosen and faithful."
In our daily struggles, in our concerns for people, in our wondering about events in the world, Gracious Lord, help us to remember Who You are. In a race between a delicately tuned race car and a bicycle with square wheels, there is no contest. Frustrations look really large to us, Lord. Disasters and violence from evil seem such clear dangers. Prejudice, hatred, selfish and violent people—all of them have square wheels, Lord. Thank You! Remind us that You are victorious from Your cross and empty tomb. Remind us that You are ascended and at the right hand of Your Father, Jesus. As we get closer to the end, as we continue to see evil around us, remind us that You are our Lord, that we can depend on You to be with us in every trial, that You give us strength to Live in every day. Remind us that You are the Lord, You are our King, and You are victorious over every evil. Remind us that You are Life, with us, in us—now, past death, and forever.

Choosing You first, in everything
Depending on You, with or without zapping
In every attack, You are King, victorious forever

Revelation 18

4 I heard another voice from heaven, saying, "Come out of her, my people, so that you will not participate in her sins and receive of her plagues."
When the enemy of the Church is finally destroyed, You graciously call Your people out of the destruction. Praises to You, Lord. Bless Your people, Lord, so that we can all look at the political world, the business world, and the communication world, (including the internet?!), around us now and not just wait for the end to come. Help us to see what is around us through Your eyes, Lord. Thank You for the faithful people of integrity and ability who are working hard in every area. Help us to see that which is not Yours, that which is contrary to Your grace and Your love. Help us to recognize those things that try to claim first place in the lives of people now. Grant that we don't wait for You to call us out of places where You are not welcome. Grant that we continue through all the days You give us to avoid idolatrous attitudes in the daily affairs we engage in. Let nothing we want, no allegiance we profess get in the way of having You first in our Life. Help us to hear Your call to come away from evil and come to You in all we do, say, think, and choose, and grant that we always are faithful to You, even now.

11 "And the merchants of the earth weep and mourn over her, because no one buys their cargoes any more."
Business often seems to have at heart, as paramount, the best interest of business first. There have been times, Lord, when there is a business who really cares about people (thank You!), and some that care about people if it is good for business. It appears that at the end, business leaders will be amazed that Someone actually cares how business operates! Thank You for the wonderful things that are available to people today. Thank You for the people who have given so much of themselves to provide goods and services that have great quality for the needs of people. Bless people who are in business now—touch their hearts,

open them to directing business in ways that really bless people. Help them to avoid putting money first. Help us all in our choosing and purchasing, to support good business and not just meeting our needs selfishly. Help us to care about people in business and help them to care about the people they serve.

20 "Rejoice over her, O heaven, and you saints and apostles and prophets, because God has pronounced judgment for you against her."
It is easy, Lord, to see things that should be better. (OK, sometimes it's a case of I'd like it my way—forgive me for imposing my selfish attitudes on others.) But often we can see things that are wrong. And we would like Justice to be done. (Thunder, lightening, Your mighty voice from heaven—those would be nice!) But here, You make clear, the day is coming. There is a celebration of right, goodness, justice coming. There is a time coming, thank You, Lord, when all that is evil will see clearly that they are not in Your will. Help us not to be depressed or discouraged now (not hearing thunder or seeing lightening!). Help us depend on You in every day, doing all we can, faithfully serving You. And grant that we take in the certainty that the celebration of justice, right, love, and all other good is coming, by Your grace. Thank You, Lord, that You are with us now and also then.

You first: Avoiding evil, coming to You
Businesses and customers: Caring about people
Faithful to You, waiting confidently for the celebration


Revelation 19

5 And a voice came from the throne, saying,
"Give praise to our God, all you His bond-servants, you who fear Him, the small and the great."

Thank You, Lord, that we get to join in the great song of praise to You.  During this time here, continue to show us Your grace and love and glory.  Help us to get to know You better through all the days of our lives.  Keep us in Your word, draw us closer to You, Lord Holy Spirit.  And when we gather as the Church to sing Your praise and glory, open us finally to be able to recognize You in all Your wonder and glory with awe and joy.  As we look forward to that song of praise, help us to see that the time is coming when the judgment is final.  That there will never again be any attack on the Church or on the people who witness to You and Your grace.  And that is a nice touch, Lord, the way You invite us all to join in, the small and the great.  Of course, speaking personally, (and incredibly with abject vanity!), I would like to be in the middle somewhere.  Sorry, Lord.  Please forgive me.  Thank You that the small are included (I will be fully satisfied in the small section!).

8  It was given to her to clothe herself in fine linen, bright *and* clean; for the fine linen is the righteous acts of the saints.  "What can we do for You, Lord, to glorify You?"  It's a question that, in our better moments, we do ask.  And I suppose, Lord, that most of us, when we ask that question expect an invitation to work in a mission on the top of a distant mountain, living on wild locusts and turnips.  It is surprising to some of us, that You give us things to do today, here, simply, faithfully for You to Your glory.  Help us to see the ways we get to add to the linen of the righteous acts of the saints, in the way we choose attitudes about people who seem grumpy or selfish, in the ways we speak with love and joy even when others seem uncaring and judgmental, in the ways we spend money and remember to be a blessing to those in need.  Show us the things we can do, the choices we can make, the words we can speak, Your love we can share in little ways today, here.  (Thank You that we can glorify You without the distant mountain, locusts, and turnips (!)).

15  From His mouth comes a sharp sword, so that with it He may strike down the nations, and He will rule them with a rod of iron; and He treads the wine press of the fierce wrath of God, the Almighty.

When I think of You, Lord, I enjoy thinking of You as my Good Shepherd. I enjoy the pictures of You as Refuge, as the One loving children, walking on the water, pulling up Peter, stilling the storm, feeding the multitudes, turning water into wine and privately smiling, speaking graciously to the woman washing and anointing Your feet, appearing on Easter to the Emmaus disciples. There are so many wonderful images of You graciously loving people, Lord. But this picture is difficult, Lord. Fire in Your eyes, riding to crush all those who are not in Your family, pouring out God's wrath upon them. I know it has to be, Lord. Make the number small, Lord. Reach with Your grace my friends, relatives, neighbors. Reach the people in businesses who are kind and gracious. Reach all those who care about those in need. Reach all those in emergency services, all those in the medical field. Well, You know, Lord. We each have a list of those we would really like You to reach and bring to You. So I suppose that means, please use us, Lord to show You, to show Your love, to invite people to You, now and into eternal joy with You.

Getting to know You, singing Your praise
Finding ways to glorify You, today
Grow Your family, Lord!


Revelation 20

3  ...and he threw him into the abyss, and shut *it* and sealed *it* over him, so that he would not deceive the nations any longer, until the thousand years were completed; after these things he must be released for a short time.

Thank You, Lord, for Your plans for completion. It seems so difficult to have a feeling here and now of completion.

Whether it is a report that I write or a preparation for a meeting, whether it is a project at home or working, I get to the point of being done. But there always seem to be pieces left over—information not used, ideas not taken into account, people not included, (little pieces of metal or plastic in fix-it projects, that I couldn't figure out how to put back!). But Your plan is for completion, not just for the little things in life, but for Your Church. Grant that we, Your people, may be part of that plan for completion today. Grant that everything we choose, everything we think, in every opportunity we have to love and respect people, we will be part of Your plan for completion. Help us not to get in the way of Your plan. Help us not to slow Your plan down. I am never quite satisfied with just being done with a project. But by Your grace, I know that I, together with all Your people, will be totally satisfied with Your completed work. I look forward to that time, Lord. Keep me in Your plan for completion, and use me as You will toward that wonderful end.

12 And I saw the dead, the great and the small, standing before the throne, and books were opened; and another book was opened, which is *the book* of life; and the dead were judged from the things which were written in the books, according to their deeds.
All our deeds are written in Your books, Lord. Talk about gigabytes of memory! And when I consider what is written there, Lord, sheesh! There are things from yesterday that I would rather not have written there. And there have been a lot of yesterdays! When a person is brought into a criminal courtroom, the charges are very clear and very limited. But to open the books on days upon days and years upon years of things I have said and done is truly mind-boggling! Thank You, Lord Jesus, that You have another book. Thank You that by Your grace the deeds that You have done through us completely cover all the things written in the first books. It's easier now for me to see the things that I have done, that are not honoring You, that are not pleasing to You, which I would really like to forget, and I would really like You to forget,

which are in the first set of books. Thank You that as I look ahead to the actual event when the books will be opened, I can be sure that the wonder of what is written in Your book of Life, will completely overshadow and obliterate everything else that is written. I know I don't deserve that. Thank You for that confidence in Your grace now and then.

14  Then death and Hades were thrown into the lake of fire. This is the second death, the lake of fire.
To look around and see no enemy to You or to Life in You! What a sight, Lord! I'm not actually conscious of looking over my shoulder now, wondering where the enemy is lurking. But when You show this picture of the event where the last enemy is gone, I can realize that I do spend time now looking for the enemy. I keep looking back at what I have said and done to see where the enemy has influenced me. When I make plans I know the part of "Lord willing" is a blessing and I can depend on Your guidance. The part "and the creek don't rise", is looking around and over my shoulder, for sure. Part of the nature of living now seems to be keeping an eye on the horizon to see what financial problem, what social difficulty, what unknown parameter is coming that will mean I have to change again. Help me to keep my eyes on You now, so that all plans I make are in Your will and protection now. And grant that I look forward with confidence and joy to the time when there is only Your good and gracious will, no matter where I look! Wow! What a sight!

Being part of Your completion, today
Graciously do good through me, today
Planning, with eyes on You, today


Revelation 21

4  "...and He will wipe away every tear from their eyes; and there will no longer be *any* death; there will no longer be *any*

mourning, or crying, or pain; the first things have passed away."

It is difficult to imagine what it will be like in heaven, Lord. Gold streets sound hard. Harps sound like music lessons. No night, sounds like getting tired. Lord, my mind is stuck on the human and broken world in which I live. So thank You, that You clarify the picture by saying take away all tears, all sorrow, all death, all fear of the end of something coming, all mourning over people, over opportunities lost, over things, all crying, all broken-heartedness, all pain, annoying, occasional, chronic, terrible, all of it. It's like You take a picture of a foggy, smoky, stormy, old city, and You pull away the fog, smoke, storm, and brokenness of age, and behold there is this beautiful, new, sun-lit metropolis, surrounded by fields, streams, mountain grandeur. Help us to picture what is coming with joy. Help us to enjoy Your presence now and desire to live in a place with You where there is nothing wrong and everything works. For those who have died and for ourselves, Lord, help us to imagine Life with no evil and no effects of evil. Lift our spirits now to look forward to the end of all those first things that You are removing. Then we can look forward to the wonderful Life we get to enjoy with You.

5, 6 And He who sits on the throne said, "Behold, I am making all things new." And He said, "Write, for these words are faithful and true." ⁶ Then He said to me, "It is done. I am the Alpha and the Omega, the beginning and the end. I will give to the one who thirsts from the spring of the water of life without cost."

What a wonderful picture, Lord! You speak and the new is created. There will no longer be any of the old, only the new, perfect and wonderful from Your rich, varied, colorful, amazing, delightful, and blessed imagination. Thank You, Lord. The part I really like is, "It is done." I've gone places that were very nice. And when I unpacked, I realized that I forgot the whatchamacallit, and sure enough, I couldn't get one there. It sounds so amazing, Lord, that You will speak and there will be forever, opening up with everything there, ready, perfect.  Nothing will be missing.  No one will show up and say, "What about the …?"  Give us confidence that You know exactly how to satisfy our needs for company, for fellowship, for joy, for wonder, for new experiences, for beauty, for feeling at home, for worship, for understanding, for questions answered, for seeing family, and for all that I can't imagine and neither can any of the rest of Your people.  Thank You that You know us, human beings as a group and as individuals, and thank You for loving us so much that You have prepared Life with You in complete satisfaction for each of us, for all of us.  You are so gracious, Lord.  When we find ourselves troubled by thinking about harp lessons or about time that doesn't end (which really hurts my head, Lord), wrap Your arms around us and give us confidence that You are really, indeed, actually preparing completely satisfying, loving, Life for us with You.

23  And the city has no need of the sun or of the moon to shine on it, for the glory of God has illumined it, and its lamp *is* the Lamb.
Thank You, Lord for the light coming.  I remember a lady whose great satisfaction was the sunshine that came into her home every day.  Through the years I have grown to understand more of her joy.  Your description of heaven is so wonderful, Lord.  We won't have to think about how much electricity we are using or whether to use an incandescent, CFL, or LED bulb.  We won't have to wonder which way our windows should face or how many windows would be good in our home.  You will be our Light.  As we wait for that great blessing, please be our Light now, Lord Jesus.  No matter what darkness tries to discourage us, lift up our spirits with the Joy and Light of Your presence.  Holy Spirit, dance with all the colors of Your Light in us and through us.  Bounce Your Light off us to others.  Father, thank You for Your love that never changes.  Let Your love Light up our hearts and fill our Living so that we may worship You now and yearn for

the joy of worshiping You in the Light of Your Gracious and Glorious Presence then.

Awaiting: The end of every evil
Confidence and patience: Complete satisfaction coming
Turning our faces to Your Light: Now and then


Revelation 22

7 "And behold, I am coming quickly. Blessed is he who heeds the words of the prophecy of this book."
There have been courses that I have taken, Lord. And I have read some great books. There have been some good seminars along the way, also, Lord. You know I have taken a lot of notes on those. Some of which I kept for years (in boxes, somewhere). The part about heeding the words is a little more direct, involving, and personal. Help me to enjoy Your word. Help me to stay in Your word regularly, faithfully. Please fill me with Your Spirit that Your word will have an effect in my thinking, feeling, speaking—in my Living. I remember those insurance policies I have bought that had a lot of words on many pages (awfully small print, too). And since I didn't intend to actually ever use those things, the words didn't seem very urgently important. But You are coming quickly, thank You, Lord. So since I plan to see You soon, I would really like to take Your words seriously, receive Your blessings, be faithful to You, and obey your words to me. Help me to keep Your words fresh and vital in my memory and Living. Grant that in each day, I look forward to seeing You, and enjoy Living in Your word as part of my current life (and not as part of a museum display I might visit occasionally).

14 Blessed are those who wash their robes, so that they may have the right to the tree of life, and may enter by the gates into the city.

Your forgiveness, Lord, is so wonderful. It gives me the right to live in Your peace. I thank You for the peace I have in myself, with You, and with others. Thank You, Lord, that there is so much more to Your forgiveness. Please, Lord, as I Live in this day, wash me clean in Your sacrifice. Cleanse my garments of Life, so that I may wear Your righteousness. Let me be aware of the wonderful wardrobe I have from You, so that I want to wear it humbly and thankfully. Grant that I live with the joy, thankfulness, and anticipation of having the right to the tree of life. What a joy to be able to see the river of the water of life and the tree of life bearing fruit every month. Thank You for that privilege coming, Lord. Let the anticipation and joy of that event show in my feelings and words, on my face and in my Life.

20 He who testifies to these things says, "Yes, I am coming quickly." Amen. Come, Lord Jesus.
In Your word, Lord, You have blessed me so much! You have encouraged me, sustained me, guided me. You have given me Your promises to hold onto. You have enabled me to listen to You. You have given me Your Spirit. You have given me the privilege of walking with You and talking to You. It just seems like the world around is getting louder all the time. There is such anger and violence, Lord. I'm really looking forward to Your coming. Help me to live with visible eagerness for Your coming. Grant me the peace and joy of Your certain coming. Thank You, that You are coming quickly, Lord. My "quickly" would be this afternoon. You know that. Whenever Your "quickly" is will be just right. (Of course, before another body part fails—they are getting expensive—would be nice.) The party! The celebration! Being with You! Satisfaction in praising You! Please, Lord, yes. Come quickly!

Your word, directing my Living
Humbly Living in privilege, now and then
Coming Lord: Come quickly!

Printed in Great Britain
by Amazon